TEACHING STUDENTS WITH MODERATE/SEVERE DISABILITIES, INCLUDING AUTISM

TEACHING STUDENTS WITH MODERATE/SEVERE DISABILITIES, INCLUDING AUTISM

Strategies For Second Language Learners In Inclusive Settings

Second Edition

By

ELVA DURÁN, Ph.D.

California State University, Sacramento

Foreword by

Leonard M. Baca, Ed.D.

Introduction by

Diane Cordero de Noriega, Ph.D.

CHARLES C THOMAS • PUBLISHER, LTD.
Springfield • Illinois • U.S.A.

Published and Distributed Throughout the World by

CHARLES C THOMAS • PUBLISHER, LTD.
2600 South First Street
Springfield, Illinois 62794-9265

© *1996 by* CHARLES C THOMAS • PUBLISHER, LTD.
ISBN 0-398-06700-7 (cloth)
ISBN 0-398-06701-5 (paper)
Library of Congress Catalog Card Number: 96-23691

First Edition, 1988
Second Edition, 1996

With THOMAS BOOKS *careful attention is given to all details of manufacturing
and design. It is the Publisher's desire to present books that are satisfactory as to
their physical qualities and artistic possibilities and appropriate for their particular
use.* THOMAS BOOKS *will be true to those laws of quality that assure a good
name and good will.*

Printed in the United States of America
SC-R-3

Library of Congress Cataloging-in-Publication Data

Durán, Elva.
    Teaching students with moderate/severe disabilities, including
autism : strategies for second language learners in inclusive
settings / by Elva Durán ; introduction by Diane Cordero de Noriega
; foreword by Leonard M. Baca. — 2nd ed.
      p.   cm.
    Rev. ed. of: Teaching the moderately and severely handicapped
student and autistic adolescent. 1988.
    Includes bibliographical references and index.
    ISBN 0-398-06700-7 (cloth). — ISBN 0-398-06701-5 (pbk.)
    1. Handicapped children—Education—United States. 2. Linguistic
minorities—Education—United States. 3. Hispanic American
children—Education. 4. Autistic youth—Education—United States.
5. Special education—United States. I. Durán, Elva. Teaching the
moderately and severely handicapped student and autistic adolescent.
II. Title.
LC4031.D836   1996
371.91—dc20   96-23691
                                                    CIP

CONTRIBUTORS

Leonard M. Baca, Ed.D. Professor and Director of Bueno Center for Multicultural Education; University of Colorado, Boulder, Colorado, is a leader in the area of bilingual-special education.

Gwendolyn T. Benson, Ph.D. Coordinator of programs for students with severe disabilities, Atlanta Public Schools, is well-known for her work with the African-American community.

Lou Brown, Ph.D. Professor in the Department of Rehabilitation, Psychology and Special Education, University of Wisconsin, Madison, Wisconsin is a leader in the area of teaching students with severe handicaps.

Patricia Thomas Cegelka, Ed.D. Professor, California State University, San Diego, is a leader in the field of personnel preparation and teacher credentialing for special educators in California.

Elba Maldonado Colón, Ed.D. Professor, California State University, San Jose, is a leader in the field of bilingual/special education.

Diane Cordero de Noriega, Ph.D. Professor/Bilingual Education and Dean of the School of Education, California State University, Sacramento.

Vivian I. Correa, Ph.D. Professor, University of Florida, has worked extensively with students of multihandicaps who are also limited English proficient in Puerto Rico and Florida.

Jorge Descamps, Ed.D. Professor in the Department of Teacher Education at the University of Texas, El Paso, has done much research and work in the area of the Mexican-American student.

Elva Durán, Ph.D. Professor, California State University, Sacramento, has contributed to the field of

v

bilingual/special education especially as it relates to the student with more severe disabilities.

Anne Y. Gallegos, Ph.D. Professor in the Department of Special Education, New Mexico State University, Las Cruces, New Mexico, specializes in the area of parent education of students with handicaps and bilingual/special education.

Paula M. Gardner, Ed.D. Assistant Professor at California State University, Sacramento, who specializes in inclusive education for students with disabilities.

William Mateer Harris, Ph.D. Professor at California State University, Sacramento, specializes in public school law and inclusion education for students with disabilities.

Norma G. Hernández, Ph.D. Professor in the Department of Teacher Education at the University of Texas, El Paso, has done much research and work in the area of the Mexican-American student.

Ming-Gong John Lian, Ed.D. Professor, Illinois State University, is well-known for his contributions to the Asian-American community and students with severe disabilities.

Bruce A. Ostertag, Ed.D. Professor, California State University, Sacramento, has done extensive work in formal and informal assessment in regular and special education.

Hyun-Sook Park, Ph.D. Associate Professor at California State University, Sacramento, conducts research in social ecology.

Eugene C. Valles, Ph.D. Assistant Professor, California State University, San Diego, is well-known for his work in bilingual/special education.

Susan Whaley, B.A. Teacher of adolescents with severe disabilities in a transition program, Sacramento City Unified School District.

Michael R. Yount, M.A. Transitional work specialist for Sacramento City Unified School District.

In memory of
Juan and Petra Durán

Dedicated to
Josephine Durán Lucero, my sister
and my other brothers who have
helped me through the years.

FOREWORD

This second and revised edition of this text represents a major and unique contribution to the field of Bilingual Special Education. The first edition of this book was heralded as the first and only text dealing with Bilingual Special Education at the severe and profound level. This revised version is not the usual cosmetic update of an important and popular text. Rather it is a book that has been completely revised. Several new chapters have been added which make it much more comprehensive and responsive to the needs of the students with severe and profound disabilities from bilingual backgrounds.

The needs of Asian and African American students have now been incorporated. Much more emphasis has been given to practical teaching strategies for working with students. The chapters on assessment and second language learning represent the state of the art in Bilingual Special Education. Both practitioners and academicians will find this to be an invaluable resource in their work.

My congratulations are hereby extended to Professor Elva Durán and her colleagues for this valuable gift to our profession.

LEONARD M. BACA

PREFACE

This book has been revised to include many new contributions in the area of teaching strategies for the second language learners. After teaching a bilingual/special education course for several years and working closely in classrooms in the public schools, this writer has come to realize from her teachers that more information is widely needed by the teachers in the field with the ever-growing populations of culturally and linguistically diverse students. The sections that have been included all represent major revisions and additions to the field of educating students with moderate to severe disabilities who are culturally and linguistically diverse. The writer is especially pleased with the research and information which has also been provided to the readers in the area of full inclusion. It is my hope that each of you will be able to take with you some of the information contained within these chapters and utilize it with some of your students presently and in the future.

ELVA DURÁN, PH.D.

INTRODUCTION

As educators, we never cease to learn, and the body of knowledge about learning and teaching continues to grow. Those of us who have been working in the education arena for the past twenty-five to thirty years have seen extraordinary changes occur, changes not only in what we know about children and how they learn, but extraordinary changes in the student population itself.

Historically, we have seen a shift with respect to the treatment of children with special needs. We went through a time when children with special needs were never allowed in public schools. Families either kept them at home or they were institutionalized. We emerged from this dark period into an era when provisions were made to have children attend special schools for children with disabilities. Later, there were special day classes within public schools where children with special needs had some limited interaction with other children. What we have learned from years of research on how children learn in general is that (1) children learn from each other as much as from the teacher, (2) high expectations result in higher achievement, (3) children with special needs mainstreamed in school will have a better chance at mainstreaming into life. Today we are taking the next steps forward in improving the educational attainment for children with special needs. We are implementing, gathering data, and documenting the results of schools' efforts at full inclusion. Children who are fully included so indeed learn from their regular education peers. The higher expectations that result from participation in a fully inclusive environment is having a positive impact on student outcomes. And finally, children fully included in general education classrooms are in fact functioning better in their adult lives.

Secondly, the changing demographics of the student population are having a profound effect on schools, educator preparation, and program design. In California, perhaps, the shift is more visible and pervasive; but clearly this is a national trend. Children who come from linguistically and culturally diverse backgrounds are increasing annually. In some larger urban areas, they comprise the majority. We have seen changes in how this population has been treated historically with respect to special education. We went through a period when language minority students were seriously overrepresented in special education classrooms. With court decisions like Larry P. and Diana, the pendulum swung in the opposite direction. Children who actually needed help were ignored for fear of misdiagnosis and misrepresentation. Clearly, children who have special needs and are also English language learners present a particular challenge.

In California, teacher candidates are preparing themselves by acquiring Cultural Language Academic Development (CLAD) certification. Candidates who are bilingual are receiving BCLAD preparation. Teachers with this preparation are uniquely qualified to address the special needs, whether they are developmental or linguistic. At California State University, Sacramento, we have a particularly unique program that combines special education, general education, and CLAD in one program. These teachers represent the model teachers of the future, prepared to teach all children whatever their needs. Today, we are preparing educators to address the total child—linguistically, culturally, and cognitively.

This book offers the latest thinking and research on some of these extremely critical issues. There are chapters that focus on full inclusion and successful transitions into vocational education, job-skill training, and post-secondary education. There are chapters that focus on the community and, more specifically, the family's role in partnership with the school to provide support for children with disabilities. Finally, there is a significant number of chapters that address culturally and linguistically diverse student populations, including one that is devoted to strategies for teaching English language learners in general as well as special education settings. This is a significant contribution to the field of education overall. Students with a multiplicity of needs have been neglected too long in the professional literature.

Dr. Elva Durán, the editor and one of the principal authors of this book, has compiled some of the most current, relevant research writing in this very important field. She clearly has her finger on the national pulse of special education trends. Her commitment and enthusiasm for her work shines through in this book and all she does. As a friend and a colleague, I am proud to have Dr. Durán as a member of our faculty. We are far richer for her presence among us.

DIANE CORDERO DE NORIEGA, PH.D.
Dean, School of Education
California State University, Sacramento

ACKNOWLEDGMENTS

The author wishes to thank all of the following people for helping her finish this book and for providing encouragement through the years:

Ruth Waugh, Ph.D., my doctoral advisor, who helped prepare me for all that was ahead in my teaching and writing and who has further offered much guidance through the years.

Ed Ekwall, Ed.D., who has patiently taught me how to organize much of my review of the literature and who also has always been there to answer many questions I have had concerning this book.

Lou Brown, Ph.D., who has inspired me through the years to provide the best possible education for populations with severe handicaps and who also gave me ideas to include in this book.

Leonard Baca, Ed.D., who gave me some suggestions to include in this book.

Norma Hernández, Ph.D., my former Dean, who helped me establish the UTEP Clinic and who has assisted me with it through the years.

Bill Dunlap, Ph.D., my former Dean, who always told me I could do whatever I set my mind to doing and who continually supported my work in special education.

Joe Ptasnik, Ed.D., Charlene Radach, Thelma Aguirre, and Art Alva, all persons involved with major positions in the various school districts I have worked in. I thank them for allowing me to try so many ideas in their districts so that it was possible to learn and put theory into practice.

Jack C. Vowell, Texas state representative, who helped obtain funding for the University of Texas, El Paso clinical programs.

The Dues & Hightower Foundation and Texas Planning Council for Developmental Disabilities which have supported the clinic financially through the years.

Kelly Woessner, my graduate assistant who helped me collect data in the schools.

My sister, Josephine Durán Lucero, who has always been so supportive of all of my efforts.

Some of my college students who are now teachers: Cheryl Boyd, Anne Ross, Sylvia Fernández, Barbara Franco, Fred Doreck, Loretta Valdespino, Katherine Wellborn Chacon, Rick Razo, Anne Wolff, Lynn Tompson, Roseanna Lee, and Mark Cline for offering me special friendship and support.

Also, to my clients and students and their parents who have come to the U.T. El Paso Clinic and to all of the other clients and their parents I have learned from also in the public schools. To you, thanks from the bottom of my heart because you have been my best teachers as I have struggled to find ways to help my college students and to teach you!

Further, to Melvin Fox, one of my medical doctors and friends, and Kenneth Wiesner who helped me stay well and gave me a positive attitude about all that I must do.

Michael John Lewis, my department chair at California State University, Sacramento, for acting as a facilitator and allowing me opportunities to pursue the personnel preparation grant which has brought the cross-cultural language academic development emphasis to our teacher training in special education.

Bruce A. Ostertag, my colleague at California State University, Sacramento for working with me as a co-project director on the personnel preparation grant that has brought a cross-cultural language academic development emphasis to our special education department.

Maurice Poe, my associate Dean, for encouraging me to revise my book and do this second edition.

Special thanks to John West, my friend and English professor, and his wife Lucy who edited the first edition of this manuscript.

Additionally, my thanks to Nancy Rzeznik who typed this entire manuscript.

Further, this writer would like to thank Dr. Lou Barber and Sacramento City Unified (Department of Special Education) for allowing her the opportunity to conduct research with second language learners in the schools.

Finally, to all my colleagues at California State University, Sacramento and other campuses who have been so gracious to complete chapters and sections for my revised edition of my book.

CONTENTS

                                                                    Page
Foreword—Leonard M. Baca   ix

Preface   xi

Introduction—Diane Cordero de Noriega   xiii
Chapter

1. BUILDING INCLUSIVE COMMUNITIES   3
    Paula M. Gardner

    Inclusive Education and Educational Reform   3

    The Civil Rights Movement   3

    Legislation   3

    The Least Restrictive Environment   4

    Special Education Reform Efforts:
        The Regular Education Initiative   5

    Inclusive Education   8

    America 2000: The Educate America Act   10

    Continuum of Services   12

    Building Inclusive Communities   13

    Teacher Acceptance   13

    Promoting, Understanding, and Celebrating
        Individual Differences   15

    Peer Acceptance   16

    Support Systems   17

    Collaboration   18

    Curriculum Adaptation and Supportive
        Instructional Practices   19

    Cooperative Inclusion   20

    Building Peer Relationships   20

    Circle of Friends   22

    Barriers to Building Inclusive Classrooms   23

    Benefits of Inclusive Classrooms   24

	Benefits of Inclusion for Typically Developing Children	24
	Discussion Questions	25
	References	25
2.	THE LEGAL SYSTEM AND PERSONS WITH DISABILITIES INTRODUCED	30

William Mateer Harris

	Introduction	30
	The Individuals with Disabilities Education Act	32
	IDEA: Free Appropriate Public Education	33
	IDEA: Due Process and the Individualized Education Plan	35
	Least Restrictive Environment	39
	Rehabilitation Act of 1973 Section 504 and the Americans with Disabilities Act (ADA) of 1990	45
	Discussion Questions	47
	References	48
3.	FUNCTIONAL LANGUAGE AND OTHER LANGUAGE INTERVENTION STRATEGIES	50

Elva Durán

	Functional Language	50
	Incidental Teaching	51
	Mand Model or Manding	52
	Delay Procedure	54
	Nonvocal Communication Approaches	55
	Manual or Total Communication	55
	What Signed System to Use	57
	Signed English	57
	Signing Exact English	57
	Other Gestural Systems	58
	Pointing and Natural Gestures	58
	Other Communication Systems	59
	Communication Booklets	61
	Facilitated Communication	63
	Vocal Systems	64
	Developing Attending Skills and Eliminating Inappropriate Behaviors which Interfere with Communication Training	66

Some Other Considerations in Teaching Language and
    Communication to Students with Severe Handicaps   67

Discussion Questions   70

References   70

4. TRANSITION AND POSTSECONDARY
    PROGRAMMING   74

    Elva Durán

    Vocational Transition Programming   75

    Individual with Disabilities Education Act   79

    Fair Labor Standards Act   80

    Programming for Postsecondary Training   85

    Beginning an Adult Transition Program   85

    Some Skills Needed by Secondary Students when They Enter
        the University Program   85

    Starting a Postsecondary Transition Program for Persons
        with Severe Handicaps   86

    Discussion Questions   92

    References   92

5. VOCATIONAL TRAINING   94

    Elva Durán

    Sheltered and Nonsheltered Vocational Training   94

    What are Some Problems with Sheltered Workshops   95

    Nonsheltered Vocational Training   95

    Training Techniques   97

    Full Inclusion Helps Prepare Students to do
        More Work in the Community   100

    Getting the Student Started to do a Job   101

    Other Training Techniques   103

    Getting a Nonsheltered Vocational Training Program Started   106

    Adolescent Students with Autism in Vocational Training   110

    Discussion Questions   115

    References   115

6. COMMUNITY–BASED INSTRUCTION   117

    Elva Durán

    Considerations to Make in Implementing
        Community Based Instruction   117

Staffing Strategies that can be Useful in
Community Based Instruction 122
A Model Community Based Transition Program:
Teaching Students to Make Informed Choices 128
Adolescent Students with Autism in the Community 135
Discussion Questions 138
References 138
7. ADOLESCENT STUDENTS WITH AUTISM 140
Elva Durán
Characteristics of the Adolescent with Autism 140
Language and/or Communication 142
Social Skills 144
Managing the Adolescent with Autism 146
Independent Skill Training 148
Self-Help Skills 149
Functional Reading 151
Inclusion and Second Language Acquisition of Students
with Autism: Qualitative Study Research Results 153
Discussion Questions 157
References 158
8. STUDENTS WITH MULTIPLE DISABILITIES 160
Vivian I. Correa
Prevalence 160
Visual Impairments 162
Assessment 163
Intervention 165
Hearing Impairments 168
Assessment 169
Intervention 170
Dual Sensory Impairments 171
Assessment 171
Intervention 172
Conclusion 174
Discussion Questions 175
References 176
9. PARENT AND FAMILY ISSUES 183
Anne Y. Gallegos

Historical and Legislative Perspective 183

Characteristics of Parents and Families of Children
with Severe Disabilities 186

The Need for Support by Families of Children
with Severe Disabilities 188

Considerations Related to Involving Parents
in Their Children's Education 191

Korean-American Families of Children with Disabilities:
Perspectives and Implications for Practitioners 194

Cultural Tradition and Disability 195

Expectations for Education and Social Relationships
of Children with Disabilities 198

Participation in Educational Systems 199

Toward Unbiased Collaboration 200

Methods for Involving Parents in School Activities 205

Summary 209

Discussion Questions 210

References 210

10. ISSUES RELATED TO LATINO STUDENTS 215

Norma G. Hernández & Jorge Descamps

Introduction 215

Demographics of Latinos in the United States 216

Employment Strategies in Various Categories 218

Unemployment Statistics 218

Educational Development of Latinos 219

Findings Disproving Genetic and Cultural Traits
as Causes of Underachievement
Among Mexican Americans 220

Variables Associated with Increased Achievement
Among Mexican American Students 224

Conclusions 229

Summary of Results 231

Discussion Questions 232

References 232

11. TEACHING ASIAN AMERICAN CHILDREN 239

Ming-Gong John Lian

Characteristics of Asian American Children 240

Uniqueness of Educating Asian American Children 243

Parents of Asian American Children   245
Suggestions for Teachers   248
Summary   251
Discussion Questions   251
References   251

12. ISSUES IN THE EDUCATION OF AFRICAN
    AMERICAN STUDENTS WITH DISABILITIES   254
    Gwendolyn T. Benson
    Introduction   254
    Trends   255
    Learning Styles   256
    Self-Esteem   257
    Family Involvement   257
    Instructional Approaches   258
    Learning Environment   259
    Discussion Questions   260
    References   261

13. THE CULTURALLY AND LINGUISTICALLY
    DIFFERENT STUDENT   263
    Elva Durán
    Who is the Culturally and Linguistically Different Student? 263
    Historical Information   264
    Cultural Implications   265
    Curricular Implications   267
    Functional Reading and Language Intervention   268
    Vocational and Community Training   271
    Discussion Questions   274
    References   274

14. STRATEGIES FOR TEACHING
    THE SECOND LANGUAGE LEARNERS   276
    Elva Durán
    Second Language Acquisition Information   276
    Total Physical Response Approach   280
    The Natural Approach   281
    Sheltered Instruction/Specifically Designed Academic
        Instruction in English (SDAIE)   284
    Other Strategies Useful in Teaching
        Second Language Learners   287

Inclusion 289

Discussion Questions 290

References 290

15. ADDRESSING CULTURAL AND LINGUISTIC
DIVERSITY IN SPECIAL EDUCATION 292

Patricia Thomas Cegelka & Eugene C. Valles

Special Education Practices 292

Developing Effective Educational Programs 295

Parent Participation and Community Involvement 310

Bilingual Special Education Teacher Competencies 311

Summary 316

Discussion Questions 317

References 317

16. CROSSCULTURAL LANGUAGE AND
ACADEMIC DEVELOPMENT 321

Bruce A. Ostertag

What is CLAD? 326

A Blueprint for a Combined Teacher Credentials Program 328

Summary 340

Discussion Questions 340

References 341

17. A PROACTIVE ASSESSMENT FRAMEWORK TO
MEET THE CHALLENGE OF DIVERSITY 343

Elba Maldonado-Colón

Concerns in Assessment 343

Understanding the Ontogeny of the
Current Educational Condition 345

A Proactive Perspective 349

Conclusion 361

Discussion Questions 361

References 362

Index 365

TEACHING STUDENTS WITH MODERATE/SEVERE DISABILITIES, INCLUDING AUTISM

Chapter 1

BUILDING INCLUSIVE COMMUNITIES

Paula M. Gardner

INCLUSIVE EDUCATION AND EDUCATIONAL REFORM

Research and legislation have played a major role in the history of special education services for children with severe disabilities. Two decades ago, programs for students with severe disabilities consisted of segregated schools and denied opportunities for integration within the community (Brown et al., 1989). As the political and moral climate began to change in the 1950s, a shift began to occur.

THE CIVIL RIGHTS MOVEMENT

The Brown v. Board of Education decision (1954) was the first case to address the issue of racial desegregation of schools (Turnbull, 1993). As Chief Justice Earl Warren ruled in the 1954 decision, separateness in education is inherently unequal. The Brown decision recognized "that if black children were educated separately, even in facilities "equal" to those of white children, their treatment was inherently unequal because of the stigma attached to being educated separately and the deprivation of interaction with children of other backgrounds" (Rothstein, 1994). The application of the principles set forth in the Brown decision provided advocates of the disabled with the vehicle to address equal educational opportunities for children with disabilities. Brown v. Board of Education was a major impetus behind impending "right to education" cases (Turnbull, 1993).

LEGISLATION

In 1960, as a result of the widespread attention "right to education" court cases were receiving, President John F. Kennedy and Vice President Hubert Humphrey established the President's Committee on Mental Retardation (Turnbull, 1993). In 1966, Congress established the Bureau of Education for the Handicapped Act, with the goal of providing leadership in special education programming (Turnbull, 1993).

By 1971, the principles set forth in the Brown v. Board of Education decision became a legal theory for two landmark decisions. These two court decisions cleared the way for reforming the way America would educate children with disabilities in the future (Marozas & May, 1988). The Pennsylvania Association for Retarded Children (PARC) v. Commonwealth of Pennsylvania and Mills v. D.C. Board of Education ruled that children with disabilities have the right of access to public education. These cases found that "denial of education to children with disabilities and denial of due process in so doing violates the Fourteenth Amendment to the Constitution, which provides that the states may not deprive anyone of "life, liberty, or property, without due process of law" nor deny anyone "equal protection of the laws" (Rothstein, 1994, p. 12). These cases not only affirmed the right to education for children with disabilities, but also the right to a *least restrictive environment* (Turnbull, 1993). In response, Congress established federal aid to those states who provided "full educational opportunities to all handicapped children" (Public Law 93-380). Congress acknowledged that Public Law 93-380 was only to serve as an interim until Congress could enact legislation that would mandate free and appropriate public education for all children with disabilities (Hallahan & Kauffman, 1993). What followed was the 1975 passage of Public Law 94-142, The Education for All Handicapped Children Act. This law provided the framework for which children with disabilities would be guaranteed comprehensive and consistent educational programming (Rothstein, 1990).

THE LEAST RESTRICTIVE ENVIRONMENT

A major component of Public Law 94-142 is the principle of integration. Integration emphasizes the education of children with disabilities in the *least restrictive environment* (Marozas & May, 1988). The goal of integration is the practice of providing students with disabilities the opportunity for interaction with and social acceptance by students without disabilities (Stainback & Stainback, 1986). Specifically, Public Law 94-142 (reauthorized 101-476, Individuals with Disabilities Act, IDEA) reflects the legal intention to educate students with disabilities in the general education environment by mandating:

... to the maximum extent appropriate, handicapped children in public and private institutions or other care facilities are educated with children who are not handicapped, and that special classes, separate schooling, and other removal of handicapped children from the regular educational environment occurs only when the nature or severity of the handicap is such that education in regular classes, with the use of supplementary aids and services cannot be achieved satisfactorily (Rothstein, 1990, pp. 317–318).

Accordingly, the education of students with disabilities has increasingly been advocated as a shared responsibility between general and special educators (Wang, Walberg, & Reynolds, 1992).

Despite the considerable progress that has been made concerning the education of children with disabilities, educators still have differing opinions on how to define, interpret, and implement the education of children with disabilities in the least restrictive environment. Gottlieb (1981) stated, "At this point in time we are more concerned with placing children in the least restrictive environment than educating them in the least restrictive environment" (p. 122). Though laudable, the interpretation of and placement in the least restrictive environment is not as simple as it seems.

SPECIAL EDUCATION REFORM EFFORTS: THE REGULAR EDUCATION INITIATIVE

Looking beyond federal legislation, recent attention in the educational literature has focused on the merger of general and special education services (Schloss, 1992). What has emerged from this highly controversial issue of least restrictive environment and integration is the political, economic, and sociological issue of reconceptualizing the goals of special education through reform efforts such as the Regular Education Initiative (REI) and full inclusion. Both the Regular Education Initiative and full inclusion have been described as full access to a restructured mainstream for all students with, respectively, mild and severe disabilities (Skrtic, 1991). These two reform proposals are still being debated. In 1986, through speeches and articles, Madeleine Will, then Assistant Secretary of the U.S. Department of Education, suggested that the "dual system" of educating students with disabilities presumes that students with learning problems cannot receive an appropriate education in the regular education classroom and, therefore, must be educated in separate remedial programs, such as a resource room or special class. This is referred to as the "pull-out approach" (Will, 1986). Will argues that the "pull-out" approach is driven by "conceptual fallacy; that poor performance in learning can be understood solely in terms of deficiencies in the student rather than deficiencies in the learning environment" (Will, 1986, p. 13). This approach would require educators to always "create a new educational environment" (Will, 1986, p. 14). Will contends that the REI is a commitment to "search for ways to serve as many children as possible in the regular classroom by encouraging special education and other special programs to form a partnership with regular education. Will stated "the objective of the partnership for special education and the other special programs is to use their knowledge and expertise to support regular education in educating children with learning problems" (Will, 1986, p. 23). In the same year, Will cited several problem areas affecting the current special education service delivery model:

(1)   Special education services are fragmented into numerous categorical programs.
(2)   Special education and regular education are a dual system of education where the responsibility for students with disabilities is passed to the special education professional.
(3)   Special education students in segregated programs are often stigmatized by their chronological age peers.
(4)   Eligibility criteria are often so rigid that disputes between parents and schools develop and impact negatively on the student's education (Will, 1986a, p. 412).

Proponents of the REI (Davis, 1989; Wang, Reynolds, & Walberg, 1986, 1987, 1988, 1989, 1992; Reynolds & Wang, 1981; Spon-Shevin, 1988; Stainback & Stainback, 1984, 1986, 1987, 1988, 1989, 1990; Gartner & Lipsky, 1987, 1989) call for "a dissolution of the present dual system in our public school system, to be replaced by a unitary educational system, which, if carefully designed and implemented, would allow for a more effective and appropriate education for all students" (Davis, 1989, p. 440). Stainback et al. (1989c) suggested that, while education is "technically a sub-system of regular education, the United States has in effect created a separate system for educating students with disabilities. The operation of separate systems has a number of disadvantages, including: (a) the instructional needs of students do not warrant the operation of a dual system; (b) maintaining a dual system is inefficient; and (c) the dual system fosters an inappropriate and unfair attitude about the education of students classified as having disabilities" (p. 15).

Proponents of the REI also contend that separating and segregating students with disabilities from their nondisabled peers results in stigmatization (Biklen & Zollers, 1986; Gartner & Lipsky, 1987; Lilly, 1988; Reynolds, Wang, & Walberg, 1987; Stainback & Stainback, 1984; Stainback, Stainback & Forest, 1989; & Wang & Birch, 1984). As a critic of the Regular Education Initiative, Kauffman (1989) argued that the negative effects of labeling a student with disabilities have been overestimated and that "the nonlabeling issue is exploitable for its public relations value . . . [and] is also consistent with the Reagan-Bush administration's approach to equity issues, which relies on the surface appeal of nondiscrimination without analysis of the deeper meanings for individuals with a history of disadvantage" (p. 265). While Hallahan and Kauffman; Lloyd and McKinney (1988) contended that the REI is not based on research, but on the opinions presented in an early paper by Margaret Wang and Maynard Reynolds (1981), Will argues otherwise. Will (1986) contended that the REI is based on empirical research outlined in studies on the inadequacies of current special education service delivery models (i.e., Heller et al., 1982; Hobbs, 1975, 1980; Wang et al., 1981). Writers commonly identified as critics of the REI (Hallahan & Kauffman, 1994; Lloyd, & McKinney, 1988; Gerber, 1988; & Keogh, 1988) advocate for a more cautious approach to the restructuring of general and special education programs. A major argument has been that the REI is "consistent with the Reagan-Bush policy objectives of reducing federal influence and expenditures for education, which have resulted in declining federal support for programs designed to ensure equity in education of the disadvantaged and handicapped" (Kauffman, 1989, p. 256). Others question general educators' willingness to educate students with disabilities (Singer, 1988). Singer asked "What leads special educators to believe that regular educators are willing to take back responsibility for special needs children" (1988, p. 416)? Additionally, critics of the REI caution against the dissolution of the current dual educational system (Kauffman & Hallahan, 1990; Byrnes, 1990). Byrnes (1990) stated, "Without clear proof that the REI is more beneficial to these children, whose current rights are hard-won, how can a teacher, principal, or special education administrator tell a parent that the old way is no longer good and that REI is better? What evidence will we bring to a court" (p. 348)? While proponents contend the REI is based on empirical research, opponents characterize the United States

Office of Special Education and Rehabilitative Services (OSERS) policy statement as a political proposal grounded in ideology.

INCLUSIVE EDUCATION

Will's (1986) advocacy to educate students with learning problems, including "those who are learning slowly, those with behavioral problems, those who may be educationally disadvantaged, those who have mild specific learning disabilities and emotional problems (p. 1) in the general education classroom (i.e., the Regular Education Initiative) has been expanded to include children with severe disabilities in the general education classroom. Full inclusion, inclusive schooling, and inclusive education are terms that have emerged to describe this practice. Full inclusion represents a statement of public policy that affects the fields of both general and special education. Full inclusion refers to the practice of educating all children in neighborhood classrooms and schools (Lipsky, & Gartner, 1989). "Full inclusion asserts that each student living within the boundaries of a particular school should be included in all aspects of life at that school" (Alper & Ryndak, 1992, p. 374). Full inclusion is a policy of placing students with disabilities "in a regular education class-room for the entire day. The necessary support services to ensure an appropriate education come to the student in the regular class setting" (Hardman, Drew, Egan & Wolf, 1993, p. 485). Full inclusion has been "heralded as critical for social, educational, legal, and philosophical reasons" (Hanline & Fox, 1993). Sailor (1991) outlined the basic components of most full inclusion models as:

(1)   All students attend the school to which they would go if they had no disability.

(2)   A natural proportion (i.e., representative of the school district at large) of students with disabilities occurs at any school site.

(3)   A zero-reject philosophy exists so that typically no student would be excluded on the basis of type or extent of disability.

(4)   School and general education placements are age- and grade appropriate, with no self-contained special education classes operative at the school site.

(5)   Cooperative learning and peer instructional methods receive significant use in general instructional practice at the school site.

(6)   Special education supports are provided within the context of the general education class and in other integrated environments (p. 10) (refer to Table I).

Debate surrounding the issue of moving from an exclusive educational system toward one where all students are included, where the primary

TABLE I
DOES FEDERAL LAW REQUIRE INCLUSION?

▼INDIVIDUALS WITH DISABILITIES EDUCATION ACT (P.L. 101-476)

Each public agency shall insure:

(a) "Each handicapped child's educational placement:
  (1) is determined at least annually;
  (2) is based on his or her individualized education program; and
  (3) is as close as possible to the child's home.

(b) The various alternative placements included under Reg. 300.551 are available to the extent necessary to implement the individualized education program for each handicapped child.

(c) Unless a handicapped child's individualized education program requires some other arrangement, *the child is educated in the school which he or she would attend if not handicapped;* and

(d) In selecting the least restrictive environment, consideration is given to any potential harmful effect on the child or on the quality of services which he or she needs." (34-CFR 300.552)

▼REHABILITATION ACT OF 1973—SECTION 504

"A recipient (of federal funds) to which this subpart applies shall educate, or shall provide for the education of, each qualified handicapped person in its jurisdiction with persons who are not handicapped to the maximum extent appropriate to the needs of the handicapped person. A recipient shall place a handicapped person in the regular educational environment operated by the recipient unless it is demonstrated by the recipient that *the education of the person in the regular environment with the use of supplementary aids and services cannot be achieved satisfactorily.* Whenever a recipient places a person in a setting other than the regular educational environment pursuant to this paragraph, it shall take into account the proximity of the alternate setting to the person's home." (34 CFT 104.34)

placement of the child is in a general education classroom, where the necessary support services (i.e., special education teacher, paraprofessionals, curriculum materials, and technology aids) to ensure that an appropriate education comes to the student in the general class setting, has very recently been at the forefront of educational concern, as exemplified in California by the Board of Education v. Holland, 1992 case. A decision by U.S. District Court Judge David E. Levi, in the 1992 Holland case, affirmed a severely disabled child's right to an inclusive school program. Judge Levi supported the testimony of significant nonacademic benefits a disabled child may receive from interaction with nondisabled peers. Judge Levi's decision reflects the fundamental purpose of the Individuals with Disabilities Education Act's integration requirement (Holland, Civ. S-90-1171-DFL). According to Disability Rights Education and defense attorney Diane Lipton (Lipton, 1994),

> The decision of the Ninth Circuit is a momentous victory for children with disabilities across the nation. The Holland case follows in the tradition of Brown v. Board of Education. It signals the end to a system that automatically excludes children with disabilities from the regular public school classroom and relegates them to segregated 'handicapped only' classes and schools.

In support of the decision, the Justice Department, on behalf of the Office of Special Education of the United States Department of Education, filed an amicus brief. On June 13, 1994, the United States Supreme Court affirmed Judge Levi's decision refusing to hear the school district's appeal, leaving the Ninth Circuit landmark decision intact.

AMERICA 2000: THE EDUCATE AMERICA ACT

The United States government has also been engaged in comprehensive school restructuring and reform efforts. In March, 1994, former President Bush embraced school reform by announcing America 2000: Educate America Act. This bipartisan reform effort provides monetary resources to states to assist in developing and implementing comprehensive educational reform. It has been described as "the beginning of a new era in school and education reform—a revolutionary, all inclusive plan to change every aspect of our education system, while at the same time aligning its individual parts with one another" (p. 1). America 2000 has four central themes: (a) better and more accountable schools for today; (b) a new generation of schools for tomorrow; (c) becoming a nation of students; and (d) making our communities places where learning happens (U.S. Department of Education, 1994). Public Law 103-227 includes six goals developed by President Bush and two additional goals established by the Clinton administration (refer to Table II).

Although the language of Goals 2000 specifically addresses the needs of "all children," many have questioned whether the legislation and terms "all children" includes students with disabilities. The new legislation is, however, clear in the bill's definition of "all children" to include not only typical learners, but also those who are from diverse cultural and ethnic backgrounds, limited English proficient, disadvantaged, and those students with disabilities.

> The terms "all students" and "all children" mean students or children from broad range of backgrounds and circumstances, including disadvantaged students and children, students or children with diverse racial, ethnic, and cultural background, American Indians, Alaska Natives, Native Hawaiians, students or children with

TABLE II
AMERICA 2000: EDUCATE AMERICA ACT

Goal 1: By the year 2000, all children in America will start school ready to learn.

Goal 2: By the year 2000, the high school graduation rate will increase to at least 90 percent.

Goal 3: By the year 2000, American students will leave grades four, eight, and twelve having demonstrated competency in challenging subject matter, including English, mathematics, science, history, and geography; and every school in America will ensure that all students learn to use their minds well, so that they may be prepared for responsible citizenship, further learning, and productive employment in our modern economy.

Goal 4: By the year 2000, U.S. students will be first in the world in science and mathematics achievement.

Goal 5: By the year 2000, every adult American will be literate and will possess the knowledge and skills necessary to compete in a global economy and exercise the rights and responsibilities of citizenship.

Goal 6: By the year 2000, every school in America will be free of drugs, violence, and the unauthorized presence of firearms and alcohol and will offer a disciplined environment conducive to learning.

Goal 7: By the year 2000, the nation's teaching force will have access to programs for the continued improvement of their professional skills and the opportunity to acquire the knowledge and skills needed to instruct and prepare all American students for the next century.

Goal 8: By the year 2000, every school will promote partnerships that will increase parental involvement and participation in promoting the social, emotional, and academic growth of children.

disabilities, students or children with limited English proficiency, school-aged students or children who have dropped out of school, migratory students or children, and academically talented students and children (Public Law 103-227).

The Office of Special Education and Rehabilitation Services (OSER) has also identified some key program features of the America 2000 initiative. One of the most important features with relation to inclusion is as follows: "All students, including those with disabilities, are a valued part of the school community and contribute unique talents and perspectives to the school. All students must be ensured equal opportunities to access activities, materials, equipment, and classrooms throughout the entire building" (Smith, 1991). Additional features of inclusive educational practices identified in Feature #2 of the America 2000 initiative are as follows:

PRACTICE 1: Schools should provide opportunities for students to have shared experiences by offering extra-curricular activities to promote a sense of belonging and to teach students how to relate to and communicate with peers.

PRACTICE 2: Peer advocate and peer tutoring programs are examples of edu-

cational strategies that equip students with the skills involving
empathy and problem solving, and that foster mutual understanding and respect.

PRACTICE 3: School programs should promote social supports and friendships
among students with disabilities and their non disabled peers.
Strategies include forming circles of friends and recruiting intact
student cliques from social networks (Smith, Hunter, & Schrag,
1991).

Quality education for all children is the goal of America 2000. It is
designed to promote educational systems that increase implementation
strategies that foster inclusive communities. It supports the collaborative
ethic inherent in full inclusion.

CONTINUUM OF SERVICES

Despite school reform efforts such as the Regular Education Initiative,
full inclusion, and Goals 2000, large gaps exist between policy and
practice. State and local agencies continue to prescribe educational
placements based on a continuum. A **continuum of services** implies
districts offer a range of different educational placement options ranging
from the most restrictive, full-time residential school, to the least restrictive,
the general education classroom. The continuum of services model
(Deno, 1970), although intended to provide a variety of service options
based on the individual skills and needs of a student, helped to create a
system of lock-stepped placements based on disability labels. Students
with severe disabilities were automatically placed in self-contained special education classrooms of students with similar disabilities. Unfortunately, this practice continues today. As a result, placements in general
education classrooms have eluded the overwhelming majority of children with severe disabilities (Wang, Walberg, & Reynolds, 1992). The
typical service delivery model is one where students are placed in a
resource or self-contained special education classroom with limited opportunity for integration with nondisabled peers. Advocates of inclusion
prefer to view the continuum of service model as one which is fluid,
placing all students with disabilities in the least restrictive environment,
the general education classroom. In this way all students with disabilities
are given the opportunity to be educated with their nondisabled peers
unless documented evidence supports a more restrictive placement on
the continuum.

BUILDING INCLUSIVE COMMUNITIES

In order for students with disabilities to be successfully included in the general education classroom, administrators, general and special education faculty and staff, and parents must demonstrate a strong commitment to the education of all children. The principles necessary for building successful inclusive school communities involves careful planning and support. Table III represents principles necessary for building an effective learning environment where all children are valued members of the school community. These principles and resulting recommendations are based on extensive research from various authorities. They include:

(1) A vision or mission statement that reflects a shared commitment to educating all children.
(2) A strong sense of community involvement in the education of all children.
(3) Strong administrative leadership.
(4) Collaboration and cooperation.
(5) An understanding of changing roles and responsibilities among both general and special educators.
(6) Support services.
(7) A commitment to the study and celebration of diversity.
(8) A partnership with parents.

The following section further elaborates on some of these principles. In addition, other specific strategies for successfully building inclusive communities have been addressed.

TEACHER ACCEPTANCE

In order for inclusion to be a positive, meaningful experience for all children, the classroom teacher must become a confident and comfortable facilitator of learning and support opportunities. This may come easily for some and not for others. In Gardner's (1994) study on exemplary inclusive general education teachers, teachers anecdotally shared such feelings as, "I wasn't sure if I was doing the right things . . . but then I began to watch how the other children were reacting . . . it all seemed so natural." Another teacher commented "I was so nervous in the beginning . . . it's hard to believe . . . he is such a joy," and "I was spend-

TABLE III
Principles for Building Successful
Inclusive School Communities

Presentation by Dr. Paula M. Gardner

ing so much time worrying and planning about how to make her fit in that I forgot to just let her be a kid." One teacher summarized her feelings by anecdotally stating "By helping her with her social interactions I helped all the children . . . it's a win, win situation." School districts can support a teacher's ability to become a facilitator of learning and support opportunities through general and special education collaboration and on-going, in-service training. By doing so, districts demonstrate a clear commitment to building successful supported inclusive communities.

PROMOTING, UNDERSTANDING, AND CELEBRATING INDIVIDUAL DIFFERENCES

Classroom teachers can promote an acceptance and understanding of differences by creating an environment of positive supports. These supports are based on the principles for building successful inclusive school communities (see Table III) and inclusion considerations outlined in Table IV. These principles and considerations assume a clear understanding of the role of the general education teacher in the inclusion process. One such role may be that of an interpreter. This is not meant in the usual context of interpreting for students with hearing impairments, but rather assuming an interpretive role in order to interpret the behavior of children with disabilities. The general education teacher can provide meaningful and valuable bits of information for nondisabled students. Exemplary inclusive teachers can be observed answering specific student questions about a disabled student's behavior and/or needs. An example of this is "Will Pammy fall down if we don't hold on to her?" or "Why is she so wobbly," or "When she screeches like that does that mean she is excited?" This additional interpretive support for example, "When Matt covers his ears like that he is telling you something . . . you are speaking too fast and/or too loud for him," or "What Anthony is trying to tell you is that he wants to be the first to roll the dice" results in an increased understanding of both the feelings and behaviors of the students with disabilities. Nondisabled students will often positively respond by saying such statements as "I hate when people speak all at one time or too loud at me, too" and "Pammy can hold on to me if she wants to." As a result, a better understanding of a child's gifts and needs are demonstrated. Robert Barth (1990), a Harvard Professor described the value of differences in a statement:

> I would prefer my children to be in a school in which differences are looked for, attended to, and celebrated as good news, as opportunities for learning. The question with which so many school people are preoccupied is, "What are the limits of diversity beyond which behavior is unacceptable?" But the question I would like to see asked more often is, "How can we make conscious, deliberate use of difference in social class, gender, age, ability, race, and interest resources for learning?" Differences hold great opportunities for learning. Differences offer a free, abundant, and renewable resource. I would like to see our compulsion for eliminating differences replaced by an equally compelling focus on making use of these differences to improve schools. What is important about people—and about school—is what is different, not what is the same (pp. 514–515).

TABLE IV
INCLUSION CONSIDERATIONS

Inclusion Considerations

✖ Fair is not the same—Fair is *getting what you need.*

✖ Special education is not a *room* or *building.*

✖ Students with disabilities are not the *only* students that present diverse needs that require individual accommodations.

Presentation by: *Dr. Paula M. Gardner*   Adapted from: *BTSA Sacramento Consortium*

PEER ACCEPTANCE

Students with disabilities need to be included in the general education classroom physically, instructionally, and socially if successful peer acceptance is to take place. Students who are included physically, but not instructionally and or socially, will continue to remain isolated from their nondisabled peers. There are several ways teachers can promote the inclusion of students with disabilities. Providing information, curricular infusion, and cooperative teaching efforts help to facilitate peer acceptance (Smith et al., 1995). In addition, limiting the number of students with severe disabilities in each class may allow for more successful positive social interactions to occur. Providing students with disabilities the opportunity to attend their neighborhood school is also a way districts can support peer acceptance. Familiarity or prior social interactions may make an important contribution to the frequency of social interactions. In a review of play behavior, Rubin, Fein, and Vendenberg (1983) reported that children tended to select and interact when in the company of a familiar peer. Doyle, Connolly, and Rivest (1980) reported similar results. Another explanation may suggest that social interactions with peers who have disabilities may be a valued source of personal growth for many nondisabled students. This finding supports Peck, Donaldson, and Pezzoli's descriptive study (1990) which investigated twenty-one nondisabled high school student's perceptions of benefits received from developing relationships with peers who had moderate or severe disabilities.

Results of the study indicated nondisabled student's relationships with students with disabilities resulted in improvements in self concept (e.g., "I felt good about myself"), growth in social cognition (e.g., "They have feelings too, and they need to have the same things we do, and they feel the same things we do"), increased tolerance of other people (e.g., "I've treated my own friends better . . . I haven't been as cold to people"), reduced fear of human difference (e.g., "You get to meet a whole range of people—so you're not afraid of the unknown anymore), development of personal principles (e.g., "If there is something personal between us then they're just going to be my friend, no matter what other people say"), and interpersonal acceptance and friendship (e.g., "I felt like I could just be myself and have fun"). The extent of benefits and/or personal satisfaction received from such interactions is an important question to address in future research.

SUPPORT SYSTEMS

In order for successful inclusive education programs to become a reality, districts must be committed to providing staff development and supplementary aid and supports services. These supports may include full or part-time instructional support personnel, peer support, technological support, and flexible planning time for general and special education teacher collaboration.

In schools such as Mariemont Elementary in Sacramento, California, neighborhood students with disabilities are included in every aspect of the school community. This has been established through careful planning, encouragement, and the belief that all children bring unique needs and gifts to the educational community.

This planning includes various steps of preparation in order to provide successful inclusive opportunities. These steps include:

Step 1: Identifying the supportive educational team;

Step 2: Getting to know the student, including identifying the strengths and areas of need;

Step 3: Developing educational goals based on both parent and teacher(s) desired outcomes;

Step 4: Identifying necessary support services;

Step 5: Developing a daily schedule of activities, peer tutoring, and or peer buddy programs;

Step 6: Establishing a regularly scheduled time for general and special education teacher collaboration;

Step 7: Establishing a regularly scheduled time for parent/teacher collaboration

Step 8: Establishing a plan for on-going evaluation of the student's needs and accomplishments;

Step 9: Personal and professional development opportunities.

COLLABORATION

General and special education teachers must regularly interact and collaborate if inclusive educational communities are to be successful. Through collaboration, teachers are given the opportunity to share their expertise and skills. Two major assumptions of effective collaboration in the schools are (Idol & West, 1991):

(1)   Educational collaboration as an adult-to-adult interactive process can be expected to have an indirect impact on student outcomes; thus, the process of educational collaboration among adult team members typically yields changes in teams member attitudes, skills, knowledge, and/or behaviors first, followed by changes in student and/or organizational outcomes.

(2)   Educational collaboration may be used as problem solving: thus, it can be an effective tool for proactive strategic planning or reactive, but efficient, problem solving in any organizational structure in the school environment (p. 72).

When implemented properly, the general and special education collaborative approach of providing services to students with disabilities promotes the concept of teaching smarter not harder.

CURRICULUM ADAPTATION AND SUPPORTIVE INSTRUCTIONAL PRACTICES

Although each effective inclusive classroom may be unique in itself, most reflect very specific common supportive instructional practices. These practices include multilevel instruction, cooperative learning, mastery learning, instructional technology, peer support, high rates of reinforcement for specific behaviors, and activity based learning. In addition, the general education curriculum is modified, adapted, and or expanded, when necessary, to reflect the diverse learning needs of each child. Table V provides a sample of possible curriculum adaptations for students with special needs.

TABLE V
INCLUSIVE EDUCATION GUIDELINES

As Is:	Students are involved in the same lesson as other students with the same objectives and using the same materials.
Providing Physical Assistance:	The teacher or support person assist a student in completing an activity by the actual manipulation of materials, equipment, or his/her body.
Adapting Materials:	Students utilizing materials that allow for participation in age-appropriate activities without having prerequisite basic motor, communicative, or cognitive skills.
Multilevel Curriculum:	Students are working in the same subject area, but working at different levels of curriculum.
Curriculum Overlapping:	Students are involved in the same activity with other students but may have a goal from a different curriculum area.
Substitute Curriculum:	Students are involved in alternative activities that meet primary instructional needs when the general education curriculum at the time does not.

Adapted from Neary, T., Halvorsen, A., & Smithey, L. (1992). Inclusive education guidelines. Sacramento, CA: California State Department of Education.

Cheney (1989) suggested that curricular modifications align the level of achievement of the student and the level of the instructional material, the characteristics of the learner and the level of the instructional material or technique, and the motivational aspects of the learner and of the material in (in Smith, Polloway, Patton, and Dowdy, 1995). This alignment will, in effect, result in all children benefiting from specialized support and assistance.

COOPERATIVE INCLUSION

Successful inclusive communities are ones where teachers prepare the environment and materials in such a way so as to lend themselves more readily to cooperative use. For example, flexible heterogeneous groups, in well-defined areas, in proximity to each other, is an excellent inclusive strategy. In the primary grades (K–3) this may include carpeted areas. The use of cooperative grouping supports previous research (Brown, Fox, & Brady, 1987) that indicated interactions are more likely to occur if children are provided with cooperative activity areas near one another. This strategy also supports research conducted by Rynders, Johnson, Johnson, & Schmidt (1980) who found that a cooperative group structure, rather than a competitive or individualistic structure, facilitated significantly more positive interactions between severely disabled and nondisabled students. Consistent with Rynders' et al. study, Slavin (1990) found that students with disabilities made significant gains in a range of educational outcomes when included in cooperative groups within the general education classroom, and without loss to the nondisabled peers in the classroom.

Wang (1988) found similar results in a series of studies of the Adaptive Learning Environments model (ALEM), a general education-based service delivery model. Wang found the ALEM model increased the occurrences of spontaneous sharing, resulting in reciprocal positive social responses by peers. In addition, teachers who briefly involve themselves in a cooperative activity accomplish a number of other goals. Not only are the teachers able to closely monitor and modify the interactions taking place between the disabled student and nondisabled peers, they are also able to demonstrate they too enjoy interacting with the disabled student. This "enjoying" behavior may include participating in the cooperative process, playing a game, laughing, joking, and or sharing. Providing an opportunity for students with severe disabilities to interact with their nondisabled peers is just one piece of the complex structure that must be created if full inclusion is to become a reality (Tally & Burnette, 1982).

BUILDING PEER RELATIONSHIPS

One of the primary reasons for advocating inclusive education is the opportunity for social interaction between students with disabilities and those without disabilities. Current research has found that teachers play a significant and critical role in facilitating strategies that address the social interactions of children (McEvoy et al., 1990). In a study by Gardner (1994), general education teacher behaviors that facilitate positive social interactions between students with severe disabilities and their nondisabled peers in an inclusive classroom were examined? This study revealed thirteen teacher behaviors that facilitated positive social interactions. These behaviors included such strategies as **praise/compliments** for desired behaviors and/or approximations toward a desired social behavior of both the disabled student and his/her nondisabled peers, **verbal prompts** when necessary, **modeling** of appropriate social interactions, **questioning** the disabled child about the activity and/or interaction, **close proximity nonverbal facilitation, elicited peer support,** giving the student with a disability **choices** of what and with whom they would like to play, **affection** toward the student with a disability, and providing the disabled student an opportunity to **assume a leadership** role within the classroom. Additionally, the teachers **initiated conversation, engaged in a cooperative activity, provided physical assistance** when necessary, and used **gesture prompts** as a means to facilitate positive social interactions between disabled and nondisabled peers.

In each of the observed inclusive classrooms, specific strategies that preceded the occurrence of a social interaction between the disabled student and nondisabled peers were manipulated by the teacher. The strategy that was used most frequently was a behavior Gardner referred to as close proximity/nonverbal facilitation. This behavior is described as standing near a student to student interaction and silently observing the social interaction. The facial expression of each of the teachers was one of approval, as validated by a smile. The teachers were not observed intervening in any way. The students did, however, appear aware of this observing behavior. On several occasions, the students glanced at the teacher, smiled, and immediately resumed the play behavior. This led Gardner to initially question whether this behavior was a teacher mediated strategy to increase or maintain positive social interactions. Soderhan and Whiren (1985) have suggested that monitoring teacher-child interaction may actually lead to increased social interactions among peers. Close proximity nonverbal facilitation allowed time for natural social interactions to occur, using positive facial expressions to support and maintain the social interaction. Gardner contends this teacher behavior is purposeful and deliberate in its attempt to promote positive social interactions between disabled and nondisabled peers, followed closely by eliciting peer support, teacher praise/compliments, verbal prompts, and teacher modeling.

Other frequently observed teacher behaviors included teacher prompt, praise, modeling, and peer support. Research supporting the use of these strategies is well documented. It should be noted, however, that some nondisabled peers may appear to ignore or respond to students with disabilities in a rather neutral way. A teacher may initially view this as an undesirable behavior. However, many inclusive teachers view this as a very normal pattern of behavior. Most nondisabled children experience both positive and negative social interactions, neutral interactions, and/or children who appear to ignore or tolerate them. In essence, the disabled students are experiencing the continuum of possible social interactions.

The results of Gardner's study supported Gottlieb's (1981) suggestion that mere placement in a regular education classroom alone is not sufficient to provide for increased social interactions between disabled and nondisabled students. Specific teacher behaviors to facilitate social interactions is an important factor in stimulating social interaction.

CIRCLE OF FRIENDS

In many inclusive classrooms, teachers use a more formalized program to increase social interactions between disabled and nondisabled peers. One such program used throughout the United States is called "Circle of Friends" (Forest, 1986; O'Brien, Forest, Snow, & Hasbury, 1989; Perske, 1988). In this program, the teacher asks for student volunteers to participate in a "circle of friends" activity. While this intervention almost guarantees substantial contact between the disabled student and their nondisabled peers, the teacher still assumes a pivotal role in the facilitation of interactions. The activity, in its intention to support social interactions between the student with disabilities and his/her peers, is equally reinforcing to all participants. The following are examples of a "circle of friends" meeting involving Matt, a fourth grade student with autism. The teacher begins:

- Matt, we are going to go around the group to discuss what our favorite sandwich is? I'll go first . . . I love tuna fish. When I was little I use to love to put potato chips on my sandwich. [students laugh] Can anyone think of a question to ask the group . . . related to what their favorite sandwich is or what they'd like for lunch? [Matt responds]

- Matt, remember . . . when we talk to someone what do we usually do first? [no response] Ask "what kind of food do you like?"
- [Matt responds] What kind of sandwich do you like?
- [Teacher] But who are you talking to?
- [Matt] Nora.
- [Teacher] Ah, so if you say Nora's name first would that get her attention?
- [Matt] Yes.
- [Teacher] Go ahead then.
- [Matt] Nora, what kind of fruit do you like?
- [Nora] Grapes.
- [Matt] I like grapes, too.
- [Teacher] Great! Did you see how Matt addressed Nora by name first? Let's see if you can all remember to do that.

Another section of the discussion went as follows:

- [Teacher] Before we go out to recess, let's share one thing we did this weekend. Anybody want to go first?
- [Matt listens to another student and then asks] What kind of bad guy?
- [Teacher] Good question Matt.
- [Student] A bad guy that was in the movie. [student continues to share].
- [Student] Matt, did you do something this weekend?
- [Matt] I went to the mountains . . . to go camping . . . I forgot what place it was.
- [Another student] Was it Truckee?
- [Matt] Yes, I went up there to have fun with my parents.
- [Student] Great.
- [Teacher] You all did something very nice. You asked questions and shared your experiences. Many of you had similar experiences. Asking questions and sharing experiences is a very nice way of keeping a conversation going.

In addition to providing support through informal discussions, the teacher was also able to model, prompt, and facilitate social interactions that may generalize to other situations and environments.

BARRIERS TO BUILDING INCLUSIVE CLASSROOMS

Although widespread support of inclusive education exists, barriers to successful inclusion should not be overlooked. Smith, Polloway, Patton, and Dowdy (1995) cite a number of barriers to the successful inclusion of students with disabilities:

- General educators have not been involved sufficiently and are, therefore, not likely to support the model.
- General educators as well as special educators do not have the collaboration skills necessary to make inclusion successful.

- There is limited empirical data to support the model. Therefore, full implementation should be put on hold until sound research supports the effort.
- Full inclusion of students with disabilities into general education classrooms will take away from students without disabilities and lessen their quality of education.
- Current funding, teacher training, and teacher certification is based on separate educational systems.
- Some students with disabilities do better when served in special education classes by special education teachers (p. 83).

Critics of inclusion continue to assert that inclusive practices are based on limited empirical evidence and that proponents of inclusion have traded rhetoric for reason. Advocates of inclusive practices remind critics of the extensive amount of research on the negative effects of labeling and separate segregated educational programming.

BENEFITS OF INCLUSIVE CLASSROOMS

There are no quick and easy magic recipes for building successful inclusive communities. The process of building inclusive communities will be one marked with questions and struggles. Those who have faced these questions and struggles (Smith et al., 1995) remind us of the benefits of inclusive educational opportunities for students with disabilities. These benefits include:

- Increased interactions between disabled and nondisabled peers.
- Less stigma than being pulled out of the classroom to receive instruction in the special education classroom.
- Increased levels of self-esteem.
- Avoidance of the problems often associated with identification and eligibility determination of students for special education.
- Closer interactions among all school personnel in working with all students.
- The dismantling of the artificial dual system of education currently provided in school (pp. 82–83).

BENEFITS OF INCLUSION FOR TYPICALLY DEVELOPING CHILDREN

Teachers, staff, and parents often question the benefits of inclusion for typically developing children. It would be an injustice not to conclude with the benefits inclusive education provides for all children.

- Classmates can develop enhanced responsibility and self-esteem.
- Classmates can build comfort, confidence, and a better understanding of the range of human diversity.
- Classmates benefit from the knowledge of a disabled students gifts as well as needs.
- Classmates are enriched by the opportunity to develop new friendships with students with disabilities.

DISCUSSION QUESTIONS

(1) How have historical events shaped inclusive reform efforts?
(2) What specific principles and strategies help to facilitate the building of successful inclusive communities?
(3) What kinds of peer support can be built for all children?
(4) How can the general education curriculum be modified in order to meet the diverse learning needs of children with special needs?

REFERENCES

Alper, S., and Ryndak, D. L. (1992). Educating students with severe handicaps in regular classes. *The Elementary School Journal, 92*, 373–384.

Barth, R. S. (1990). *Improving schools from within.* San Francisco: Jossey-Bass.

Biklin, D., and Zollers, (1986). The focus of advocacy in the LD field. *Journal of Learning Disabilities, 19*, (10), 579–586.

Board of Education, Sacramento City Unified School District, v. Rachel Holland, Civ. S-90-1171-DFL, March, 1992.

Brown, W. H., Fox, J. J., and Brady, M. P. (1987). The effects of spatial density on the socially directed behavior of three and four year old children during freeplay: An investigation of a setting factor. *Education and Treatment of Children, 10*, 247–258.

Brown, L., Long, E., Udvari-Solner, A., Schwarz, P., Van-Deventer, P., Ahlgren, S., Johnson, F., Gruenewald, L., and Jorgensen, J. (1989). Should students with severe disabilities be based in regular or in special education classrooms in home schools? *Journal of The Association for Persons with Severe Handicaps, 14*, 8–12.

Brown, L., Schwarz, P., Udari-Solner, A., Kampschroer, E., Johnson, F., Jorgensen, J., Duxstad, J., and Gruenewald, L. (1990). *How much time should students with severe intellectual disabilities spend in regular education classrooms and elsewhere?* Paper supported by grants to University of Wisconsin and Madison Metropolitan School district.

Brown, L., Schwarz, P., Udvari-Solner, A., Kampschroer, F., Johnson, F., Jorgensen, J., Duxstad, J., and Gruenewald, L. (1991). How much time should students with severe disabilities spend in the regular classroom? *Journal of The Association for Persons with Severe Handicaps, 16*, 39–47.

Brown v. Board of Education, 347 U.S. 483, (1954).

Byrnes, M. (1990). The regular education initiative debate: A view from the field. *Exceptional Children, 56*(4), 345–349.

Cheney, S. B. (1990). A modification perspective of special education curriculum: Introduction. *Academic Therapy, 25*(4), 391–394.

Davis, W. E. (1989). The regular education initiative debate: Its promises and problems. *Exceptional Children, 55*(5), 440–446.

Davis, W. E. (1990). Broad perspectives of the regular education initiative: Response to Byrnes. *Exceptional Children, 56*(4), 349–351.

Deno, E. (1970). Special education as development capital. *Exceptional Children, 37,* 231–237.

Doyle, A., Connolly, J., and Rivest, L. (1989). The effects of playmate familiarity on the social interactions of young children. *Child Development, 51,* 217–223.

Gardner, P. M. (1994). Unpublished dissertation. A study of exemplary general education teacher behaviors that facilitate positive social interactions between disabled and nondisabled students in a full inclusion classroom.

Gartner, A., and Lipsky, D. (1987). Beyond special education: Toward a quality system for all students. *Harvard Educational Review, 57,* 367–395.

Gartner, A., and Lipsky, D. (1989). *The yoke of special education: How to break it.* Rochester, NY: National Center on Education & the Economy.

Gerber, M. (1988). Tolerance and technology of instruction: Implications for special education reform. *Exceptional Children, 54,* 309–314.

Gottlieb, J. (1981). Mainstreaming: Fulfilling the promise? *American Journal of Mental Deficiency, 86,* 115–126.

Hallahan, D., and Kauffman, J. (1994). *Exceptional Children: Introduction To Exceptional Children* (6th ed.). Boston: Allyn & Bacon.

Hallahan, D. P., Kauffman, J. M., and Lloyd, J. W. (1988). *Introduction to learning disabilities* (3rd ed.). Englewood Cliffs, NJ: Prentice-Hall.

Halvorsen, A. T., and Sailor, W. (1990). Integration of students with severe and profound disabilities: A review of the research. In R. Gaylord-Ross (Ed.) *Issues and research in special education: Volume 1,* 410–472. New York: Teachers College Press.

Hanline, M. F., and Fox, L. (1993a). Learning within the context of play: Providing typical early childhood experiences for children with severe disabilities. *Journal of the Association for Parents with Severe Handicaps, 18*(2), 121–129.

Hanline, M. F. (1993b). Inclusion of preschoolers with profound disabilities: An analysis of children's interactions. *The Journal of the Association for Persons with Severe Handicaps, 18*(1), 28–35.

Hardman, M., Drew, C., Egan, M., and Wolf, B. (1993). *Human Exceptionality* (4th ed.). Boston: Allyn & Bacon, Inc.

Heller, K., Holtzman, W., and Messick, S. (1982). Placing children in special education: A strategy for equity. Washington, DC: National Academy of Sciences Press.

Hobbs, N. (1975). *The futures of children: Categories, labels, and their consequences.* San Francisco: Jossey-Bass.

Hobbs, N. (1980). An ecologically oriented service-based system for the classification of handicapped children. In E. Salzinger, J. Antrobus, and J. Glick (Eds.), *The ecosystem of the "risk" child* (pp. 271–290). New York: Academic Press.

Idol, L., and West, F. (1991). Educational collaboration: A catalyst for effective schooling. *Intervention in School and Clinic, 27,* 70–78.

Jenkins, J. R., and Pious, C. G. (1991). Full inclusion and the REI: A reply to Thousand and Villa. *Exceptional Children, 57*(6), 562–564.

Jenkins, J., Pious, C., and Jewell, M. (1990). Special education and the regular education initiative: Basic assumptions. *Exceptional Children, 56*(6), 479–491.

Kauffman, J., Gerber, M., and Semmell, M. (1988). Arguable assumptions underlying the regular education initiative. *Journal of Learning Disabilities, 21*(1), 6–11.

Kauffman, J. (1989). The regular education initiative as Reagan-Bush education policy: A trickle-down theory of education of the hard to teach. *The Journal of Special Education, 23*(3), 256–278.

Kauffman, J., and Hallahan, D. (1990). What we want for children: A rejoinder to REI proponents. *The Journal of Special Education, 24*(3), 340–345.

Kauffman, J. (1993). How we might achieve the radical reform of special education. *Exceptional Children, 60*(1), 6–16.

Keogh, B. (1988). Improving services for problem learners: Rethinking and restructuring. *Journal of Learning Disabilities, 21*(1), 19–22.

Lieberman, L. (1985). Special education and regular education: A merger made in heaven? *Exceptional Children, 51,* 513–516.

Lilly, S. (1988). The regular education initiative: A force for change in general and special education. *Education and Training in Mental Retardation, 23*(4), 253–260.

Lipsky, D. K., and Gartner, A. (1987). Capable of achievement and worthy of respect: Education for handicapped students as if they were full-fledged human beings. *Exceptional Children, 54*(1), 69–74.

Lipsky, D., and Gartner, A. (1989). *Beyond separate education-quality education for all.* Baltimore: Paul H. Brookes.

Lipton, D. (1994). Victory in landmark "full inclusion" case. *Disability rights education and defense fund news,* September, 1994.

Marozas, D., and May, D. (1988). *Issues and practices in special education.* New York: Longman.

McEvoy, M. A., Shores, R. E., Wehby, J. H., Johnson, S. M., and Fox, J. J. (1990). Special education teachers' implementation of procedures to promote social interaction among children. *Education and training in mental retardation, 25*(3), 267–276.

O'Brien, J., Forest, M., Snow, J., and Hasbury, D. (1989). *Action for inclusion.* Toronto: Frontier College Press.

Peck, C. A., Donaldson, J., and Pezzoli, M. (1990). Some benefits non-handicapped adolescents perceive for themselves from their social relationships with peers who have severe disabilities. *Journal of the Association for Persons with Severe Handicaps, 15*(4), 241–249.

PEERS: Inclusive education/supported education. (1992). California State Department Of Education.

Perske, R., and Perske, M. (1988). *Circles Of Friends.* Nashville, TN: Abingdon Press.

Reynolds, M. C., and Wang, M. C. (1981, September). *Restructuring "special" school programs.* Paper presented at National Invitational Conference on Public Policy and the Special Education Task of the 1980s, Racine, WI.

Reynolds, M. C., Wang, M. C., and Walberg, H. J. (1987). The necessary restructuring of special and regular education. *Exceptional Children, 53*(5), 391–398.

Rothstein, L. (1990). *Special education law.* New York: Longman.

Rubin, K. H., Fein, G. G., and Vandenberg, B. (1983). Play. In E. M. Hetherington (Ed.), *Carmichael's manual of child psychology: Socialization, personality, and social development.* New York: John Wiley & Sons.

Rynders, J., Johnson, R., Johnson, D., and Schmidt, B. (1980). Producing positive interaction among Down syndrome and nonhandicapped teenagers through cooperative goal structuring. *American Journal of Mental Deficiency, 85,* 268–283.

Sailor, W. (1991). Special education in the restructured school. *Remedial and Special Education, 12*(6), 8–22.

Schloss, P. (1992). Mainstreaming revisited. *Elementary School Journal, 92*(3), 233–244.

Singer, J. (1988). Should special education merge with regular education? *Educational Policy, 2,* 409–424.

Skrtic, T. (1991). *Behind special education.* Denver: Love.

Slavin, R. E. (1990). General education under the regular education initiative: How must it change? *Remedial and Special Education, 11*(3), 40–50.

Smith, A., Hunter, D., and Schrag, J. (1991). *IMPACT: Feature issue on inclusive education, 4*(3), 4–5. Minneapolis: University of Minnesota Institute on Community Integration.

Smith, T. E., Polloway, E. A., Patton, J. R., and Dowdy, C. A. (1995). *Teaching children with special needs in inclusive settings.* Boston: Allyn & Bacon.

Soderhan, A., and Whiren, A. (1985). Mainstreaming the young hearing impaired child: An intensive study. *Journal of Rehabilitation of the Deaf, 18*(3), 7–14.

Spon-Shevin, M. (1988). Working towards merger together: Seeing beyond distrust and fear. *Teacher Education and Special Education, 11,* 103–110.

Stainback, W., Stainback, S., and Jabin, T. (1981). Providing opportunities for interaction between severely handicapped and nonhandicapped students. *Teaching Exceptional Children, 13,* 72–75.

Stainback, W., Stainback, S., Rasche, D., and Anderson, (1981). Three methods of encouraging interactions between severely retarded and nonhandicapped students. *Education and Training of the Mentally Retarded,* Oct., 1981.

Stainback, S., and Stainback, W. (1984). A rationale for the merger of special and regular education. *Exceptional Children, 51,* 102–111.

Stainback, S., and Stainback, W. (1986a). One system, one purpose: The integration of special and general education. *Entourage, 3*(1), 12–16.

Stainback, S., and Stainback, W. (1986b). The merger of special and regular education: Can it be done? *Exceptional Children, 51,* 517–521.

Stainback, W., and Stainback, S. (1987). Facilitating friendships. *Education and Training in Mental Retardation, 22*(1), 18–25.

Stainback, S., and Stainback, W. (1988). Educating students with severe disabilities. *Teaching Exceptional Children, 21*(1), 16–19.

Stainback, S., and Stainback, W. (1989a). Using qualitative data collection procedures to investigate supported education issues. *Journal of the Association for Persons with Severe Handicaps, 14*(4), 271–277.

Stainback, S., Stainback, W., and Forest, M. (Eds.) (1989b). *Educating all students in the mainstream of regular education.* Baltimore: Paul H. Brookes.

Stainback, S., Stainback, W., and Bunch, G. (1989c). A rationale for the merger of regular and special education. In S. Stainback, W. Stainback, and M. Forest, (Eds.), *Educating all students in the mainstream of regular education* (pp. 15–26). Baltimore: Paul H. Brookes.

Stainback, W., and Stainback, S. (Eds.). (1990). *Support networks for inclusive schooling: Interdependent integrated education.* Baltimore: Paul H. Brookes.

Talley, R. C., and Burnette, J. (Eds.) (1982). *Administrators handbook on integrating America's mildly handicapped students. Special education in transition.* Annadale, Va: JWK International Corp.

Turnbull, H. (1993). *Free appropriate public education.* Denver: Love.

20 U.S.C. 1412 (5)(B); 34 C.F.R. 300.551. See also Rothstein, L. (1990). *Special education law.* New York: Longman.

U.S. Department of Education, 1994. *Goals 2000: Educate America act.* Washington, D.C.

Wang, M., and Birch, J. (1984). Comparison of a full-time mainstreaming program and a resource room approach. *Exceptional Children, 51*(1), 33–40.

Wang, M., and Reynolds, M. (1985). Avoiding the "catch 22" in special education reform. *Exceptional Children, 51*(6), 497–502.

Wang, M., Reynolds, M., and Walberg, H. (1986). Rethinking special education. *Educational Leadership, 44*(1), 26–31.

Wang, M., Reynolds, M., and Walberg, H. (1987). *Handbook of special education: Research and practice: Vol. I. Learner characteristics and adaptive education.* Oxford, England: Pergamon Press.

Wang, M., Reynolds, M., and Walberg, H. (1988). Integrating the children of the second system. *Phi Delta Kappan, 70,* 248–251.

Wang, M., Reynolds, M., and Walberg, H. (1989). Who benefits from segregation and murkey water? *Phi Delta Kappan, 71*(1), 64–67.

Wang, M., Walberg, H., and Reynolds, M. (1992). A scenario for better-not-separate special education. *Educational Leadership, 50*(2), 35–38.

Will, M. (1986a). Educating children with learning problems: A shared responsibility. *Exceptional Children, 52*(5), 411–416.

Will, M. (1986b). *Educating students with learning problems—A shared responsibility.* A Report to the Secretary, Office of Special Education and Rehabilitative Services, U.S. Department of Education.

Chapter 2

THE LEGAL SYSTEM AND PERSONS WITH DISABILITIES

WILLIAM MATEER HARRIS

INTRODUCTION

I t seems clear that the intent of law is to protect persons from infringements on their agreed upon constitutionally guaranteed rights, to offer a more objective view toward the settlement of disputes between persons, and to offer standards of behavior that allow all of the elements of a civilization to exist together as a single society without tearing itself apart.

Sometimes it is forgotten that the most critical function of the law is to bring people together in collaborative relationships to solve problems. Too often, observations of our legal system at work notice only its competitiveness, its advocacy, its opposing sides, and conclude that in order to be successful one must prevail in a court of law.

Another and much more effective view is that if a community of persons collaborates in the process of making the law and using the law as a community standard of conduct then disagreements and disputes more often result in successful efforts at resolution without recourse to a court of law. In order to achieve this more nonlitigious culture, as it relates to persons with disabilities, it will be necessary for all elements of the community, including parents, community leaders, teachers, students, and school administrators to learn together and to work together in establishing codes of conduct that both protect civil rights and allow full social participation without discrimination based upon disability.

The foundation for civil rights comes from Article 1, Section 8 of the Constitution of the United States which states that the Congress " . . . shall have the power to . . . provide for . . . the general welfare." The Fourteenth Amendment to the Constitution states that " . . . No State shall make or enforce any law which shall abridge the privileges or immunities of citizens of the United States; nor shall any State deprive any person of life, liberty, or property, without due process of law; nor deny to any person within its jurisdiction the equal protection of the laws." These are the legal cornerstones for all subsequent civil rights legislation including that relating to persons with disabilities. These constitutional provisions not only allow Congress the power to legislate in the area of civil rights but also guarantees to each person certain rights that cannot be infringed upon by any legislation.

There is a growing body of federal legislation and case law concerned specifically with persons with disabilities. It is built upon and intertwined with legal precedents from the fields of civil rights and education. Taken together, these form a network of individual educational rights and protection from unlawful discrimination for persons with disabilities.

There are two major types of legislation that have an impact on persons with disabilities. First, legislation that grants certain educational rights to persons with disabilities, ages three to twenty-one years, can be found in the Individuals with Disabilities Education Act (IDEA, 1990) becoming law in 1990. This Act renamed and included all of the provisions of the existing Education of the Handicapped Act (EHA, 1970) and its amendments, including the Education for All Handicapped Children Act (EAHCA, 1975) which became law in 1975. Currently, all fifty states have applied for and receive federal financial assistance for providing educational services to students with disabilities and, as a result, have agreed to meet certain minimum requirements established by the Act.

The main requirements of IDEA are that all students with disabilities, ages three to twenty-one years, will: (1) be provided with a free and appropriate public education as evidenced in a state plan that is submitted to the federal Secretary of Education for approval; (2) be able to ensure their rights under the Act through procedural safeguards and due process; (3) have an individualized educational plan (IEP); (4) be educated in the "least restrictive environment."

Second, legislation that prohibits discrimination against all persons with disabilities of any age and in most locations including public schools is found in the Federal Rehabilitation Act of 1973, Section 504 and the Americans with Disabilities Act (ADA, 1990) which became law in 1990.

While Section 504 established that discrimination was prohibited in all programs receiving federal financial assistance, the ADA extended this protection to all private sector enterprises with fifteen or more employees. In addition, the ADA excluded drug addiction as a disabling condition under the Act. The major provision of Section 504 and the ADA is that all persons with disabilities of any age are protected from discrimination which is based solely on their disability if they are "otherwise qualified."

THE INDIVIDUALS WITH DISABILITIES EDUCATION ACT

Beginning with the Education of the Handicapped Act in 1970 (Title VI of the Elementary and Secondary Education Act, Public Law 98-750, 1966, represents the first congressional attempt to assist the states in providing special education) and extending through all of its amendments through 1990 including the Education for All Handicapped Children Act of 1975, the development of this legislation was in response to a very uneven and discriminatory set of educational practices throughout the public and private schools of the United States. Many students with disabilities were excluded from any educational services. Others were not able to obtain services they needed in order to learn. Still others could find adequate services in one location but not in another (Hearings before the Senate Committee on Labor and Public Welfare, 93rd Congress, May, 1973).

This legislation also was a response to a growing body of case law brought by dissatisfied parents as well as cases out of the civil rights movement. In 1954, the U.S. Supreme Court ruled in the first of many Brown v. Board of Education (1954) decisions that black children educated in a nonwhite segregated school when compared to white children educated in an all-white segregated school did not receive an education that offered an equivalent opportunity to develop as adults and to pursue their constitutionally guaranteed rights. Brown set the stage for subsequent civil rights legislation relating to persons with disabilities since it used psychological and educational arguments to establish that a group of persons had been denied their constitutional rights under the Fourteenth Amendment to the Constitution. Education was established as a property right. The Civil Rights Act of 1871 (CRA, 1871), in part, usually referred to as Section 1983, already had established the right of a person to file a claim against a governmental body when that body deprives the person of a constitutional right.

In 1972, a federal district court in Pennsylvania in the case of Pennsylvania Association for Retarded Children v. Pennsylvania (1972) stated that mentally retarded persons from age six to twenty-one years were entitled to a free public education and that together with other students with disabilities they should be educated in regular classrooms when possible.

In 1972, a federal district court in the District of Columbia, in the case of Mills v. Board of Education of District of Columbia (1972), decided that all school-age children with disabilities were entitled to a free public education.

IDEA: FREE APPROPRIATE PUBLIC EDUCATION

The Act defines this requirement as "special education and related services that: (a) have been provided at public expense, under public supervision and direction, and without charge; (b) meet the standards of the State educational agency; (c) include an appropriate preschool, elementary, or secondary school education in the State involved; and (d) are provided in conformity with the individualized education program required under Section 1414(a)(5)" (IDEA, Section 1401[18]). Special education is defined as " . . . specially designed instruction at no cost to parents or guardians, to meet the unique needs of a child with a disability, including: (a) instruction conducted in the classroom, in the home, in hospitals and institutions, and in other settings; and (b) instruction in physical education" (IDEA, Section 1401[16]).

Children with disabilities is defined as " . . . (i) (a) children with mental retardation, hearing impairments including deafness, speech or language impairments, visual impairments including blindness, serious emotional disturbance, orthopedic impairments, autism, traumatic brain injury, other health impairments, or specific learning disabilities; and (ii) who, by reason thereof, need special education and related services. (b) the term 'children with disabilities' for children aged three to five, inclusive, may, at a State's discretion, include children: (i) experiencing developmental delays, as defined by the State and as measured by appropriate diagnostic instruments and procedures, in one or more of the following areas: physical development, cognitive development, communication development, social or emotional development or adaptive development; and (ii) who, by reason thereof, need special education and related services" (IDEA, Section 1401[1]).

Free clearly means at public expense. When school districts have tried to disqualify some students from special education or any educational program at all due to the severity of their disabilities, the courts have responded with a firm requirement for providing a free, appropriate education to all students with disability who qualify under the law. In the case of Timothy v. Rochester School District (1989), a federal appeals court rejected a school district's conclusion that a student with severe disabilities including severe spasticity, cerebral palsy, brain damage, joint contractures, cortical blindness, and nonambulatory quadriplegia could not profit from an education. The court held that the student was handicapped under the meaning of IDEA and therefore the school district was required to provide him with a free, appropriate public education.

The major issue in this area litigated in the courts has been the definition of "appropriate." What is an appropriate education? The basis for the answer to that question comes from the U.S. Supreme Court in a 1982 decision in the case of Board of Education of Hendrick Hudson Central School District v. Rowley (1982). The court stated, "(C) When the language of the Act and its legislative history are considered together, the requirements imposed by Congress become tolerably clear. Insofar as a State is required to provide a handicapped child with a 'free appropriate public education' we hold that it satisfied this requirement by providing personalized instruction with sufficient support services to permit the child to benefit educationally from that instruction. Such instruction and services must be provided at public expense, must meet the State's educational standards, must approximate the grade levels used in the State's regular education, and must comport with the child's IEP.

In addition, the IEP and, therefore, the personalized instruction, should be formulated in accordance with the requirements of the Act and, if the child is being educated in the regular classrooms of the public education system, should be reasonably calculated to enable the child to achieve passing marks and advance from grade to grade." If it can be shown that a student with disabilities can "benefit educationally" from the instruction offered, has an individualized educational plan that conforms to the IDEA requirements, and, in the case of students with disabilities in regular classes, has an educational program that is "reasonably calculated" to enable the student "to achieve passing marks and advance from grade to grade," the student is receiving a free, appropriate public education.

In this case, while the court upheld the constitutionality of PL 94-142, it ruled against the request by Amy Rowley to have an American Sign Language interpreter accompany her while in her regular classes. They took this action because Amy was successful in these classes without an interpreter. The court rejected an argument from Amy Rowley and the U.S. Court of Appeal that "appropriate" should mean that Amy's I.E.P. should allow her to reach her "maximum potential."

The courts have also interpreted appropriate to include related services such as transportation, physical therapy, and counseling, as found in IDEA. One area which has resulted in extensive litigation involves what is included in related medical services. IDEA only allows medical services for diagnostic and evaluation purposes although it defines related services as " . . . transportation, and such developmental, corrective, and other supportive services (including speech pathology and audiology, psychological services, physical and occupational therapy, recreation, including therapeutic recreation, social work services, counseling services, including rehabilitation counseling, and medical services, except that such medical services shall be for diagnostic and evaluation purposes only) as may be required to assist a child with a disability to benefit from special education . . . " (IDEA, Section 1400[17]). In one case, the U.S. Supreme Court required a school district to provide clean, intermittent catheterization (CIC) service to an eight year old student with spina bifida since CIC is not a medical service but may be performed by a lay person with some training or fits that category of service usually provided by a typical school nurse (Irving Independent School District v. Tatro, 1984).

Excluded then from IDEA requirements are the provision of medical services that would need to be performed by a physician or a specially trained or full-time registered nurse or medical equipment that would be so costly that its use would negatively affect the education of other students with disabilities in the district.

IDEA: DUE PROCESS AND THE INDIVIDUALIZED EDUCATIONAL PLAN

IDEA guarantees parental and/or student involvement in all educational decision making regarding the education of students with disabilities. Each stage in the process requires their consent. Assessment, identification, placement, and the individualized educational program all require parental and school district agreement and approval (IDEA, Section 1415).

In the area of assessment, parents must be notified in writing and consent to any test or evaluation procedure that will be used for purposes of placement in special education. The state education agency must establish

> ... procedures to assure that testing and evaluation materials and procedures utilized for the purposes of evaluation and placement of children with disabilities will be selected and administered so as not be racially or culturally discriminatory. Such materials or procedures shall be provided and administered in the child's native language or mode of communication, unless it clearly is not feasible to do so, and no single procedure shall be the sole criterion for determining an appropriate educational program for a child (IDEA, Section 1412[5]).

This requirement for the use of multiple assessment procedures to determine eligibility for special education has been important since, in many instances, students with disabilities have been denied services because they did not meet a single threshold test such as a particular IQ score or a discrepancy between potential and achievement.

In the areas of identification, placement, and content of the individualized educational program (IEP), parents must be notified in writing and consent to the initiation of any IEP and school placement or any change or refusal to change that program. They must be notified in a language easily understood by the general public and in their native language if feasible. Individualized educational programs are devised at an IEP meeting conducted by an IEP team. Parents are important members of the IEP team for their child or children.

An Individualized Educational Program Team is an interdisciplinary team including a school administrator, the student's present teacher, one or both of the parents of the student, the student if appropriate, and other persons and professionals chosen by the district or the parents who are necessary to arrive at an "appropriate" individualized educational plan.

This team meets and an Individualized Educational Program (IEP) is devised (1) when it is the result of an initial assessment; (2) at least annually; (3) whenever the student evidences a lack of progress toward meeting IEP goals; (4) upon parental request; (5) once every three years as a result of a complete re-assessment process (34 C.F.R., Section 300.340).

The federal regulations stipulate the contents of an IEP.

> The IEP for each child must include: (1) A statement of the child's present levels of educational performance; (2) A statement of annual goals, including short term instructional objectives; (3) A statement of the specific special education and related services to be provided to the child and the extent to which the child will

be able to participate in regular educational programs; (4) The projected dates for initiation of services and the anticipated duration of the services; and (5) Appropriate objective criteria and evaluation procedures and schedules for determining, on at least an annual basis, whether the short term instructional objectives are being achieved (34 C.F.R., Section 300.346).

The effect of the individualized educational plan or the individual family service plan in the case of children from birth to five years of age or the individualized transition plan in the case of students sixteen to twenty-two years of age has been to offer parents and teachers the opportunity to create an educational program that brings consistency between home and school environments. It has also provided for the involvement in planning by all those who may have a positive impact upon the education of children with disabilities.

In the area of due process, the IDEA sets out a series of very specific procedural safeguards to be followed when one or more parties to the IEP disagree or when one party to the process perceives that one or more legal requirements have not been met (IDEA, Section 1415). These include the timelines stipulated concerning the notification and consent for assessment (school district has fifteen days to develop an assessment plan after parental consent to assess is obtained and parents have fifteen additional days to consider it), the development and implementation of the IEP (a total of fifty calendar days not including long holidays or summer vacations between parental consent for assessment and the IEP meeting), the inclusion of parents in all decisions concerning the education of their child(ren), the notification to parents of their rights at each step in the process, and the appeal process for parents and districts when they do not agree.

A parent or public education agency (school district) may initiate an impartial due process hearing concerning any of the procedural safeguards or any proposal or refusal by the education agency to act. This hearing is conducted by the State Education Agency. The public education agency must " . . . inform the parent of any free or low-cost legal and other relevant services available in the area . . . "

Any party to the hearing has a right to: (1) Be accompanied and advised by counsel and by individuals with special knowledge or training with respect to the problems of children with disabilities; (2) present evidence and confront, cross-examine, and compel the attendance of witnesses; (3) Prohibit the introduction of any evidence at the hearing that has not been disclosed to that party at least five days before the hearing; (4) Obtain a written or electronic verbatim record of the hearing; (5) Obtain written findings of fact and decisions (34 C.F.R., Section 300.506–300.508).

The decision of the due process hearing officer may be appealed to the State Education Agency.

Any party aggrieved by the decision of the State Education Agency may bring a civil action in a court of competent jurisdiction. Usually, these cases are appealed to the appropriate federal district court.

In regard to decisions by school districts in suspending or expelling students with disabilities, the courts have interpreted the IDEA free and appropriate requirements and have arrived at a very controversial set of procedural safeguards. This interpretation has resulted in the protection of students with disabilities from unilateral school district decisions.

In a case involving several students identified at the time as "educable mentally retarded," a court in S-1 v. Turlington (1981) stated:

> Accordingly, we hold that under the EHA, Section 504, and their implementing regulations: (1) Before a handicapped student can be expelled, a trained and knowledgeable group of persons must determine whether the student's misconduct bears a relationship to his handicapping condition; (2) an expulsion is a change in educational placement thereby involving the procedural protections of the EHA and Section 504; (3) expulsion is a proper disciplinary tool under the EHA and Section 504, but a complete cessation of educational services is not.

In 1988, the U.S. Supreme Court in Honig v. Doe (1988) affirmed the procedural safeguards and due process provisions of the EHA (now IDEA). Their decision stated: " . . . the Act establishes a comprehensive system of procedural safeguards designed to ensure parental participation in decisions concerning the education of their disabled children and to provide administrative and judicial review of any decisions with which those parents disagree." This case dealt with the unilateral decision on the part of a school district to suspend indefinitely two emotionally disturbed students, although the decision only applied to one of those students. The decision goes on to state:

> We think it clear, however, that Congress very much meant to strip schools of the unilateral authority they had traditionally employed to exclude disabled students, particularly emotionally disturbed students, from school. In so doing, Congress did not leave school administrators powerless to deal with dangerous students; it did, however, deny school officials their former right to "self-help," and directed that in the future the removal of disabled students could be accomplished only with the permission of the parents or, as a last resort, the courts.

These decisions require a school district to plan for and implement a set of procedures for suspension and expulsion for students with disabilities that is different from that used with typical students. In most cases, an IEP meeting must be held since either recommendation would result in a change of placement (if the suspension is longer than three days). All usual procedural safeguards are in place. At this meeting, it must be determined that the behavior resulting in the recommendation for suspension and/or expulsion did not result from the disability or from an inappropriate placement. If such a causal connection is established, the recommendation for suspension and/or expulsion is not appropriate and alternate means must be devised to continue to work with the student. During the pendency of these procedures, the school must continue to offer an appropriate educational program to the student.

These provisions regarding suspension and expulsion have resulted in an effort by school districts to change the IDEA during its reauthorization in 1995–1996 so that they might have greater control over what is perceived to be dangerous behavior on the part of some students with disabilities. Also of concern to school districts is the double standard that appears to result when dealing with issues of misbehavior on the part of typical students and students with disabilities.

LEAST RESTRICTIVE ENVIRONMENT

The IDEA requires that:

The state has established . . . procedures to assure that, to the maximum extent appropriate, children with disabilities, including children in public or private institutions or other care facilities, are educated with children who are not disabled, and that special classes, separate schooling, or other removal of children with disabilities from the regular educational environment occurs only when the nature or severity of the disability is such that education in regular classes with the use of supplementary aids and services cannot be achieved satisfactorily . . . (IDEA, Section 1412[5][B]).

The federal regulations that clarify this legislation, in addition to containing the same language as that cited above, adds:

Continuum of alternative placements: (a) Each public agency shall ensure that a continuum of alternative placements is available to meet the needs of children with disabilities for special education and related services. (b) The continuum . . . must—(1) Include the alternative placements listed in the definition of special education . . . (instruction in regular classes, special classes, special schools, home instruction, and instruction in hospitals and institutions); and (2) Make provision for supplementary services (such as resource room or itinerant instruction) to be provided in conjunction with regular class placement (34 C.F.R., Section 300.551).

Despite these provisions and perhaps because persons with disabilities had always been segregated or excluded from the typical school population, most special education placement decisions (with some exceptions) until the 1990s were based on a process of labeling a student then placing her/him in a classroom with similarly labeled students in a segregated classroom.

This separate and segregated special education system exists today but is under increasing scrutiny as educational views towards persons with disabilities change and increasing academic and social success on the part of students with disabilities is demonstrated by schools that combine regular education and special education services in typical classrooms regardless of labels.

There are an increasing number of schools that are attempting to keep students who qualify for special education services in typical, nonsegregated classes. This structure of service delivery has been called "inclusive, supportive education" or "full inclusion" and, initially, it was called "mainstreaming."

This movement toward the inclusion of students with disabilities in typical classes has occurred at the same time as increased political activism on the part of persons with disabilities and their supporters has begun to change the way people think about disabilities and has concentrated attention on their civil rights.

The issue of Least Restrictive Environment has been litigated many times and a consistent body of case law has emerged. In Roncker v. Walter (1983) the court stated,

> The Act does not require mainstreaming in every case but its requirement that mainstreaming be provided to the maximum extent appropriate indicates a very strong congressional preference.... In a case where the segregated facility is considered superior, the court should determine whether the services which make that placement superior could be feasibly provided in a nonsegregated setting. If they can, the placement in the segregated school would be inappropriate under the Act. Framing the issue in this manner accords the proper respect for the strong preference in favor of mainstreaming while still realizing the possibility that some handicapped children simply must be educated in segregated facilities either because the handicapped child would not benefit from mainstreaming, because any marginal benefits received from mainstreaming are far outweighed by the benefits gained from services which could not feasibly be provided in the non-segregated setting, or because the handicapped child is a disruptive force in the non-segregated setting. Cost is a proper factor to consider

since excessive spending on one handicapped child deprives other handicapped children.

This case concerned a disagreement over the placement of a nine-year-old "severely mentally retarded" student. The district wanted to place the student at a county school which was attended exclusively by "mentally retarded" children. The parents wanted to maintain a placement in a segregated class for "mentally retarded" children at a regular school site because they believed their child benefitted from contact with typical students. The parents requested a due process hearing and subsequently filed suit.

The court, in agreeing with the parents, cited several critical factors in determining whether mainstreaming is indicated: (1) Would the academic benefits of the segregated setting be balanced by the academic and social benefits derived in a supported environment in a mainstreamed setting? This is clearly the question with the highest value. (2) Is the cost of providing that support so great that the education of other children with disabilities in the district will be negatively affected? If so, then mainstreaming would be not be indicated. (3) Is the child so disruptive that an excessive amount of teacher time is consumed with attention to the mainstreamed student that the education of other students in the class is negatively affected? If so, then mainstreaming would not be indicated.

In the case of Daniel R. R. v. State Board of Education (1989), a different court was concerned with a six-year-old student with Down syndrome who had been placed at parental request in a regular prekindergarten class. The district, finding that Daniel required constant, individual attention from the teacher and that he failed to master any of the skills taught, decided to return him to a special education early childhood class where they made arrangements for him to participate with typical students in nonacademic activities.

The parents requested a due process review of the placement. The court, agreeing that the school district had adhered to the requirements of the Act, stated, however,

> We recognize that some handicapped children may not be able to master as much of the regular education curriculum as their non-handicapped classmates. This does not mean, however, that those handicapped children are not receiving any benefit from regular education. Nor does it mean that they are not receiving all of the benefit that their handicapping condition will permit. If the child's individual needs make mainstreaming appropriate, we cannot deny the child access to

regular education simply because his educational achievement lags behind that of his classmates.

This court places consideration of overall educational benefit above academic benefit when making a decision to mainstream or not. The court goes on to state,

> Thus, the decision whether to mainstream a child must include an inquiry into whether the student will gain any educational benefit from regular education. Our analysis cannot stop here, however, for educational benefits are not mainstreaming's only virtue. Rather, mainstreaming may have benefits in and of itself. For example, the language and behavior models available from non-handicapped children may be essential or helpful to the handicapped child's development. In other words, although a handicapped child may not be able to absorb all of the regular education curriculum, he may benefit from nonacademic experiences in the regular education environment.

The court goes on to say that a determination of mainstreaming should be based upon a careful examination of each individual case and that labels and administrative structures and needs should not take precedence.

The court continues noting the limitations to mainstreaming. For example, if a student with a disability took up so much of the teacher's time, that the education of other students in the regular class was negatively affected, or if to modify the regular curriculum and provide support would change it "beyond recognition," mainstreaming would not be indicated. Where a student is placed in a special class, the court specifies that other contact with non-handicapped peers must be sought, such as " . . . providing interaction with non-handicapped children during lunch and recess."

IDEA regulations also speak to the location of a child's school in relationship to his/her home. "Each public agency shall ensure that: (a) the educational placement of each child with a disability (b) Is as close as possible to the child's home . . . (c) Unless the IEP of a child with a disability requires some other arrangement, the child is educated in the school which he or she would attend if non-disabled" (34 C.F.R., Section 300.552).

In a 1992 decision of a United States District Court, upheld by the U.S. Court of Appeals, specific guidelines to use in consideration of least restrictive environment were stipulated and form a summary of case law to that time. In Board of Education, Sacramento City Unified School District v. Rachel Holland (1994), the court stated:

The federal appellate courts have recognized the following factors as relevant to determining if a placement is appropriate: (1) The educational benefits available to the child in a regular classroom, supplemented with appropriate aids and services, as compared to the educational benefits of a special education classroom; (2) the nonacademic benefits to the handicapped child of interaction with non-handicapped children; (3) the effect of the presence of the handicapped child on the teacher and other children in the regular classroom; and (4) the costs of supplementary aids and services necessary to mainstream the handicapped child in a regular classroom setting.

This case concerned Rachel Holland, nine years old, whom the school district wanted to place half-time in a segregated special education class and half-time in regular classes. Rachel's parents felt she would benefit from a full-time placement in regular classes with support and pursued a due process hearing. The school district appealed the hearing officer's ruling to the federal district court. The court found that the appropriate placement for Rachel was " . . . in a regular second grade classroom, with some supplemental services, as a full-time member of that class." The decision of the hearing officer was affirmed.

In a case involving principles of free, appropriate public education, procedural safeguards, due process, and the least restrictive environment, the U.S. Supreme Court in 1993 explicitly expanded a parent's ability to contravene school district authority. In this case, the parents' idea of appropriate included more special education services with higher expectations. In the case of Florence County School District Four v. Carter (1993), a high school student was classified as learning disabled and her public school IEP provided for instruction in regular classes except for three periods of individualized instruction per week. The IEP also set goals for reading and math which would require four months growth in these areas over the entire school year. The parents felt the IEP was not appropriate and requested a due process hearing. The hearing officer found that the public school IEP was appropriate but the parents had already unilaterally taken their youngster out of public school and placed her in a private school for children with learning disabilities. At this school, she averaged one year's growth in reading and math for each year of attendance.

This suit was filed by the student's parents in 1986, claiming that the public school IEP was inappropriate and sought tuition and other cost reimbursement. The federal district court, the U.S. Court of Appeals, and the U.S. Supreme Court agreed with the parents. The U.S. Supreme Court stated,

> ... public educational authorities who want to avoid reimbursing parents for the private education of disabled children can do one of two things: give the child a free appropriate public education in a public setting, or place the child in an appropriate private setting of the State's choice. This is IDEA's mandate . . .

The court noted the financial risk of the parents in following the path taken in this case. "They are entitled to reimbursement only if a federal court concludes both that the public placement violated IDEA, and that the private school placement was proper under the Act." Finally, this decision broke new ground in allowing for parents to unilaterally remove their child from a placement while due process proceedings were occurring when the IEP is inappropriate and in granting tuition and cost reimbursement subsequent to the unilateral change (although other cases cited herein also point in this direction).

Today, there is a growing opinion among many special education professionals and parents that school districts should concentrate on providing appropriate special education support services (as determined by an individual's IEP) in neighborhood schools of regular attendance in typical classes to all those needing that support and focus less on the place where that support occurs.

Special education, then, is a support service, not a place. For this to occur, however, substantial change will need to occur in the entire educational system and in the attitudes of the public in general. Communities will need to view themselves as inclusive rather than exclusive, embracing all of its members in all activities. This would mean that regular education teachers, special education teachers, employers in the community, and those involved in social services, as well as all residents must view persons with disabilities as permanent parts of their communities. Persons with disabilities and persons with fewer disabilities (sometimes referred to as persons without disabilities) would all be seen as persons with individual and unique abilities that each has a unique contribution to make. All would have an equal right of access to opportunities so that those contributions could be made. In this writer's opinion, nothing else is acceptable under the U.S. Constitution.

REHABILITATION ACT OF 1973 SECTION 504 AND THE AMERICANS WITH DISABILITIES ACT (ADA) OF 1990

These Acts prohibit discrimination against persons of any age who meet the definition of handicapped (Section 504) or person with a disability (ADA). Section 504 applies to persons in programs receiving federal funds while the ADA expands this coverage to include private enterprises of fifteen or more employees and makes specific provisions in the areas of telecommunications, transportation, and public accommodations. The federal regulations for Section 504 state: "No qualified person with disability(ies) shall, on the basis of this disability, be excluded from participation in, be denied the benefits of, or otherwise be subjected to discrimination under any program or activity which receives or benefits from Federal financial assistance" (34 C.F.R., Section 104.4).

> The regulations define persons with disabilities as . . . any person who (i) has a physical or mental impairment which substantially limits one or more major life activities, (ii) has a record of such an impairment, or (iii) is regarded as having such an impairment . . . physical or mental impairment means (a) any physiological disorder or condition, cosmetic disfigurement, or anatomical loss affecting one or more of the following body systems: neurological; musculoskeletal; special sense organs; respiratory, including speech organs; cardiovascular, reproductive, digestive, genitor-urinary; hemic and lymphatic; skin, and endocrine; or (b) any mental or psychological disorder such as mental retardation, organic brain syndrome, emotional or mental illness, and specific learning disabilities. Major life activities means functions such as caring for one's self, performing manual tasks, walking, seeing, hearing, speaking, breathing, learning, and working (34 C.F.R., Section 104.3[j]).

Section 504 and the ADA, while prohibiting discrimination on the basis of disability, require that the person with disability be "otherwise qualified" which means that they can perform the essential functions of the job or task with "reasonable accommodation" on the part of the employer or agency. For schools, reasonable accommodation includes the provision of equal opportunity for participation in extracurricular events, physical access to programs offered to nondisabled students, and access to programs that are basically the same as those that are offered to nondisabled students. In addition, schools must plan reasonable accommodations and modifications in a Section 504 service plan or accommodation plan. This is a regular education responsibility and is often part of the function of the student study team or the child study team. Many of the requirements of Section 504 and ADA as they apply to students in schools are close to those of the IDEA. For example, due process procedures are stipulated, although they begin by the victim filing a complaint with the Office of Civil Rights of the Department of Education within one hundred eighty days of the causal incident.

As to modifications required of academic programs, the regulations state,

> (a) Academic requirements. A recipient to which this subpart applies shall make such modifications to its academic requirements as are necessary to ensure that such requirements do not discriminate or have the effect of discriminating, on the basis of disability against a qualified applicant or student with disability. Academic requirements that the recipient can demonstrate are essential to the program of instruction being pursued by such student or to any directly related licensing requirement will not be regarded as discriminatory within the meaning of this section. Modifications may include changes in the length of time permitted for the completion of degree requirements, substitution of specific courses required for completion of degree requirements, and adaptation of the manner in which specific courses are conducted. (b) Other rules. A recipient to which this subpart applies may not impose upon students with disability(ies) other rules such as the prohibition of tape recorders in classroom or of dog guides in campus buildings, that have the effect of limiting the participation of students with disability in the recipient's education program or activity (34 C.F.R., Section 104.44).

Additional regulations require modifications as reasonable accommodations in the areas of course examinations and in the provision of auxiliary aids.

Many students that meet the Section 504 and ADA definition of disability(ies) may not qualify for services under the IDEA. For example, some students diagnosed with Attention Deficit Hyperactivity Disorder but do not need the intensity of special education services in order to be successful in school still qualify for a 504 Accommodation Plan which is intended to help the institution avoid discriminatory practices. Other students designated as having this disorder may qualify under IDEA as other health impaired if they require special education support services to "benefit from" an education. In another example, students who are HIV positive for the HIV virus would qualify for protection under Section 504 and not under IDEA. Students whose performance is declining due to the presence of opportunistic infections as a result of an active AIDS disease would qualify under IDEA as "Other Health Impaired" since it may be assumed that they would need special education support in order to "benefit from" an education.

The courts have interpreted the "otherwise qualified" provision as requiring program modifications but not a lowering of program standards. In Southeastern Community College v. Davis (1979), the U.S. Supreme Court decided a case in which a student was applying for admission to a nursing program. The student had a bilateral, sensorineural hearing loss that, with appropriate modification, resulted in a lack of assurance that the student could understand normal spoken speech. The school recommended that she not be admitted to the nursing program. The school had the student evaluated in an appropriate manner as to her hearing loss. The court stated,

> ... An otherwise qualified person is one who is able to meet all of a program's requirements in spite of his handicap ... It is undisputed that respondent could not participate in Southeastern's nursing program unless the standards were substantially lowered. Section 504 imposes no requirement upon an educational institution to lower or to effect substantial modifications of standards to accommodate a handicapped person.

In the case of School Board of Nassau County v. Arline (1987), the U.S. Supreme Court stated:

> Allowing discrimination based on the contagious effects of a physical impairment would be inconsistent with the basic purpose of Section 504, which is to ensure that handicapped individuals are not denied jobs or other benefits because of the prejudiced attitudes or the ignorance of others. By amending the definition of "handicapped individual" to include not only those who are actually physically impaired, but also those who are regarded as impaired and who, as a result, are substantially limited in a major life activity, Congress acknowledged that society's accumulated myths and fears about disability and disease are as handicapping as are the physical limitations that flow from actual impairment.

As with IDEA, school districts and agencies should reexamine their attitudes and program options as they relate to persons with disabilities and assume a proactive stance concerning Section 504 and ADA regulations. By allowing persons with disabilities to become full citizens in not only their opportunities but also in the hearts and minds of everyone in the community, Section 504 and the ADA will become a community standard rather than a needed protection.

DISCUSSION QUESTIONS

(1) Why has legislation guaranteeing a free and appropriate public education to all infants, children, and youth with disabilities followed the granting of these rights by court decisions? What was

the role of the professional education community in these legal
developments?

(2) Although it is required by case law and legislation, many persons
do not think that students with disabilities should be educated
with support services in regular classes with their nondisabled
peers. What are the reasons that are used to support this view and
what effective arguments could be developed that support full
inclusion?

(3) Do you think that the legal educational requirements of the
IDEA and the nondiscrimination provisions of the Vocational
Rehabilitation Act of 1973, Section 504 and the Americans With
Disabilities Act will be sustained by the courts in the future?
What changes do you anticipate?

(4) What are the characteristics of the value system that a community
would need to have in order to fully integrate persons with
disabilities? What would the characteristics of a value system be
for a community that decided there should be no special protec-
tions or additional expenses for persons with disabilities?

(5) What role will you play in the continuing struggle of persons with
disabilities to achieve equal rights in education and in life in the
community?

(6) Why isn't there a category under the Individuals With Disabilities
Act for children with Attention Deficit Hyperactivity Disorder?

(7) In the past, students who were linguistically or culturally or
ethnically different from the majority of students were placed in
special education classes because of these differences, rather than
for educational reasons. How could this occur? Are the protec-
tions in the Individuals With Disabilities Education Act sufficient
to prevent this from happening in the future?

REFERENCES

Americans with Disabilities Act. 1990. 42 U.S.C. 12101.

Board of Education of Hendrick Hudson Central School District v. Rowley. 1982.
458 U.S. 176, 102 S.Ct. 3034, 73 L.Ed. 2d 690.

Board of Education, Sacramento City Unified School District v. Holland. 1994. 14
F. 3d 1398 (Ninth Circuit), cert. denied, 129 L.ed. 2d 813.

Brown v. Board of Education. 195f4. 347 U.S. 483.

Civil Rights Act of 1871. 42 U.S.C., Section 1983.

34 C.F.R., Section 104.3(j).

34 C.F.R., Section 104.44.

34 C.F.R., Section 300.340–300.350.

34 C.F.R., Section 300.346.

34 C.F.R., Section 300.506–300.508.

34 C.F.R., Section 300.551.

34 C.F.R., Section 300.552.

Daniel R. R. v. State Board of Education 874 F.2d 1036 (5th Cir. 1989).

Education of the Handicapped Act, Public Law 91-230 (1970).

Education for All Handicapped Children Act, Public Law 94-142 (1975).

Florence County School District Four v. Carter 114 S.Ct. 361 (1993).

Hearings before the Senate Committee on Labor and Public Welfare, 93rd Congress (May, 1973–March 1974).

Honig v. Doe 484 U.S. 305, 108 S.Ct. 592, 98. Ed. 2d 686 (1988).

Individuals with Disabilities Education Act (IDEA, 1990). 84 Stat. 175, as amended, 20 U.S.C. Section 1400 et seq.

IDEA, 20 U.S.C., Section 1400(7).

IDEA, 20 U.S.C., Section 1401(1).

IDEA, 20 U.S.C., Section 1401(16).

IDEA, 20 U.S.C., Section 1401(18).

IDEA, 20 U.S.C., Section 1412(5)(B).

IDEA, 20 U.S.C., Section 1412(5)(C).

IDEA, 20 U.S.C., Section 1415 and 34 C.F.R. Section 300.482–300.515.

IDEA, 20 U.S.C., Section 1415 and 34 C.F.R. Section 300.486–300.515.

Irving Independent School District v. Tatro 468 U.S. 883 (1984).

Mills v. Board of Education of District of Columbia 348 F. Supp. 866 (D.C. 1972).

Pennsylvania Association for Retarded Children v. Pennsylvania 343 F. Supp. 279 (E.D. Pa. 1972).

Roncker v. Walter 700 F. 2d 1058 (Sixth Circuit 1983).

S-1 v. Turlington 635 F. 2d 342 (Fifth Circuit 1981).

Southeastern Community College v. Davis 442 U.S. 397, 99 S. Ct. 2361, 60 L. Ed. 2d 980 (1979).

School Board of Nassau County v. Arline 480 U.S. 273,107 S. Ct. 1123, 94 L. Ed. 2d 307 (1987).

Timothy v. Rochester School District 875 F. 2d 954 (1st Cir. 1989), cert. denied, 493 U.S. 983 (1989).

Vocational Rehabilitation Act of 1973, Section 504 (1973), 29 U.S.C. 794.

Vocational Rehabilitation of 1973, Section 504 34 C.F.R. Section 104.4.

Chapter 3

FUNCTIONAL LANGUAGE AND OTHER LANGUAGE INTERVENTION STRATEGIES

ELVA DURÁN

Before a teacher can begin to work with a child on any level, some means of communication must be established. With the wide range of problems involved in teaching handicapped and autistic children, fulfilling this need is no less basic. Some have limited motor abilities, some have undeveloped speech abilities, many have emotional problems, and others have any number of interferences that the teacher must overcome. But of them all, the need for communication—in verbal form or some other means of language—is most fundamental. This chapter will define functional language and will give information on the language intervention strategies which can be used with populations with moderate to severe handicaps.

FUNCTIONAL LANGUAGE

Language, to be functional, must be used in a communicative interaction (Warren and Warren, 1985); that is, it must affect the listener in specific intended ways. For example, a student will communicate with another person by pointing with his/her finger, with or without words. The listener will understand the student and will not "Yes" to the student after he/she has pointed to a particular object or has noted something to the person. Functional language also means that the words that are to be used are words that the student will need in his/her later life. For instance, some functional words may include vocabulary like "exit," "women," "stop," and "water."

It should also be noted that for language instruction to be useful in everyday life the teacher must use techniques that can be used with students with handicaps in the child's natural environments. In summary, the child's language instruction should include words from his/her environments—home, school, and community. In order to teach these words, the teacher should utilize approaches which would result in language instruction to be taught as the child or student is eating at the cafeteria or is making a sandwich at home.

In the next section of this chapter, natural approaches or techniques which are utilized to teach language to students with handicaps will be discussed.

INCIDENTAL TEACHING

According to Halle (1982), in incidental teaching, there is an interaction between an adult and a child that arises naturally in an unstructured situation and is used by the adult to teach information or give the child practice in developing skills. In incidental teaching, the teacher may arrange the environment so that the child will be encouraged to talk or request various items. For example, a series of objects will be placed on a table where the child can see them. These objects should be things the student wants or would like to have. It is important when teaching language to help create in students a desire so that the child will want to speak. Also, in incidental teaching, the teacher, or the parents, will do will be in various places, in such different environments as the cafeteria, outdoors, at home, at a grocery store, and/or at a fast food restaurant.

Thus, the teacher or parent may ask the child a question about the environment during a particular time. For instance, the teacher may say to the child, "Look at the people standing in line. Let us count the people." The teacher may also say, "Look at Juanita's jacket. What color is it?" According to Halle (1982) incidental teaching produces spontaneous variety in language among students with handicaps who are disadvantaged or come from environments where they are not normally stimulated to speak.

This language model also works well with a student with more moderate handicaps such as one who has Down's syndrome, with the student with severe handicaps, and with the student with autism. Some examples to illustrate this are seen when students with the above handicaps are engaged in vocational and community-based training (learning to shop in grocery stores, or learning to order their food in fast food restaurants) in their own nearby environments and vocational sites.

Teachers or practicum student trainers may ask students questions about their work or purchases they are going to make at stores or restaurants. Students will respond by using short word phrases, will answer teachers or trainers by one word utterances, or perhaps by pointing.

The writer has noticed as she visits schools where teachers and students are engaged in training that once teachers and trainers are aware of how to ask questions, and further encourage students to talk, these students begin to communicate more in varied locales than they did when language instruction was done just in classrooms or in one environment. It is also important to remember that in incidental teaching the student should be reinforced for initiating a request or should be reinforced for communicating with the adult person. As the child is praised or verbally reinforced for communicating or initiating a request, the child's desire to communicate continues to increase. This reinforcement may be as simple as saying to the student, "Good talking" or "I like the way you said that word" (whatever word or words the student said in the environment).

The effectiveness of using incidental teaching has been widely researched and reported. Hart and Risley (1975) found that using this approach produced spontaneous language in many students who have moderate disabilities. Cavallaro (1983) also found that spontaneous speech increased for several students with moderate handicaps. Further, Cavallaro and Bambura (1982) discovered that incidental teaching was effective in increasing rates of two-word requests in a language-delayed preschooler. Warren and Kaiser (1986) found that using incidental teaching often generalized to other environments. Hart and Risley also found that incidental teaching resulted in substantial increases both in the frequency of language use and in vocabulary growth. Warren and Kaiser (1986) have noted that students tend to use language in a more functional way, or in ways more meaningful to themselves, when they are taught by means of the incidental language approach, rather than in isolated, nonenvironmental situations.

MAND MODEL OR MANDING

Another technique which is part of functional language teaching is manding, a method of interaction which *demands* a verbal or other response. Like incidental teaching, manding is used more successfully and efficiently in the child's natural environment. In manding, a response is requested from a child. For instance, the teacher or parent may say to the child, "Tell me what you want" or the teacher may say, "Show me what you want," or "Tell me what you'd like." The teacher during the language instruction session provides the students with interesting materials that will cause the student to request desired object. Objects are given to the student only if the student explains to the teacher what he/she wants. The teacher will often not give the student the object unless the child points to it or asks for it in a one or two word utterance.

According to Halle (1982), the mand model is especially helpful with moderately to severely language-delayed students. This writer has found the mand model especially useful when adolescents (or students of any age) who may have moderate to severe handicaps are supposed to complete a sequence of steps. The teacher may remind them of the step or steps they are forgetting to complete by commanding them to show the teacher what to do next. For example, at the University of Texas at El Paso this writer directed an adolescent and young adult all day program. In the program the students or clients were required to wash dishes, bake, cook, and do many other independent types of skills. Since many of the clients in the program had very poor memories due to their extreme mental retardation and/or brain damage, they often forgot the sequence of steps they were to complete for various tasks. In one instance, one of the students was drying dishes and forgot what to do after washing and rinsing the dishes. The writer of this program cued the client by saying, "Show me what to do next." The student then remembered to place the dried dishes in the cabinets.

At the University of Texas at El Paso there is an after school intervention program where students of all ages and varied handicapped conditions are assisted in language and communication intervention, functional academics, and other areas where teachers and families feel students may need help. In this after school program the mand model has also been extremely useful when teaching students language and/or communication. Undergraduate college practicum students may be teaching several language concepts—for instance, learning labels or common noun object names. If the teacher is at a point where he/she wants to see if his/her student remembers a series of words just learned, the teacher may command the child to point to the various objects or vocally to say the names of each object. The teacher can say, "Mary, point to the table" or "Mary, tell me what you want."

In manding the teacher must remember to show the child interesting materials or objects. If the child responds minimally or not at all, the teacher may model for the child a more satisfactory response. Studies done by Rogers-Warren and Warren (1980) indicated that the verbalization rates of three children with moderate to severe language delays increased at least twofold from their baseline levels when a manding model was introduced. Vocabulary and complexity of utterance increased, as did the children's display of newly trained words and grammatical forms. McQuarter (1980) found that use of the mand model technique resulted in higher verbalization rates for the children studies, and the student's language complexity increased when the reinforcement pattern changed to include two-word rather than one-word utterances. Manding also showed that generalization—transfer from an initial environment situation to one in another environment—was successful if this procedure was used in a number of environments rather than in a single one (McQuarter, 1980).

DELAY PROCEDURE

Another technique used in functional communication training is the delay procedure. In the delay procedures the teacher or trainer stands at least three feet from the client or student (Halle, 1982; 1987) and waits at least five seconds to see whether the student will give the appropriate response. If the student does not give an appropriate response, then the teacher can model, or give the appropriate response, to the student. It is important to note that the teacher or trainer should not rush to vocalize the response for the student until there has been sufficient time—five seconds at least—for the student to attempt a response. As part of the delay procedure in teaching language, the teacher or adult trainer places a toy or other pertinent object out of reach of the client and delays giving it to him/her until the student properly requests it. Such a procedure has proven very effective in the Special Education Clinic at U.T. El Paso, where college students learn what particular objects to teach first to students, by placing objects on a table away from the student's immediate reach. Students soon realize that the college student trainer is not going to give them the material they want until they ask for items (or point to the item if they are nonvocal students).

In research conducted by Lovaas (1976) and Halle, Marshall, and Spradlin (1979) using the delay procedure proved effective with clients who had learned some words or vocabulary prior to using this approach.

In each case, "waiting out the child" helped increase the child's vocabulary. Halle, Marshall, and Spradlin (1979) found that an even longer delay procedure was effectively used with students with moderate handicaps. The researchers showed the students food trays and waited fifteen seconds before giving what was on the tray. The fifteen second delay procedure helped the student learn to request their food trays effectively more often than before this procedure was used. Halle (1982) noted that, taken together, all of these procedures are capable of making moderately and severely handicapped children, with very low rates of initiation and small expressive vocabularies, into fluent communicators. Thus, it is important to use all of these approaches. When teaching moderately to severely handicapped students language, a combined or integrative model can help increase students' vocabularies, as well as the ease with which they can communicate.

NONVOCAL COMMUNICATION APPROACHES

Nonvocal communication approaches are varied and include several techniques which must be carefully evaluated by the teacher in order to determine which technique is the best approach for teaching communication to a student who is nonverbal or who has some capacity to learn to communicate if given the appropriate stimulus. In the following section, the writer will explain some of these approaches used to teach nonverbal children and will also provide some considerations a teacher can use to determine if a student should be taught by means of a particular technique.

MANUAL OR TOTAL COMMUNICATION

Total or simultaneous communication is referred to as manual communication, a technique which has the teacher or trainer orally saying the word as the sign is modeled for the child. This is signing such as that used by students who are deaf or are partially deaf. The purpose of signing or total communication is to facilitate verbal communication for a student with an intact vocal mechanism. Selection of a total communication approach may be considered, according to Alberto et al. (1983), under a variety of conditions: (1) if the student has poor articulation; (2) if the student has an intelligibility problem; (3) if the student has a minimum vocabulary pool; (4) if the student has more of a receptive ability than an expressive one; (5) if the student has minimal degree of language generalization; or, (6) if the student has some inhibition because of emotional problems.

When teaching a child manual or total communication, it is important to remember to begin with functional words or action words that the child needs in order to communicate in his/her various environments. Brown (1979) noted that using an environmental inventory (Goetz, 1981) can help a teacher or trainer discover words to teach a child that are found in the child's home, school, and community. The teacher can develop a table where there are different columns with labels of "Home," "School," and "Community," and the basic words appropriate to each environment listed separately in each column. Functional words are then selected for instruction in each child's environment. The words are prioritized and the most important ones are listed first on each of the columns.

TABLE VI
ENVIRONMENTAL INVENTORY FUNCTIONAL WORD SELECTION
FOR LANGUAGE COMMUNICATION

Home	School	Community
water	bus	store
glass	pencil	street
bread	paper	car
mild	desk	bus
food	toilet	restaurant

After experimental use of the assumed priorities, the teacher can go through each column and decide which items are in fact more important and therefore should be listed first and should be taught first. Parents can also be encouraged to take part in deciding what their son or daughter should be taught in communication instruction.

Some other considerations which should be noted when teaching students to sign or learn manual communication are to use body movement and facial expression and say the word clearly when the sign is made for the child. The teacher and/or trainer and the student should face each other while the training is being conducted (Dayan et al., 1977). Further, the student should be reinforced for learning correct signs. If the students sign correctly for a particular food item he/she is learning, the student should be rewarded, perhaps by being given some of the food he/she is learning to sign during the lesson.

Additionally, when training the student, it is important to use real objects, concrete objects, and photographs or pictures to help stimulate the student to make the proper sign. The training session should not be confined just to teaching the student in the classroom, but the teacher and parent should stress that the student sign for various objects or other stimuli in the different environments where the student lives, works, and plays. Prizant (1983) found that successful training is more widely seen when the students practice their vocabularies in their various training environments. Again, careful, continuing reexamination of the lists described in Table VI is indicated, stressing particularly those vocabulary words with utility in a variety of situations.

WHAT SIGNED SYSTEM TO USE

There are several educational systems that a teacher can use in teaching signs to students. This particular section will discuss some of these systems and research related to the system.

SIGNED ENGLISH

Signed English is an educational signed system. It has the same syntax as spoken English (word order, use of auxiliary verbs, articles, inflections, etc.). The syntactic correspondence among signed and spoken and written English makes possible the close linkage between the two in the teacher's, and, later, the child's or student's signing (Schaeffer, 1980). Signed English has been reported to be useful in teaching students with autism, those from nonverbal populations, and the severely mentally retarded.

SIGNING EXACT ENGLISH

Signing Exact English is another educational signed system that was developed to improve other educational systems. This particular signing system consists of nearly 4000 signs. Words in Signing Exact English are considered basic, compound, or complex. Basic words are root words with no additions, no plurals or inflected forms such as "girl," "talk," or "sit." Signing Exact English was developed as a manual communication system to represent English for educational purposes (Musselwhite, St. Louis, 1982; 1986). Signing Exact English parallels the English language and is often used by students who have developed competence in understanding English but who cannot speak it. Alberto (1983) noted that Signing Exact English is not as transparent or ionic—i.e., not as realistic or concrete, so that the concept is less easily grasped with a little imagination—and, therefore, is not as easily remembered by students learning these particular signs. These two educational manual systems are noted here because they are most often used. There are other educational manual systems used with students with autism and those students who have severe handicaps.

OTHER GESTURAL SYSTEMS

One gestural system that has shown great promise is the American Indian Sign or gestures developed by Skelly (1979) from the Iroquois Indians to be used with nonverbal students. It is noted that observers can interpret 50 percent to 80 percent of the signs without previous instruction. The American Indian Sign or gesture system is highly **ionic** and is used by many students who have been placed in many other systems and have failed to learn to sign (Daniloff, 1981). In the American Indian sign or gesturing system, the core of signals centers around actions and objects that pertain to the daily needs and desires of students. In a study completed by Daniloff (1981), twenty-one students who were labeled severely and/or profoundly handicapped made progress learning gestures. Some learned one gesture, while others learned thirty gestures. It should be noted that in all manual systems, what is helpful in increasing the number of gestures the students learn is to have all the people who come in contact with a particular student (parents, teachers, etc.) practice the gestures with the student. This involvement by others helps to insure maintenance and generalization from one environment to another.

POINTING AND NATURAL GESTURES

In the U.T. El Paso Special Education Clinic, over the past eight years, the practicum students and this writer have found that the use of pointing and other natural gestures are very helpful in teaching some form of communication to students who are severely mentally retarded, since they are less able to learn manual or other types of signed systems. Many are adolescents or young adults when they come to the program, and their parents or guardians have not been able through the years to teach the person any form of communication system. Since time becomes a major factor for these older students, the simpler the communication system is for them the faster they will be able to use these systems in the various environments where they live, work, and play. Many are taught to use natural gestures and to point to various things they want or desire. In our experience, if the students are training in the Student Union cafeteria, for example, and need to communicate that they are tired and need a break, we have taught them to gesture naturally by placing their hand over their forehead and wipe their forehead clean of sweat. This immediately cues the workers or supervisor of the student that the clients should be allowed to take a five-minute break in the lunchroom.

Pointing is also widely used by students and their trainers as the students are crossing streets or are grocery shopping. The clients or students point to the light when it is green and they know they can cross the street. If the light is red the trainer points to the student so that he/she may look up and the student stops the moment the trainer points to the red light. Many older students are not able to learn signs as readily as younger students, and pointing or gesturing naturally is the only way they are able to communicate or understand how to get around in their different environments. As part of the programming, parents and/or guardians are taught how to point or gesture naturally so they can do the same once their sons and/or daughters are at home or are with them in community environments. Some of the students who are enrolled in the All Day Program for Adults with Autism and Other Severe Handicaps come to the program not knowing basic gestures or pointing, and can now after several months move about the community and can let others know what they would like or can request various objects or food from their environments.

Nietupski (1977) noted that natural gestures are easily understood by others, and no additional equipment is needed to have the students participate in communicating with other people around these particular populations. Natural gestures and pointing can easily supplement other communication systems.

OTHER COMMUNICATION SYSTEMS

Communication boards can be effectively used with nonverbal students in order to teach them to communicate. The communication board can be made of cardboard or other firm material and is usually divided into small squares that are neatly divided by lines running vertically and horizontally to separate each square from the other square. The square and line pattern is much like a Chinese checker board or a tic-tac-toe board. Each square on the communication board is big enough to hold a picture or photograph so that the student can point to the picture or photograph in order to tell others what he/she wants or needs.

The board is organized in the Fitzgerald key and the organization is usually one row for the subject or agents such as "I" or "me." There is an additional column for the verbs such as "want" and there is a column for prepositions such as "in." Finally, there are columns for objects such as "big" and an additional column for nouns which represent objects; for instance, one of the object names placed on this particular column may be a commonly used food item such as "milk." Also, at the top of the communication board there is a place for a "Yes" on the upper left hand corner of the board. There will also be a "No" placed at the upper right hand corner. The "Yes" and "No" are used by the student to communicate wanting or not wanting certain items. Numbers one through ten are also placed at the upper right-hand corner for the student so that he/she may communicate how much or how little of each he/she would like of various things. The alphabet (in upper case letters) is placed toward the bottom of the communication board. As the student learns the alphabet, he/she will also learn that he/she can spell different words with the letters of the alphabet. Again, the words (nouns) placed on the communication board should be words that are used very often by students.

The environmental inventory that was discussed earlier as being useful for helping the teacher discover words for the students to learn is practical here as well. The same procedure should be used to help students learn words from the communication board. Verbs "want" and "go" should be taught to the student immediately, since they are action words that are commonly used to express various activities. On the communication board, the printed word should appear above each picture or symbol, for fullest utility. Thus, if there is a drawing or a photograph of milk or bread, the printed word "MILK" or "BREAD" should appear above it. Some instruction or cueing should be given to the student so he/she can learn to respond to the object pictured or photographed on the communication board. For example, the teacher or adult teaching the student to communicate using the board can say,

"What do you want?" (Dayan et al., 1977; Snyder, 1975; Firling, 1975). If the student does not respond to the teacher's inquiring after the teacher has waited approximately five seconds, then the teacher can ask the question once again and at this time place the student's hand over the photograph or picture being requested. This type of practice is important to do with a student learning to use the communication board because such practice will help train the student so that if he/she is asked such a question, then the student can learn to use the communication board to request items from the environments he/she participates in.

Obviously, in order for the board to be useful to the student in different environments it must be portable. Placing a small handle on the board will help the student carry the board from one place to another.

COMMUNICATION BOOKLETS

Communication booklets are becoming widely used by special education teachers who teach students with severe handicaps (Sailor, 1985; Wilcox, 1984; Brown, 1987). Communication booklets are often made quite easily by placing colored photographs in a 5 × 7 spiral notebook. Pictures or photographs can also be placed on cards and then laminated so they will not become destroyed and can be used over and over by the student. As with the booklets, the printed words are usually written above each photograph to allow the student the opportunity to read or learn to recognize the words. Vocabulary selected for the booklets, of course, should be chosen by using the environmental approach that was noted earlier in this chapter.

In the U.T. El Paso Special Education Clinic, the communication booklet has been widely and successfully used with several students who attend the program for remediation and/or additional help. For example, a boy I will call Rene was one student who made excellent progress learning languages by using the communication booklet. He was a Spanish-dominant, severely language-delayed student. He was five years old when enrolled in the Clinic. He was nonverbal and quite aggressive. Rene would cry most of the time he was being taught language or any other skill area; he was extremely stubborn and inflexible. His mother naturally wanted desperately for Rene to be able to communicate some of his desires. We first completed an inventory to see which words the student would learn from home, school, and community. A total communication system approach was used with the student. Along with a signed speech approach and/or total communication, an alternative system consisting of a communication booklet was used with the student. Rene's mother was instructed to teach him utilizing this approach. After six months he had learned several signs. His aggressive behavior diminished almost completely. During the hour and a half instruction (for the first six months) at the Clinic, the student was also given help learning to use the communication booklet. He was also taught signs and the use of the booklet at home and in other environments. Rene learned to also request various items using his communication booklet. His communication booklet was organized into several sections, involving each of his environments, including one for restaurants. Photographs useful in each of the different areas were included in the appropriate section.

As the student needed to learn additional vocabulary items, more photographs were placed in each section. He used his booklet daily, and by the end of the year had increased considerably the number of symbols he comprehended, as well as developing more and more facility in using his communication booklet. Both his mother and his teacher continued to observe that his aggressive actions decreased markedly in addition, probably because he had become less frustrated with matters of communication.

In using an alternative mode of communication such as a picture or photography booklet, it is obviously important to involve the parents. They must be taught how to use such a system or any system of communication used with the child. If they learn to use the system being employed, their son or daughter will increase in functional vocabulary, and parents themselves will add more items to the booklet as they become increasingly aware of the usefulness of this communication device and of the importance of enriching it. In the eight years this writer has been working with parents of language-delayed students, both at the University Clinic and as a consultant in public schools, she has noted repeatedly that when parents are not fully behind a procedure or technique, the son or daughter will make considerably less progress, whatever system is used.

It should be pointed out that little information has been written on the effectiveness of using communication booklets because this technique has only recently come into use as an alternative system of communication for students who have been successful learning by other systems. The versatility of the booklet, and the ease with which it can be carried about by students, gives this means of communication great promise for wider use with language-delayed populations. And, as in this case, the gratification the student receives from achieving success where little or none was felt before has infinite possibilities.

FACILITATED COMMUNICATION

Crossley (1988, 1992) and Biklen (1990, 1992) defined facilitated communication as an augmentative communication method that permits individuals with severe disabilities such as autism to demonstrate unanticipated and, in some cases, extraordinary communication skills (Simpson and Myles, 1995).

It has been reported by Biklen (1990) that many students with autism and severe disabilities can, through facilitated communication, communicate for the first time in their lives.

Crossley, an Australian, is acknowledged as the developer of facilitated communication (Simpson and Myles, 1995). Crossley worked at St. Nicholas Institution in Melbourne with individuals with multiple disabilities. It is reported that she worked with a young woman by the name of Anne McDonald who had cerebral palsy. Anne could not effectively communicate, walk, or talk (Simpson and Myles, 1995). Crossley believed that Anne could do more than she was given credit for. She supported her index finger and she identified many objects in her environments. By using facilitated communication, Anne was able to read and write letters (Simpson and Myles, 1995).

Crossley continued using facilitated communication with other clients in Australia who had been diagnosed as having severe communication disorders. Many of these clients also had severe physical disabilities and it was shown to be effective with them.

Biklen is given credit for introducing facilitated communication in the United States (Biklen, 1990, 1993). He introduced facilitated communication to the Syracuse, New York public schools. He wrote articles about the success of facilitated communication there. Biklen and Schubert (1991) reported many positive facilitated communication interventions with twenty-one students with whom they worked. Biklen suggested that if the scientific community attempted to assess the effectiveness of facilitated communication, individuals using this method would not communicate and would resist the probing that would be done because they could not communicate with more than one facilitator.

Some others believe that facilitated communication is not a valid and reliable procedure (Prior and Cummins, 1992). The *Advocate* newsletter of the Autism Society of America reported that "there is no hard evidence for facilitated communication" (1992–1993, p. 19). Data by several investigators in the field (Myles and Simpson, in press; Calculator, 1992) noted that when facilitators lack information related to questions asked of an individual being facilitated, the individuals are not able to communicate independently (Simpson and Myles, 1995).

According to Rimland, several horror stories occurred because some adults were typing that they had been sexually abused. It turned out later that these reports were proven untrue when a new facilitator was asked to assist the person to type. This caused grave harm to many of the individuals, according to Rimland, because they were removed from their homes due to the reports that they made originally which could not be substantiated later.

According to Simpson and Myles (1995), when individuals have been tested further, many cannot communicate independently once the facilitator ceases to help them and many also do not even know the alphabet.

Simpson (1995) and many others in the field of autism along with individuals with severe disabilities believe that many schools, agencies, and professionals are reluctant to commit significant resources to facilitated communication without having clear evidence that it works. According to Rimland (1992b), Schopler (1992), and Simpson (1993), there must be a validation of facilitated communication before it is widely adopted.

Biklen (1992) still believes that facilitated communication cannot and should not be evaluated and analyzed critically.

This writer believes that teachers and parents should look closely at all the research before deciding to change all communication strategies for individuals with disabilities. Teachers should further let parents know all the data that explains the problems and lack of validation which has not been accomplished before they decide that this will be the only communication means used with their child.

VOCAL SYSTEMS

There are few programs that have the special features that are needed to teach students who have some ability to say one-word or two-word phrases. The Functional Speech and Language Program has appeared in the literature several times as being a very worthwhile program to teach verbal students with language delays (Haring and Brown, 1976; Guess et al., 1976; Booth, 1987; Musselwhite, 1982; Bullo and Bullo, 1984; Wilcox, 1984). This program is a behavioral approach designed to increase the student's expressive language. Unlike the few other programs that have been developed for nonvocal students, it is a program that is designed to increase the student's vocalization because the structured program stresses generalization training. The program is divided into four parts. The program emphasizes Persons, Things, Action with Persons, and Action with Things. Other content areas include Possession, Color, Size, Relation, and Morphological Grammar (plurals, suffixes, tenses, inflections). The program has easy-to-follow lessons where the teacher or trainer is told the exact dialogue to say to the child. For example, in the first lesson, the student is asked by the teacher, "What want?" At this point, the teacher holds up one object at a time as she asks the child the above question. As the child responds to the object name, the teacher records a "+" in the space next to the object. This indicates the student responded correctly. This continues until all the objects are shown to the student for that lesson's objective. The teacher or trainer is given suggestions as to which object to use in each lesson.

It is important to remember that when teaching students with severe language delays, there have to be very motivating objects shown to the student at first to help create a desire to want to communicate. Few students with severe language delays learn language unless a strong desire is created to communicate (Warren and Warren, 1985). This writer has used the Functional Speech and Language Training Program in the U.T. El Paso Special Education Clinic for approximately four years and has found it to be very helpful for various students who have come to the program with some expressive language abilities.

Roberta was a four-year-old with extreme mental retardation and language delay. She could vocalize only a few words, and the words she vocalized were not easily understood. In conferencing with Roberta's parents, we learned that Roberta cried and became extremely aggressive with others when she was not given what she demanded. The student acting as her tutor interviewed one of the parents and did an environmental inventory on Roberta in order to determine what words in home and community she needed to know. The public school teacher provided the practicum students with words that were important for Roberta to know in school.

After completing the child's environmental inventory, the practicum student started with the first lesson in the program. The parent and teacher also reinforced the same lessons with Roberta at home and school. She was taught twice weekly in the clinic for one hour each session. At first, all words selected for Roberta were functional. Later some functional words were interspersed with words that would be also highly motivational to her. Roberta, for example, found music and toys highly motivational, and these were often added to each of her language lessons. In one year, Roberta began speaking one-word and two-word utterances. By the end of two years, she started to request more items and also asked more questions as she went around her different environments. Roberta continues to be in the Functional Speech and Language Training Program and continues to make more progress daily. Her vocabulary has increased to the point that she is requesting and naming approximately ten more items in her immediate environment on a weekly basis.

DEVELOPING ATTENDING SKILLS AND ELIMINATING INAPPROPRIATE BEHAVIORS WHICH INTERFERE WITH COMMUNICATION TRAINING

As with many nonvocal programs, the few vocal programs that have been developed, including the Functional Speech and Language Training Program, do not have guide manuals explaining the areas in which a teacher can develop attending skills. Attending skills are seen when a student looks at the item or training object or person or teacher who is attempting to get a response from the student (Campbell and Campbell, 1982; Warren and Warren, 1985; Snell, 1987). Attending skills, simply stated, involve the ability to pay attention, to respond appropriately to the teacher, parent, or as the situation demands.

When beginning any language or communication program, the first thing a teacher or trainer must do is to teach the student to look at the stimulus or object that the teacher is using to teach the student (Snell, 1987). The teacher begins by teaching the student to look at the teacher when the teacher says, "Look at me." The teacher should give the student reinforcement, or praise the student for looking at the object or stimulus the teacher is holding in his/her hands. If the student is aggressive or swings at the teacher or trainer, the teacher can hold the student's hands for about three seconds and say "No hitting" (Lovaas, 1981; Prizant, 1983). If the student kicks, the teacher can also hold down the student's legs for three seconds and say, "No kicking."

As the teacher or trainer holds the stimulus, and the student responds by not kicking and looks at the trainer, then the trainer should continue praising the student. For example, the trainer should say, "Good not kicking" or "Good looking." With constant reinforcement (Wehman, 1974) and work, the delayed-language student will gradually begin to focus on the training object or stimulus and will further learn to replace kicking with other less aggressive behaviors.

It has been the experience of this writer that many students who have not had training in language make more progress when they are taught how to attend and to be less aggressive. It usually takes several lessons, plus consistent training time at home, before attending becomes a major part of the student's repertoire. As the instruction continues, the student needs a continuation of this type of instruction in attending and in eliminating his/her interfering behaviors. Students with autism and those with autism plus severe mental retardation have the most difficulty learning to attend. Also, students with autism have extreme difficulty learning new behaviors such as kicking and hitting.

In the U.T. El Paso Clinic, approximately eight students with autism have been assisted in language training. With all of the students some time was spent initially teaching them to sit up and look at the trainer or teacher. With some it took approximately one week, and with others it took two to three weeks to accomplish these goals. Unless these particular skills are taught, the students make little progress in their language instruction.

SOME OTHER CONSIDERATIONS IN TEACHING LANGUAGE AND COMMUNICATION TO STUDENTS WITH SEVERE HANDICAPS

In the past five years, much has been written about teaching functional and chronological age appropriate materials to students with severe handicaps (Brown, 1979, 1980; Wilcox and Bellamy, 1984; Sailor, 1984). It is important to remember that students who are severely and/or developmentally delayed need to be shown materials that are age-appropriate. For instance, a seventeen-year-old nonverbal student with handicaps should not be instructed in a separate speech room and taught the colors and the letters of the alphabet, as one would teach developmental skills to young children who are beginning to learn language. It would be far more appropriate to teach a nonverbal seventeen-year-old how to order food in a restaurant, or buy groceries, by using picture or photograph cards as he/she goes out into the community.

In short, rather than using an artificial approach, one should use a natural one, reaching the student language in context, not in meaningless isolation. By following this method, the student is taught to generalize, applying what is learned in one environment to another environment; once again, this generalization is necessary in making certain that students learn language or how to communicate with others.

It should be obvious that basic to successful language instruction is teaching elementary age student material which is functional and appropriate to the environments in which they live. But all too often there are language programs which devote themselves to nonfunctional, illogical vocabulary almost entirely unrelated to the student's real life. The majority of words used are school-related, and the program had few if any words from other environments.

Another important consideration in teaching students with severe handicaps language is allowing time to train or teach parents to use or learn the different manual or vocal systems. It has been the experience of this writer that if parents are not given instruction on how to teach their son or daughter the different language or manual systems, generalization will not carry over to other environments. In the U.T. El Paso Special Education Clinic, parents are instructed at the beginning of each semester, when they bring their son or daughter for tutoring in how to use the appropriate language or communication system.

The college student and/or clinic director who works with a child gives the parent(s) correction feedback on how well the parents have learned the particular language system. Parents have repeatedly indicated that if it had not been for the training sessions and correction feedback, they would not have been able to use the manual or communication system at home.

Too often teachers have indicated that many parents do not work with their son or daughter on language or communication training at home. If more time is taken to teach parents how to use various programs or techniques, then they will try harder to use these particular materials with their child at home. Language and/or communication systems are considerably less effective unless parents teach these systems at home and in the other environments where their son or daughter may live, work and/or play (Firling, 1975; Brown, 1987; Warren and Warren, 1985). Parents work with their child at least two or three times weekly for twenty-minute sessions. Natural use of these techniques on a daily basis is an easy addition to the training.

Another important aspect of language training is to consider the sequence of instruction for the students. Schaeffer (1980) believes that students should be taught to express their desires first, because students with developmental delays, or those who are severely handicapped, express desires more easily and naturally than they address people or ask questions. Earlier in this chapter when speaking about signing communication, some of the actions that could be taught were indicated.

When deciding what noun labels to teach, it is important once again to do an environmental inventory and select words from the child's home, school, and community. Evaluating daily where the student is successful in learning words is important, because that gives the teacher information on what words should be taught once again, reviewed, or presented by using different objects or materials to teach the concepts. The student's progress on the various language concepts being presented can be noted as follows: a plus (+) is used for correct words and a minus (−) is used for incorrect words. If a student does not respond, a "N" is placed beside the word. This progress can be noted each time the trainer or teacher teaches the child in his/her particular language lesson. Additionally, when teaching language and/or communication strategies to students with disabilities, it is necessary to consider the student's primary language as part of his/her instruction. The teacher should determine if the student, who may be from another country, speaks English or another language as the primary language. If the student is nonverbal, the teacher should also determine the student's primary language at home. Receptively, the student whose first language is not English still needs support and instruction in his or her primary language no matter what system(s) of communication is/are employed by the teacher. Parents, by law, can request that some primary language support be allowed for their son and/or daughter at school. Parents should request primary language support for their son and/or daughter in their child's individualized education program.

In conclusion, when teaching language instruction to students with severe handicaps, it is necessary to realize that there are many different approaches and systems that are available to teach these populations. Further, it is important to consider many systems in order to decide on the best one for a particular student. Finally, the vocabulary taught to the students should be age-appropriate and should more importantly include words from the different environments where the student lives, works, and plays.

DISCUSSION QUESTIONS

(1) What is functional language?
(2) Define incidental teaching. Explain how it is used with persons with moderate handicaps.
(3) What is manding and how is it used with moderately handicapped students?
(4) What is the delay procedure?
(5) List and explain two nonvocal approaches.
(6) What is Signed English and when should you use this manual communication?
(7) What other communication systems can you use with nonvocal students?
(8) How are inappropriate behaviors eliminated in students with severe handicaps?
(9) What are the pros and cons of using or not using facilitated communication?

REFERENCES

Alberto, P. et al. (1983). Selection and initiation of a non-vocal communication program for severely handicapped students. *Focus on Exceptional Children, 15*(7), 1–16.

Biklen, D. (1990). Communication unbound: Autism and praxis. *Harvard Educational Review, 60*(3), 291–314.

Biklen, D. (1992). Typing to talk: Facilitated communication. *American Journal of Speech and Language Pathology, 1*(2), 15–17.

Biklen, D. (1993). *Communication unbound: How facilitated communication is challenging traditional views of autism and ability.* New York: Teachers College Press.

Biklen, D., and Schubert, A. (1991). New words: The communication of students with autism. *Remedial and Special Education, 12*(6), 46–57.

Biklen, D., and Schubert, A. (1992). *Communication unbound: The story of facilitated communication.* Paper presented at 1992 National Symposium, Current Issues in the Nature and Treatment of Autism. St. Louis: Missouri Department of Mental Health Conference.

Booth, T. (1978). Early receptive language training for the severely and profoundly retarded. *Language, Speech and Hearing Services in School, IX,* 142–150.

Brown, L. (1979). A strategy for developing chronological age appropriate and functional curricular content for severely handicapped adolescents and young adults. *Journal of Special Education, 13*(1), 81–90.

Brown, L. (1987). *Transition and educating the person with moderate to severe handicaps.* Paper presented at workshop, El Paso Independent School District, El Paso, Texas.

Calculator, S. N. (1992). Perhaps the emperor has clothes after all: A response to Biklen. *American Journal of Speech and Language Pathology, 1*(2), 18–20.

Calculator, S., and Singer, K. (1992). Letter to the editor: Preliminary validation of facilitated communication. *Topics is Language Disorders, 13,* ix–xvi.

Campbell, R. C., and Campbell, K. (1982). Programming loose training as a strategy to facilitate language generalization. *Journal of Applied Behavior Analysis, 15*(2), 295–301.

Cavallero, C. (1983). Language interventions in natural settings. *Teaching Exceptional Children, 16*(1), 65–70.

Cavallero, C. C., and Bambura, L. M. (1982). Two strategies for teaching language during free play. *Journal of the Association for the Severely Handicapped* 1982, 7(21), 80–92.

Crossley, R. (1988, October). *Unexpected communication attainments by persons diagnosed as autistic and intellectually impaired.* Unpublished paper presented at International Society for Augmentative and Alternative Communication, Los Angeles, CA.

Crossley, R. (1992a). Communication training involving facilitated communication. In DEAL Communication Centre (Eds.), *Facilitated communication training,* (pp. 1–9). Melbourne, Australia: DEAL Communication Centre.

Crossley, R. (1992b). Who said that? In DEAL Communication Centre (Eds.), *Facilitated communication training,* (pp. 42–54). Melbourne, Australia: DEAL Communication Centre.

Daniloff, J. (1981). A gestural communication program for severely and profoundly handicapped children. *Language, Speech and Hearing Services in Schools, XII,* 258–268.

Dayan, M., et al. (1977). *Communication for the severely and profoundly handicapped.* Denver: Love.

Firling, J. D. (1975). Functional language for a severely handicapped child: A case study. *AAESPH Review, 1*(7), 54–71.

Gullo, D.F., and Gullo, J. C. (1984). An ecological language intervention approach with mentally retarded adolescents. *Language, Speech and Hearing Services in Schools, 15,* 182–191.

Halle, J. W. (1982). Teaching functional language to the handicapped: An integrative model of natural environment teaching techniques. *TASH Journal, 7,* 29–37.

Halle, J. W. (1987). Teaching language in the natural environment: An analysis of spontaneity. *Journal for the Association for Persons with Severe Handicaps, 12*(1), 28–37.

Halle, J. B., and Spradlin, D. (1981). Teacher's generalized use of delay as a stimulus control procedure to increase language use in handicapped children. *Journal of Applied Behavior Analysis, 14,* 389–409.

Haring, N. G., and Brown, L. (1976). *Teaching the Severely Handicapped.* New York: Grune and Stratton.

Hart, B., and Risely, T. R. (1975). Incidental teaching of language in the preschool. *Journal of Applied Behavior Analysis, 8,* 411–420.

Lovaas, I. O. (1981). *Teaching developmentally disabled children the me book.* Baltimore: University Park Press.

Lovaas, I. O. (1976). A program for the establishment of speech in psychotic children. In J. K. Wing (Ed.), *Childhood autism.* Oxford: Pergamon.

McQuarter, R. (1980). Milieu language training: A functional alternative to traditional remediation strategies. Master's thesis, University of Kansas.

Musselwhite, C. R., and St. Louis, K. (1982). *Communication programming for the severely handicapped vocal and nonvocal strategies.* San Diego: College Hill Press.

Musselwhite, C. R. (1986). Using signs as gestural cues for children with communicative impairments. *Teaching Exceptional Children, 19*(6), 32–35.

Myles, B. S., and Simpson, R. L. (1994). Facilitated communication with children diagnosed as autistic in public school settings. *Psychology in the Schools, 31,* 208–220.

Nietupski, H. (1977). Curricular strategies for teaching selected nonverbal communication skills to severely handicapped students. In L. Brown, et al., *Curricular strategies for teaching nonverbal communication, functional object use, problem solving and mealtime skills to severely handicapped students, 7,* (Part 1). Madison, WI: University of Wisconsin-Madison and Madison Metropolitan School District.

Prizant, B. M. (1983). Language acquisition and communication behavior in autism toward an understanding of the whole of it. *Journal of Speech and Hearing Disorders, 48*(3), 286–296.

Rimland, B. (1992a). A facilitated communication "horror story." *Autism Research Review, 6*(1), 1, 7.

Rimland, B. (1992b). Facilitated communication: Problems, puzzles, and paradoxes: Six challenges for researchers. *Autism Research Review, 5*(4), 3.

Rimland, B. (1993). Facilitated communication under siege. *Autism Research Review International, 7*(1), 2, 7.

Sailor, W. et al. (1976). Functional language for verbally deficient children: An experimental design. *Mental Retardation,* 27–29.

Sailor, W. (1985). Strategies for teaching persons with severe handicaps. Paper presented at a workshop held at the University of Texas at El Paso, El Paso, TX.

Sailor, W., and Guess, C. (1982). *Severely handicapped students: An instructional design.* Boston: Houghton Mifflin.

Schaeffer, B. (1980). Teaching signed speech to nonverbal children theory and method. *Sign Language Studies, 26,* 29–63.

Simpson, R. L., and Myles, B. S. (1995). Facilitated communication and children with disabilities: An enigma in search of a perspective. *Focus on Exceptional Children, 27*(9), 1–16.

Simpson, R. L., and Myles, B. S. (1995). Effectiveness of facilitated communication with children and youth with autism. *Journal of Special Education, 28*(4), 424–439.

Skelly, M. (Ed.). (1979). *American-Indian gestural code based on universal American Indian hand talk.* New York: Elsevier North Holland.

Snell, M. (1987). *Systematic instruction of persons with severe handicaps* (3rd Ed.). Columbus: Merrill.

Snyder, L. K., et al. (1975). Language training for the severely retarded: Five years of behavior analysis research. *Exceptional Children, 7*–15.

Warren, S. F., and Kaiser, A. P. (1986). Incidental language teaching: A critical review. *Journal of Speech and Hearing Disorders, 15,* 291–299.

Warren, S. F., and Warren, A. K. (1985). *Teaching functional language, language intervention series.* Austin, TX: Pro-ed.

Wehman, P. (1979). *Curriculum design for the severely and profoundly handicapped.* New York: Human Services.

Wilcox, B. (1984). Teaching language to persons with moderate to severe handicaps. Lecture series from workshop taken at the University of Oregon, Eugene OR.

Wilcox, B., and Bellamy, T. G. (1984). Programming for secondary students with severe handicaps. Lecture series given at the University of Oregon, Eugene, OR.

Chapter 4

TRANSITION AND POSTSECONDARY PROGRAMMING

Elva Durán

This chapter will define transition and will note some programming information that should be considered when developing transition procedures in the schools and in community agencies. There will also be some information given on starting a postsecondary program for students who are leaving the public schools to enter the world of work and living in a nonsheltered environment.

The entire area of transition is getting more and more attention in the public schools because more students are enrolled and are leaving at the ages of twenty-one and twenty-two. Many of these students are not becoming productive members of society. As this writer was reviewing the literature, she became aware that there are still many communities that are not doing enough for transition. Unfortunately, little has been written concerning transition, and what does exist is still very much in the stages of discovery. However, the literature does attempt to point out what has been helpful or not helpful in this very new area in special education.

According to Wehman (1986), transition is a carefully planned process which may be initiated either by school personnel or by adult service providers, to establish and implement a plan for either employment or additional vocational training of a handicapped student. When the student reaches late adolescence, the student will graduate or leave school in three to five years and such a process must involve special educators, vocational educators, parents, and/or the student, an adult service system representative, and possibly an employer. There are several components that are extremely important in developing transition within the schools so that students will have special skills once they leave their public school placement. A number of researchers (Brown, 1980; Ballantyne, 1985; Wehman, 1986; Johnson, 1987; Rusch & Phelps,

1987) note that some of the following components are essential in starting transition within the schools and community: (1) there must be members of multiple disciplines involved in the program, and service delivery must participate; (2) there must also be parental involvement; (3) further individualized vocational transition planning must occur well before the student becomes twenty-one years of age; (4) the process must be planned and systematic, and the vocational service must be of a high quality. All of the above components are extremely important, and in order to explain how each of them work, this writer will present how transition has been developed in two large public school districts where she acts as a consultant.

VOCATIONAL TRANSITION PROGRAMMING

For the past four years, the author has started with a few students—approximately thirty from one large school district and forty from another—to try to prepare them to obtain jobs once they leave school. The students became involved in this vocational transition project when they were between the ages of fifteen and eighteen. Many had moderate to severe handicaps, and more than ten had been classified as having autism or having many characteristics of autism. The administrators of each of these large districts was cooperative and flexible in making adjustments where changes were needed as the programming continued. In order to begin the vocational programming, university program personnel brought the students in both districts to the campus four times weekly. During this time, as has already been explained in Chapter Two, the students learned to do meaningful or real work in food service, in janitorial and clerical areas, and several learned to work in a convalescent home for senior citizens. Before the actual training started in each of the areas, the teachers and the author met with each of the managers or supervisors of the employment areas to explain to them how their cooperation was needed in allowing students with all kinds of handicaps to work in their businesses or places of employment. This stage, as the literature describes as being very crucial for successful transition, was most important in placing students in various training areas around the city where the programming was initiated.

One of the difficulties with having members of the different multiple disciplines and service delivery areas participate in the transition process was that in this particular project there was not a main liaison or person from the school districts to help organize and get the community agencies, teachers, and school personnel more involved. There was no one person concerned with helping place students permanently in jobs. Since this on-going communication and actual search for jobs for these students did not take place, some of the employers did not make a commitment to hire students involved in training. According to Benz and Halpren (1987), there must be a team or committee designated in each school with the direct responsibility of coordinating transition. Benz and Halpren (1987) note further that if this team or committee is not set up within the schools where the vocational training and transition is being attempted, the responsibility for finding jobs for these students is usually given to the special education teachers, and many of them are already so busy that the goals of transition do not truly take place.

In coordinating several transition projects with two major school districts, experience has shown that establishing a transition committee to spearhead transition must be accomplished in order to have the objectives of transition reached. Without this team or committee, transition often remains in the training phase for excessively long periods of time.

This author has further discovered that the program director and/or teachers involved in transition programming are not the only ones who should meet and talk to the employers. There must be a team or committee designated by the school to assist the program director and teachers in meeting with the agencies and employers, in order to get them committed to hiring students who are involved in training.

The literature, as has already been noted, also mentions that there must be parental involvement in order for transition to be successful. Parents must be involved in planning with the schools, adult agencies, and employers in developing an individualized transition plan (Benz and Halpren, 1987; McCarthy, 1985; Wehman, 1985) for students preferably when they reach the age of sixteen (Wehman, 1985). If parents are not involved from the beginning, they will not realize the importance of their involvement in planning for their sons and/or daughters once they complete their public school programming at ages twenty-one or twenty-two.

It has been this writer's experience that many parents do not stop to think, until it is late in their son's and/or daughter's education, about what did happen to their son and/or daughter upon graduation from the public schools. The transition meetings designed to develop the individualized transition plan are a very important component, enabling the parents to understand that they need to request vocational training which is meaningful, or will lead to future employment possibilities for their sons and/or daughters.

Effective transition takes place most successfully if the individualized transition plan is implemented for the student and the process begins well before the student is twenty-one years of age. Some transition leaders suggest that the plan for each student should be formalized when the student is sixteen years old. In the public school programming that this writer started four years ago with the public schools, some of the older students who were getting ready to graduate at ages twenty-one or twenty-two were placed in the vocational transition programming. Other students who were part of the programming were seventeen or eighteen years old. For the ones who were seventeen or eighteen, there was greater opportunity to train them to learn to do work. They would have more years in school and could learn each of the tasks presented to them. It was noted that the older students had already established many behaviors that were often hard to remove and they had difficulty learning how to do some of their tasks at an acceptable rate.

The earlier that training is started for these populations, the sooner they will be ready to learn how to do the particular work. Many of the teachers and aides involved in the vocational programming were often more hesitant to work or train the older student who had never received training. When asked why they did not want to train the older students, many of them responded that it was more difficult to teach them because they had for so long learned behaviors that were inappropriate and breaking these patterns was extremely difficult. These comments were accurate. Some students were inappropriate in their behaviors and had to be placed in sheltered environments where they could be worked with in more secluded areas until they learned compliance training. When students are older and have not had early vocational training, it becomes more difficult and it takes longer to teach them new behaviors.

In the vocational transition programming organized through the schools, there are some students who may require as many as two trainers each because they have not learned earlier to do meaningful tasks. Some students who begin training much later in their years can learn some of the steps in their particular jobs, but many of them often are not able to learn to work fast enough to keep up with everything they must do.

Another important component that must be part of the vocational transition process is that a program must be planned and systematic. Additionally, the vocational service must be of high quality. In the vocational transition projects this writer coordinates, much planning is required with school administrators, teachers, aides, college student trainers, and employers. Teachers and aides have to be trained to work with all kinds of students in different jobs. In-service sessions must be planned and organized for teachers and aides.

There must be a clear check to see that every student who is nonverbal has his/her communication booklet and money to teach him/her how to purchase foods in restaurants. Some students often do not have any money and teachers or P.T.A. groups often have to secure funds to help these students. Fund raising activities are often helpful. If students still do not have enough money, then many make their lunches or participate in the school's free lunch program. Students can take lunches with them to the community training. These students do purchase soft drinks and, as a result, get some training paying for items and obtaining receipts or change, but they miss the fuller opportunity of selecting and purchasing a wider variety of items.

Transition planning also has to include explaining to employers when on-the-job training for the students begins in their places of employment after school starts. Careful planning includes getting transportation for the students and setting up particular times when program directors will meet with employers to see how the students are doing in training. The follow-up with employers should include discovering if there are any particular problems that are seen among students, coworkers, and the overall training of students. This writer often spends six to eight hours weekly following up all activities that have to be coordinated with students and their training in the particular job sites. The work is exhausting and continuous, but it is important to follow-up with everyone concerned, because communication and constant observation are of utmost importance when working with so many different people.

Every area of the country is different, and that what may work in one area may not always work in another. Over time, the author served as a consultant to other school districts that were starting vocational transition planning in their communities and shared with them some of what she learned in her area. Many of these considerations were helpful to others attempting transition planning.

INDIVIDUAL WITH DISABILITIES EDUCATION ACT

Congress amended the Individuals with Disabilities Education Act (IDEA PL 101-476) in 1990 to include transition service requirements. The provisions of IDEA include a set of coordinated activities for a student which include movement of a student from school to postschool activities, including postsecondary education, vocational training, and integrated employment, including: supported employment, adult education services, independent living, or community participation (Simon & Cobb, 1994).

According to the IDEA, to provide transition services, students' preferences and needs must be included as part of a coordinated curriculum. The law further states that students will be evaluated functionally and they will acquire daily living skills. Additionally, the law suggests that simulated vocational activities do not lead to employment for students with disabilities. The law in part suggests less emphasis on simulated activities. The law emphasizes that students be allowed to work and be paid while working in the community as part of their work experiences. Further, the law notes that students who are fourteen years and older can engage in some nonpaid vocational exploration, assessment, and training experiences.

The community-based vocational education has the following components: (1) vocational exploration, (2) vocational assessment, (3) vocational training, (4) cooperative vocational education.

Vocational Exploration

In this section students are urged to be exposed to a variety of work settings to help them make future career decisions. Their interests, values, and beliefs are brought to the work experience so that they can determine if they would like certain types of work. Students watch work being performed and talk with employers. The information helps to develop the student's individual education plan.

Vocational Assessment

This particular section helps determine a student's individual training objectives. In this area, the student works in several community sites under the supervision of school personnel. As the student participates in the various community sites, assessment data is collected on his/her special interests, aptitude, special needs, learning styles, work habits, behavior, and work tolerance (Simon & Cobb, 1994).

Vocational Training

As part of this component it is encouraged that students with disabilities be placed in the community at various work sites. A detailed plan should be developed determining what competencies are to be developed, and what methods of instruction will be used to train the student. People responsible for placing students in the community work sites are encouraged to rotate them to various sites.

Cooperative Vocational Education

This is the fourth component of the community-based vocational education section of the IDEA section relating to transition services. In this section there is an arrangement made between schools and employers in which each contributes to the student's education and employment in various ways. One of the ways is to pay the student for work performed in the employment setting. Also, students may receive money from their employer, from the school's cooperative vocational program, and another employment program operating in the community. Students are paid the same wages as nondisabled employees performing the same work. The school and employer reach a written agreement before the student enters the cooperative vocational education component. The agreement includes a clear stipulation of student's wages and benefits. The agreement may include follow along services for the student.

FAIR LABOR STANDARDS ACT

A very important act which has become a significant component of community-based vocational education is the Fair Labor Standards Act. According to the Act, community-based vocational education takes place in the community, therefore, these activities must comply with the provisions of the Fair Labor Standards Act. The Fair Labor Standards Act is federal legislation establishing minimum wage, overtime pay, record-keeping requirements (personal employees information, wages, hours) and child labor regulations (Simon & Cobb, 1994). Employees, under the Act, are entitled to a regular wage of $4.25 per hour and overtime pay of at least one and one-half times their regular wage for all hours over forty hours in a work week. The Act further notes that some states have labor laws and the most stringent laws apply.

The Fair Labor Standards Act comes into effect only in an employment relationship. Prior to this, when students were in a work setting, it was not clear if students were in the work place for vocational training or for work. According to Simon and Cobb (1994), schools were careful not to set up programs for fear they would be violating the law.

The Fair Labor Standards Act has a statement of principles and a set of guidelines that apply to students with disabilities. The guidelines include participation of students with disabilities for vocational exploration, assessment, or training in a community-based work site and under general supervision of public school personnel. The guidelines include that participants in the vocational programming in the community will be youth with physical and mental disabilities for whom competitive employment at or above minimum wage level is not immediately obtainable and who because of their disability will need intensive on-going support to perform in a work setting (Simon & Cobb, 1994). The Act defines community-based placements as clearly defined components of individual education programs developed and designed for the benefit of each student. The statement of needed transition services established for the exploration, assessment, training, or cooperative vocational education components will be included in the individual education plan of the student.

The guidelines further note that information contained in student's individual education plan will not have to be made available, but documentation of the student's enrollment in the community-based placement program will be made available to the Department of Labor and Education. A student and his/her parent or guardian must be fully informed of the individual education plan and community-based placement component and have indicated voluntary participation with the understanding that participation in such a component does not entitle the student-participant to wages. The activities of the student at the community-based placement site do not result in an immediate advantage to the business.

The guidelines also indicate that no displacement of employee or vacant positions have been left unfilled nor have employees been relieved of assigned duties and students are not performing services that, although not ordinarily performed by employees, clearly are of benefit to the business (Simon & Cobb, 1994).

Additionally, it is clearly noted in the guidelines that students are under continued and direct supervision by either representatives of the school or by employers of the business. Such placements are made according to the requirements of the student's individual education plan and do not meet the labor needs of the business. Also, it is indicated in the law that periods of time spent by students at any one site or in any clearly distinguishable job classification are specifically limited by the individual education plan.

In terms of number of hours that determine an employment relationship, the guidelines suggest that while existence of an employment relationship exists, this employment relationship will not be determined exclusively on the basis of the number of hours. As a general rule, each component will not exceed the following limitation during any one school year: (1) vocational exploration—five hours per job experience; (2) vocational assessment—ninety hours per job experience; (3) vocational training—one hundred twenty hours per job experience (Simon & Cobb, 1994).

Additionally, the guidelines indicate that students are not entitled to employment at the business at the conclusion of their individual education plan, but once a student has become an employee, the student cannot be considered a trainee at that particular community-based placement unless it is a clearly distinguishable occupation. The guidelines go on to suggest that if a student is paid for work performed in the employment setting, an employment relationship does exist.

Schools and businesses are subject to all the provisions of the Fair Labor Standards Act. These provisions would include minimum wage, overtime pay, record-keeping requirements, and child labor. This is true whether the student is paid by the business, the school, or a third party.

Students aged fourteen and fifteen years, under the Fair Labor Standards Act child labor provisions, may work in various jobs outside school hours no more than three hours on a school day with a limit of eighteen hours in a school week, no more than eight hours on a nonschool day with a limit of forty hours in a nonschool week, nor before 7:00 A.M. or after 7:00 P.M. except from June 1 through Labor Day, when the evening hour is extended to 9:00 P.M. These students may not work in jobs declared hazardous by the Secretary of Labor (Simon & Cobb, 1994). Further, the guidelines note for sixteen- and seventeen-year-olds, under the child labor provisions, students may work any time for unlimited hours in all jobs not declared hazardous by the Secretary of Labor.

Student learners (full-time students aged sixteen years and older and enrolled in a vocational education) can be employed at a special minimum wage rate of not less than 75 percent of the minimum wage (for example, $3.19 under the present $4.25 per hour minimum wage), provided authority is obtained from the Department of Labor Regulating Office of the Wage and Hour Division before the students begin employment.

Trainees, under the Fair Labor Standards Act, are also provided a training wage of $3.62 per hour, or 85 percent of the applicable minimum wage, whichever is greater, to be paid to most employees under twenty years of age for up to ninety days under certain conditions. Individuals under twenty years of age may be employed at this training wage for a second ninety-day period by a different employer under certain conditions. Individuals may not be employed at the training wage in any number of jobs for more than one hundred eighty days. Employers may not displace regular employees to hire those eligible for the training wage.

Workers with disabilities in supported work programs, as indicated by section fourteen of the Fair Labor Standards Act, are allowed to be employed at wage rates that may be below the statutory minimum. Still, the workers with disabilities are often compared with nondisabled peers in order to see if the worker with disabilities is just as productive when completing similar tasks and their nondisabled peers.

In order to pay a wage rate below the statutory minimum, an employer must have a certificate from the Regional Office of the Wage and Hour Division of the U.S. Department of Labor. The employer must obtain the certificate before employing a worker with a disability at less than minimum wage.

Documentation is needed for students to participate in community-based vocational education. This should be in the form of a letter of agreement outlining the Department of Labor and Department of Education requirements listed above and signed by participants and on-going case notes, for example, attendance records and progress reports. Schools and businesses should consult their U.S. Department of Labor, Employment Standards Administration Wage and Hour Division Regional Office for additional guidance.

PROGRAMMING FOR POSTSECONDARY TRAINING

In the past, the author has coordinated an adult transition program on her university campus, and learned—sometimes the hard way—some considerations that can make transition stronger for those students preparing to leave the public schools at ages twenty-one or twenty-two. The first part of this section will explain what is involved in beginning such a program; the second part will give information on what may be helpful in the transition process (Durán, 1988).

BEGINNING AN ADULT TRANSITION PROGRAM

Funding for the adult transition program came through a grant this writer wrote and submitted to the Texas Planning Council for Developmental Disabilities in Austin, Texas. The funding was for approximately $30,000 for the first year. At the program's inception, there were about fifteen students, whose ages ranged from twenty-two to forty years. Many of the students in the program had been classified as having severe to profound handicaps. Several came directly from the public schools, while others came to the program from state institutions. The program was designed to teach the students independent skills such as cooking, cleaning, shopping, and others. The other major goals of the program were designed to teach the students how to work and how to stay with an on-the-job training program.

This program was appropriately situated in a university environment where the students, like the university students training the clients, were usually of similar ages to the clients. According to Sailor (1985), adults in transition are very appropriately located at a university campus.

Staff for the program included a teacher who was certified in special education and college student assistants who were available when there were not enough college practicum students to help assist with the training. The transition program was open from 8:00 A.M. to 4:00 P.M. daily. During most of the day, students were either involved in on-the-job training or were in the community shopping. One day a week they spent learning to prepare their meals. Much of this learning was done either in homes near the university area, or in homes near to those of the clients. The home training was implemented in addition to the work training and the practice in going out into the community to make purchases, because the students learned skills best when they practiced in several different environments. Other times of the day the students were taught hygiene skills in order to be clean and groomed for their job training. Because the program was organized with structured objectives, few of the students had any time to act inappropriately or to spend their time doing activities that they were not supposed to do.

SOME SKILLS NEEDED BY SECONDARY STUDENTS WHEN THEY ENTER THE UNIVERSITY PROGRAM

Upon entering the postsecondary program on campus, 95 percent of students did not have enough skills to be independent. This lack became very apparent to the teacher, parents or guardians, and the program director (Durán, 1988). Many of the students who came to the adult program had previously done only academics in the classroom; a few had done nonfunctional activities such as coloring, pasting, and putting puzzles together. This previous experience is one of the main reasons the transition program's goals initially had to include some independent, self-help, and personal hygiene along with vocational skill training.

Further, many of the students, especially those from institutional programs, would wear mismatched clothes or would be totally uncoordinated in what they wore. Also, students walked, acted, and often (for those who spoke) asked or said inappropriate things to college students with whom they came in contact.

During the few months of the program, the author believed that the older students, who were from institutions, would not be able to make the transition quickly enough to keep from being too obtrusive with other college students. But after almost a year of training, many of them started to normalize more among themselves and their college peers. Several students, for example, wanted to wear some jewelry or clothing which would make them more like their peers. College students also started to become more adjusted to the students of the program. They started to be more accepting of the students, who at first had seemed so strange to them. As the months passed, the college students learned from the students of the program and the students learned from the college student trainers. Many very important socialization skills, among others, were learned by the students, who very much needed good models that many had not even seen prior to being placed on a university campus.

Other important skills the students in the transition program did not know were vocational. None of the students were able to do a variety of tasks for long periods of time. Still others were not able to stay on task any longer than five to ten minutes. One or two who had been involved in transition training before entering the adult program at the university were more normalized in their behaviors, and could do some work and other independent skills for longer periods of time during the training day. It was very clear to the trainers, the program teacher, and the director that the majority of students in the program had not been prepared adequately to live and work in the adult world.

It was evident that many of the students in the adult program had not learned to generalize skills from one environment to another. Brown (1980), Wilcox (1984), and Sailor (1985) all note that secondary students need functional and meaningful skill training which will generalize from one environment to another. It becomes more evident what is meant by this type of training after one sees secondary students leave the public schools and not know what to do. It becomes very evident that secondary students need to begin their vocational training early in their adolescence because so many young adults do not have the necessary skills to remain on their jobs or know how to do various independent tasks.

Further, secondary students attending high school programs need at least three hours daily of vocational training and, as the students get older and are getting ready to leave their public school placements, according to Brown (1987), they need to work from half a day to an entire day. In order to accomplish some of these goals, teachers need to understand how to train students with appropriate vocational techniques such as those discussed in the chapter on vocational training. Teachers and/or trainers need to understand how to do a variety of jobs and be committed to training students in the community, where many of these jobs are located.

STARTING A POSTSECONDARY TRANSITION PROGRAM FOR PERSONS WITH SEVERE HANDICAPS

Little has been written concerning postsecondary programs which are community-based, although during the last five years there has been more emphasis on adult programming because of awareness of the importance of transition. When this writer started an adult vocational transition program three years ago, she discovered that the majority of information that existed concerned adult programs which were not community-based but were more like segregated or institutional place ments. This section will describe how to begin a community-based program for adults with moderate to severe handicaps.

The U.T. El Paso Adult Program started with some federal and state grant monies. There were seventeen clients or students who were first enrolled in the program. These clients had moderate to severe impairments, and were from public school settings and institutions. The main goals of the program were to teach students independence and to help as many as possible find jobs.

Because many of the students had never received any training to do any kind of job, many of them started from the beginning of the programming to learn a variety of jobs in food service, or janitorial and clerical duties. To date, three of the students enrolled in the program have been placed in permanent employment. The other students or clients are currently (1987) involved in vocational training. They work approximately six hours daily in food service functions, and receive some free food, such as their lunches, for the work they complete. Many of these students are not able to complete the work as a regular employee would be able to do and, as a result, are working in food service as volunteers. According to Brown (1987), if students with severe handicaps cannot do their work as regular employees, then in some cases these students can become volunteers and partially participate—that is, have some trainers help them finish some of the work that needs to be complete. The employers can work directly with program supervisors to determine what will be paid to the clients or students for their work. Since the program is located on a university campus in a college of education, many of the students who help train or teach the clients or students in the adult program are college students who are preparing to be regular or special education teachers. This situation is an excellent one, because not only are the college students receiving training but also they are around their peers and age-appropriate models.

Every three months the students' goals, objectives and progress are reviewed in a conference held with the parents of the student or client. In the individualized habilitation plan conference, the program director and teachers meet with the client's parents. At this time the student's current progress is reviewed, and progress sheets or task analyses coding sheets are summarized for parents. The parents are now free to ask questions and make suggestions concerning their son's and/or daughter's individualized plan. The parents are informed about how their sons and/or daughters are performing on community-based training, which include grocery shopping and learning to use the community. The parents are shown data as to how their sons and/or daughters are performing in vocational training or on the actual job site. The parents are given information on when their sons and/or daughters may possibly begin permanent employment. If one of the students or clients will not be able to become competitively employed, then the parent is told during the conference that her/his son and/or daughter may be able to do volunteer work or can partially participate in some type of job training. The parent conferences are held on Saturdays, making it more convenient for working parents to participate.

The program has reached a stage where some of the clients or students who started originally in the program now need to be placed permanently in jobs, or else they will have to be placed on the job most of the day with college student practicum assistants. According to Sailor (1985), good adult transition programs are examined periodically by the program director to determine the impact of the program on the original clients.

Sailor (1985) suggests that after three years, clients of such programs should be moved to another—such as in a community college—to prevent the students from staying in one place too long and without achieving other goals. This writer finds that in her particular city and surrounding area, there are no other programs which are community based and which could take some of the clients or students into their programs. Thus, the program teacher must begin placing these students in more permanent jobs at once.

Job placement in such programming involves first training students in food service, clerical and janitorial jobs. After the students or clients receive training in these different places, the program teachers and director begin calling various job site areas to see where the students can be permanently placed. This process is long and involved. If the employer seems interested with the initial and first phone conversation, a time is set aside to meet personally with the employer. Meeting personally with the employer is extremely helpful because at this time many questions posed by the prospective employer can be answered by the program teacher or director. The employer can also see that there is a person who will be at the job site for the client or student, if there is a problem, as the job training begins. Employers are more receptive in accepting students or clients with moderate to severe handicaps if they know that a person is there to help when students act inappropriately or need special assistance. Phone numbers of the program teacher and director should also be given to the employers in case the employers may need to call about a student or client who may be absent from work too often or may be having difficulties with on-the-job training.

Periodically, it is extremely important to check personally with employers, because they need to know that someone who is responsible for the job coaching will be there to assist with any difficulties which may arise. In directing the adult transition program, this writer discovered that employers were more receptive to accepting clients if they knew that either this writer or the program teachers would be on hand if there was a problem. Some of the employers, for example, were concerned especially about the students with autism who were often unpredictable and bizarre in their behavior.

It should be noted in starting a postsecondary program for persons with moderate to severe handicaps that the clients' or students' goals or long-term objectives should be kept in mind daily; otherwise some of the clients might remain in the program for long periods of time without becoming employed. One of the main reasons for reviewing the program's as well as the clients' objectives is to prevent clients or students from remaining in the program without beginning some type of job training. If the students' objectives are not in the forefront, the program's objectives often do not get accomplished. Also, if the program's goals or objectives are not reviewed, students will remain in the program and there will not be openings for new students who should be enrolled. It is necessary to find jobs for students so that new clients can come into the program, and job training situations can be obtained for the new students entering the program.

Additionally, other important considerations that need to be made in starting a postsecondary program for persons with moderate to severe handicaps is to constantly be aware that initially many regular students or people have little or no understanding of students or clients who show inappropriate or bizarre behavior, and consequently may be amazed or shocked when clients display such behavior. If regular students do complain or show intolerance of inappropriate behavior, it is important to explain to them what the particular disability is; and it is necessary to explain to the college students what the different characteristics of various disabilities involve.

During the first year of the project, many questions were raised concerning the students in the program and their disabilities. After the regular students saw the clients or students on a daily basis around the campus, they became more tolerant of them and slowly developed a better understanding of them and their particular behaviors. Presently, the clients or students are better accepted by regular education students and faculty.

An important area to consider when starting a program is the necessity of maintaining good communication between the local school districts and the postsecondary program staff, since the school districts will likely continue to serve as feeders for such programs, forwarding their students for further training.

Further, the postsecondary program will often need letters of support from school districts for inclusion in grant proposals which are written to obtain more funding for the program's continued operation. It is important to maintain a good relationship with the public schools, because providing a destination for students completing their years in the school district relieves the districts of the responsibility of continuing training for students to whom they can offer nothing further. The success of such programs encourages the school districts and the community at large to continue their support, without which no postsecondary program can survive.

Another important aspect to consider in beginning a postsecondary program is to plan from the very beginning how the program will be funded after grant monies end. It may take anywhere from $25,000 to $30,000 yearly to operate such a program. Some of the expenses of a postsecondary program, of course, are the salaries of the director, teachers, and other paid members of the training staff. Occasionally, circumstances relieve some of the pressure produced by expenses; for example, this writer teaches at the University of Texas at El Paso, so her directorship of the program does not cost anything for a grant director's salary, saving money for other aspects of the program. Obtaining local foundation support for the program has also been helpful to supplement federal grant monies. Parents in the postsecondary program are generally not financially able to pay monies to keep their son and/or daughter in the training program, but they often organize and do fund raisers to give additional financial assistance to the program. The parents see the importance of having their son and/or daughter come to a skills training program, because they know that keeping a program such as this alive will help their sons and/or daughters and other students to learn some vocational skills before becoming permanently employed.

The directors of the program need to be encouraged to become close to their state legislators, because lawmakers can be very helpful when funding is needed for the postsecondary program. This writer, acting as director of an adult program, knows how important it is to maintain close communication with state legislators. Jenson (1987) notes that because state funding for programs for persons with handicaps is so competitive, people involved in programming must keep a close contact with their state legislators. He stated that his legislators have repeatedly helped him get funding for autism programs he has coordinated in his state.

Finally, it should be noted that beginning a postsecondary program is a major responsibility, because many students' lives and the lives of their parents become a direct responsibility of the program and staff. The main concern for everyone in the program is trying to find jobs where the students will become permanently employed. Great disappointments result if students do not find at least a part-time job after vocational training has ended. Parents need to be told at the time they enroll their son and/or daughter in the postsecondary program what steps will be followed in order to help them get a job. It is also extremely important that, soon after the vocational training begins, parents should be told if it is apparent to the staff that their son and/or daughter will be able to do only volunteer work, or will be able to work for only a few hours a day. Parents, for the most part, are happy to see their son and/or daughter learn independence and, above all, learn to do some type of useful work. Regular and candid parents' and staff conferences are vitally important, because parents should be informed on a regular basis of the actual progress their sons and/or daughters are making in the program.

The effort involved in teaching students to become more independent is hard work and requires much patience from the program staff. It is important to have excellent communication among the staff. The communication helps relieve stress that may be found among different staff members. Communication may further bring new and fresh ideas into the programming.

Thus, transition involves having a plan in place for the students long before they are to leave their public school placements, and transition also involves constant reviewing of the students' and parents' goals to assure that students will become employed. Transition also involves postsecondary programming where students continue with vocational training.

DISCUSSION QUESTIONS

(1) What is transition? Discuss and list some of the components that make for effective transition.

(2) What is the importance of having an individualized transition plan?

(3) What is an individualized transition plan? When should such a plan be formalized for a student with handicaps in secondary programs?

(4) What is a postsecondary program and how can one be started?

(5) What are some advantages and disadvantages to having a postsecondary program?

(6) What are some difficulties or obstacles in implementing a transition program?

(7) Discuss the different components of the Fair Labor Standards Act as it is related to transition services.

REFERENCES

Ballantyne, D. (1985). *Cooperative programs for Transition from School to Work*, pp. 1–117. Washington: U.S. Department Office of Special Education and Rehabilitation Services, National Institute of Handicapped Research.

Benz, M. R., and Halpren, A. S. (1987). Transition services for secondary students with mild disabilities: A statewide perspective. *Exceptional Children, 53*(6), 507–514.

Brown, L. et al. (1980). *Strategies for generating comprehensive longitudinal, and chronological age appropriate individualized educational programs for adolescent and young adult severely handicapped students.* Manuscript done in cooperation with University of Wisconsin and Madison Metropolitan School District, pp. 1–18.

Brown, L. (1987). From school to adult living: A forum on issues and trends. *Exceptional Children, 53*(6), 546–554.

Brown, L. (1987). *A vocational follow-up evaluation of the 1984–1986 Madison Metropolitan School District graduates with severe intellectual disabilities.* Paper completed in cooperation with the University of Wisconsin and Madison Metropolitan School District.

Butterworth, J., Jr., and Strauch, J. D. (1994). The relationship between social competence and success in the competitive work place for persons with mental retardation. *Education and Training in Mental Retardation and Developmental Disabilities, 29*, 118–133.

Durán, E. (1988). Adults with handicaps at a university-based program. *Reading Improvement.*

Jenson, W. (1987). Teaching persons with autism. Lecture workshop series presented to students, parents and teachers at the University of Texas at El Paso, El Paso, TX.

Johnson, D. R. et al. (1987). Meeting the challenge of transition service planning through improved interagency cooperation. *Exceptional Children, 53*(6), 522–530.

Kleinhammer-Tramill, J. P., and Tramill, J. (1994). Early intervention and secondary/transition services: Harbingers of change in education. *Focus on Exceptional Children, 27*(2), 1–8.

McCarthy, P. et al. (1985). Transition from school to work: Developing the process for individuals with severe disabilities. *Journal for Remedial Education and Counseling, 1*, 463–472.

Rusch, F. R., and Phelps, A. L. (1987). Secondary special education and transition from school to work: A national priority. *Exceptional Children, 53*(6), 487–492.

Sailor, W. (1985). *Teaching persons with severe intellectual disabilities.* (Workshop presented at the University of Texas at El Paso, El Paso, TX, special education teachers and administrators).

Simon, M., and Cobb, B. (1994). *Meeting the needs of youth with disabilities.* Handbook for implementing community-based vocational education programs according to the Fair Labor Standards Act, U.S. Department of Education, Office of Special Education and Rehabilitation Services, Cooperative Agreement H15862002, Washington, D.C., pp. 1–17.

Wilcox, B. (1984). *Transition and employment issues for persons with severe intellectual disabilities.* (Lecture presented in a course entitled: Secondary Program for Persons with Severe Handicaps, University of Oregon, Eugene, OR).

Wehman, P. et al. (1986). Transition from school to adulthood for youth with severe handicaps. *Focus on Exceptional Children, 18*(5), 1–12.

Wehman, P. et al. (1985). A supported employment approach to transition, *American Rehabilitation*, pp. 12–30.

Chapter 5

VOCATIONAL TRAINING

Elva Durán

Vocational training for persons with moderate to severe handicaps has made large strides in the last ten years. Presently, more persons with such handicaps are beginning to be placed in the community (Rusch and Chadsey-Rusch, 1985). Still, with all of these gains, many such persons remain unemployed. This chapter will define vocational training and will present various training techniques which are effective in teaching individuals with moderate to severe handicaps. Also, an explanation will be given of how students should be effectively trained to complete a task. In addition, this chapter will explain how to start vocational training programs in the community and will finally note how adolescents with autism are managed in vocational skill training.

SHELTERED AND NONSHELTERED VOCATIONAL TRAINING

In sheltered vocational training, students with moderate to severe handicaps are placed in a work setting where each person completes a specific part of a series of tasks that has been contracted for by some industry for the students to carry out. Students, for example, may have to perform some simple but multistep function such as packaging computer cables. One student may take a cable from a container and place it on an assembly table; another student may put the cable in a plastic bag; a third student may seal the ends of the bag shut with a pressing iron; a fourth may put the sealed bag into a container with other completed units for shipping to the warehouse or the retailer. At the same time, on the opposite side of the assembly table, another group of students may be doing a similar series of tasks, completing a contract for the same contractor or for another company. Whatever steps in the process that cannot be completed by the handicapped students in the workshop are usually finished by "lead" persons (Bellamy, 1981), who are regular supervisors or other employees who work in the sheltered workshop, supervising and otherwise helping the students with handicaps.

WHAT ARE SOME PROBLEMS WITH SHELTERED WORKSHOPS?

Sheltered workshops often do not accept the students or clients with more severe disabilities (Brown et al., 1983). Many of these sheltered facilities have clients on waiting lists, some as long as three years. Often there is not enough work for the students to do in the workshop and some of the completed work students have done is undone in "make-work" manner so the students will repeat the tasks, just so they will have something to do. As students sit and wait for more work to do, many of them become unoccupied and start to make inappropriate noises while others self-stimulate or move their hands in the air, for example, or flap their arms. Some bang their heads and abuse themselves. Other more severe students or clients displaying these behaviors will become models for other students. Soon they begin to imitate the disruptive behavior.

Besides the problems posed by inappropriate behaviors, shelters generally do not provide enough pay for the work students complete, some receiving as little as 50 cents a day. Further, students who are placed in these facilities seldom receive any type of work benefits such as medical and dental insurance. According to Brown et al. (1983), sheltered workshops may cost as much as $5,000 per year to operate per client. As important as sheltered workshops are, such costs become a burden to the taxpayer, as is obvious when one notes that there may be as many as twenty students in one facility at a time, and there are many such sheltered workshops in operation.

NONSHELTERED VOCATIONAL TRAINING

In nonsheltered vocational training, the clients or students are placed in training in various jobs around the community. Brown (1983) noted that in some instances the students are not paid directly, because they are learning to do various jobs. Some are often not paid directly because of their inability to complete tasks as quickly as someone who does not have severe intellectual disabilities. Brown (1983) reported that many handicapped workers do learn to complete their jobs with a good work rate or speed, and these students are paid directly. In some instances, however, students are not paid the minimum wage even after they have been in training for some weeks because many require supervision on the job, and often a coworker may need to prompt each of them to complete the tasks which have been assigned them. Despite these drawbacks, it is more important for students with severe intellectual handicaps to have an opportunity to do work for some part of the day, instead of having to sit at home and be idle for days or even years (Brown, 1983).

Before students are placed in various areas where they can do work, the teacher should survey the area near the school. This concept is called ecological or environmental inventory. When a teacher completes such an inventory, he/she can discover what jobs or industry are near the school in order to place students in these particular sites. After completing such an inventory, the teacher can further discover what nearby jobs are available where she/he can place students in training. In some instances, schools may be located at a distance from any industry and the teacher will need to survey other jobs available around the school that students may be able to complete.

This writer has helped two major school districts in the Southwest begin nonsheltered vocational training or training of these students utilizing various jobs around the community. In one of the districts, some of the schools are not located near any type of industry; as a result, the teachers in these schools have surveyed their campuses and have discovered many different jobs the students can do at their campuses. Some of the jobs have included food service (including all the different work tasks involved in the school cafeterias), and other job possibilities have included various kinds of clerical work in school offices such as filing, stamping envelopes, and placing mail in teachers' boxes. In some school situations, where there are no nearby industries or businesses that lend themselves to training programs for the handicapped, school administrators have approved the use of work opportunities on the university campus, with teachers, aides, and volunteers going along to work with the students undergoing training. These students often get another opportunity for learning to live in the "real" world by having to take public transportation to and from the university campus. One of the job areas that students can complete is the union food service, which involves busing tables, operating the automatic dishwasher, and sorting silverware. In the student alumni office, students find such work as stamping and sorting out-going mail, filing, and some even assist the office clerks in answering the phone. Other possibilities include a variety of janitorial work, such as cleaning the dormitories and main offices.

Near the university, students are also placed in fast food restaurants and convalescent or retirement homes. In fast food restaurants, students may wash and slice lettuce, tomatoes, and prepare other food items for hamburgers and sandwiches. In convalescent or retirement homes, students may learn to pour juices and other drinks in drinking glasses. They can also learn to fold linens and assist with washing of dishes in the automatic dishwasher.

There are many different types of jobs that students can complete in different work places; it is important to survey each work area carefully so that students can be placed in different jobs during the time they are in training. Students should be rotated periodically from job to job, a practice which will give students an opportunity to learn how to do a variety of jobs. For example, in the vocational training programs of the University of Texas at El Paso and the El Paso Public Schools, the students are rotated from one job to another every three to six months. This period has been chosen as an optimum because it takes approximately that long for some students with even moderate handicaps to learn a job. This extended period also gives teachers fuller opportunity to observe how the students are doing in acquiring their different skills. Further, giving the students three to six months of training allows the trainers enough opportunity to see how the students are performing tasks utilizing those skills. On another level, it is a good idea to rotate students because they thus learn to complete a wider variety of tasks. A standard practice in any vocational programming is to develop a regular sequence of learning opportunities. At U.T. El Paso, for example, a student is often started in the food service, moving on to clerical duties or janitorial tasks. Keeping records of which students have learned to perform which jobs is important, so that students can be rotated intelligently as they develop one set of skills and are ready to learn new ones.

TRAINING TECHNIQUES

In order for students to complete their work in vocational training, it is important for the people training these populations with moderate to severe handicaps to know training techniques that will assist the students to complete various tasks. One of the training techniques that is helpful is the use of verbal cues. Verbal cues or brief instructions can be given to the student who is learning to do a particular task. For example, if the student is ready to start the dishwashing machine and he/she is about to press the wrong button, the student can be verbally cued by the trainer, "No, try this one." Another type of training cue that can be given to students is physical guidance cues. When using physical guidance, the teacher or trainer may guide the student's hands or fingers by placing his/her hand or hands over those of the student, guiding the hands correctly so that the student can complete the task. Physical guidance cueing is very helpful to the student, especially when trying to prevent the student from making an error in the on-the-job training. In addition, proper motor skills are developed in the student by guiding these motions, which then can better be imitated and repeated correctly.

Other training techniques used with students are modeling and demonstration. In modeling the teacher or trainer shows the student how to do one or more steps on the job. For example, the student may not understand how to place certain food items in a grocery cart. The teacher may say, "Look at me," placing the item properly so the student can see the right manner before returning to the job. Demonstration works in a very similar manner, in that the teacher or trainer shows the student how to complete the entire task. Of course, it is necessary when using modeling and demonstration techniques that the student look at or attend to the trainer. The trainer, as well, should look at the student and make certain that the student is not looking away when modeling is being done, or when a particular demonstration is being performed. Gesturing and pointing are good training techniques that can help to keep the student from becoming confused. Another technique which can be used to train students is color coding. Color coding is often used to highlight or emphasize a particular part of the task that may not be very visible for the student. For example, if the student has to sort socks or linens in a convalescent home, the trainer may color code the box where the socks needing mending may need to go. The other socks which can be worn after they have been sorted may be placed in a regular box or bin which has not been color coded. As with any other prompting technique, color coding can be phased out as soon as the student has learned to do the task.

Another important training technique is to have the trainer stand behind the client or student. In this position the trainer or teacher correct the student with pointing, gesturing, or verbal cues so that the student can see what to do correctly without the trainer obstructing the work. It has been noted (Bellamy, 1979) that standing to the side or in front of a client while training the student can result in the student not being able to complete the job because he/she will be distracted by looking at the trainer. Also, if the trainer stands to the side of the student, the student will try to capture a "shadowing" glance of the teacher or trainer.

If the trainer continues standing beside the client or student, the student will continue "shadowing" or watching from the side of his/her eyes in an attempt to get some cues from the trainer or teacher. The trainer or teacher also must understand that he/she should continue standing farther and farther away from the client, until he/she is able to fade away completely from the student performing the task.

This writer has found that if it is not emphasized that the trainer must stand behind the student or client, then the trainer seems to want to continue to help the trainee, often increasing the trainer's involvement to the point that it becomes interference or takeover of the task—a situation in which the trainee learns little.

It is necessary to have workshops where some training techniques that have been discussed in this chapter can be shown and demonstrated to people or job coaches who will be helping with the training of students or clients. This writer has found that providing training workshops for vocational trainers or job coaches saves a lot of confusion and time initially if people know clearly what to do and are aware of what is expected of them.

Periodically, people involved in training these populations need to be observed and given feedback as they teach. It helps the teacher or trainer to go over the feedback with trainers, pointing out positive and negative points collected through observations of their training of students or clients. Many other training techniques have been found useful. For one thing, trainers must be careful to be as unobtrusive as possible when out in the community or in the work place. When observing or supervising a variety of trainees, co-workers and people in general are more accepting of the student trainees if they are not constantly having to listen to trainers giving a multitude of loud directions to the students. In some instances, co-workers have become distracted and complained to their supervisors that they are being interfered with by the noise and disruptive actions of the trainers. In one case, a co-worker was so bothered by the noise level produced by the job coaches involved in training their students that he complained to his supervisor, who then asked the director of the program not to send that particular trainer back to the job site. A few weeks later, the supervisor asked that all the clients and their trainers stop training at his work site, because one of the co-workers simply could not complete his work due to the noise level produced by the on-the-job training activities.

Thus, it should be clear that stressing to trainers that they should be as low-key as possible is vital to the success of a training program; unobtrusiveness is central in helping coworkers be accepting of handicapped trainees, and keeping the doors open to such training sites. Teaching trainers to be unobtrusive is also important so that students involved in training will not be as aware that someone is standing over them, assisting them in completing their tasks or helping them to do their work. The too-obtrusive trainer undermines the student's self-confidence as well, undoing much of the progress that might otherwise be made.

FULL INCLUSION HELPS PREPARE STUDENTS TO DO MORE WORK IN THE COMMUNITY

Inclusion of students with moderate to severe disabilities in regular education classrooms can be helpful in teaching students how to do various jobs in the community (Whaley, 1995). As a teacher of young adult students with severe disabilities, Whaley (1995) noted that having students in regular education classrooms when they are younger could be most helpful to teachers of high school programs. According to Whaley (1995), they developed the very social skills they needed in order to be in the community accomplishing a variety of jobs. Durán (1995) notes in her qualitative research study that parents noted that students with autism who had difficulty prior to being in a fully inclusive classroom were now more willing to follow directions and wanted to participate in different activities at home and at school. Durán (1995) also notes that the general education students model for the students with moderate to severe disabilities in how to participate in cooperative groups. Also, the general education students are able to model for the more severe students in how to share materials in groups and take turns completing various tasks.

Whaley (1995) noted how much better students do their activities in secondary vocational/community-based programs when they are part of full inclusion programs for several years before entering middle and high school programs. Further, because the students with severe disabilities were included in elementary classes, many in high school vocational programs can also be part of general education classes in the high school. Thus, parents need to be told the value from the beginning of how important full inclusion can be during the experience and much later when the students with moderate to severe disabilities are in high school.

This writer has observed that students with autism who were placed in the community early on through preschool and elementary years were more likely to follow directions and stay on the job for more hours than those students who never left their homes. More data is needed to discover the positive effects of full inclusion with students with autism. The author has also noted that the more students with autism are allowed to participate with general education peers, the more they become tolerant of them as they do similar activities with students in general education classrooms. For the past forty years, students with autism have been educated on a one-to-one type of intervention in order for them to learn many of their academic as well as functional skills. Many of these students can perform many tasks, but many who have been educated by the one-on-one model are not able to stay on a job for a long period of time. Could it be that these students never acquired more social skills that are vital to remaining on jobs in the community? Again, more research is needed in this crucial area.

GETTING THE STUDENT STARTED TO DO A JOB

Once the trainer is aware of the various training techniques that are necessary to help clients or students do a particular task, the trainers can begin with the student in actual on-the-job training. The client or student needs to be taught to attend or look at what he/she is completing. Often just pointing to the particular button, for instance, that he/she should be pressing while working with a dishwasher will be helpful to the client or student. This simple action will cause the student to focus his/her attention on the part of the work he/she should be completing. Students with autism, for instance, have great difficulty looking at what they are doing in on-the-job training, but with pointing, gesturing, and/or verbal cues, the student begins to learn to look at what he/she is doing.

This writer has found in coordinating several vocational projects, and carrying out her own programs through the university, that the older the student is before he/she begins vocational training the more difficult it is to teach the student to concentrate on what he/she is doing. As the training continues, it is often necessary to use a variety of reinforcements to get students, especially those with autism, to complete their work. With some students with autism and other severe handicaps this writer has tried a variety of reinforcers to get the student to stay on task. Sometimes what works is not what one would ordinarily expect. For example, Jose, a fifteen-year-old severely autistic adolescent working at a convalescent home washing and rinsing food trays, was initially given three five-minute coffee breaks during his three-hour training shift. These frequent interruptions of the routine were found to be disruptive, producing interfering behavior. A new reinforcement strategy and schedule was begun, and Jose's reward—one five-minute break and a cup of coffee in the break room at the end of his three hour shift—has turned him around and made it possible for him to work steadily for the entire three hours with no disruptive behavior.

Other reinforcement strategies may include having the student select from a menu of reinforcers to be earned if he/she completes his/her job. When selecting a menu of reinforcers for the student, the trainer must remember to change the reinforcers periodically; otherwise the student will have a tendency to choose one reinforcer too often or will not choose any reinforcer and will not be motivated to increase his/her level of work (Durán, 1987).

If the trainer observes that the student is making too many errors on different steps of the job, the trainer or teacher can also utilize different reinforcement strategies to get the student to practice the steps he/she is having difficulty completing. For instance, in the various vocational projects this writer coordinates, it is first noted which steps the students may have difficulty completing. Five minutes before the actual vocational training begins, the trainer tells the student, "Maria, if you work hard to do this right, you get to drink juice." The student should be rewarded after the five minutes of training or practicing on steps he/she has been doing incorrectly. To further remind the student about his/her reward, a photograph of juice is placed near the student's work area. Rewarding the student in this manner encourages the student to practice on steps he/she has missed on the job. Also, rewarding the student after he/she has completed the practice helps him/her realize that this was part of his/her work and is not a form of punishment. If practice is planned before the student's actual work begins and no reinforcement is given to the student, the student often does not want to practice on steps he/she is missing on the job.

Once a week it may be necessary for staff members to get together and talk about students who are involved in the training. They can discuss what reinforcements may be needed to help students produce more work during on-the-job training. During these staff meetings any particular information that was noted concerning the students' behaviors on the job can also be discussed. Weekly staff meetings are crucial in keeping excellent communication among all who work closely with the students involved in training.

OTHER TRAINING TECHNIQUES

The author earlier discussed students learning to attend to a particular task. This attending problem can cause difficulty in a student's acquisition of a particular task. Acquisition is a very important component of vocational training. In acquisition training, the trainer or teacher must help the student learn how to do a particular job, utilizing appropriate training techniques, reinforcement strategies, and by giving students time to practice difficult steps of a task. Also, acquisition for the student is greatly improved if the student's environment is assessed for different obstacles which may be keeping him/her from starting or completing the job (Wehman, 1982).

If there are problems in the environment or place where the students are working, then they will be unable to acquire or learn how to do a job. Some problems which may arise that may prevent acquisition are unusual or different noises that are not part of the work environment originally.

Another source of interference in acquisition training can involve a break in pattern—like having materials that the student trainee needs to complete a task moved from the usual locations or misplaced accidentally by coworkers. For example, one of the students from the public schools who worked at the union cafeteria was originally trained to get detergent to wash the dishes from a shelf area near the automatic dishwasher. When the shelf area broke and the detergent was moved to another location, the student spent twenty minutes looking for the detergent and became quite upset when he couldn't find it. That morning the student did not accomplish any work on his job. Changing the environment and not leaving necessary materials exactly where they are normally placed can cause major difficulties as the student is learning to do a task. Another problem, giving students incomplete or unclear directions, often keeps them from acquiring needed skills or learning to perform a task. Directions to students should be brief and brisk. According to Gold (1980), Schloss (1987), Hill (1982), and Brown (1987), giving verbal directions to students is important not only in helping them learn to do a job, but also in assisting them to do it accurately. Gold (1980) suggested such directions as "Try another way" or "This way." These are examples of brief statements that tell a student to do the job in another manner if he/she is not completing the job steps as instructed.

Another important area in on-the-job training involves skill maintenance. In skill maintenance, the student or client continues doing the job that has been learned, as time passes. Also, students need to be trained by several different trainers and some of these trainers must be coworkers who work with the student. If the coworkers are not involved in the training, then when trainers leave the actual work site, the coworkers will not know how to help the students or clients and the students may forget certain steps and eventually the job may not be completed as it should be. Skill maintenance also allows the student to learn to work in one setting and learn certain skills and be able to transfer the learning of similar steps to another job. This growth can take place because the student maintains what he/she learned originally in on-the-job training.

Similarly, another important training technique which students need to strive toward achieving is production. In production, various factors must be emphasized by the trainer if the student is to learn how to do a particular job satisfactorily, so that the work is done rapidly enough as well as accurately enough to be acceptable. Work rate, quality, and endurance are important considerations of on-the-job training, and are components of production. In work rate the trainer is concerned with teaching the student to complete the task at speeds much like those of a regular worker. By correcting steps the student does incorrectly and increasing or adding different reinforcers, work rate can often be increased.

Another important aspect of vocational training is work quality. Work quality involves having the student complete work accurately and according to the way job supervisors want it completed. In work quality the trainer is concerned with having the student make as few errors as possible. Also, if students do make errors, it is important that practice time be given to students so that they will get opportunities to learn steps they have missed as part of the task.

Another important aspect of training and work is for the worker to have endurance on the job. Work endurance means that the student will be able to work more and more hours of the day without too many pauses or breaks. Developing work endurance among students with handicaps takes time, and with some students it requires that time spent on training be increased gradually until they are working more hours of the day independently. These are some very important components that make up the area of production. Without emphasizing the need for the student to do work quality, rate, and endurance, the production on-the-job training would not be increased, and the student would not develop the skills needed for success.

Three other components of vocational training are error correction, evaluation of the work the student has completed, and follow up. Error correction procedures involve making the student aware of the steps he/she is missing. One type of error correction procedure is verbally stating to the student that he/she has made an error. For instance, the trainer will say, "No, like this." Here, the trainer has verbally corrected the student and has modeled for the student the correct procedure, or the correct step. Another technique that can be used to correct a student is to have the trainer physically guide the student's hands so that the student can learn to make the necessary corrections on the step he/she may have done incorrectly. These error correction procedures can be used in combination, or each procedure can be used by itself. Following all of these techniques the student should also get practice training on the missed step(s) for five minutes before the actual training begins, as has already been explained earlier in this chapter.

Another technique that is necessary in vocational training is periodically evaluating the student's or client's progress. This evaluation should also be done as explained in the chapter on language training, by using a task analysis coding sheet. Keeping track of how students do each time they train on the job is important so that if they are not learning the job, it may be necessary to retrain them to do difficult steps, or it may be necessary to increase or change the reinforcement.

Parents, principals, and other school administrators want to know the progress of their students in learning to do a particular job or jobs. They want to see the results of on-the-job training, because many have set up as a priority helping students with moderate to severe intellectual handicaps find jobs once they leave their public school placements. This writer works with several school administrators and is often asked how students are doing on the job. Also, administrators want to know if students have completely learned the job or part of the job. Therefore, having task analyses coding sheets in order to evaluate students' vocational training progress is vital in order to keep such programs always open to these populations.

Another important component of a good vocational training program is follow-up. Follow-up includes seeing how students have done if they have been placed in various jobs. When students begin working and training in various jobs, their progress must be checked to make certain that they are not having any major difficulties with coworkers or supervisors, and it is also important to check to see that they are adjusting to their work environments. The author has learned firsthand the importance of checking on or directly observing the students as they are involved in training. It is important to observe both the students who are in training and those who are already working, at least once weekly. At this time one can talk to job managers or supervisors and sees how students are getting along with their coworkers. This writer regularly spends time talking to everyone involved in the direct on-the-job training with the student. Communication and observation of the entire work site are crucial in keeping students working for a long-term basis.

GETTING A NONSHELTERED VOCATIONAL TRAINING PROGRAM STARTED

When beginning a nonsheltered vocational training program there are several recommended considerations that need to be made in order to make such programming successful. First, someone must talk to public school administrators and explain to them what this type of training is and what it involves. Further, an explanation must be given to these school personnel of the objectives of such type of programming. School administrators need to realize that this type of vocational training is necessary so that students who are still in the public schools can possibly obtain jobs once they leave their placements, at age twenty-one or twenty-two.

Following this orientation with top school administrators, it is time to begin surveying the school environments where students who are involved in training attend school. The environmental or ecological survey (Brown,

1983) will reveal to those who are going to conduct the training what businesses and/or industries are located near the schools. The director in charge of programming will need to talk to job managers or supervisors of these companies so that possible work sites can be obtained for the students involved in training.

During the interviews with the job managers, the program director or person coordinating the programming should have a prospectus prepared (Duran, 1988), including the goals and overall purpose of the nonsheltered vocational programming. The paper should include most of the components which are listed in Table VII. Employers are usually very helpful if they know the overall purpose of the program and are aware of whom they may call if there is a problem. Also, employers are usually very helpful if they know that students will be assisted by trainers to help them learn to work. Many will even let some of their coworkers teach students if time allows. The program director should make certain that he/she understands how to do different jobs and, if possible, should take some other trainers to the job site so they can also learn how to do various jobs.

Once jobs are secured and the program director and trainers know how to do the jobs, then it is time to begin training principals and teachers about what they will need to know concerning job coaching in nonsheltered placements. An in-service training workshop for the teachers, aides, volunteers, and school principals should include a slide presenta-

TABLE VII
NONSHELTERED VOCATIONAL TRAINING INFORMATION
FOR JOB EMPLOYERS

I. What is Nonsheltered Vocational Programming?
   A. Define
   B. Explain what it leads students to obtaining
   C. Types of jobs students with handicaps can do
II. Practice on the Job Site
   A. Days per week
   B. Actual time spent on training per week
III. Supervision & Follow-Up
   A. Who will do the supervision?
   B. How often will supervision be done with students?
   C. Contact person for problems
   D. When and how often will follow-up occur?
   E. Who will do follow-up?
IV. Parents
   A. What should co-workers do if parents visit their son/daughter?
   B. Manager's and job coach's role in assisting parents.

tion of the different job sites. Also, this workshop should provide training for teachers on correct training procedures, as explained earlier in this chapter.

Additionally, workshop training should include information for all persons concerned with the program on how to correct, evaluate, or code the student; and, further, the workshop director should explain how students with handicaps can be retrained to correct missed steps on their particular jobs. The workshop participants should see models and demonstrations of the various training procedures so they can understand how to train students correctly. The latter part of the workshop should include some actual training, where the participants train students to do work on different jobs. Besides the program director, there should be at least one other trainer on hand at the workshop in order to give correction feedback to workshop participants.

Procedures go more smoothly the first day of training if teachers, aides, principals, and volunteers all know how to teach persons with handicaps to learn to do a job. Once training is underway, the job coaches and other volunteers involved in the actual vocational program should continue to get feedback of what they are doing correctly and incorrectly with the on-the-job training.

After vocational trainers have been oriented and have been shown what to do as part of vocational training, it is important to have a short meeting with the parents of students who will be involved in training. During the meeting, the principal should express his/her desire and excitement about having the students participate in this type of programming. If school principals do not convey their interest in having such a program as a part of their campus, many parents and teachers will not become committed to the entire program. In the long run, all of these attitudes will hurt the day-to-day programming.

During the parent meeting, parents should have explained and demonstrated to them the importance of having their son or daughter find work, once they leave the public schools. Too many parents fail to see beyond their child's early school years and, unless all of this is fully explained, parents will not stress this in their own contributions to their son's or daughter's individualized education program. It should be fully explained to parents that unless they request such training for their sons or daughters in their child's individualized program, no school time can be allowed for such training. Parents should further be invited to come and see vocational training, once it all begins. When parents come to the job sites, they should be welcomed, and any questions which they have should be answered. There should be very good communication between parents, teachers, and all concerned, so that the training may prosper and the programming can be continued.

Once all have been trained and there seems to be a good communication among all concerned, it is important to try to locate and secure as many additional job sites as can be obtained. If the school environment can provide only one or two training sites, then other areas must be carefully looked at to assist the students with more training opportunities. This writer has discovered that her own university campus has provided many job possibilities for training students. Some have already been mentioned earlier in this chapter. If no jobs are located near the schools where training will begin, it is important that additional nearby areas be surveyed so that students can take public transportation to go to those particular job training sites. The more sites that students have to work, the better will be the possibilities of their obtaining jobs at the end of their public school programming.

The acquisition of a sufficient number of training sites requires a lot of time, especially if many students are potentially needing this kind of vocational training. If the city is large and there are many public schools in the area, finding jobs and training sites will take long hours and much patience. If adequate time is designated by the teacher and program director, it is possible to locate new training sites and jobs. Of course, a program that is successful for students, employers, and those involved in the training is excellent evidence to provide to prospective employers.

At the beginning of the vocational programming with which this writer was involved, there were only about five different types of jobs that students could engage in. Presently, with teachers, trainers, administrators, and parents working together, a total of more than twenty different types of jobs have been secured for students to learn.

As the different jobs for vocational training and employment are secured, everyone concerned with the training will want to know how often and how long students should be involved in training. According to Brown (1983), as students become older, every effort should be made to place them in training for more hours of the day and more days of the week until eventually they are working at their jobs almost all day by the time they are twenty-one or twenty-two. Brown (1983) and Wehman (1979) both noted that for best results, vocational training should begin when the student is twelve or thirteen years of age.

Students who become involved in training early—even those who are more severely and intellectually impaired—have a better prognosis for finding some work once they leave the schools than those who begin much later in their years to do any type of vocational training. Students who begin training later have a longer and more difficult time learning different tasks, and often near graduation even leave school without having learned appropriate job training skills. Prognosis for these late starters is often not as good as for those who started training early in their years.

ADOLESCENT STUDENTS WITH AUTISM
IN VOCATIONAL TRAINING

Except for some work of Schopler and Mesibov (1983), Lettick (1979), Durán (1987), and Durán (1990), not much has been written concerning the adolescent with autism who is involved in vocational training. This next section will explain some of the considerations which must be recognized in placing these students in nonsheltered training. It will also discuss the author's experience in placing them.

First, the greatest difficulty in placing autistic adolescent students in training is their often bizarre and inappropriate behaviors. As many go through puberty they become very hard to teach in on-the-job training. This writer has observed that some of the procedures which seem to help college students who are doing the training is to first of all warn the managers and coworkers about what may happen with an autistic adolescent at work. This preparation will prevent coworkers from becoming overwhelmed when an adolescent with autism throws water on the floor, for instance, if he is washing dishes, or throws himself on the floor when not wanting to work. Of course, coworkers should also be informed about these students who are involved in training, because many may complain that the trainers are being too firm, or may not understand why the students are being made to complete their work.

It is extremely important for trainers to remember that adolescent students with autism must learn that they cannot get out of work by acting inappropriately. Autistic adolescents must be taught that if they work and complete their tasks, their rewards will be greater for being productive than if they are being nonproductive and inappropriate. The author's experience has shown that being persistent and adding to the vocational training time as the students stay on task will help them gradually learn their particular jobs. This persistence and adding to their time on the job have helped many stay on task for longer periods.

Adolescent students may act unusual, for example, by throwing themselves on the floor or hitting themselves, or they may attempt to destroy materials found on the job. Also, the adolescent students with autism may physically attack their trainers. Several remedies to help with the bizarre behavior have been tried. First, it is important for a trainer to lift the student from the floor if he/she drops himself/herself. If at all possible, the student should be kept on task and working. Further, if the student hits the trainer, sometimes soft tie bands can be placed on the student's hands, leaving enough slack for him/her to use his/her arm and finish working (Lettick, 1979). The tie bands are removed after two minutes, and if the student does not hit others or himself, he/she is rewarded with something he/she likes very much. If something is not done to prevent severe aggression, such as using soft tie band restraints and/or rewards when the student is not engaging in these behaviors then the behaviors often continue and the student gradually becomes worse in these types of behavior.

Adolescents with autism soon learn that inappropriate behavior exhibited in on-the-job training will not be easily tolerated and consequently they will become more productive through the rest of their training period. Also helpful is briskly and firmly saying, "No, not like that." The first, brisk voice almost seems to snap many of these students back to reality as they are about to act inappropriately for on-the-job training. The author has also used some time-out procedures with students with autism to help reduce the frequency of their inappropriate behaviors, but these aggressive or inappropriate behaviors are not always diminished. Some students with autism enjoy being placed by themselves and, further, some may like not having to complete their work. Some seem to almost test new trainers and often see how much they can get away with during the training. Trainers who have never worked with autistic students must realize that they must be consistent and firm, especially when students are learning new tasks or are moving from one activity to another. Once a student realizes that the trainer means business and is the boss (Lovaas, 1981) he/she will work for longer periods of time.

This writer has worked with several public school principals and other school administrators and has learned that not too many people have faith that autistic students can complete their work. This belief is held by many people because they become completely scared of the aggression and self-abuse students with autism frequently display. The author often tells administrators and teachers that if training is started early and consistently with these populations, then many do learn more appropriate behavior in their vocational and other skill areas. She also helps administrators realize that some students can learn to act appropriately in on-the-job training if they are given firmness and structure.

In one school district, some administrators and teachers did not believe that the students could ever learn to stay on task for long periods of time, due to the students' aggressive behaviors. One administrator agreed to try and did allow students in his district to begin some vocational training in the community. He believed that the students in his schools could learn some tasks. After four years that the students have been in training in vocational sites around the city, these students have improved markedly as far as their aggressive behaviors are concerned. Many of them can work on a job or jobs for about four to five hours daily. They do require some breaks during their work period, mostly restroom breaks, and the time spent on these breaks is not longer than five minutes. All of the teachers, parents, and volunteers have worked hard to keep the cueing similar with these students across all environments. Everyone in the program strives to be consistent and firm. The trainers have taught the adolescent students with autism to comply with directions and perform all that they had to do in their on-the-job training. Compliance training has resulted from having the students complete their tasks. Since everyone works together to be firm, there is always a consistency presented to all students in whatever they do. If they want to throw tantrums or attempt to become aggressive, this behavior is corrected by the methods and ideas presented earlier in this chapter.

This writer is aware that there is much criticism presently about using some management procedures, including firmness, raising of the voice, structure, and aversive techniques such as using soft tie band restraints in training these populations. But as Rimland (1987) noted, the techniques that Ivar Lovaas (1981) used, such as firmness and structure, are intense, but are not excessively harsh. Care should be taken not to use aversive procedures with students with disabilities.

The author has used many management techniques of Lovaas and Lettick (1979) and many other approaches in teaching these populations and has found some of these ideas to be very helpful in working with students with autism who have severe, aggressive behaviors. It has also been noted that when one is in the community, with some students who become noncompliant, it is difficult at times to get them to do as they are supposed to in their vocational and other tasks. Many drop themselves on the floor, break materials in the vocational setting, and others are so self-abusive that even covering their arms often does not keep them from hurting themselves. After much hard work with these students they begin to show more on-task behavior appropriate for on-the-job training.

This writer has seen good results from using firmness, structure, and reinforcement with some adolescents with autism. Many students have become more normalized in their behaviors because of the consistency, firmness, and structure in their instruction. Parents who do not believe at first that their son or daughter could work at a job for even twenty minutes are astounded when they see that person finally working for one hour and then gradually working for even more hours without demonstrating inappropriate behavior. As the time on the job increases for these young adults with autism, and they become more compliant in following directions and doing what they are supposed to do, many of their aggressive, self-abusive, and tantruming behaviors cease. Eventually, as years pass, many become more normalized in their behavior while at work.

Employers who have some autistic students in their sites have commented on how scared they were at first when they allowed these students to come to their facility to train and learn how to do a job. Many feel they never believed the students would ever calm down and work. When they see the students improving on a day-to-day basis, they understand that there is hope for even the most bizarre students to learn to do work.

Employees should never feel that they are alone in handling students with autism in their work areas. The supervisors and program directors must always be visible, so that a good communication and dialogue can exist between program staff and employers in the community. In the end, when employers grow and become more flexible about allowing other students with autism to work in their places of business, it becomes worthwhile to have offered such support to the people in the employment arenas.

Also, when one sees an adolescent with autism it is important, therefore, to be aware that there are many methods that have been presented to teach adolescents with autism. There are some ideas or suggestions which exist in the behavior modification literature for teaching the student with autism who has severe aggression and noncompliance in vocational training; many of these ideas are excellent and, above all, work. Some of these are: (1) reinforcing appropriate behavior that the student demonstrates while ignoring the bad behavior; (2) using a five-minute time-out with the aggressive student; (3) and reinforcing the student intermediately when he/she is performing the appropriate task (Lettick, 1979; Lovaas, 1981).

A good teacher or trainer should review all effective research and attempt all such methods that seem to fit a situation; many may indeed be helpful in improving a student's behavior. A good teacher or trainer is one who is not an extremist in any one management approach or technique, but rather stays in the middle and attempts a variety of proven and well-documented management strategies.

Further, it is necessary also for the teacher to attempt a variety of management techniques because the goal ultimately is to get the student to become more independent in vocational training. The teacher needs to realize additionally that he/she must have conferences and communicate with parents concerning intervention strategies used with a particular student.

Additionally, the teacher should be aware that he/she does not have an absolutely free hand to alter the program strategies at will. Both teacher and parents should know precisely what management procedures have been specified in the student's individual education plan and approved, in writing, by the parent. No deviation from that plan can be initiated by the teacher without parental approval and signature. Communication between the teacher and parents is of utmost importance in attempting to manage autistic students, and others with severe handicaps in the community.

Finally, using punishment or any form of aversives should be used as a last resort and should not be used as an intervention. Whenever possible, using reinforcement strategies or finding what the student enjoys or likes is important, because often the adolescent student is larger than the persons on the staff, and using any form of punishment may only increase the student's level of aggression. What may happen if punishment is used is that the student may attack the trainer or coworker and, because the student is often larger and stronger, especially during this period of adolescence, he becomes extremely difficult to handle. The student's lack of responsible control of that strength is also a factor.

In conclusion, vocational skill training for the adolescent with autism and other students with moderate to severe handicaps is an exciting area to attempt to develop, but within the entire training area there are strategies and knowledge of the jobs that must also be considered. With appropriate management techniques, and placing more moderate to severe students in general education classrooms early in their education, even the student with the most severe handicaps can often be successfully put to work and taught to complete a task.

DISCUSSION QUESTIONS

(1) Define and compare sheltered with nonsheltered vocational training.
(2) What are some specific difficulties with sheltered workshops?
(3) Discuss three training techniques used by people to help training moderately and severely handicapped students to do a job in a vocational training facility.
(4) Discuss and list three considerations that must be taken into account when beginning a nonsheltered vocational program.
(5) What training techniques can be used in assisting an adolescent with autism to do a job?
(6) What is the role of full inclusion for the students with moderate to severe handicaps in vocational/community-based programs?

REFERENCES

Bellamy, T. G. (1981). Vocational habilitation training. (Lecture presented at the University of Oregon for a class entitled: Teaching the Severely Handicapped).

Bellamy, T. G. (1979). Vocational habilitation of severely retarded adults: A direct service technology, pp. 3–233. Baltimore: University Park Press.

Brown, L. et al. (1983). Teaching severely handicapped students to perform meaningful work in nonsheltered vocational environments. Manuscript done in cooperation with University of Wisconsin and Madison Metropolitan School District, pp. 1–97.

Brown, L. (1987). A vocational follow up evaluation of the 1984–86 Madison metropolitan school district graduates with severe intellectual disabilities. (Paper done in cooperation with Madison Independent School District and University of Wisconsin, Madison) pp. 3–115.

Duran, E. (1987). Overcoming people barriers in placing severely aberrant autistic students in work sites and community. *Education*, *17*(3), pp. 333–337.

Durán, E. (1988). Adults with handicaps at a university based program. *Reading Improvement*.

Durán, E. (1990). Parent interviews of their students with autism, University of Texas at El Paso.

Gold, M. (1980). *Did I say that? Articles and commentary on the try another way system.* Champaign, IL: Research Press.

Hill, J. (1982). Vocational training. In L. Sternberg and G. L. Adams (Eds.). *Educating Severely and Profoundly Handicapped Students,* pp. 269–311. Rockville, MD: Aspen.

Lettick, A. L. (1979). *Benhaven then and now,* pp. 120–149. Benhaven Press. New Haven, CT.

Lovaas, I. O. (1981). *Teaching developmentally disabled children: The me book,* pp. 1–129. Baltimore: University Park Press.

Rimland, B. (1987). *Autism Research Review International* (Institute for Child Behavior Research), *1*(1), pp. 1–7.

Rusch, F. R., and Chadsey-Rusch, J. (1985). Employment for persons with severe handicaps curriculum development and coordination development and coordination of services. *Focus on Exceptional Children, 17*(9), pp. 1–8.

Schopler, E., and Mesibov, G. (1983). *Autism in adolescents and adults,* pp. 411–433. New York: Plenum.

Schloss, P. J. (1987). Self-management strategies for adolescents entering the work force. *Teaching Exceptional Children, 19*(4), pp. 39–43.

Wehman, P. (1982). Vocational training. In L. Sternberg and G. L. Adams (Eds.), *Educating severely and profoundly handicapped students,* pp. 269–311. Rockville, MD: Aspen.

Wehman, Paul (1979). *Curriculum design for the severely profoundly handicapped,* pp. 111–145. New York: Human Services Press.

Whaley, S. (1995). Transition programming for students with severe disabilities. Presentation made in transition course, California State University, Sacramento.

Chapter 6

COMMUNITY–BASED INSTRUCTION

ELVA DURÁN

This chapter will define what community based instruction is and will also explain how community-based instruction works by reviewing various models described in the literature. In addition, it will discuss some actual community based training that is being completed by this writer and several teachers in two large school districts.

Community-based instruction involves teaching students the skills they will need in their everyday lives (Snell & Browder, 1986). For example, some will need to cross streets or buy food in restaurants. In order to determine what skills students need, an environmental or ecological inventory (Brown, 1980) must be conducted, as discussed before. According to Snell and Browder (1986), community-based instruction had its beginnings with the idea of normalization as defined by Wolfensberger in 1972. Normalization, which was popular in Scandinavia in the 1960s, set forth an ideal of community living for all people, with or without handicaps. First, normalization assumes the importance of teaching skills for adult life in the community and, second, normalization sets some guidelines for social validation of the results.

CONSIDERATIONS TO MAKE IN IMPLEMENTING COMMUNITY–BASED INSTRUCTION

In reviewing the literature, not many articles were found which explain how to actually set up community-based instruction. There were even fewer articles which explain what difficulties can result from beginning such programming in schools.

First of all, community-based instruction can occur in school environments, nonschool environments, and in the community at large. Sailor et al. (1984) and Falvey (1984) noted that it is necessary to do training in all of the above environments so that students with moderate to severe handicaps can generalize from one place to another. It is also important to consider that community-based training should be age appropriate and functional for students who are receiving the instruction (Falvey, 1984 & 1986). Once it is clear where the training will take place, then there are several other factors that need to be considered in developing community-based instruction. Some of the factors include: (1) liability and insurance, transportation; (2) cost; (3) student factor; (4) environments for community-based instruction; (5) teacher factors; and (6) the amount of time students with handicaps should spend training in the community (Sailor et al., 1984; Nietupski, 1982). Liability and insurance should be carefully looked into, because one of the things that often prevents training in the community from taking place is that administrators are afraid of what may happen if teachers transport students in their cars or vans.

Experience has shown that many school principals as well as area superintendents are afraid to let students off campus unless they travel in school or city buses. Legally, permission slips will not keep a school or school district from being liable in case an accident occurs and the parents can prove negligence. This aspect was explained to this writer by a lawyer in her city when she was involved in assisting two school districts to begin community-based instruction. Thus, checking carefully to see what the public schools have in terms of insurance is of utmost importance. Also, making certain that students are well supervised when they are out in the community is important—in insuring that the students are safe in crossing busy intersections or when buying their food at restaurants. In discussing liability and insurance, transportation is a chief factor.

It is also important to note that students need to be well supervised while they ride city buses, but they should also be well supervised if they ride in vans or parents' cars as they are doing community training. When students have been long accustomed to riding school buses and they make a change to city buses or buses for handicapped populations furnished by the city, many experience difficulties in adjusting to these new means of transportation. Some adolescent students with autism, for instance, may exhibit unusual behaviors such as crying, or pulling the cord that activates the alarm or bell system on the bus. Other students with autism may encounter difficulty in departing from the bus in a quiet, still fashion. Some, for example, may run from the bus, or will not get off the bus as they are supposed to do. The teacher preparing the students with severe handicaps and autism may have to work very closely with parents of these particular students, as well as the bus drivers, until caretakers or persons responsible for the students are all implementing similar intervention strategies.

This cooperation is essential to help extinguish some of the unusual behaviors that adolescents with autism may exhibit initially when having students ride a city bus or bus for persons with handicaps for the first time in their lives. The case of Manny will help illustrate this point. Manny was an eighteen-year-old autistic student, attending the public school during the school year, but in the summer attending a university based transition program. When Manny was first picked up at his home in a city bus for persons with handicaps, he was not able to keep from ringing the bus's interior alarm system. Also, Manny ran furiously out of the bus each time he reached his destination and the door opened. The bus driver, parent, and teacher worked together to remind Manny that if he stopped running out of the bus and did not ring the alarm, he would get to eat some of his favorite food snacks at the end of his destination. At first Manny was rewarded with some of these favorite snacks each time he did not do either of the problem actions. Later he was reinforced every other time he did not engage in the inappropriate behaviors. By the end of the summer, Manny was given only verbal praise by his mother and teacher when he did not engage in the inappropriate behaviors that were slowing his progress in riding a bus.

This writer, acting as program director of the community-based and/or transition program Manny was attending during the summer, realized the importance of working on the problems immediately. Sometimes bus drivers become intolerant and will complain to the point that some students with handicaps have to participate in more restricted types of transportation due to their display of inappropriate behaviors.

Thus, the area of transportation is critical and involves not only liability and insurance but has to do with students' behaviors, which must be worked on at the first sign that the inappropriate behaviors could cause problems to the student and other passengers in the bus.

Another aspect to consider in community-based instruction is cost. Most of the cost that comes from such programming involves the cost of the school buses and cost of the food and drinks that students buy as they learn to use grocery stores and fast food restaurants. Local parent associations often help students pay for some of their food or bus fare training costs. When it becomes a burden for parents who are in economic hardship, then students can take their lunches and buy only a beverage. Falvey (1984) notes that teachers can give students money so that they can buy some of their groceries or other food items. Sailor (1984) notes that students and teachers can even train in nearby areas to cut the cost of transportation.

The author has not seen that the community instruction has become a financial burden for either the district or the families of the students, because the principals and teachers have meetings with the parents of the students involved in the instruction. During these meetings the principals and teachers discuss with parents exactly who will be involved in supervising the clients or students. Also, the principals and teachers ask parents if they have any concerns about actual programming of the clients or students in the community. One of the campuses where the severely handicapped students regularly do community training also has bake sales to help with the cost of the training.

Another important consideration in community-based instruction is the student factor. When students are younger, community instruction can involve teaching students how to utilize, for example, the campus, playground, and a nearby park. Training for students to use these can include one or two hours a week. As students become older and reach adolescence and late adolescence, training should become part of their vocational activities, and more and more time should be spent in the community and less time should be spent in the classroom. This type of scheduling is especially true as students are getting ready to leave their public school placement. Brown (1987) notes that by the time students with severe handicaps are getting ready to leave their public school placement at ages twenty-one and twenty-two, it becomes more critical for them to learn the various skills they may not have learned previously.

Student factors also indicate that many students with moderate to severe intellectual handicaps are unable to participate fully in the various community training activities but, as Brown et al. (1981) note, they can partially participate according to their abilities. The example of Lynn, a young adult with multiple handicaps—severe mental retardation as well as cerebral palsy—will help illustrate the operation of partial participation. She could not grasp items normally with both hands, so she was taught to do what she could do—order and grasp food items in a restaurant with one hand when she went with her classmates. With modeling and cuing, she was taught to use the abilities that she had, rather than attempt a procedure with which she would be unsuccessful.

Many parents often do not want their children to be part of community training because they fear that people will make fun of their disability or will ridicule them for not participating, as other students, in various activities. As time passes, parents who may exhibit this hesitation may become more accepting that their son and/or daughter, who may not be able to totally participate in activities, but may still do some things to the best of his/her ability, and should be encouraged to try to do so.

Another factor to look at in community based instruction is noting to see what environments will be used by students. The environmental inventory should indicate what restaurants, shopping areas, and stores are near the school so that the student can participate in these particular areas. If no shopping areas or restaurants are nearby, then it is important to see which other shopping and restaurant areas are in close proximity to the school. The teacher and students can then take a city bus to available sites. It is necessary to keep in mind that students with moderate to severe handicaps need to shop in different stores and restaurants, because they need practice in generalization training. In the vocational and community based program this writer coordinates, teachers and students make a list of the stores and restaurants they will be able to use for training, and weekly the stores and restaurants are placed on a schedule so that students may go to different areas each time they are involved in community-based instruction.

Another important consideration in community-based instruction is teacher factors. This includes in-service training activities for the teachers so they can learn the techniques involves in training students in the community. Teachers and/or trainers need to be taught how to code or evaluate students as they participate in different activities in the community, as has already been explained. They also need to develop a communication system—for example, having the use of a picture or photograph communication booklet so that the students may order their food in restaurants or purchase food items at grocery stores.

Teachers and/or trainers need to know how to train students by standing behind them in an unobtrusive manner (as described in vocational training). For example, when students are crossing a busy intersection, it is necessary that trainers walk behind them individually so that they will not become too dependent on the trainer to give cues on waiting for the street light to turn green, or waiting for the trainer to cue when to cross the street. Teachers, volunteers, and college practicum students learn quickly to do community-based instruction techniques if they are required to participate in actual training, using the routes and materials that the students will use when they begin to do the actual training in the community. Because of the time that has been taken in the in-service training to acquaint teachers and trainers with the techniques they will need to operate a program of community-based instruction, greater success can be anticipated, as well as a smoother operation.

The other factor which needs to be considered in community-based instruction is the amount of time students with handicaps should spend in community training. This point has been discussed earlier, but it is important to understand that the older students with moderate to severe handicaps are, the sooner they will be leaving school and it thus becomes more critical to teach them to learn different skills in the community. In addition, older students are often slower to learn needed skills, so priorities should be established as to what skills are most vital, so they can be emphasized in training sessions.

STAFFING STRATEGIES THAT CAN BE USEFUL IN COMMUNITY BASED INSTRUCTION

Staffing patterns become highly critical in community based training, since they make a difference in how many students can be taken to the community at one time. Also, staffing patterns can help teachers with extra hands which can make a difference in community-based instruction. This section will review some staffing patterns which have been found useful in other programs where community-based training is in operation. Each type of staffing pattern will be followed with a brief explanation of how the different patterns actually work (Baumgart & Van Wallenghem, 1986; Martin, 1982; Coon, 1981). Some of the staffing patterns which have been found helpful in community-based training are: (1) consultants; (2) volunteers and peer tutors; (3) related staff; (4) staggered implementation of community-based instruction; (5) substitutes or paraprofessionals; and, (6) team teachers (Baumgart & Van Wallenghem, 1986).

One of the first staffing patterns described in the literature utilized a consultant to help a teacher or teachers in a district begin community-based training. Consultants can be extremely helpful, especially if they have been instrumental in helping other teachers and school districts organize such training. The actual experiences they have had in helping other schools start community-based instruction can be useful in helping other districts learn from the difficulties or problems that consultants have already encountered through actual experiences. Baumgart and Van Wallenghem (1986) note that it might be thought expensive to bring in a consultant to help organize such training, but they feel that one or two days of help a consultant might be able to give is useful enough to help offset the cost of having such assistance. Baumgart (1986) notes that there are ways through federal and state monies to pay a consultant's fees.

Another staffing pattern noted uses volunteers and peer tutors. Volunteers and peer tutors can usually be found if the teachers, or even other parents who are involved in various organizations, can check to see who could be available to help teachers take students out in the community. In community-based programs this writer is involved with through the schools, she and the teachers have utilized grandparent volunteers and college practicum students very effectively in the programming. Since the college practicum students are in this writer's vocational class, all of the students must complete a practicum training students with moderate to severe handicaps who are involved in the programming through the public schools. The college students receive their training as part of the class instruction. All of the college students report that they are better prepared because of the actual hands-on experience they have obtained as part of their special education undergraduate vocational class instruction.

During the summers in the community-based program at the university that this writer coordinates, high school students from various area schools participate as peer volunteers for students or clients involved in the community-based training. It is helpful to have peer volunteers, because students with handicaps adjust better if a peer volunteer helps them learn various tasks, since persons with handicaps learn to model some behaviors after their peers. In speaking recently to four high school volunteers after they had completed their summer months at the university program, the writer found that all of them felt that they would like to help in the university program again.

The private industry council and other summer youth programs can often place high school-age students in various work training opportunities, and it is a good idea to have teachers call these agencies to see if secondary students are available to assist with students with handicaps in the community. Slovic et al. (1987) noted additionally that college student fraternity and sorority members can also be another source of volunteers for community-based training of persons with moderate to severe handicaps.

Similarly, as with peers, volunteers, and college practicum students, some related staff—nurses, occupational therapists, and speech-language pathologists—can schedule time when they can assist teachers with the various community training activities. By scheduling these related staff to do some of their job duties with students at different blocks of time, the related staff people could be free during certain times of the day to help with specific students out in the community.

Additionally, another staffing pattern noted in the literature was staggering implementation of community-based instruction. With such creative scheduling, some of the students could be completing training at school in the lunchroom while a few other students could be spending their time going shopping or buying groceries at a nearby grocery store. Such staggering in the schedule could be helpful for times when there may not be enough volunteers or practicum students to assist the students who require a one to one ratio, allowing some students in class to work with the few volunteers who are available and do some community-based instruction. According to Baumgart (1986), when there is inadequate staffing, many of the students may not receive enough training unless their schedules are alternated so that all students in class can receive a turn at completing their training in the community.

Another staffing pattern that can be considered in accomplishing community-based instruction is team teaching. In this particular type of staffing pattern, one teacher is in charge of a segment of the class and does some community-based instruction, while another group of students with a second teacher does vocational skill training. The groups are then alternated so that students doing vocational training also do community training, and vice versa. Team teaching is helpful also in that teachers or staff working together may help each other and make suggestions to one another about training which is taking place. It has been this writer's experience that if there is more than one teacher involved in training, teachers share their ideas and exchange thoughts concerning what works and what does not work. Also, teachers working together can be helpful to one another because if one teacher does not observe a particular aspect of the training, someone else may, and this will be helpful to the entire programming.

The next section of this chapter describes some of the community-based programming which this writer coordinates with two major school districts in her area, explains how the vocational programming got started and what was involved in the training of teachers and aides who were part of community-based instruction.

In order to begin community-based instruction, there must be a person who acts as a catalyst to help explain the need for such programming to administrators in the public schools. Once administrators understand how such community based instruction works, many principals and superintendents usually become very supportive. There needs to be an in-service training session given to the teachers, aides, volunteers, and principals, where community-based instruction will begin. The in-service training should be given by someone who is enthusiastic about such programming. The in-service training can usefully include slides of the students who have been involved in community-based instruction. The presenter should give the workshop participants an overview of the nature of community-based instruction. Also, the participants should learn various techniques of how to train students to gesture and point, and how trainers can physically guide, giving verbal cues to the students who are involved in the actual training—techniques which have been explained in the chapter on vocational training.

Another important aspect of community training in-service is to have the workshop participants practice doing some actual shopping with students in grocery stores, restaurants, and also have participants practice teaching students to cross streets. This in vivo practice will assist workshop participants to understand more clearly what they need to do when they begin attempting the actual training. It has been this writer's experience that having such training for workshop participants is very worthwhile because the correction feedback given to participants at this particular time is extremely important and will make actual training go more smoothly for each of the participants. Thus, a suggested outline for an in-service for training teachers and other care givers is presented in Table VIII.

In organizing a community-based program, transportation, time, and the schedule of when the students come to programming; supervision of students with handicaps; and follow-up of all program activities must be considered. In projects this writer coordinates, students from both districts in her area come to the nearby university campus on school buses. The buses are parked near the sites where the students will be shopping or buying their food. The buses wait for the students until they have done their grocery buying, etc. Many of the parents of students who participate in community training activities take turns riding on the bus so that they can assist the teachers in supervising the students.

As mentioned earlier, scheduling when students can participate in the

TABLE VIII
COMMUNITY BASED INSTRUCTION INSERVICE OUTLINE

I. Overview of What is Community Based Instruction?
II. Slide Presentation of Students Involved in Training.
III. Present Techniques of What is Involved in Training.
  A. Physical Guidance
  B. Verbal Cues
  C. Gestures
  D. Modeling
  E. Combination of All of the Above
IV. In-Vivo Practice with Students from the Community
V. Correction—Feedback
VI. Questions and Answers

programming is another area that is necessary to consider in community-based instruction. According to Brown (1981) and Sailor (1984), as students reach later years of adolescence, they need to be involved in community training more and more hours of the day and they also need to train more days of the week. Brown (1987) suggested that as many as four days of the week with a minimum of three hours each day should be considered in the training of these students. In the vocational/community-based training this writer helps coordinate, one school district has its students participate four days a week with four hours allowed for community training during each of the days. In the second school district, students participate three days weekly with a total of three hours daily devoted to community-based training. This writer and teachers of the programming have noted that students who did not get the training early in their years, starting late in receiving some training in the community, were not able to learn many of the skills as quickly, because of generalization difficulties and starting late.

An important factor in the scheduling of community-based training is setting sufficient time when the students can go to different stores and restaurants during the week. If teachers do not schedule time on a monthly or even a biweekly basis to do this training, students will not be exposed to a variety of different grocery stores and restaurants.

Similarly, another important component in community-based training is adequate supervision of students who are involved in training. In the programming this writer coordinates, college students have been helpful in acting as job coaches for students with moderate to severe handicaps. Sailor (1985) noted that college students help make community-based programs very successful. Often a student with multiple or severe handicaps must be coached or supervised by two college student trainers. When taking students into the community who have severe inappropriate behaviors—for example, students who are autistic—it is important to remember that the students may need more individual attention, from additional trainers or coaches, in order to help prevent them from running wildly or becoming noncompliant. This writer has observed that many adolescents with autism need much community coaching, because they often have not had the necessary practice previously to learn to act appropriately in different parts of the community.

Thus, managing students with autism and other students who display inappropriate behaviors becomes especially difficult during community-based instruction, and appropriate supervision must be available to help students with their difficult moments.

Other supervisors, who can also be utilized for community-based instruction, are peers and volunteers. In districts where this writer is most familiar with community-based instruction, grandfather volunteers have proven very efficient in supervising and training students with moderate to severe handicaps. The most important characteristics of these grandparent volunteers is that they need to be dependable and should be there when they are needed.

Another important consideration of community-based instruction is the follow-up on what needs to be accomplished as students go out into different places in the community. Some coordinator or person who is in charge of the overall program needs to observe the training and students in operation so that the problems or special difficulties students may have can be dealt with immediately, before problems become even more pronounced. An example to help illustrate this point would be when people from the community question why students with handicaps are shopping or buying groceries in different stores. If a coordinator or overall supervisor is aware of this questioning, the supervisor can talk to people in the community who may be wondering why students with handicaps are in the stores. During recent community training, a college student was coaching an autistic student in a nearby grocery store to stand in line and pay for his food item; because the student with autism started to make strange noises, a lady in the store was about to complain to the store manager. The supervisor observed the lady becoming angry and decided to speak to her briefly about the programming. After she understood why the students were at the grocery store, she no longer complained nor insisted on speaking with the grocery store manager. This is an instance where it is important for some person closely related to the community-based programming to carefully follow-up all aspects of the instruction. Such follow-up will keep major problems from surfacing and becoming unresolved.

A MODEL COMMUNITY BASED TRANSITION PROGRAM: TEACHING STUDENTS TO MAKE INFORMED CHOICES

MICHAEL R. YOUNT AND SUSAN L. WHALEY

This section will describe what students with severe disabilities are learning about decision making in a high school community-based/vocational program. The curriculum described focuses on teaching students how to make choices in their environments. The first part of the section will give the audience some information on how students with severe disabilities are empowered to make informed choices.

As persons with severe disabilities enter and succeed in more environments, four things become apparent. First, when given the opportunity, persons with severe disabilities thrive in diverse environments, especially when taught in the environment itself. Second, this capacity to thrive always existed. For example, students with severe disabilities now work in paid jobs, ride public transportation to and from activities, and live independently. Third, independence occurred in large part from the fact that students with severe disabilities were given opportunity to participate in new environments. Finally, it appears that the real "mental challenges" occur for teachers who self-fulfilling limits create barriers for persons with severe disabilities. For example, in one instance known to the writers, a student greatly enjoyed weekly integrated activities which included trips to pizza parlors, game rooms, and weekend camping. However, the teachers planning the activities always controlled transportation and when transportation was not available the second year, the student could not attend activities in the community. Therefore, in addition to building knowledge, the challenge for teachers is to examine their mental limits concerning the capabilities of people with disabilities, and to teach the basic skills required for students with disabilities to gain control within and between environments.

For a person, gaining control of their decision making required making meaningful choices between activities, solutions, or environments using a broad information base, and this cannot be done unless one knows something about the choices. That is, "before students can think, . . . they need something to think about" (Olsen, 1982). This is the first part of informed choice, and the basis of empowerment. The second part to this skill is the *way* one chooses. In other words, a basic skill important to selecting options is to be a thinker, and "to be an efficient and effective thinker, the learner should be able to monitor his or her degree of understanding, be aware of the knowledge possessed, be conscious of the task demanded, and know the strategies that facilitate thinking" (Wilen & Phillips, 1995). This last statement generates another question. Why is effective thinking important for persons with severe disabilities, and can they learn this difficult task?

The answer to the first part of the above question contains several parts, the first of which concerns safety. To negotiate between environments requires critical judgment, such as: when to reveal personal information, what to do in an emergency, or deciding when to get help. Second, by demonstrating competence, persons who control environmental access can fade their role. Finally, gaining control over decisions through effective thinking empowers persons with severe disabilities.

The answer to the second section of the preceding question helps the readers consider: Can students with severe disabilities learn difficult thinking skills? This is best answered by describing the community based transition program with which these writers are involved in Northern California. The program teaches students critical thinking skills. Eighteen to twenty-two-year-old students with severe disabilities participate in this community based class of fourteen. The students are based in a one bedroom apartment with a city-wide "campus" of twenty-five square miles.

Before entering this school district program, students go through regular high school graduation at one of three comprehensive high schools and begin following the local community college schedule. Student composition reflects the multiethnic and multicultural make-up of this Northern California city, including African American, Caucasian, Latino, and Asian with significant numbers of immigrants from Southeast Asia and Russia. In fact, forty-seven different languages are spoken in the homes of local students. Additionally, all students are ambulatory, some classified as nonverbal and some able to read primary grade material. The staff directly serving these young men and women consists of two teaching assistants and one certificated teacher. In addition, the school district provides other services such as speech and language therapy and work experience.

Sometimes these students do not see a teacher all day or only for a few minutes. Other days staff members seldom see each other. They all keep in contact through a phone in the apartment, a cellular phone and two pagers. The curriculum is functional and community based, but also teaches the young adults to think by emphasizing critical thinking skills which are taught in context of their functional instruction. For example, the students are taught to be aware of time management across activities such as work, recreation, community college classes, household chores, or shopping.

The thinking skills part of this curriculum uses Ann Brown's (1982) metacognitive process as outlined by Wilen and Phillips (Table IX). The transition classroom first follows the awareness outline. Using the time management example, purpose means to determine an aim or goal for subsequent action. In time management, students must use their time efficiently, effectively, independently, and they must determine how to complete their selected activities. Second, they are posed with the question which means what information does the student have concerning the goal? Here, students know they must work, attend school, do apartment chores, eat, shop, and save time for leisure and recreation. Another part of the awareness outline attempts to teach the students the value of what do I need to know? Thus, students need to know work schedules, class schedules, appointments, and how much leisure and recreation time they want, within the schedules of public transportation. Finally, the additional part of the outline asks the student what facilitates their learning? In this particular case, it means planning a schedule and completing the schedule. This is community based instruction combining basic critical thinking skills and time management. "Research shows that students learn both skills and subject matter if they are taught concurrently" (Beyer, 1988).

Teachers in special education often teach basic skills by imbedding them in concrete activities. The transition staff reinforces his strategy by individual and small group instruction in an apartment that has been assigned to the students as part of their community based instruction.

They especially model the behavior through "thinking out loud" and the teachers open their thinking processes to students by analyzing and openly discussing the steps in making decisions. In one instance the teacher might consider with the assistant the invitation to go to lunch at a fast food restaurant. The following dialogue may take place with a student:

> Let's see, I enjoy the person's company and want to go. I ate lunch yesterday at the same restaurant, but I could order something else. I only had toast for breakfast so I am hungry. I don't have much money, but if I don't order a drink I can afford it. I have my bus pass. I'll check my calendar to see if I have time before my gym class. I'll get my gym clothes out now so I won't forget them. I think I'll go.

In the above example, the teacher goes over feelings, hunger, finances, transportation, scheduling, and a strategy for enhancing memory. In another example, such as when a stranger approaches, the thinking process must be timely, but also needs training. Students will need to determine if they know the person, how well, and where they stand in relation to other people (e.g., in class, on the street).

Next, the action portion of the metacognitive process includes: planning, checking, evaluating, revising, and remediating. To teach the above, teachers help students plan by starting with a blank monthly calendar, then listing their activities and prioritizing them. They first enter set activities such as daily work experience or community college classes. After this they determine other necessary tasks and schedule them, e.g., shopping for food. Then they look at free time on the calendar and decide what to do for fun and who to have fun with. This all must include time for transportation. One strategy students find helpful is to break the day down into three natural time periods such as morning, lunch, and afternoon. With two free time blocks, they can participate in a longer activity or one farther away from the home base. If the students have a little free time, activities must remain short.

The calendar becomes the action plan and the vehicle to teach time management and critical thinking. Students check the calendar (their plan) and follow it. At first they often ask the staff what to do today? However, the staff responds, "I don't know; check your calendar." Soon students stop asking and refer to their calendars automatically. In fact, often the teaching staff must find out from the students what they planned. In one case, the teacher wanted to talk to a student but had to make an appointment with her for the next day because of the student's busy schedule.

Evaluating means checking the action plan and determining if the plan works to one's satisfaction. In other cases, it takes time to determine success or failure. For example, one student worked, took community college classes, and ate her lunch in the community college cafeteria. However, on her first calendar during all of her free time blocks she chose to sit in the cafeteria. She did not go out to lunch, go to a movie, shop, get groceries, or visit friends. After a couple of weeks of seeing her friends going out every day and having fun, she approached the teacher and said, "Maybe next month I'll add some activities on my calendar." This student made a plan, checked it, and did not like the outcome. This encouraged her to revise the next month's plan and remediate the action.

This strategy does not mean that students make choices without guidance. Earlier in this section the authors discussed "thinking out loud" to reveal thinking processes to students. Additionally, students need to experience many different activities to make informed choices. For example, the teacher might say, "This time I want you to try it. If you don't like it, next time you can choose something else." Even with something as important as work, the students choose this option. When problems arise on the job, the teacher may recommend that "If you don't like your job, you need to tell the boss and still do the job until a replacement can be found, or give two weeks notice." They may also be reminded that there will be no pay if the job terminates. As a result, students make choices and have guidance based on their needs, experience, and natural consequences.

As one might expect, when first entering this program everything does not run smoothly for students and the teaching staff. First, students often have little experience making choices. In most cases, they follow the decision of authority figures. Sometimes, they just pretend to follow instructions. Students may overtly agree with the suggestion of the teacher and continue to engage in whatever action they selected. For example, one student said that he liked a particular job and wanted to work, but often would hide on the way to the bus, or get off the bus on the way to work. He then would eat dinner and show up at home as if nothing happened. He never said that he disliked the job, but his actions communicated otherwise. This behavior is not the most common problem. As mentioned earlier, even when students have real preferences, they too often follow the direction of whomever is in authority. That is, they do not make decisions for themselves, but try to seek the cues given by the teacher to direct them. The teaching staff then must take great pains not to decide on the options for the student.

Recreation and leisure activities play another large part of the community transition class. Informed choice effects this aspect strongly, and extends beyond the boundaries of the normal school day and time. Students fill most of their spare time with leisure activities including going to lunch, shopping, going to the movies, or going to the mall with a "buddy." The buddy goes as a companion and also for safety reasons. These buddies ride the bus together, shop together, and help each other make decisions. Even in "safe" environments, companionship is more prudent and reassuring to parents. Students often plan for after school or weekend activities with a buddy. In addition to leisure activities, most students engage in some type of physical exercise. Many go to the YMCA, others take physical education classes at the community college, two take a marshal arts class at a local dojo, and one plays basketball in three regular night leagues.

The domestic skills aspect of this program primarily occur in the apartment where students cook, clean, and garden. They plan and cook lunch for themselves and invited guests. This necessitates shopping, budgeting, using recipes, running out for the last forgotten ingredient, and "making do" with the wrong utensil because the last person did not wash the right one, or did wash it and put it away where only he or she can find it.

At transition meetings, parents agree to support domestic skills by training students at home and letting them cook a meal at least once a week. Parents often remark how responsible and how well their children clean up at the apartment as compared to home. As one can see, this program extends the time and space of typical community based or transition programs.

Students in the transition program also benefit from an extensive work experience starting from the time they entered high school. They start on a part-time basis in situational assessment settings. This includes one of dozens of exploratory, community based work sites with job coaches. The range of explorations include offices, warehouses, hospitals, restaurants, schools, plant nurseries, parks, cafeterias, hardware, toy, clothing and variety stores. By the time students reach the transition classroom all of them sample at least seven jobs. The majority of students also participate in regional occupational programs and/or summer youth programs with the goal of having each student in a paid position or attached to a supported employment agency by the time they leave. They learn that they enjoy some things and dislike others. For example, one student developed back problems every time he went to work in a state office building. However, when he changed work to a warehouse, he made the warehouse workers actively think of more he could do. With informed choices, students generally feel empowered enough to be more open with their preferences.

In summary, all of the normal community based instruction components are part of this program. These include work experience, transportation training, domestic skills training, leisure, recreation and participation in the community. These components are vehicles to teach the most important part of the curriculum such as thinking skills, respect, and making informed choices. Students who participate in this curriculum demonstrate that critical thinking is part of their thinking skills. This occurs because of extensive experience, and infusion of thinking skills across functional activities. (The writers wish to thank Cathy Barone, Stacey Hoffman, Tasha Norris, Pam Zaharie, Yvonne Acuesta, Linda Kawahara-Matsuo, and Dr. Lou Barber for their dedication and individual contributions to this program. The writers also thank Dr. Hyun-Sook Park for including this community program as part of her on-going research in the area of social ecology.)

TABLE IX
METACOGNITIVE PROCESS

  I. AWARENESS
    A. Purpose
    B. What one knows
    C. What one needs to know
    D. What facilitates learning
  II. ACTION
    A. Planning
    B. Checking
    C. Evaluating
    D. Revising
    E. Remediating
(Wilen & Phillips, 1995)

ADOLESCENT STUDENTS WITH AUTISM IN THE COMMUNITY

The literature in the area of placing adolescent students with autism in community based instruction is once again not very prevalent. According to Lovaas (1981), much of the reason for such a limited number of articles on the adolescent and young adult is that we have been teaching the young child with autism for many years and have not focused our attention on older subjects until more recently. Also, Lovaas feels that for many years there was little assistance for the student with autism and, as he/she became older, the only hope there was for these young adults was to place them in institutions. With the work of Lou Brown in Madison, Wisconsin, in the 1970s, there has been a greater emphasis on placing students with severe handicaps and autism in the community. The section which follows will provide some information this writer has learned through the years in coordinating several community based programs for students with autism. There have been more than fifteen young adults with autism who have received various kinds of training through the districts in this writer's area.

The main difficulty faced by most teachers or trainers who begin taking autistic students out into the community is to teach them compliance training. While some students will have received compliance training in the classroom when they are younger, far too often that is all the training they have received, with none in normal community settings. For these students there is a real problem with generalization, a problem that becomes even more critical as the students grow older, stronger, bigger, and become less agreeable to accepting instruction. Teachers must teach students with autism in several environments.

Since many young adults do not either receive compliance training early in their education or are not taught generalization training by different trainers and across various environments, it is suggested that some compliance training in the form of simple commands be done in the classroom and other environments before the students are taken out into the community to learn to use this information. The teacher or trainers can tell the student to pick up their food trays and go to a table and eat. This command can be given to the student several times by different trainers and in different rooms and/or locations until the student does this particular command with little hesitation.

A student should be verbally praised for completing a task with less hesitation each time he/she is asked to do the task. The student should also be given the task to clean his/her table area of food wrappers. Different trainers should give the student the command and the student should be asked to clean his/her area in different environments. Praise or other reinforcement should be made to the student after he/she does the appropriate task. After a few weeks of compliance training in the classroom and other environments is accomplished, the student should be taken to a grocery store or restaurant near the school to see how well he/she can follow directions in an actual community setting. Gradually, if the student continues to follow directions in the first training areas of the community, second and third areas can be added for the compliance training. Jenson (1987) notes that compliance training is of utmost important for students with autism. He further states that if compliance training is done regularly for a few minutes of the student's instructional day, the student will be more inclined to respond to various commands given to him/her in the community.

When teaching students to cross busy streets and intersections, it may be necessary to have them cross less busy ones first, then gradually have them train in streets which are busier. Some adolescents with autism may be runners, or may want to step out in front of the traffic as they are waiting for the light to change to green. It has been helpful with some students to have them do some street crossing trials when the traffic is not as busy. The student should be cued or told (in a firm voice) by the trainer before he/she crosses the streets that he/she is not to walk or run in front of the cars. The student can be shown by the trainer the appropriate way to stand and wait on the curb until the traffic light changes. When the student accomplishes the goal of waiting properly for the light to change, and learns not to run as he/she crosses the street, then some verbal praise should be given to the student. The verbal praise should be done quietly, so that other people standing at the street corner do not even hear the trainer tell the student. Also, the praise should be phased out as the student learns to do each skill without being prompted by the trainer. In some instances, the trainer should stand closer behind the student if the trainer feels the student has not generalized fully and may attempt to run in front of cars. If the trainer is close at hand, the trainer or practicum student can easily get hold of the student's arm, shirt or blouse if he/she becomes impulsive and attempts to run away from the trainer and onto the street.

It should be noted that street crossing becomes of major importance because many autistic adolescents are unaware of the dangers that result from wrong movements on a busy street. By being firm, consistent, and giving the student much needed compliance training before the major tasks are to be accomplished, the trainer can instruct the autistic adolescent to be successful in street crossing.

A major part of community based training is to teach students with autism how to go to restaurants and/or grocery stores without acting out of the ordinary or being unusual in their behavior, as is typical of many autistic adolescents who are beginning community training. The students' behavior can be unpredictable, and the trainer or teacher must be ready to observe and prevent, if possible, while training a student in a restaurant.

Because students often have to stand in line and place an order, or they have to learn to wait in some restaurants until they have finished eating, the time they have to wait often precipitates certain noises in them or other behaviors which can bring attention to the student in the restaurant. If the student continues bringing attention to himself/herself while at the restaurant, it is suggested that the student be taken out as quietly as possible from the restaurant with the assistance of another trainer (if needed). Similar problems can arise in grocery stores, and are handled similarly. Usually waiting out doors for a few minutes will help the student realize that he/she will not return inside until he/she is no longer making the inappropriate noises or behaving unacceptably. When the trainer or trainers are outside with the student, one of them should firmly tell the student that because he/she has made noises inside the restaurant or store he/she cannot go inside for the remainder of the time. Further, the student is told that he/she will not get a dessert or the student's preferred food until he/she has learned to stop making noises.

As part of all of this intervention, it is always important to tell a student why he/she has done wrong; otherwise the student may not be aware why he/she has been removed from the public facility. Upon returning with the student to the restaurant, he/she must be reminded by the trainer once again that he/she must not make noises in the restaurant or grocery store. The student must also be reminded about the privileges he/she will lose if he/she makes noises or acts inappropriately while at a public eating place or grocery store. Since people eating in restaurants or buying groceries, unfamiliar with persons with some kind of handicaps, may stop and ask trainers or the food or restaurant manager about the students, it is a good idea to take time to explain to curious people about autism and why the students are shopping or are in a restaurant. Taking time to do this type of explanation to people in the community becomes helpful in that they realize the importance of having persons with handicaps learn how to behave. Because autism is a condition that is so unpredictable, it is often necessary to spend time explaining to store and restaurant managers about autism. If this is done, it is easier for the store or restaurant managers to explain to customers when they ask questions about any of the adolescents with autism who may be acting inappropriately.

Thus, it takes much concentrated effort to teach adolescents with autism to be successful in the community. It requires that the adolescent with autism be taught to act appropriately, and encouraged to do so through practice. It is necessary that the general public be educated about autism and its unpredictability. Without everyone working together and communicating clearly about the condition, the programming for these populations may not always be successful.

DISCUSSION QUESTIONS

(1) What components must be considered before a good program in community based instruction is implemented? Discuss these points.
(2) What are some staffing considerations that need to be considered when implementing a community based program?
(3) What is the concept of partial participation that can be implemented successfully in community based instruction? Describe this concept and give an example of how it can work.
(4) Define the concept of normalization and explain how it relates to community based instruction.
(5) What are specific problems that are seen among some adolescents with autism in community based training? What are some solutions that can be used to solve the problems of acquainting autistic adolescents with life in the community?
(6) Describe how students with severe disabilities can be taught to make choices?

REFERENCES

Baumgart, D., and Van Wallenghem, J. (1986). Staffing strategies for implementing community based instruction. JASH, *Journal for the Association for Persons with Severe Handicaps, 11*(2), 92–102.

Beyer, B. K. (1988). *Developing a thinking skills program.* Boston, MA: Allyn & Bacon.

Brown, L. et al. (1987). Longitudinal transition plans in problems for severely handicapped students. Manuscript done in cooperation with the University of Wisconsin and the Madison Metropolitan Schools District, pp. 1–9.

Brown, L. (1987). Vocational training for persons with severe handicaps. Workshop presented at El Paso Public Schools and sponsored by Region 19 Education Service Center, El Paso, TX.

Brown, L. (1980). Strategies for generating comprehensive longitudinal, and chronological age appropriate individualized educational programs for adolescent and young-adult severely handicapped students. Manuscript done in cooperation with University of Wisconsin and Madison Metropolitan Schools District, pp. 1–18.

Coon, M. E. et al. (1981). Effects of classroom public transportation instruction on generalization to the natural environment. JASH, *The Journal for the Association for Persons with Severe Handicaps, 6*(2), 46–53.

Falvey, M. et al. (1984). Developing and implementing integrated community referenced curriculum. In D. Cohen and Ann Donnellan (Eds.), *Handbook of autism and disorders of atypical development,* pp. 1–24. New York: Wiley.

Falvey, M. (1986). *Community based curriculum instructional strategies for students with severe handicaps,* pp. 1–241. Baltimore, MD: Paul Brooks.

Jenson, W. (1987). Behavior management strategies for teaching students with autism. Workshop presented at U.T. El Paso and sponsored by Region 19 Education Service Center for teachers who work with students with autism.

Lovaas, I. (1981). *Teaching the developmentally disabled children: The me books,* pp. 1–243. Baltimore, MD: University Park Press.

Martin, J. E. et al. (1982). Teaching community survival skills to mentally retarded adults: A review and analysis. *The Journal of Special Education, 16*(3), 243–263.

Nietupski, H. S. et al. (1982). Implementing a community based educational model for moderately/severely handicapped students: Common problems and suggested solutions. JASH, *Journal of the Association for Persons with Severe Handicaps,* pp. 38–43.

Olson, G. O. (1995). "Less" can be "more" in the promotion of thinking. *Social Education, 59,* 130.

Sailor, W. (1985). Teaching the severely handicapped. Workshop presented at U.T. El Paso for teachers and undergraduate students who teach populations who are severely handicapped.

Sailor, W. et al. (1984). Community intensive instruction. In R. Horner et al. (Eds.), *Education of learners with severe handicaps: Exemplary severe strategies,* pp. 1–57. Baltimore, MD: Paul Brookes.

Slovic, R. et al. (1987). G-u-i-d-e-s Aid transition for severely handicapped students. *Teaching Exceptional Children, 20*(1), 14–18.

Snell, M. E., and Browder, D. M. (1986). Community referenced instruction: Research and issues. JASH, *The Journal for the Association for Persons with Severe Handicaps, II*(1), 1–11.

Wilen, W. W., and Phillips, J. A. (1995). Teaching critical thinking: A metacognitive approach. *Social Education, 59,* 135–138.

Chapter Seven

ADOLESCENT STUDENTS WITH AUTISM

ELVA DURÁN

This chapter will give some historical information on the adolescent student with autism, information on some of the characteristics of the adolescent with autism, and, additionally, some intervention strategies that can be used with these students. Information will be noted on some particular programming techniques that can be used with these students in the public schools and in a university based program.

The adolescent student with autism was given little attention by researchers or in programming until 1974 (Kilman, 1978; Cheney, 1987). Prior to this time, it was generally believed that many of these young adults should be placed in institutions, because it was felt that they did not have the capacity to learn. Because of these students' unusual behaviors, many people believed that they were extremely harmful and were afraid to be around them for fear that they would harm the people who came in contact with them.

CHARACTERISTICS OF THE ADOLESCENT WITH AUTISM

Autism is defined as a developmental syndrome or, more recently, as a pervasive developmental disorder; pervasive means essentially that the individual diagnosed with autism has many of the original characteristics of the syndrome that were described by Kanner in 1943.

Autism is a lifelong condition that is characterized by some of the following characteristics: The student in many cases is without language, and when language is present in these students, the literature notes that they make grammatical errors such as pronoun reversals, etc. (Baltaxe, 1977). They have few social skills and are egocentric in a sense (Kilman, 1978). They may talk without regard to who is paying attention to them or talk without noting if anyone has interest in what they may be saying.

140

Many of the adolescent students with autism remain ritualistic and repetitive in their behaviors throughout their lives. They may stare at lights, or say something over and over, if they have some capacity to communicate. Many are aggressive and self-abusive as children and remain so during adolescence. According to Schopler (1981), the ones who have lower intelligence tend to have more severe symptoms of autism. Many of these young adults with lower intelligence reach adolescence and are then institutionalized. Other characteristics of the autistic adolescent include their inability to answer questions when someone is talking to them. They will ask abstract questions which reflect their aimless curiosity (Isaev & Kagan, 1974). They are often greatly lacking in creative, spontaneous language abilities. If someone asks them a question or talks to them about something, they are unable to go beyond what has been asked of them. They may respond with a quick "yes" or "no," and, unless they are further cued by the other person who is talking to them, they do not add other information to the conversation. Many also have orientation problems, poor specific motor habits, and difficulty learning simple movements.

It has been this writer's observation as she has worked with students with autism, and especially the adolescent with autism, that at the beginning of puberty or at the onset of adolescence, many of these young adults show severe intensity in their behavior patterns, and parents have reported to the writer that their son and/or daughter with autism becomes very difficult to handle and live with in the home during this period. This writer has observed that it is not usually until young adults reach later years in adolescence that they become somewhat more normalized in behavior. Parents have indicated that the onset of adolescence and some years thereafter is a more trying period than can be imagined by anyone who lacks personal experience with such a situation.

Additionally, the size of the adolescent makes it difficult to manage his/her behavior. Parents have often explained to the writer that the autistic adolescent seems to have energy which is so bountiful and unmanageable at times that many parents become afraid of them. It has also been this writer's direct observation in her consulting work with these populations in the public schools, and in her own university-based program, that the greatest challenges in trying to educate the adolescent with autism are also seen in trying to assist the parents of these young and most active almost adults.

LANGUAGE AND/OR COMMUNICATION

In Chapter One on language and/or communication strategies, much information has already been discussed on how to teach the student with moderate and severe handicaps and autism. This section will note some intervention strategies to keep directly in mind when teaching communication skills to them. In reviewing the literature in this area, one finds that little if any information has appeared on how to assist or help the adolescent in the area of language or communication training. There is some information given in a few articles on the characteristics or problems a student with autism may have in learning language or some form of communication (Dewey, 1974). There were even some descriptions published on difficulties these students had in speaking (Baltaxe, 1977; Schuler, 1980), but no direct and specific information was found concerning teaching language and/or communication to the adolescent with autism. By the time the student with autism reaches adolescence, many of his/her means of communication have already been established. There are a few things that can be done which will allow the student to communicate more fully in his/her environments. This writer has worked with several adolescents with autism through the years, and has implemented some approaches which follow. It should be kept in mind that whatever is presented to these students should be functional (Brown, 1978; Schuler, 1980; Carr, 1980). Functional, in this sense, means that the student will be able to use the vocabulary or language material, because it is found in his/her various environments. Functional also means that the student is taught in the context of his/her particular environments. Once again, this means that material selected for the student's instruction is vocabulary that is taught because the student can use the material in whatever environment he/she is living, working, or playing.

As was already pointed out in the chapter on language and communication and other intervention strategies, an environmental inventory should be completed by the teacher and the student's parents in order to determine what words or vocabulary should be emphasized to the student. If, for example, the student is learning to do a job, he/she should learn words related to what he/she is performing in his/her work. For instance, the adolescent student with autism may learn that "on" is the red button on the dishwasher and that if he/she wants the button to activate the machine, then he/she needs to press the red button. Here, the student is learning language in the context of his/her particular job training (Durán, 1986 and 1987). Also, if the student is unable to communicate verbally, he/she can learn to point or gesture to whatever he/she would like to obtain. Communication booklets containing photographs of foods and/or other materials he/she may need to request or purchase at a grocery store or department store can also be used by these students. The communication booklets are small enough so that students can carry them easily in the community. Color photographs are taken frequently in order that they may be inserted; new photographs will expand the materials that the student can learn by means of the booklet. With repeated practice in all environments, and by cuing by all the people who work with the adolescent, the student can learn to use his/her booklet in whatever environment(s) he/she may be associated with.

Some students who have learned total or simultaneous communication during these early years of training continue to do very nicely, learning a few more functional signs during adolescence. According to Carr (1980) and Schafer (1980), total communication helps a student with autism learn communication because he/she is actively involved in a variety of environments, and this stimulation acts as a strong motivation for the students. It is highly recommended that if the student with autism is learning or continuing with total communication or learning signs from childhood, then an alternative form of communication, such as teaching him/her to use a communication booklet, would be helpful.

Sailor and Guess (1983) note that when an alternative form of communication is presented to the adolescent with autism, he/she is more likely to be understood by others. Sailor and Guess (1983) agree that the communication booklet is one effective alternative form that can be used in addition to teaching these students to use signs.

It has been the experience of this writer that adolescent students with autism and other severe handicaps learn to communicate faster in other environments if they are taught to use photographs to request and obtain various materials, along with teaching them other forms of communication. Michael, a fourteen-year-old with autism, who attends a public school integrated setting, was taught signs at age five. He has learned more than eighteen signs presently. When photographs or a communication booklet was also made part of his language intervention, he learned to point to more pictures and request items in different environments. This writer believes that Michael learned to communicate even faster, using the booklet, because his parents then understood what Michael wanted.

Whatever means of communication are used to teach the adolescent with autism, it is important to include the parents in all that must be done so that generalization training with the student can be more easily accomplished. It has been the experience of this writer that parents who bring their sons and/or daughters to the university special education programming twice weekly often are not aware of how important it is to get actively involved with teaching. Once they do help their son and/or daughter learn the material at home and wherever their young adult lives, works, and plays, then they become more enthusiastic about teaching their son and/or daughter at home.

SOCIAL SKILLS

The area of social skill training, like language training, is also very important for the student with autism. This area of training is especially important if the autistic student is also an adolescent. Many adolescents with autism do not get jobs or have extreme difficulties living in their communities because they act inappropriately. Schopler (1983) noted that this is one of the main reasons the adolescent fails to get a permanent job. Once again, not much literature has been written concerning the autistic adolescent's social skill development. Because the adolescents are going through many bodily changes, many of their behaviors will be even more pronounced and severe than at other stages of their lives.

According to Mesibov (1984), the adolescent student with autism can be taught social skill development by teaching the student to role play. During the role playing process, the student is taught to smile and shake hands and is taught directly how to respond to another person when the person says, "Hi, how are you?" Mesibov (1984) suggested that the role playing should be done in different environments with the student, so that the student will learn appropriate behaviors in each of the environments where he/she may be active.

At the U.T. El Paso Special Education Adult Program, parents are asked to come into the program area practice with their son and/or daughter, and observe the practicum students as they have the student respond if someone says, "Hi, how are you?" The parents are taken to the other locations where their son and/or daughter may be participating in a variety of activities. As this is done, parents learn how they are to cue their son and/or daughter so he/she can respond to questions directed to them.

Also, to help develop the students' social skills, college students, parents, and other people who work closely with the autistic adolescents and adults in the university program provide each of them with a variety of social skill activities. When students are participating in various recreation activities, the practicum students talk and ask the students questions about the various games or activities in which they may be participating. For example, if the students are tossing the ball to each other, they are asked, "Who has the ball?" If they are verbal, they learn to look at the person who has the ball and call out the person's name. If they are nonverbal, they are taught to look at the person who has the ball or point to the person who has it. Teaching them to respond to various questions helps them learn to be more attentive to one another. Students with autism have to be shown how to be aware of others who are in their nearby space or environments. Parents or guardians are shown how to do this also, so that all such learning can transfer from one environment to another. More recently, in a study in progress (Durán, 1995), this writer has begun to gather data on some students with autism who have been fully included in a kindergarten and first grade classes. The data collected has shown that the students with autism and pervasive disorder have acquired several social skills by participating with general education peers. Some of the social skills include sharing materials with each other and engaging in some circle activities with general education students. It will be important to follow these children into the various elementary grades to see how they continue to gain in social skill development and thus continue to improve in their management skills because of their gains in social skills and language development.

It is important for the people working with these populations to realize that special time must be set aside in order to develop social skills among these particular students. Further, questions, must be asked of these students while they are participating in various natural activities, so they can know when and how to respond and look at people who are talking to them.

MANAGING THE ADOLESCENT WITH AUTISM

Because the adolescent with autism gets larger as he/she grows older, the autistic adolescent becomes more difficult to manage. He/she will ordinarily be undergoing some major bodily changes, may be aggressive, and once again difficult to manage. It has been the direct experience of this writer in working with autistic adolescents for more than eight years that no other disability or age group presents more of a challenge than do these students. It is recommended when working with an adolescent in the community, or whatever environment, that some of the following guidelines be followed:

(1) Use positive reinforcement with the adolescent student with autism. Find out what he/she likes and tell him/her that if he/she completes the task or does not engage in self-abusive or self-stimulatory behaviors, he/she can choose what he/she would like to do (preferred activity) or eat, or have (some particular object he/she would like to have, whatever object is reinforcing to the adolescent).

(2) Oftentimes, just saying in a very firm manner, "No, put your hands down," will be enough to keep the student from being aggressive toward a particular person. In order for this technique to be effective, the student must know the person means business, and this form of control must also be used consistently so that the student will know to respond.

(3) Have conferences with the student and his/her parents. Face the student with autism, and have him/her look at you also. Tell him/her what he has done to make you upset and/or his/her parents. Tell the student in a firm manner that you are disappointed in his/her behavior. Tell him/her what you and the parents expect of him/her. Have the parents also tell their son and/or daughter what they expect. Let the student know what they will be rewarded with if he/she does not do that bad behavior or action again. Tell him/her you will ask his/her mother or father if he is trying hard to act appropriately at home. Keep your voice firm and with an even volume throughout the conference. Conferences are very effective if done with one or both of the parents present. The conferences are also effective if they are done consistently to eliminate inappropriate behavior.

(4) Always keep the parents informed at all times concerning their son's and/or daughter's behavior in the program. A brief phone

call to one of the parents can be very helpful in keeping parents abreast of their son's and/or daughter's inappropriate, abusive or severe aggressive behavior. Parents appreciate being kept informed about their son's and/or daughter's behavior, good or bad. Too often we wait to notify the parents until something very serious has happened to the student or wait until the student has done something serious to another student in the classroom or program and forget to report the good actions being achieved.

(5) Have literature available with guidelines explaining the types of students who are enrolled in the class or program and also the types of intervention strategies that may be used in the program. Have several copies available to give to interested community persons or parents who may want to read further about the various intervention strategies being used in your program.

(6) Have workshops about the type of students being worked with, as well as information on management strategies parents, coworkers, and other people who have contact with your students may be able to use. Such workshops will pave the way for your autistic adolescents with people in the community who often do not know about autism, or are sensitive to the fact that students with handicaps also have a right to be in the community.

(7) On file or your clipboard where you keep your data collection on your student's progress, keep information as to when the inappropriate behavior started and the number of times the student may be engaging in such behavior. This data will help you analyze what may be causing the student to engage in the inappropriate behavior, especially if patterns may be observed.

(8) Have parents sign their names at the individual plan meeting beside all intervention strategies you will be performing with their sons and/or daughters. Keep them informed weekly or biweekly about the effectiveness of the various strategies used at school or in the program. Ask them how the intervention strategies are working at home with their son and/or daughter.

(9) Have activities planned throughout the day for the adolescent with autism. Idleness or inactivity often causes the student to act inappropriately (La Vigna, 1980; Olley, 1985). Some physical activities are important to include for the adolescent with autism because he/she often becomes full of excessive energy and has a

tendency to be very aggressive if no physical activity is provided for him/her at some time during the day (Wing, 1983).

(10) Keep your principal and other administrators informed about management techniques used in your program. If you are out in the community with your students and one acts inappropriately, someone may complain to your school principal or other administrators; and if these officials are well informed about the management strategies you use and your difficulties in managing students, they can act as advocates for you if you are not on hand when someone calls from the community inquiring about a student or a procedure used with the students.

(11) Begin including the students as often as possible in general education settings. Full inclusion can be helpful in managing the student's behavior because they become more normalized as they spend time and engage in some activities with general education students (Durán, 1995).

(12) Often redirecting the student to engage in a different activity can be helpful in reducing inappropriate or self-destructive behavior (Meyer, 1995).

The entire area of management requires the teacher to be a skilled communicator with the public and, above all, requires the teacher to try a variety of positive programming in teaching the students with autism.

The areas of vocational skill training and community training for autistic students have been discussed in the chapters which are devoted to these particular areas. Additional management strategies are described there.

INDEPENDENT SKILL TRAINING

The area of independent skill training is of continuing utmost importance in teaching the adolescent with autism. In fact, it takes a dedicated commitment to teach the students these skills, with reinforcement training repeatedly required from time to time over the years in order to maintain the desired skills (Lovaas, 1981). Little literature has been found by this writer on specifically what to teach or how to teach adolescents with autism. Much of the information and most of the examples which follow in this section have been tested experimentally and have been used to teach clients in the All Day Adult Program and the Special Education Clinic located at U.T. El Paso. Home training, a great part of each of the client's or student's curriculum, plus other information given in this section, derives from direct experiences of teachers in training these students with moderate to severe impairment in their home and public school environments. Information shared here has been accumulated for the past nine years.

SELF–HELP SKILLS

In order to teach students skills that involve learning to care for themselves, it is suggested that parents be asked what specifically their son and/or daughter needs to learn. After the parents provide this information, the individual's needed skills should be prioritized or rank ordered, with the important skills being labeled number one or two, while others will be labeled as of lesser importance. Some of the skills parents feel their son and/or daughter should learn are washing hands and face, brushing teeth, wiping the mouth while eating, chewing with the mouth closed, teaching them to comb and brush their hair, helping them keep their fingernails clean and trimmed, teaching them to put on clean and appropriate clothes for different occasions, and helping them learn to apply deodorant. Some of the specific strategies which help students learn these particular skills include letting them see a picture or photograph of what clean teeth look like, or what constitutes appropriate clothes to wear for different activities.

A strategy which is helpful in teaching these students self-help skills is physically guiding their hands momentarily so they can become aware of the appropriate strokes to use when brushing their teeth, for instance. The trainer or teacher should also stand in back of the student as the student is trained to learn a particular skill. Standing in back of the student will not allow the student to keep following the teacher or trainer with his/her side vision and will teach him/her to focus forward on his/her own to get his/her task completed. Different trainers should have the student do the task. These same skills should be practiced under parental supervision in the student's home environment. All of these techniques help to bring about generalization of the skills. Parents especially should be encouraged to take the time to teach the student at home (Falvey, 1984). Home training accomplished with different members of the family is extremely important; otherwise skills taught to the student in other environments will not be generalized from one place to another.

It should be noted that some other important independent skills to teach the students are to have them learn to cook simple meals, clean their homes, cross streets, and take the city bus to and from their work and homes. In order to teach cooking skills, photographs should be taken of the different steps involved in making a sandwich or enchiladas, for example. The photographs cue the student to follow different steps in recipe sequences. With practice, students learn to cook independently by imitating actions in the photographs. Colored photographs should be glued to a large file folder, laminated to a file folder so that the file folder can be folded, and placed in a recipe file or file cabinet when not in use. All these recipe files should be titled according to the different recipes they represent, for example, "Making a sandwich" or "Making sugar cookies." Thus, when the file folders are placed in the file cabinet, the title of each recipe will show for ease in having the student select recipes. A similar set of these photographs should be sent home so that parents will make use of the photographs to have their son and/or daughter cook at home.

In order for the students to become independent in learning to perform some cleaning tasks, such as mopping and sweeping, they need to be given practice in performing these activities both at school and at home. A task analysis sheet which indicates the incorrect and correct steps they are performing, in the proper sequence of steps, should be kept on each student in order to see what areas they will need more assistance in, or to indicate that they are ready to move on to learn new skills. Again, learning to mop and sweep are important skills that must also be practiced wherever the student lives. Such practices will assist with generalization training for the student, who will need help practicing in various environments before he/she can learn to do the various skills independently. When the student is completing a task incorrectly, it is important to model for the student how to do various steps correctly for a particular task. Oftentimes, modeling different steps for the student can be helpful in teaching the student how to complete each step of the task correctly, and in the proper sequence.

During parent/staff conferences, it is necessary to ask parents how their sons and/or daughters are doing at home with the various independent training skills. If parents know that the staff will ask them questions about their son's and/or daughter's home training, they will more likely make an effort to have them do more training of different skills at home. During parent conferences, it is necessary to reevaluate what is being taught to students and, if necessary, help should be given to parents so that they can reprioritize new skill areas. There should be constant feedback coming from the teacher and other staff persons and the parents. Only with open communication and constant feedback will the adolescents' programming improve satisfactorily.

FUNCTIONAL READING

As with all areas of instruction for the student with moderate to severe handicaps, the area of reading instruction for these populations should be functional and should include words that the student will encounter in different environments. Lettick (1979) noted that the most important function of teaching a person with autism to read is for that student to be able to get around in his/her different environments. As with all material that is taught to students or persons with moderate to severe handicaps, an environmental inventory (Brown, 1978) should be completed to determine what words the student needs to learn in order to function in all environments. The words should also be age appropriate. Thus, words like "city bus," "cafeteria," and "work" are more age appropriate for the adolescent than words like "blue" or "one" etc.

It is important when teaching any skill to a student with moderate to severe learning problems to ask oneself, "Why am I teaching this particular skill to this student?" (Sailor, 1985). Another important question to ask is, "If I do teach this skill, how will it help the student?" If one cannot answer these questions, then it would probably be better to teach a different skill or not teach the skill at all. This evaluation is vital to consider, because adolescents' time in the public schools gets shorter and shorter, since students will be leaving the public schools at the ages of twenty-one or twenty-two. Teaching time becomes extremely important when one considers that it takes students with severe handicaps a long time to learn and then to make use of what they have learned.

Once the student's vocabulary is selected for instruction, the words are printed on flash cards. To help the student generalize from one printed word to another, the words which will be taught should also be typed on three-inch by five-inch cards or on a sheet of white unlined paper. The student will read the flash cards and words typed on the white paper. Such precautions will once again help the student read the same words when they come to other printed material. When the student does not learn to read or instantly recognizes the different word, photographs can be shown to the student with the word. For example, if the student cannot instantly recognize the word "sandwich," a photograph of a sandwich should be shown to the student along with the printed word. Later the photograph can be phased out, and only the word can be shown to the student. For the student with moderate handicaps or one with higher abilities, he/she can be shown the photograph or just the word and later can be taught to spell the word. Also, this student can be taught to read additional words by having the teacher or staff utilize the language experience approach with some of the words. In this approach, the teacher or person teaching the student selects a photograph or an actual object. The teacher asks the student questions such as, "What kind of sandwich are you going to eat?" The student who may have more verbal capacity will respond, perhaps, "Ham sandwich." The teacher will print what the student says. The teacher proceeds to ask the student another question about the sandwich or whatever photograph or concrete object is being used for the lesson. The teacher prints out each time what the student is saying in response to the teacher's questions. When the teacher feels the student has talked all he/she can about the picture, the teacher lets the student point to each word and the student reads out loud (Ekwall, 1987) all the words and sentences he/she has said to the teacher during the lesson.

During another session a story about a sandwich can be typed (double spaced) and shown again to the student. Typing the story will help with generalization training. The language experience approach can be utilized again and again. Each time the approach is used, the student's oral and reading vocabulary will increase. The students soon learn to read more and more words and, eventually, will not have to point to the words in the stories. Another approach which can be used with students who have moderate handicaps is to have them purchase items at the grocery store by having them read from a grocery list. Students who are higher functioning will soon learn to find different items by reading the grocery list. It is important to follow the student around to make sure that he/she is learning to read and find the appropriate item that is printed on the grocery list.

Students with moderate handicaps can see the picture or actual food item label of what they are going to buy and can be taught to note the written name for each of the items. For instance, if the student is going to buy a can of soup and one of tomato sauce, the student can learn to read the words "soup" and a "tomato sauce." Flash cards can be prepared utilizing the same words from the items being purchased from pictures or labels. The students can be shown the label and the printed word which appears on a flash card. This will give the student additional practice seeing and recognizing words on labels and flash cards. If the student comes across the particular words, he/she may recognize them because of the constant practice in seeing the words in different formats. Parents should be given help on how to carry out this instruction, so that information presented to their son and/or daughter in the community can also be taught at home. Parents should be encouraged to take their son and/or daughter grocery shopping often. Lower functioning students can learn to use and read some words accompanied with pictures. Many of them will not recall the word without the picture or photograph clue, but some of the students will be able to learn to point to or read some words when asked to tell or point to the word which is being called. Functional reading is an important part of the instruction of some persons with autism. It is important to ask oneself if the words or phrases being taught to the student will be helpful to the students in their environments and in the various activities they are performing.

INCLUSION AND SECOND LANGUAGE ACQUISITION OF STUDENTS WITH AUTISM: QUALITATIVE STUDY RESEARCH RESULTS

Pre and Post Inclusion Data with Students with Autism at a School in Northern California

Even though this chapter emphasizes the adolescent student with autism, this writer would like to share this research which is still in progress because she cannot emphasize enough the importance of including students in general education classrooms as much as all people concerned with the student feel is possible. What follows is a summary of some of the beginning research results which have been collected and analyzed up to this date.

As more and more general education classrooms begin opening their doors to students with severe disabilities, the research data and information that is conducted will become increasingly important in order to see the long-term effects of full inclusion among all the students in the different classrooms. This investigator has been collecting data on five students who have been labeled as having autism or a pervasive developmental condition first in their self-contained classroom and secondly in their fully included site. The report will give accounts of self-contained and regular classrooms where the students were assigned.

Pre-Test Data in Self-contained Site on First Campus

In the self-contained classroom the five students were placed in a room with one special education teacher and two instructional aides. The teacher had a curriculum in the self-contained classroom which included oral language development activities such as singing, nursery rhymes, stories enhanced with puppets, free play activities, and shared literature. The students also had speech development with a speech and language pathologist during the week. Also, as part of the curriculum, the students participated in art and music activities.

The aides and teachers spent a considerable amount of time developing activities so the students could learn as much language or means of communication in order for some of their inappropriate behaviors to decrease. Research indicates (Durand, 1990; Durán, 1988; Durán, 1990) that the more the student with autism can communicate, the more his or her inappropriate behaviors will decrease.

The curriculum of the students also included some physical exercise which was greatly encouraged by the teacher and instructional aides during recess.

This investigator collected data twice weekly for approximately two to two and one-half hours each visit. The qualitative study was based on research collection information developed by Bogand and Biklen (1994) using an alpha program to help the investigator visually see the various variables which were increasingly evident as the observations continued throughout the year.

The variables that repeatedly became evident in the various observations were a rich language environment, students with disabilities were talking and socializing with one another or the staff of the classroom. Additionally, some other behavior variables which were noted were some tantruming behaviors from the students with autism during the day. The students with autism also engaged in self-stemming and, at times, self-hitting behavior. Additionally, the students showed poor attending skills whenever any stimulus or modeling was done by the staff. Often inappropriate social skills were seen by the students as they pulled things from one another during free play and other more structured times. Much crying behavior was seen especially as the staff changed some of the activities for the students.

The one Hmong child with autism who was on a preproduction level of language development would frequently not respond to any of the curricular activities designed to enhance his English knowledge and language development. The Hmong student often tantrumed and one of the aides or the teacher would sit beside the student in order to offer him enough support so that he could attend for some of the time as the language activities were being presented. The Hmong student continued his inappropriate behavior and shouted words in his Hmong language.

The classroom teachers and the investigator conferred weekly as this writer presented the teachers with copies of the observation data. Both teachers and investigator shared weekly what the data was revealing and all concerned talked about how changes could be made in order to help improve some of the behaviors of the children. The students' behavior and language development remained the same. Data collection in this particular classroom stopped in June as the school year came to an end. Thus, the first year of predata was concluded.

Fully Included Site in Another School—Year II of Study

During the summer, the students with autism and pervasive developmental disorder participated in the regular activities of a regular kindergarten classroom. No data was taken by the investigator during the summer months, but the special education teacher noted verbally to the writer that much planning was done with the regular kindergarten teacher in order to see how all the children would respond to each other. Full inclusion started with these students with special challenges in June, 1994. By Fall 1994, the students, teachers, and instructional aides were invited to fully participate in the kindergarten classroom with twenty regular kindergarten children and two regular education teachers.

This investigator obtained permission from the director of special education of the district and the principal of the new school site to continue the qualitative research study and follow the students of the general education classroom to see how their oral language development was progressing.

During the fall semester the investigator and the research assistant went twice weekly for two to two and one-half hours each time to observe the progress of the students with special needs in the fully-included classroom.

Some of the variables or characteristics which started to evolve as the year progressed in the fully-included site were as follows:

(1) Much oral language development was seen in evidence as the regular and special education teachers planned daily to add shared literature units, finger plays, and riddles to the curriculum. Music and use of puppets and art activities were continued as part of the curriculum.

(2) Centers or various group activities were planned in order for the students to sit beside one another and share materials and conversation.

(3) The teachers placed regular education students beside the students with special needs so the general education students could assist the children. The Hmong child with special needs increased his English vocabulary and socially did not require as much assistance as he had previously in the self-contained classroom, or the first site where the data was started.

Two of the regular education students who were Asian imitated the Asian special education teacher and constantly offered assistance to the students with autism and other pervasive disorders. Buddies naturally evolved and developed as the year progressed.

One of the students with autism who had previously been assigned to a one to one intervention and home program started to attend to lessons being presented by the staff. His crying ended. He went to the centers and stood by the regular education children and participated with other general education students. During circle time, which is a large part of the curriculum in this kindergarten classroom, the students with special needs sit beside the general education students and participate in all of the circle time activities. These circle time activities include shared literature units, singing, reading, math, and dancing.

Outside at recess or other free play activities the students with special needs played with general education students, by themselves, and often observers commented that one could not tell which child had the disability.

Social relationships and friendships also developed among the general education children and the students with autism and other pervasive developmental disorders. The students with autism tantrumed very little if at all in the new setting as the year progressed.

By the end of the school year in June, the students with special needs were reminded by the regular education children that everyone had to participate and not make a lot of noise. Good modeling from the general education students was evident throughout the day.

Parents of both groups of children have commented on the benefits all the children have received. The parents further believe that more growth has taken place this school year than was ever imagined. The parents of the children with special needs and the regular education students have commented to the teachers about how happy they are with the progress all the children have achieved.

Thus, the postdata results in the fully included, general education classroom setting reveal that the students have grown socially, have developed language, and have learned to profit from much of the general education curriculum which is rich and varied in this kindergarten classroom. The general education students have also benefited as they are now more tolerant to people who are slower or less talkative than they may be. The extra help from the special education teacher and her staff has also enriched the children in the general education setting. The qualitative study will continue as the students with special needs go to first grade classrooms with some of their old and new classmates.

[Qualitative Study supported by personnel preparation grant: (Durán and Ostertag) MS/SH/CLAD MS/LH/CLAD grant number: H029E-40008. Data collected by Elva Durán, Ph.D. and Kelly Woessner, research assistant.]

DISCUSSION QUESTIONS

(1) What are some characteristics of autism?

(2) What are some strategies you use in teaching language and/or communication with the adolescent with autism?

(3) Explain some social skills you can teach adolescents with autism.

(4) List at least three management strategies you can try with an adolescent with autism who acts inappropriately.

(5) What are some independent living skills you can teach adolescents with autism?

(6) What are some strategies to consider when teaching functional reading to a student with moderate or severe handicaps?

(7) Explain how the language experience approach is used in teaching reading to adolescents with autism who have moderate impairments.
(8) Explain the importance of inclusion of students with autism and other pervasive disorders in general education classrooms.

REFERENCES

Baltaxe, C. A. M. (1977). Pragmatic deficits in the language of autistic adolescents. *Journal of Pediatric Psychology, 2*(4), 176–180.

Bogdan, R., and Biklen, S. (1992). *Qualitative research for education: An introduction to theory and methods,* 2nd ed. Boston, MA: Allyn & Bacon.

Brown, L. (1978). *A strategy for developing chronological age appropriate and functional curricular content for severely handicapped adolescents and young adults.* Paper published in cooperation with the University of Wisconsin, Madison and the Madison Metropolitan School District, pp. 1–11.

Carr, E. (1980). Generalization of treatment effects following educational intervention with autistic children and youth. In Barbara Wilcox and Anneke Thompson (Eds.), *Critical issues in educating autistic children and youth,* 2nd ed., pp. 118–134. Washington, DC: U.S. Department of Education Office of Special Education.

Cheney, C. O. (1987). The comparative effectiveness of four instructional techniques with autistic adolescents. Unpublished doctoral dissertation, Indiana University.

Dewey, M. (1974). The near-normal autistic adolescent. *Journal of Autism and Childhood Schizophrenia, 4*(4), 348–356.

Durán, E. (1986). Developing social skills in autistic adolescents with severe handicaps and limited English competencies. *Education, 107*(3), 203–207.

Durán, E. (1987). Overcoming people barriers in placing severely aberrant autistic students in work sites and community. *Education, 107*(3), 333–337.

Durán, E. (1990). *Managing students with autism.* Lecture presented to transition class at California State University, Sacramento.

Durán, E. (1995). How students acquire English in full inclusion classrooms, paper presentation at TASH (The Association for Persons with Severe Handicaps) Conference, San Francisco, CA.

Durand, M. (1990). *Severe behavior problems, a functional communication training approach.* New York: Guilford Press.

Ekwall, E. E. (1987). Utilizing the language experience approach as a strategy to teach disabled readers. Lecture presented to a developmental reading course, the University of Texas at El Paso, El Paso, TX.

Falvey, M. (1984). Teaching persons with severe handicaps. (Lecture given at the University of Texas at El Paso, summer 1984).

Isaev, D. N., and Kagan, V. E (1974). Autistic syndromes in children and adolescents, *Acta pae dop sychiatrica, 40*(5), 182–189.

Kilman, B. (1978). The communicative competence of autistic adolescent. Doctoral dissertation presented at Claremont Graduate School in California, pp. 6–74.

La Vigna, G. (1980). Reducing behavior problems in the classroom. In Barbara

Wilcox and Anneke Thompson (Eds.), *Critical issues in educating autistic children and youth*, 2nd ed., pp. 135–153. Washington, DC: U.S. Department of Education Office of Special Education.

Lettick, A. (1979). *Benhaven at work*, pp. 3–510. New Haven, CT: Benhaven Press.

Lovaas, I. (1980). Child with developmental delays, Converence paper presented at National Autism Society meeting, California.

Mesibov, G. B. (1984). Social skills training with verbal autistic adolescents and adults: A program model. *Journal of Autism and Developmental Disorders, 14*(4), 395–404.

Meyer, L. (1995). Quality inclusive schooling for students with severe behavioral challenges. Unpublished manuscript, partnership for statewide systems change, New York.

Olley, G. J. (1985). Current issues in school services for students with autism. *School Psychology Review, 14*(2), 166–170.

Sailor, W. (1985). Strategies for teaching students with autism. Lecture presented at the University of Texas at El Paso, El Paso, TX.

Sailor, W., and Guess, D. (1983). *Severely Handicapped Students: An Instructional Design*, pp. 1–339. New York: Boston, Houghton-Mifflin.

Schopler, E., and Mesibov, G. (1983). *Autism in Adolescents and Adults*, pp. 3–100. New York: Plenum.

Schuler, A. (1980). Teaching functional language. In Barbara Wilcox and Anneke Thompson (Eds.), *Critical issues in educating autistic children and youth*, 2nd ed. Washington, DC: U.S. Department of Education Office of Special Education.

Chapter 8

STUDENTS WITH MULTIPLE DISABILITIES

Vivian I. Correa

The problems of students with multiple disabilities are severe enough and probably frequent enough to warrant special consideration (Orelove and Sobsey, 1991), and the educational needs of this heterogeneous population are extremely varied. Typically, students with multiple disabilities have been defined as students having one or more impairments (Warren, 1985), and it is important for educators to become increasingly aware that students who evidence severe disabilities often have additional sensory impairments requiring diverse intervention programs (Ellis, 1986; Orelove and Sobsey, 1991). The definition of multiple disabilities specified in IDEA states: "Multiple disabilities means concomitant impairments (such as mental retardation-blindness, mental retardation-orthopedic impairments, etc.), the combination of which causes such severe educational problems that they cannot be accommodated in special education programs solely for one of the impairments. The term does not include deaf-blindness" (IDEA, 34 C.F.R., Part 200, Sec. 300.7). This chapter presents information on the student with multiple disabilities who evidences sensory impairments, including blindness and deafness. Although IDEA creates a separate categories for students who are deaf-blind, information on this disability will also be reviewed. It identifies the major aspects of visual and auditory impairments and discusses assessment and intervention procedures. Educational implications for working with students with multiple disabilities, who are also limited English proficient (LEP) will also be discussed.

PREVALENCE

It is difficult to delineate the numbers of students who evidence multiple disabilities. The U.S. Department of Education's Fourteenth Annual Report to Congress (1992) revealed that 80,272 students ages six to twenty-one were served in 1990–91 under IDEA's part B programs for students with multiple disabilities. Overall, the prevalence of severe and multiple disabilities is between 1 percent and 1.9 percent (Turnbull and Turnbull, 1995).

Although there exists a paucity of studies addressing this issue, researchers agree that students with severe disabilities often have sensory impairments. In general, two out of every five students with severe and multiple disabilities will have sensory impairments (Sobsey and Wolf-Schein, 1991). For example, Cress, Spellman, DeBriere, Sizemore, Northam, and Johnson (1981) reported that as many as 75 to 90 percent of persons with severe and profound disabilities evidence visual impairments. Similarly, Ellis (1986) reported that the prevalence of visual impairments among mentally retarded persons was ten times higher than in the normal population, and Wolf and Harkins (1986) estimated that 30.2 percent of children with hearing impairments had additional handicapping conditions, with 9.5 percent of those having two or more additional disabilities.

According to the census count, 9,783 children ages birth to twenty-one years are deaf-blind and of those, at least 85 percent have additional disabilities (Baldwin, 1994). The most common additional disabilities are mental retardation, speech or language impairment, and orthopedic impairment. Although gathering the annual census has improved over the years, Davidson (1993) warns that many children who are deaf-blind are still undercounted. Best (1986) reports that although the numbers of Rubella children under the age of ten has decreased, the number of deaf/blind children who are non-Rubella, with multiple sensory defects and additional disabilities has increased. The most common causes of deaf-blindness are due to prematurity, hydrocephaly, meningitis, Ushers syndrome, and post-rubella syndrome (Baldwin, 1994; Ward and Zambone, 1992).

There are almost no data available on the number of students with multiple disabilities who are limited English proficient. One source of information on the prevalence of Hispanic disabilities children is the Texas Education Agency's Annual Special Education Statistical Report (1982–1983). This document shows that 27 percent of students with visual disabilities and 28 percent of students with multiple disabilities ages zero to twenty-two in Texas were of Hispanic background. In an article describing the need for bilingual special education personnel, Ortiz and Yates (1983) stated that 63 percent of children who were

Hispanic and had visual disabilities were served by special education in Texas, leaving 37 percent not receiving services.

While the prevalence figures are inconsistent and difficult to obtain, it is evident there exist a higher incidence of sensory impairments among persons with severe disabilities than among other persons with mild disabilities. The growing concern that many students with severe disabilities evidence problems with visual and/or hearing is clearly indicated by these figures. Further, to compound the problem, there is a growing number of students with multiple disabilities whose primary language and cultural background is different from the majority Anglo population. For example, Kirchner and Peterson (1981) suggest that children from ethnically diverse backgrounds are statistically more likely to have severe visual impairments, due to premature births and prenatal care in women who are ethnically diverse and poor. To better understand this group of students, basic assessment and intervention information on sensory impairments is necessary, and educational implications for providing services to students from ethnically diverse backgrounds with multiple disabilities must be considered.

VISUAL IMPAIRMENTS

The leading causes of visual impairments among school-age children are due to congenital cataracts (opacity of the crystalline lens of the eye), *optic nerve atrophy* (destruction of the optic nerve), *retinopathy of prematurity* (overgrowth of blood vessels from retina in premature infants) (Ward, 1986). For students to be diagnosed as *legally blind,* they must evidence vision of no better than 20/200 in the better eye after correction or a visual field of less than 20°, and *partially sighted* children are defined as having vision of 20/70 to 20/200 after correction (Sobsey and Wolf-Schein, 1991). The diagnosis of vision in children with multiple impairments requires a transdisciplinary approach.

There are many professionals working in the area of visual disabilities who can support the teacher of students with multiple disabilities. Ophthalmologists, optometrists, and low-vision specialists are among the team of professionals that evaluate and prescribe optical lenses and aids. Certified vision teachers and certified orientation and mobility specialists are professionals who assist in providing educational intervention in areas such as braille, low-vision training, cane travel, and skills of daily living. For the student who is multiply and visually disabled, occupational and physical therapists serve an important role in developing programs for movement, posture, hand function, and oral-motor skills.

Furthermore, if students are from culturally and/or linguistically diverse backgrounds, professionals in bilingual education, English for speakers of other languages (ESOL) education, and migrant education can assist in developing appropriate educational programs for the students. Rainforth, York, and Macdonald (1992) provided an excellent model for collaborative teamwork among professionals who work with students with severe and multiple disabilities and their families. The complex assessment and intervention needs of students with multiple disabilities requires that professionals work within a transdisciplinary team model.

ASSESSMENT

There exists a paucity of psychoeducational assessment instruments available for use with students who are multiply and visually disabled. General guidelines for interviewing families, teachers, and other relevant professionals have been developed by Bradley-Johnson (1994) to help organize information obtained from various sources for students who are visually impaired or blind. Langley (1986) proposes an approach which is individually tailored, process-oriented, and includes the use of multiple assessment batteries along with informal observation. Some of the instruments suggested for use with this population are outlined in Table X (Bradley-Johnson, 1994; Langley, 1986).

As discussed in previous chapters, assessment of students with severe disabilities must be ecological in its approach and result in functional curriculum planning (Brown, 1987; Helmstetter, 1989; Orelove and Sobsey, 1991).

Additionally, the assessment of functional vision in students with multiple disabilities is difficult. Nevertheless, functional vision assessment is critical to the evaluation and intervention process for this population. Among the instruments most suggested for use with students with multiple disabilities are the Functional Vision Inventory (Langley, 1980); Functional Vision Screening for Severely Handicapped Children (Langley and Dubose, 1989); the STYCAR Battery (Sheridan, 1973); and a functional vision assessment developed by Bolduc, Gresset, Sanschagrin, and Thibodeau (1993). Additionally, Cote and Smith (1983) and Jose, Smith, and Shane (1980) provided excellent suggestions for assessment and intervention techniques appropriate for use with students who are multiply disabled and partially sighted.

TABLE X
ASSESSMENT INSTRUMENTS USEFUL WITH STUDENTS
WITH MULTIPLE DISABILITIES AND VISUAL IMPAIRMENTS

Instrument	*Author*
Adaptive Performance Instrument	(Gentry, 1980)
Easement, Evaluation, and Programming System Measurement for Birth to Three Years	(Bricker, 1992)
Brigance Diagnostic Comprehensive Inventory of Basic Skills	(Brigrance, 1983)
Callier-Azusa	(Stillman, 1978)
DASI	(Fewell and Langley, 1984)
Griffiths Mental Development Scales	(Griffiths, 1954 and 1970)
Informal Assessment of Developmental Skills for Visually Handicapped Students	(Swallow, Mangold, and Mangold, 1978)
Oregon Project for Visually Impaired and Blind Preschool Children	(Anderson, Boigon, and Davis, 1986)
Reynell-Zinkin Scales	(Reynell, 1979)
Uzgiris-Hunt Ordinal Scales of Psychological Development	(Uzgiris-Hunt, 1975)
Vineland Adaptive Behavior Scales — Expanded	(Sparrow, Balla, and Cicchetti, 1984)
Vulpe Assessment Battery	(Vulpe, 1977)

For students who have limited English proficiency, the dilemma of assessment has been well documented (Baca and Cervantes, 1984; Barona and Barona, 1987). The implications for assessing students with visual and multiple disabilities are clear. Instruments discussed in this chapter are not available in other languages, and unless the examinee is fluent in Spanish, for example, the LEP student must receive assessment instruction in English. To illustrate, let us look at the case of Ricardo, a student from the Dominican Republic, living in Miami.

> At the age of seven Ricardo, a student with multiple disabilities and limited English proficiency was given the STYCAR, functional vision assessment in English and he did not understand the instruction "find the same one", the examinee concluded that Ricardo could not see from a distance and asked the parents to take him to an ophthalmologist. Ricardo's parent were very confused but followed through on the referral. After a very expensive office visit to an ophthalmologist, it was determined that Ricardo had no visual problems and refractive lenses were not prescribed. Ricardo's parents were relieved but also upset with the school examinee because of the cost of the visit. Additionally, in

their native country going "outside" of the family to solve problems was not common and had made the family uncomfortable.

The case described above illustrates not only the potential damage that can occur due to language barriers but also the cultural barriers that must be understood by professionals working with students who are multiply disabled and limited English proficient and their families.

INTERVENTION

Intervention with students who are multiply and visually disabled should not be much different than intervention with students who have normal vision (Sobsey and Wolf-Schein, 1991). Currently, Scholl (1986b) has presented the most comprehensive text on effective practices for evaluating and educating students with visual disabilities. Perhaps the most important aspect of intervention for students with multiple disabilities incorporates both the fields of vision and severe disabilities. The ecological approach to curriculum development advocated by many researchers in severe disabilities relies heavily on the interventions outlined below (as cited in Turnbull and Turnbull, 1995, p. 304):

- Functional and chronologically age-appropriate objectives must be taught in their natural context (Brown et al., 1979).
- Interdependence and partial participation are valid educational goals (Ford et al., 1989).
- Objectives should be based on the wants, needs, preferences, and culture of the student (Falvey, 1989).
- Preferences and choice-making should be incorporated into each educational objective (Reichle, York, and Sigafoo, 1991).
- Inclusion into general education classes is an essential element of an appropriate education (Stainback and Stainback, 1992).
- Parent participation is a crucial component of the instructional process (Neel and Billingsley, 1989).

For students with multiple disabilities and visual impairments, specific areas of concern for intervention include early intervention (Ferrell, 1986), maximizing residual vision (Sobsey and Wolf-Schein, 1991), orientation and mobility (Hill, 1986), and decreasing maladaptive behaviors (Sims-Tucker and Jensema, 1984).

Early intervention for young children with visual disabilities is a critical phase of the service delivery continuum. The focus of early intervention is to provide the infant with visual disabilities with appropriate and systematic sensory stimulation in order to facilitate maximum development, and provide the families with support to better understand the development and special needs of their child. A program developed by Ferrell (1985) provided parents and teachers with excellent suggestions for early intervention with young students with visual disabilities. The *Reach Out and Teach* materials also address the needs of children with multiple disabilities.

Maximizing residual vision is also a major focus of educational programs for children with visual disabilities. Interventions include use of optical lenses and aids, electronic aids (e.g., Visualtek, Viewscan, Versabraille), and environmental modifications (e.g., lighting). For many students who are multiply disabled, the use of sophisticated electronic aids is difficult, and the focus of stimulating vision is more functional in nature. Systematic and age-appropriate visual stimulation should occur during functional daily routines (Orelove and Sobsey, 1991). For example, training a student to visually track an object can be taught within the functional routine of eating with a spoon, in which the spoon becomes the object for tracking. Similarly, stimulation programs involving the other senses (tactile, auditory, olfactory, gustatory) should be taught systematically, and within a student's functional routines. Correa, Poulson, and Salzburg (1984) present data on an effective systematic prompting procedures for teaching young infants who are blind and severely disabled to reach and grasp sound making toys. Sensory bombardment is no longer justified in programs serving students with multiple disabilities with sensory impairments. Goetz and Gee (1987) provided an excellent functional vision training program for students with severe disabilities. The five steps to developing the vision program include:

Step 1. Determine the targeted visual skill.
Step 2. Select the skill contexts that require visual behavior for accurate task performance.
Step 3. Design the instructional program for teaching the vision skill.
Step 4. Select the instructional strategies that will be used to teach the functional skills.
Step 5. Implement and monitor the program that has been designed.

Orientation and mobility (O&M) is yet another critical component of the service delivery package for students who evidence multiple disabilities. Today, O&M specialists are receiving extensive training in working with preschoolers and students with multiple disabilities. The idea of independent cane travel may not be realistic for many students with multiple disabilities; thus, the definition and parameters of O&M have broadened (Hill, Rosen, Correa, and Langley, 1985; Gee, Harrell, and Rosenberg, 1987; Joffee and Rikhye, 1991). The O&M training arena is not just teaching formal cane travel around schools and communities. Instead, the training occurs in daily living areas such as kitchens, bathrooms, and bedrooms. Furthermore, concept development (the process of utilizing sensory information to form ideas of space and the environment), sensory training, and motor development become a major part of the O&M curriculum for students with multiple disabilities. In addition, physical and occupational therapists are becoming more involved in the O&M process (Harley, and Hill, 1986; Hill, 1986), by providing teachers with excellent guidance for early movement and posture development using techniques such as described in neurodevelopmental treatment (Bobath and Bobath, 1984).

Lastly, intervention techniques for decreasing maladaptive behaviors (self-injury, self-stimulation, aggression, withdrawal) are often needed with students with multiple disabilities. Perhaps, due to the lack of sensory input, communicative function, or motivation, many of these students must be involved in behavioral treatment programs to decrease maladaptive behaviors. There is an abundance of literature on the treatment of maladaptive behaviors (Donnellan, Mirenda, Mesaros, and Fassbender, 1984; Evans and Meyers, 1985; Gast and Worley, 1987; Snell, 1993; Westling and Fox, 1995), and most behavior specialists emphasize the use of nonaversive treatment options for students with severe maladaptive behavior. Only with the most severe behavior is it advisable to consider aversive treatments. A professional team is required to closely monitor treatments that include time-out, restraints, or other forms of punishment. Unfortunately, many teachers do not have available to them the support of a behavior specialist or psychologist trained in nonaversive as well as aversive treatments. Additionally, families of students with severe maladaptive behavior are often opposed to implementation of punishment techniques. For example, a Puerto Rican family who wants to overprotect their child with disabilities, would be opposed to implementing any procedures that would make the child suffer.

Clearly, the educational needs of students with multiple disabilities are diverse, and the roles of professionals working with them are varied.

Students from language minority cultures will require added support. Intervention must meet the cultural expectations of the family from a diverse background. As described in the following situation, there is often conflict between the perceived needs of family and the educational system.

> Anita is a sixteen-year-old, Mexican-American student who evidences multiple disabilities and blindness. The O&M specialist has requested that Anita's parents reinforce the use of cane travel for independent mobility during times when she is not in school. Unfortunately, Anita's parents, and particularly her grandfather, oppose this request. They do not believe Anita should travel by herself, and should always be chaperoned by an older sibling or other family member.

Anita's situation is all too common. In this instance, Anita's family values dependence, particularly for a young women like Anita; it is not proper for her to go places alone. Anita comes from a large extended family who will always be available to provide her with sighted-guide. Independence and particularly the use of a cane (sometimes a stigma of blindness) are in conflict with the values inherent within Anita's Mexican-American culture.

Whether the focus of an educational program is on early intervention, visual stimulation, O&M training, or teaching positive social behaviors, the professional working with the culturally diverse student with multiple disabilities needs the support of parents and other professionals in order to execute a quality program. However, as discussed, the program must be sensitive to the diverse needs and values of students and families from different cultures.

HEARING IMPAIRMENTS

According to Kropka and Williams (1986) the leading causes of hearing impairments in school-aged children with mental retardation are *otitis media* (inflammation of middle ear occurring in the presence of chronic Eustachian tube dysfunction); *viral infections* (Rubella and cytomegalovirus—CMV); *hereditary diseases* (Norrie's disease and Usher's syndrome); *Rh factor;* and *low birth weight.*

Hearing impairments are traditionally classified into three categories: *conductive hearing loss* caused by disease involving problems with the sound conducting pathways of the outer and middle ear and *sensorineural loss* caused by disease to the cochlea (inner ear) and neural auditory pathway (Kropka and Williams, 1986). In some cases, when both conductive and sensori-neural losses occur in the same individual, it is regarded as *mixed hearing loss* (Sobsey and Wolf-Schein, 1991). In conductive hearing loss, typical sounds are not loud enough to stimulate normal hearing, due to an impairment in the outer or middle ear. Amplification may improve the problem by increasing sound sufficiently to bypass the damaged area, and initiate reception by the cochlea and auditory nerve. Yet, with sensori-neural loss, an increasing amplification of sound does not improve its clarity. In this case, the cochlea or the auditory nerve pathway is damaged and the brain does not receive the sound vibrations (Roberts, Helmstetter, Guess, Murphy-Herd, and Mulligan, 1984). Additionally, Sobsey and Wolf-Schein (1991) present another way of understanding the typical classifications of hearing impairment. Table XI outlines these classifications by the average amount of loss in frequencies or decibel.

TABLE XI
CLASSIFICATION BY DEGREE OF HEARING LOSS

Class	Classification	Decibel	Characteristics
1	Mild	20–40 (dB)	Hear most speech sounds
2	Moderate	41–55 (dB)	Problem with speech sounds
3	Moderate/Severe	56–70 (dB)	Hear little speech range
4	Severe	71–90 (dB)	Problems with other environmental sounds
5	Profound	>90 (dB)	Hear no speech and very little other sound

Adapted from Sims-Tucker and Jensema, 1984

ASSESSMENT

As with the student with multiple and visual disabilities, assessment of the student with multiple disabilities and hearing impairments requires sophisticated procedures (Bond, 1986). Standardized nonverbal tests which may be used in the assessment of hearing-impaired students include: WISC–R for the Hearing Impaired (Anderson and Sisco, 1976); Hiskey Nebraska Test of Learning Aptitude (Hiskey, 1966); Leiter International Performance Scale (Leiter, 1969); Columbia Mental Maturity Scale (Burgemeister, Blum, and Lorge, 1972); and Merrill Palmer Performance tests. For students with hearing impairments and more severe cognitive delays, assessment is best approached from an ecological, multifactored perspective as mentioned in the previous section on students who have multiple and visual disabilities (Langley, 1986; Sobsey and Wolf-Schein, 1991; Westling and Fox, 1995). The emphasis of assessment and intervention for students is on communication development.

Assessment of functional hearing is also an important component to the complete assessment of the student with multiple disabilities and hearing impairments. Instruments such as the Auditory Behavior Index (Northern and Downs, 1984) can be adapted easily for students with multiple disabilities.

For the limited English proficient student with multiple disabilities and hearing impairments, assessment is not as difficult, since nonverbal assessment procedures are usually employed. Structured observations of the student performing daily life routines is the most valuable means of gathering data on students potential. Using materials and skills that are most common to the students environment is recommended. For example, when evaluating object/picture matching with a Puerto Rican student with multiple disabilities and hearing impairments, the teacher must use objects that are familiar to the student, such as matching pictures with foods like mangos, pineapples, guavas, plantains, acerolas, and coconuts. Clearly, sensitivity to cultural differences during the assessment is necessary.

INTERVENTION

Intervention for students with multiple disabilities and hearing impairments is primarily focused toward the development of communication and the enhancement of auditory potential (Sobsey and Wolf-Schein, 1991; Niswander, 1987). Various communication systems, including oral, gestural, and symbolic modes are used with students who are hearing impaired. The most frequently used with students with multiple disabilities and hearing impairments include gestural, sign, and total communication systems. Of course, if there is residual hearing, amplification is the desired treatment.

For students from language minority cultures, special sign systems may be employed. Although American Sign Language (ASL) is the most commonly used signing system, translation of those signs into Spanish have become necessary for families and students of limited English proficiency (Luethke, 1976; McLean and Mendez, 1986).

DUAL SENSORY IMPAIRMENTS

Although most often referred to as students with deaf-blind, it is important to note that deaf-blindness rarely means total loss of vision and hearing (Baldwin, 1994; Huebner, Kirchner, and Prickett, 1995; Stillman and Battle, 1986; Ward and Zambone, 1992). It is estimated that close to 94 percent of individuals labeled deaf-blind have some functional hearing and/or vision (Fredericks and Baldwin, 1987). Further, the intellectual level of students with dual sensory impairments ranges from giftedness to profound mental retardation (Heward, 1995).

According to federal legislation (Section 1422 of P.L. 101) the definition of deaf-blindness is:

> Children and youth having auditory and visual impairments, the combination of which creates such severe communication and other developmental and learning needs that they cannot be appropriately educated in special education programs solely for children and youth with hearing impairments, visual impairments, or severe disabilities, without supplementary assistance to address their education needs due to these dual, concurrent disabilities.

Furthermore, Roberts, Helmstetter, Guess, Murphy-Herd, and Mulligan (1984) stated that "the Helen Keller National Center defines a student as certifiably deaf-blind when central visual acuity is 20/200 or less in the better eye with corrective lenses, and when a chronic hearing impairment is so severe that most speech cannot be understood, even with optimum amplification" (p. 3). Today, Rubella is no longer the leading cause of deaf-blindness. Rather, it occurs from prematurity in infancy, genetic syndromes (Rubella, CHARGE, Down, trisomy 13, Usher), and multiple congenital anomalies (microcephaly, cytomegalovirus, anoxia, hydrocephaly). Yet, during the rubella epidemic of 1963–64, approximately twenty to thirty thousand children were disabled in utero by the rubella virus (Cherry, 1974). Today, those children are in their thirties having exited school programs, and in need of rehabilitation services, vocational training, job placement, and supported living arrangements (Dantona, 1986; Marks and Feeley, 1995).

ASSESSMENT

The assessment needs of students with deaf-blindness are similar to those of students with multiple disabilities and visual impairments or hearing impairments. Few instruments are available that are specifically designed for assessing students with dual sensory impairments. However, the Callier-Azusa (Stillman, 1978), the Callier-Azusa: H (Stillman and Battle, 1985), the INSITE Developmental Checklist (Morgan et al., 1989); and the Assessment, Evaluation, and Programming Systems Measurement for Birth to Three Years (Bricker, 1993) are the most frequently used scales for this population. Additionally, Dunlap (1984) reported on the development and validation of the Severely Disabilities Progress Inventory for use with deaf-blind students. Finally, functional and ecological approaches to assessment (Brown, 1987; Snell, 1993; Westling and Fox, 1995) should also be used in assessing students with deaf-blindness, and should be related closely to curriculum development.

Assessment of sensory intactness in deaf-blind students can be done by using functional vision instruments previously mentioned (Bolduc, Gresset, Sanschagrin, and Thibodeau, 1993; Langley, 1980; Langley and Dubose, 1989; Sheridan, 1973), and by using functional auditory assessment instruments designed for use with students with dual sensory impairments and multiple disabilities (Kukla and Connolly, 1978; Sailor, Goetz, Utley, Gee, and Baldwin, 1982).

INTERVENTION

Educational programs for deaf-blind students have been discussed in many books and articles (see Bullis, 1985, 1986; Roberts, Helmstetter, Guess, Murphy-Herd, and Mulligan, 1984; Stillman and Battle, 1984; van Dijk, 1986; Giangreco, Edelman, Dennis, and Cloninger, in press; Cloninger and Giangreco, 1995; Luiselli, Luiselli, DeCaluwe, and Jacobs, 1995). Similar to the program priorities for students with multiple disabilities and visual or hearing impairments, the student who is deaf-blind will require intervention in the areas of visual and auditory training (Sims-Tucker and Jensema, 1984), orientation and mobility (Geruschat, 1980), social and communication development (MacFarland, 1995; van Dijk, 1966, 1986).

Perhaps one of the most commonly used approaches to educational programming for deaf-blind students has been developed by van Dijk (1986). The major philosophy guiding the van Dijk approach is its emphasis on the attachment or bonding process between a child and an adult, and the child's motivation for environmental exploration. The attachment component of the curricula includes three steps:

(1) Co-active movements and responsiveness ("hands-on" method of shared movement with child and adult in as many daily living activities as possible)
(2) Structuring the child's daily routine (structuring daily living routines and building a sequence of expectations)
(3) Characterization (providing the child with the opportunity to develop an association with the adult through use of an "ear-ring" or recognizable characteristic, such as a pipe for the father, a scarf for the mother, and a bowl for the sister) (van Dijk, 1986).

When students become aware of their control over the environment, the educational goal is the development of a formal system of communication. A variety of formal communication systems can be used depending on the degree of visual and auditory impairment evidenced by the deaf-blind student. Table XII outlines the most commonly used communication systems used by persons who are deaf-blind. However, for more severely involved students with deaf-blindness, more concrete and pragmatic ways of communicating must be used.

Intervention strategies for culturally and linguistically diverse students who are deaf-blind have not been documented in the literature. If the student is non-English speaking, communication systems such as the alphabet glove method (see Table XII) will have to be taught in the student's native language. For students with more severe disabilities who are LEP and deaf blind, functional signs and gestures can more easily be taught to the family with the use of a translator. For example, an LEP student who is taught a sign for "eat," can use that sign at home to represent the Spanish word "comer" even if the parents are non-English speakers. However, the syntax sequencing of two or more words does require the teachers to understand the basic elements of Spanish. To further illustrate, an LEP child who wants to communicate the phrase "hot water" during a dishwashing lesson, would sign "agua caliente," thus reversing the syntax.

The major role of the teacher is to communicate with the parent in their native language and instruct them in the use of signs. This instruction has been most successfully done in parent groups with other families of children who are deaf, and are instructed by a bilingual teacher using sign books printed in Spanish (McLean and Mendez, 1986).

For students who require a total communication approach (speech and sign) to language, the teacher will need to speak in basic Spanish phrases. Silberman and Correa (1989) have developed a list of common Spanish-English survival words and phrases to be used by non-Spanish

TABLE XII
MOST COMMONLY USED COMMUNICATION SYSTEMS
FOR PERSONS WHO ARE DEAF–BLIND

System	Description
Palm Writing	*Block letters printed on palm of hands*
Fingerspelling	One manual sign for each letter of the alphabet
Morse Code	Dots and dashes signalled gesturally, transmitted to any part of the body
Braille Hand Speech	Reproduces braille dots in palm
Sign Systems	Hand over hand in accordance to customary sign language, also used with spoken communication for total communication approach
Glove Method	Glove with letters and numbers imprinted upon surface of the palm, sender touches area of glove assigned to the letter
Tadom Method	Hand on face of person for sensing speech sounds
Braille	Traditional braille system
Typing and Script Writing	Traditional typing and script-writing
Telephone Communication Systems	TTD's or TTY's covert type input to an audio-frequency which is converted back to letter/braille
Augmentative Communications Systems	Including symbol systems (e.g. Bliss, Rebuses); picture communication boards, electronic communication boards, speech-output communication systems, etc.

Adapted from Bullis, 1986

speaking teachers who work with Hispanic families and students with multiple disabilities. The list provides the teacher with vocabulary often associated with the education of students with multiple disabilities, such as medication (medicina), seizures (convulciones), visual impairment (impedimentos de vision).

CONCLUSION

This chapter has reviewed a variety of assessment and intervention strategies used in educating students with multiple disabilities and sensory impairments. These students have typically been considered the most difficult population to educate, due to the severity and multiplicity of their impairments. The education of students with multiple disabilities requires teachers to not only have skills in generic teaching practices for educating students with severe disabilities but, also specific knowledge of sensory impairments, alternative communication systems and orientation and mobility techniques. Ideally, families and professionals should be involved in a collaborative effort to provide an optimal educational and home environment for developing independence and enhancing the quality of life of these individuals.

For students and families from culturally and linguistically diverse backgrounds, the educational process becomes more complex. The field of special education culturally diverse students with severe disabilities is in its infancy. The future directions of research and personnel preparation must bring into focus the importance of cultural patterns associated with culturally and linguistically diverse populations and provide educators with the tools to most effectively intervene with diverse students with multiple disabilities and their families.

DISCUSSION QUESTIONS

(1) List the causes and prevalence of sensory impairments among children.

(2) Define the following terms: legally blind, partially sighted, conductive hearing loss, sensori-neural hearing loss, mixed hearing loss.

(3) List two assessment instruments appropriate for evaluating the following groups of students with multiple disabilities:
   (a) multiply disabilities/visually disabilities
   (b) multiply disabilities/hearing impaired
   (c) deaf-blind

(4) What assessment instruments are available for assessing functional vision and hearing in students with multiple disabilities?

(5) Provide three appropriate curricular objectives for each of the following groups of students with multiple disabilities:
   (a) multiply disabilities/visually disabilities
   (b) multiply disabilities/hearing impaired
   (c) deaf-blind

(6) Discuss the broadened definition of orientation and mobility for students with multiple disabilities.

(7) Discuss the major components of the van Dijk approach for educating students who are deaf-blind.

(8) Define the following terms associated with van Dijk theory:
   (a) co-active movement

(b) "ear-ring"

(c) "hands on" method

(9) List and describe the communication systems most often used with persons who are deaf-blind.

(10) What special considerations must a teacher take into account when working with the families of culturally and linguistically diverse students with multiple disabilities?

REFERENCES

Anderson, S., Boigon, S., and Davis, K. (1986). *The Oregon Project for visually impaired and blind preschool children (5th Ed).* Medford, OR: Jackson County Education Service District.

Anderson, B., and Sisco, F. H. (1976). *Standardization of the WISC–R performance scale for deaf children.* Washington, D.C.: Gaulladet University.

Baca, L. M., and Cervantes, H. T. (1984). *The bilingual special education interface.* St. Louis, MO: Times Mirror/Mosby.

Baldwin, V. (1994). *Annual deaf-blind census.* Monmouth, OR: Teaching Research Publications.

Barona, A., and Barona, M. S. (1987). A model for the assessment of limited English proficient students referred for special education services. In S. Fradd and W. Tikunoff (Eds.), *Bilingual education and bilingual special education,* (pp. 183–209). Boston, MA: College-Hill Publication.

Barraga, N. C. (1980). *Program to develop efficiency in visual functioning: Diagnostic assessment procedure (DAP).* Louisville, KY: American Printing House for the Blind.

Best, C. (1986). The multi-sensorially impaired (deaf-blind) in the mentally disabilities population. In D. Ellis (Ed.), *Sensory impairments in mentally disabilities people* (pp. 61–68). San Diego: College-Hill Press.

Bobath, B., and Bobath, K. (1984). The neurodevelopmental treatment. In D. Stratton (Ed.), *Management of the motor disorders of children with cerebral palsy.* Philadelphia: J.B. Lippincott.

Bolduc, M., Gresset, G., Sanschagrin, S., and Thibodeau, J. (1993). A model for the efficient interdisciplinary assessment of young visually impaired children. *Journal of Visual Impairment and Blindness, 87,* 410–414.

Bond, D. E. (1986). Psychological assessment of the hearing impaired, additionally impaired and multidisabilities deaf. In D. Ellis (Ed.), *Sensory impairments in mentally disabilities people* (pp. 297–318). San Diego: College-Hill Press.

Bradely-Johnson, S. (1994). *Psychoeducational assessment of students who are visually impaired or blind: Infancy through high school* (2nd Edition). Austin, TX: PRO-ED.

Bricker, D. D. (1992). *AEPS measurement for birth to three years.* Baltimore: Brookes.

Brigance, A. (1983). *Brigance diagnostic comprehensive inventory of basic skills.* North Billerica, MA: Curriculum Associates.

Brown, F. (1987). Meaningful assessment of people with severe and profound disabilities. In M. Snell (Ed.) *Systematic instruction of persons with severe disabilities* (pp. 30–63). Columbus, OH: Merrill.

Brown, L., Branston, M. B., Hamre-Nietupski, S., Pumpian, I., Certo, N., and Gruenewald, L. (1979). A strategy for developing chronological, age-appropriate and functional curricular content for severely handicapped adolescents and young adults. *The Journal of Special Education, 13(a),* 81–90.

Brown, L., Branston, M. B., Hamre-Nieptupski, S., Pumpian, I., Certo, N., and Gruenewald, L. (1979). A strategy for developing chronological-age-appropriate and functional curricular content for severely disabilities adolescents and young adults. *Journal of Special Education, 13,* 81–90.

Bullis, M. (Ed.) (1985). *Communication development in young children with deaf-blindness: Literature review I.* (Monmouth, OR: Oregon State System of Higher Education, Deaf-Blind Communication Skills Center.

Bullis, M. (Ed.) (1986). *Communication development in young children with deaf-blindness: Literature review II.* (Monmouth, OR: Oregon State System of Higher Education, Deaf-Blind Communication Skills Center.

Burgemeister, B., Blum, L., and Lorge, I. (1972). *Columbia Mental Maturity Scale.* New York: Harcourt Brace Jovanovich.

Cherry, J. (1974). Rubella: Past, present and future. *Volta Review, 76*(8).

Cloninger, C. J., and Giangreco, M. F. (1995). Including students with Deaf-Blindness in general education classes. *Journal of Visual Impairment and Blindness, 89,* 262–266.

Correa, V. I., Pouslon, C., and Salzburg, C. (1984). Training and generalization of reach-grasp behavior in blind, retarded young children. *Journal of Applied Behavior Analysis, 17,* 57–69.

Cote, K. S., and Smith, A. (1983). Assessment of the multiply disabilities. In R. T. Jose (Ed.), *Understanding low vision* (pp. 379–401). New York: American Foundation for the Blind.

Cress, P. J., Spellman, C. R., DeBriere, T. J., Sizemore, A. C., Northam, J. K., and Johnson, J. L. (1981). Vision screening for persons with severe disabilities. *Journal of the Association for the Severely Disabilities, 6*(3), 41–50.

Dantona, R. (1986). Implications of demographic data for planning of services for deaf-blind children and adults. In D. Ellis (Ed.), *Sensory impairments in mentally disabilities people* (pp. 69–82). San Diego: College-Hill Press.

Davidson, R. (1993). Personnel preparation: Reaction. In J. W. Reiman and P. A. Johnson (Eds.), *Proceedings from the national symposium on children and youth who are deaf-blind* (pp. 159–164). Monmouth, OR: Teaching Research Publications.

Donnellan, A. M., Mirenda, P. L., Mesaros, R. A., and Fassbender, L. L. (1984). Analyzing the communicative functions of aberrant behavior. *The Journal of The Association for Persons with Severe Disabilities, 9*(3), 201–212.

Dunlap, W. C. (1984). The development and validation of an assessment instrument for use with the deaf blind: The severely disabilities progress inventory. *Educational and Psychological Measurement, 44,* 1067–1071.

Ellis, D. (1986). The epidemiology of visual impairment in people with a mental handicap. In D. Ellis (Ed.), *Sensory impairments in mentally disabilities people* (pp. 3–34). San Diego: College-Hill Press.

Evans, I. M., and Meyer, L. H. (1985). *An educative approach to behavior problems.* Baltimore: Paul H. Brookes.

Falvey, M. A. (1989). *Community-based curriculum: Instructional strategies for students with severe handicaps* (2nd Ed.). Baltimore: Paul H. Brookes.

Ferrell, K. A. (1985). *Reach out and teach.* New York: American Foundation for the Blind.

Ferrell, K. A. (1986). Infancy and early childhood. In G. T. Scholl, *Foundations of education for blind and visually disabilities children and youth: Theory and practice,* (pp. 119–135). New York: American Foundation for the Blind.

Fewell, R. R., and Langley, M. B. (1984). *The developmental activities screening inventory, II.* Austin, TX: Pro-Ed Corporation.

Ford, A., Schnoor, R., Meyer, L., Davern, I., Black, J., and Dempsey, P. (1989). *The Syracuse community-referenced curriculum guide for students with moderate and severe disabilities.* Baltimore: Paul H. Brookes.

Fredericks, H. D., and Baldwin, V. (1987). Individuals with sensory impairments: Who are they? How are they educated? In L. Goetz, D. Guess, and K. Stremel-Campell (Eds.), *Innovative program design for individuals with dual sensory impairments* (pp. 3–14). Baltimore, MD: Paul H. Brookes.

Gast, D. L., and Wolery, M. (1987). Severe maladaptive behaviors. In M. Snell (Ed.), *Systematic instruction of persons with severe disabilities* (pp. 300–332). Columbus, OH: Merrill.

Gee, K., Harrell, R., and Rosenberg, R. (1987). Teaching orientation and mobility skills within and across natural opportunities for travel. In L. Goetz, D. Guess, and K. Stremel-Campell (Eds.), *Innovative program design for individuals with dual sensory impairments* (pp. 77–97). Baltimore, MD: Brookes.

Gentry, D. (1980). *The adaptive performance inventory.* Moscow, Idaho: University of Idaho.

Geruschat, D. R. (1980). Orientation and mobility for the low functioning deaf-blind child. *Journal of Visual Impairment and Blindness, 74,* 29–33.

Giangreco, M. F., Edelman, S., Dennis, R., and Cloninger, C. (in press). Use and impact of COACH with students who are deaf-blind. *Journal of the Association for Persons with Severe Handicaps.*

Goetz, L., and Gee, K. (1987). Teaching visual attention in functional contexts: Acquisition and generalization of complex motor skills. *Journal of Visual Impairment and Blindness, 81,* 115–117.

Graham, M. (1968). *Multiply-impaired blind children: A national problem.* New York: American Foundation for the Blind.

Griffiths, R. (1954). *The abilities of babies.* Great Britain: Association for Research in Infant and Child Development.

Griffiths, R. (1970). *The abilities of children.* Great Britain: Association for Research in Infant and Child Development.

Harley, R., and Hill, M. (1986). Mobility training for visually impaired mentally disabilities persons. In D. Ellis (Ed.), *Sensory impairments in mentally disabilities people* (pp. 408–428). San Diego: College-Hill Press.

Heward, W. (1996). *Exceptional children: An introduction to special education* (5th Ed.). Columbus, OH: Merrill.

Hill, E. W. (1986). Orientation and mobility. In G. T. Scholl, *Foundations of education for blind and visually disabilities children and youth: Theory and practice,* (pp. 313–340). New York: American Foundation for the Blind.

Hill, E. W., Rosen, S., Correa, V. I., and Langley, M. B. (1984). Preschool orientation and mobility: An expanded definition. *Education of the Visually Disabilities, 16,* 58–72.

Hiskey, M. (1966). *Hiskey Nebraska Test of Learning Aptitude.* Amon, Nebraska: Amon College Press.

Huebner, K. M., Kirchner, C., and Prickett, J. G. (1995). Meeting personnel training needs: The deaf-blind self-study curriculum project. *Journal of Visual Impairment and Blindness, 89,* 235–243.

IDEA 20 U.S.C. Secs. 1400–1485.

Jacobson, J. W., and Janicki, M. P. (1985). Functional and health status characteristics of persons with severe disabilities in New York State. *Journal of the Association for Persons with Severe Disabilities, 10,* 51–60.

Joffee, E., and Rikhye, C. H. (1991). Orientation and mobility for students with severe visual and multiple impairments: A new perspective. *Journal of Visual Impairment and Blindness, 85,* 211–216.

Jose, R. T., Smith, A. J., and Shane, K. G. (1980). Evaluating and stimulating vision in the multiply impaired. *Journal of Visual Impairment and Blindness, 74,* 2–8.

Kirchner, C., and Peterson, R. (1981). Estimates of race-ethnic groups in the U.S. visually impaired and blind population. *Journal of Visual Impairment and Blindness, 75,* 73–76.

Kropka, B. I., and Williams, C. (1986). The epidemiology of hearing impairment in people with a mental handicap. In D. Ellis (Ed.), *Sensory impairments in mentally disabilities people* (pp. 35–60). San Diego: College-Hill Press.

Kukla, D., and Connolly, T. T. (1978). *Assessment of auditory functioning of deaf-blind/multidisabilities children.* Dallas: South Central Regional Center for Services to Deaf-Blind Children.

Langley, B., and Dubose, R. E. (1989). Functional vision screening for severely handicapped children. In *Dimensions: Visually impaired persons with multiple disabilities* (pp. 47–51). Selected papers from *The Journal of Visual Impairment and Blindness.* New York: American Foundation for the Blind.

Langley, M. B. (1980). *Functional vision inventory for the multiple and severe disabilities.* Chicago, IL: Stoelting.

Langley, M. B. (1986). Psychoeducational assessment of visually impaired students with additional disabilities. In D. Ellis (Ed.), *Sensory impairments in mentally disabilities people* (pp. 253–296). San Diego: College-Hill Press.

Leiter, R. G. (1969). *The Leiter international performance scale.* Chicago, IL: Stoelting.

Luethke, B. (1976). Questionnaire results from Mexican-American parents of hearing impaired children in the United States. *American Annals of the Deaf, 121,* 565–568.

Luiselli, T. E., Luiselli, J. K., DeCaluwe, S. M., and Jacobs, L. A. (1995). Inclusive education of young children with deaf-blindness: A technical assistance model. *Journal of Visual Impairment and Blindness, 89,* 249–256.

Marks, S. B., and Feeley, D. (1995). Transition in action: Michigan's experience. *Journal of Visual Impairment and Blindness, 89,* 272–275.

McLean, M., and Mendez, A. (1986, November). Working with Hispanic parents of deaf children: Cultural and linguistic considerations. Paper presented at the meeting of the CEC Symposia on Ethnic and Multicultural Concerns, Dallas, Texas.

Morgan, E. C., Watkins, S., Terry, B. G., Snow, P. S., Boyle, P., Watts, J., Morrison, A., and Jensen, D. L. (1989). The INSITE developmental checklist. Logan, UT: SKI–HI Institute.

Neel, R. S., and Billingsley, F. F. (1989). *IMPACT: A functional curriculum handbook for students with moderate and severe disabilities.* Baltimore: Paul H. Brookes.

Niswander, P. S. (1987). Audiometric assessment and management. In L. Goetz, D. Guess, and K. Stremel-Campell (Eds.), *Innovative program design for individuals with dual sensory impairments* (pp. 99–126). Baltimore, MD: Paul H. Brookes.

Northern, J. L., and Downs, J. P. (1984). *Hearing in children* (3rd edition). Baltimore: Williams and Wilkins.

Orelove, F. P. and Sobsey, D. (1991). *Educating children with multiple disabilities: A transdisciplinary approach* (2nd Ed.). Baltimore: Paul H. Brookes.

Orelove, F. P., and Sobsey, D. (1994). *Educating children with multiple disabilities: A transdisciplinary approach.* Baltimore: Paul H. Brookes.

Ortiz, A. and Yates, J. (1983). Incidence of exceptionality among Hispanics: Implications for manpower planning. *Journal of the National Association for Bilingual Education, 3,* 41–53.

Rainforth, B., York, J., and Macdonald, C. (1992). *Collaborative teams for students with severe disabilities: Integrating therapy and educational services.* Baltimore: Paul H. Brookes.

Reichle, J., York, J., and Sigafoos, J. (1991). *Implementing augmentative and alternative communication: Strategies for learners with severe disabilities.* Baltimore: Paul H. Brookes.

Reynell, J. (1979). *The Reynell-Zinkin scales: Developmental scales for young visually disabilities children—part 1: Mental development.* Slough: NFER.

Roberts, S., Helmstetter, E., Guess, D., Murphy-Herd, M. C., and Mulligan, M. (1984). *Programming for students who are deaf and blind.* Lawrence, KS: University of Kansas.

Sailor, W., Goetz, L., Utley, B., Gee, K., and Baldwin, M. (1982). *Auditory assessment and program manual for severely disabilities deaf-blind students.* Parsons, KS: Words and Pictures Corporation.

Scholl, G. T. (1986b). *Foundations of education for blind and visually disabilities children and youth: Theory and practice.* New York: American Foundation for the Blind.

Scholl, G. T. (1986a). What does it mean to be blind?: Definitions, terminology, and prevalence. In G. T. Scholl, *Foundations of education for blind and visually disabilities children and youth: Theory and practice* (pp. 24–33). New York: American Foundation for the Blind.

Sheridan, M. D. (1973). *Children's developmental progress from birth to five years: The STYCAR sequences.* Slough: NFER.

Silberman, R., and Correa, V. I. (in press). Spanish survival words and phrases for use with families of Hispanic students with multiple disabilities. *Journal of the Division for Physically Disabilities.*

Sims-Tucker, B., and Jensema, C. (1984). Severely and profoundly auditorially/visually impaired students: The deaf-blind population. In P. Valletutti and B. Sims-Tucker (Eds.), *Severely and profoundly disabilities students: Their nature and needs* (pp. 269–317). Baltimore: Paul H. Brookes.

Snell, M. E. (1993). *Instruction of students with severe disabilities* (4th Ed.). New York: Merrill/Macmillan.

Sobsey, D., and Wolf-Schein, E. G. (1991). Sensory impairments. In F. P. Orelove and D. Sobsey (Eds.), *Educating children with multiple disabilities: A transdisciplinary approach* (2nd Edition) (pp. 119–154). Baltimore: Paul H. Brookes.

Sparrow, S. S., Balla, D. A., and Cicchetti, D. V. (1984). *Vineland adaptive behavior scales — expanded or survey version.* Circle Pines, MN: American Guidance Service.

Stainback, S., and Stainback, W. (1992). *Curriculum considerations in inclusive classrooms: Facilitating learning for all students.* Baltimore: Paul H. Brookes.

Stillman, R. (1978). *Assessment of deaf-blind children: The Callier-Azuza scale.* Reston, VA: Council for Exceptional Children.

Stillman, R., and Battle, C. (1985). *Callier-Azusa scales (H): Scales for the assessment of communicative abilities.* Dallas, TX: University of Texas.

Stillman, R., and Battle, C. (1986). Developmental assessment of communicative abilities of the deaf-blind. In D. Ellis (Ed.), *Sensory impairments in mentally disabilities people* (pp. 319–335). San Diego: College-Hill Press.

Swallow, R., Mangold, S., and Mangold, P. (1978). *Informal assessment of developmental skills for visually handicapped students.* New York: American Foundation for the Blind.

Texas Education Agency (1982–83). *Annual special education statistical report.* Austin, TX: Texas Education Agency.

Turnbull, A. P., Turnbull, H. R., Shank, M., and Leal, D. (1995). *Exceptional lives: Special education in today's schools.* Columbus, OH: Merrill.

U.S. Department of Education. (1992). Fourteenth annual report to Congress on the implementation of the Education of the Handicapped Act. Washington, DC: Office of Special Education, Data Analysis Systems.

Uzgiris, I. C., and Hunt, J. (1975). *Assessment in infancy: Ordinal scales of psychological development.* Urbana, IL: University of Illinois Press.

van Dijk, J. (1966). The first steps of the deaf-blind child towards language. *Journal of Education of the Blind,* 114–122.

van Dijk, J. (1986). An educational curriculum for deaf-blind multi-disabilities persons. In D. Ellis (Ed.), *Sensory impairments in mentally disabilities people* (pp. 374–382). San Diego: College-Hill Press.

Vulpe, S. G. (1977). *Vulpe assessment battery.* Toronto, Ontario, Canada: National Institute on Mental Retardation.

Ward, M. J., and Zambone, A. M. (1992). The U.S. federal data-collection process for children and youths who are deaf-blind. *Journal of Visual Impairment and Blindness, 86,* 429–435.

Ward, M. E. (1986). The visual system. In G. Scholl (Ed.), *Foundations of education for blind and visually disabilities children and youth: Theory and practice,* (pp. 35–64). New York: American Foundation for the Blind.

Warren, D. (1985). *Blindness and early childhood development.* New York: American Foundation for the Blind.

Westling, D. L., and Fox, L. (1995). *Teaching students with severe disabilities.* Columbus, OH: Merrill.

Wolf, E., and Harkins, J. E. (1986). Multihandicapped students. In A. N. Schildroth and M. A. Karchmer (Eds.), *Deaf children in America* (pp. 55–83). San Diego: College-Hill Press.

Wolf, E., Delk, M., and Schein, J. (1982). *Needs assessment of services to deaf-blind individuals.* Final report to the U.S. Department of Education.

Chapter 9

PARENT AND FAMILY ISSUES

ANNE Y. GALLEGOS

The family has been described as one of the most resilient systems in the world. The birth of a child can have a significant effect on the dynamics of a family. However, it has been noted that families of children who have disabilities are often faced with a unique set of challenges. Where a severe disability exists, the effects of resultant stress and increased need for support may be profound (Hallahan and Kauffman, 1994). Because of the extensive involvement of parents and other family members in the daily lives of a child with a disability, and because of the provisions for parent involvement mandated by the Individuals with Disabilities Education Act (IDEA), the role of the family and its needs must be given serious consideration. In this chapter several topics related to the characteristics and roles of parents and families of children with severe disabilities will be explored. These topics include: (a) historical and legislative perspective, (b) characteristics of parents and families of children with severe disabilities, (c) need for support from the school and community, (d) considerations related to involving parents, and (e) methods for involving parents in school activities.

HISTORICAL AND LEGISLATIVE PERSPECTIVE

According to Knoblock (1987), the history of disability in America is related to social, economic, and political events. During early colonial times, families were characterized by their economic capacity. The presence of a disabled member indicated an impaired ability to work. Because schooling was available mainly to the rich, families who had a weakened member were often poor and undereducated. During the seventeenth century, families with a child with a disability were seen as a unit, so that their inability to function fully was not perceived as the fault of the one, lone member.

183

Knoblock (1987) points out that throughout the eighteenth century, many cities and towns created almshouses for the disabled and poor. These almshouses became warehouses for the physically and mentally disabled, so that other family members could work and contribute their share to the common responsibility. Whereas in the previous century, families were perceived of holistically, in the eighteenth century they were sometimes split apart for cost-efficiency.

During the nineteenth century, the states and other outside authorities began to assume a greater role in families' lives (Turnbull and Turnbull, 1990). Various fields of professionalism were developed as a means of guiding and reforming parental practice. From the perspective of the new educators and psychologists, families were blamed for creating disabilities out of both moral and biological inadequacies. The solution in the nineteenth century, then, became one of removing the innocent disabled children from their homes, and placing them in asylums and residential schools.

According to Turnbull and Turnbull (1990), the eugenics movement (1880–1930) contributed greatly to the notion that parents were the source of a child's disability. The movement, which sought to link heredity to either strength or weakness in offspring, resulted in restrictive laws related to marriage between persons with intellectual abilities, compulsory sterilization, and increased institutionalization. The tradition of paid caretakers displacing parents of children with disabilities became more widespread in the twentieth century. Families were encouraged to rely upon the expertise of medical, social, psychological, and educational professionals rather than on their own abilities to overcome special problems.

Especially since World War II, both medical and political models for remediation have been adopted. In the decades since 1960 increasingly, federal, state, and local governments have become involved in mandating the type and extent of services that must be provided persons with disabilities, both in society in general, and in schools specifically.

In 1973, Congress enacted Section 504 of the Vocational Rehabilitation Act. Section 504 is a civil rights act for persons with disabilities prohibiting the recipient of federal funds, such as schools, from discriminating on the basis of disability. Based on the need for more detailed legislation, Congress passed the Education for All Handicapped Children Act (P.L. 94-142) in 1975. That law (later amended to be called the Individuals with Disabilities Education Act, or IDEA) outlined a basis for family involvement in the education of disabled children, especially in the areas of assessment, due process, placement and programming efforts. The law stipulated that each state must:

(1) Make available a free, appropriate public education to all handicapped children between the ages of three and twenty-one.

(2) Locate and identify all children who have disabilities, evaluate their educational needs, and determine whether those needs are being met.

(3) Develop an Individualized Education Program (IEP) for every child with a disability in the state.

(4) Submit to the federal government a state plan for the education of children with disabilities, and revise the state plan yearly.

(5) Describe the means by which those children will be identified and referred for diagnosis.

(6) Avoid using racially or culturally discriminatory testing and evaluation procedures in placing children in special classes and administer tests in the children's native language.

(7) Protect the rights of children with disabilities and their parents by ensuring due process, confidentiality of records, and parental involvement in educational planning and placement decisions.

(8) Provide a comprehensive system for personal development, including in-service training programs for regular education teachers, special education teachers, school administrators, and other support personnel.

(9) Educate children with and without disabilities together to the maximum extent that is appropriate. Children who are disabled will be placed in special classes or separate schools only when education cannot be achieved satisfactorily in regular classes, even with special aids and services.

P.L. 94-142 was amended in 1986 (Part H), to include provision of services to infants and toddlers and their families. While the regulations apply to children from birth to three years, the basic approach to individualization and appropriateness are similar. Probably the most striking difference between P.L. 94-142 and P.L. 99-457 is the inclusion of the Individual Family Service Plan (IFSP) rather than an IEP. According to the amendment, the IFSP must:

(1) Be developed by the family and appropriate qualified providers of early intervention services.

(2) Be based on the multi-disciplinary evaluation and assessment of the child and the assessment of the family; and

(3) Include the services that are necessary to enhance the child's development and the family's capacity to meet the child's special needs (Hallahan and Kauffman).

The 1990 passage of the Americans with Disabilities Act (ADA), P.L.

101-336, extends the principles introduced in P.L. 94-142 by mandating civil rights protection for *all* individuals with disabilities. ADA specifies that private employers, telecommunication carriers, public services and accommodations, and transportation systems cannot exclude services to persons because of their disability. Therefore, successful transitions for special education students into community life should be more accessible, and stress on families of older children with severe disabilities possibly decreased (Meyen and Skrtic, 1995).

In summary, the history of family involvement in the lives of their children with disabilities has changed from century to century in the United States. Whereas at one time families were perceived as characteristic units, by the twentieth century, individual members had been singled out for observation and treatment. Based on current political, economic, and social thought, families of persons with disabilities are presently provided a variety of services through the community and school, and are included in decision-making processes as specified by law.

CHARACTERISTICS OF PARENTS AND FAMILIES OF CHILDREN WITH SEVERE DISABILITIES

Reaction to a Disability

The birth of a child with a disability into a family is certain to impact both individual family members and the system as a whole. Various authors (Baca and Cervantes, 1989; Drotar, Baskiewicz, Irvin, Kennell, and Klaus, 1975; Marion, 1981) have traditionally described the reactions of parents to such a birth as including projection of blame, guilt, denial, sorrow/grief/mourning, withdrawal, and rejection. Recently authorities have begun to question the notion of the "stage approach" to understanding parental reactions. According to Turnbull and Turnbull (1990), while parents often struggle with questions related to diagnosis, causation and remediation, every family is different and will react out of its own set of needs and strengths. Turnbull, Barber, Kerns, and Behr (1995) have identified three variables which they believe affect the different ways families react to a disability. These are: (a) characteristics of the disability itself; (b) characteristics of the family, including its cultural background and structure; and (c) the collective personal values and coping styles of the family members. According to the authors, the severity of the exceptionality, the adaptations needed to accommodate it, and services readily available to support the child and family members define the "acceptability" of the disability. Cultural background may also influence a family's reaction to the birth of a child with a disability. Understanding of child development, family roles and responsibilities and religious beliefs are aspects of culture which may impact both the perceptions of a disability and willingness to be involved in his education (Meyen and Skrtic). Family size, economics, and cohesion also affect the way in which it accommodates a disabled member. Finally, family values, goals, available support systems, and interactive strengths (between spouses, siblings, parents, and children) additionally impact the way in which a family will adjust to the birth of a child with a disability.

Effects of Stress on Families

All families who have children with severe disabilities experience circumstances which create unusual stress. Lutzker and Campbell (1994) have discussed the tensions which arise as a result of dealing not only with the pressures that face every family in American society, but additionally, those that come with raising a child with a disability. The authors have named such factors as the age of the child and his/her diagnostic category as significant stressors. They have contended that as age increases, the child may become more difficult to manage, and more noticeably different than his peers. They additionally suggested that parents of children in certain severe diagnostic categories (autism especially) report more distress, probably due to the temperament, behaviors, health conditions, and care-giving demands of those children.

Other variables which seem to affect the stress experienced by families who have children with severe disabilities include the expectations of the parents regarding the potential of the child; parents' attitudes about their ability to affect change in their and their children's lives; the socioeconomic status of the family—its ability to cope with the extra expenses necessitated by the need for special equipment and medical care; and societal reactions to the appearance and behavior of the child with a disability.

The stress which affects families of children with severe disabilities is not always evenly distributed. For example, it appears at times that parents don't seem to be affected equally by the responsibility of taking care of the child. Much of the research related to reactions and responses of parents of children with disabilities seems to be limited to reports by mothers (Hallahan and Kauffman, 1994). Husbands and fathers who have children with severe impairments reported feeling neglected and uninvolved with activities related to the disabled child (Doyle, Goodman, Grotsky, and Mann, 1979). While Beckman (1991) noted that mothers of children with developmental disabilities suffer from depression more often than mothers of nondisabled children, Krauss (1993) stated that fathers in his study reported stress related to their children's temperaments.

Turnbull and Turnbull (1990) have pointed out that siblings who have brothers and sisters with severe disabilities may resent the amount of time and resources parents invest in the disabled child. Marion (1981) stressed the need for siblings to be well informed about the disability of the brother or sister, and to be allowed to discuss feelings of anger or guilt. The authors suggested that the school might take an active role in the development of instructional units through which nondisabled siblings might interact with one another, reflect on their roles in the family, and formulate questions for discussions as one means of promoting sibling involvement.

The model, based on a Family Systems Approach, bases its services on the premise that *all* parts of the family are interrelated and therefore, must be addressed. In summary, it must be recognized that when a child with a disability is born into a family, a variety of factors affect the feelings, attitudes, and reactions of individual family members, and interaction in the unit as a whole. The characteristics of both the child and his/her family influence the directions the family takes and the nature and extent of the support it requires.

THE NEED FOR SUPPORT BY FAMILIES OF CHILDREN WITH SEVERE DISABILITIES

When a child with disabilities is born into a family, the challenge is to find ways to structure human interactions and attachments so that support is provided to those who are in need and so resources may be exchanged (Gottleib, 1981). This support might be social, professional, legal, or practical.

Social Support

Cobb (1976) described social support as information leading a person to believe he/she is: (a) cared for and loved, (b) esteemed and valued, and (c) part of a network of mutual communication and obligation. According to Cobb (1976), this support is generally derived from family, friends, and individuals in the helping professions, and may engender better morale, reduce complaints, and lessen depression. Dunst, Trivette, and Deal (1988) have described a social support systems approach as one which focuses on informal sources of support such as friends, neighbors and extended family. It additionally focuses on helping families help themselves by encouraging the family to accept responsibility for setting and achieving needed goals. With this approach, the family, not a professional, assume the primary decision-making role (Hallahan and Kauffman, 1994).

Professional Support

Professional support for the parents who have children with severe handicaps most often comes through medical or educational channels. Families with a child with a disability generally spend far more time consulting with professionals in these areas than do parents of children without disabilities. When disabilities are apparent at birth, it is essential that the hospital or physician in charge explain to the family what it may expect and whom they may contact for further information and assistance (Schleifer, 1981). Family doctors, dentists, visiting nurses, health aides, medical equipment outlets, and specialists may need to be recommended.

Families that have children with severe disabilities also need to become aware of the importance of early educational intervention (Turnbull and Turnbull, 1990). They need to be provided with information related to physical, social-emotional, and cognitive development of their child, so that they can both provide stimulation at home, as well as seek out a program designed for infant or early childhood development. With the advent of early childhood legislation, at birth parents may become familiarized with procedures for identification and placement of children in special education in public and private schools and residential programs. Teachers, administrators, counselors, and diagnosticians should not only provide information related to the family's legal educational rights, but also discuss with the family possible alternatives for programming which meet the needs of the student and address the concerns of the parents at every stage of their child's development.

Legal Support

Legal support for parents of severely disabled children may involve providing them with information related to financial concerns or to concerns of planning and documentation. Financially, families may need assistance in obtaining aid for the considerable costs of hospitalization, doctor visits, therapies, equipment, and medication that usually are required. Even income tax deductions may need to be explained (Doyle, Goodman, Grotsky, and Mann, 1979).

The transition out of the home and into adult life can be stressful. Employment, supported living arrangements, and information related to guardianship, wills and trusts, life insurance, and social security is critical. The local chapter of the Association for Retarded Citizens, or the Council for Exceptional Children should be able to help, as should the Legal Aid Society, and special education divisions of local public schools and nearby universities.

Practical Support

Many parents who have children with severe disabilities seek assistance with problems associated with day-to-day caretaking. Their questions typically relate to concerns such as feeding, dressing, hygiene, toilet training, mobility and communication, and the answers they seek are practical ones. Often, the support these parents need may come from books or articles, community or school training sessions, or from other parents.

In summary, parents with children with severe disabilities need an immense amount of support. Family and friends, social service agencies, medical experts, educational personnel, lawyers, library literature, and parent groups are all valuable sources of assistance. It is important that persons involved in providing services to these families not only understand the nature of their needs, but be informed and provided information about resources available.

CONSIDERATIONS RELATED TO INVOLVING PARENTS IN THEIR CHILDREN'S EDUCATION

Because the family who has a child with a severe disability requires extensive support, and because by law and in practice much of that support comes from the education system, it is important to consider the interaction between the family and the school. Most educational systems encourage their personnel to involve parents of children with disabilities. In addition to the law, there exists a solid rationale for that involvement. There also exist several concerns regarding parent involvement that the school must consider before planning an approach.

Rationale for Parent Involvement

Involving parents in the education of their child with disabilities makes sense, because it is the parent who spends the most time, especially in the early years, with the child. That is the time, according to Benjamin Bloom (1964), when the greatest amount of intellectual development takes place. Studies by Bloom indicated that in terms of intelligence measured at age seventeen, about 50 percent of that develops between conception and age four, about 30 percent between ages four and eight, and about 20 percent between ages eight and seventeen. Bloom's findings support the contention that the quality and nature of early learning experience have an affect on the child's long-term development. Two conclusions may be drawn here: (a) that because parents are actively involved with their child at a critical time in his/her development, they are most likely to understand the child's personality, habits, preferences, etc.; and (b) that interaction between home and school at the earliest possible time is critical, so that the greatest amount of support and stimulation may be provided the child and the family as he/she develops.

Along similar lines, it has been said that family background plays a profound role in the development of achievement, not only through the social and economic well-being of the family, but through the values its members hold with regard to education, and the activities that parents and parental surrogates engage in with their children to make these values operational (Mayeski, 1973). Parents have been seen as agents for increasing children's progress and achievement. The notion that parents *can* be effective teachers is often translated by many professionals to mean that they *should* be (Turnbull and Turnbull, 1990).

It appears, then, that the informal education that families provide for their children makes a tremendous impact. The means by which parents solve problems with regard to language, discipline, locomotor ability, and social development provide the child with an identity and create a basis for both the personality of the school-aged child and the nature of the contribution the family makes to the educational process. It is to the advantage of educators to understand and draw from the family's position and from its experience as teacher, care giver and decision maker (Morrison, 1978).

Concerns Regarding Parent Involvement

Prior to designing strategies for involving parents who have children with severe disabilities in the education of their child, these parents must be considered in terms of several factors that may influence the nature and extent of their involvement: parents' perception of schooling, linguistic and cultural background, and socioeconomic status.

Parents' Perception of Schooling

Gallegos and Gallegos (1987) reported that some parents have perceptions of schooling that prevent them from extensive involvement in the education of their children with disabilities. Parents who did not complete high school, or who had some difficulty in school, are not as likely to feel comfortable in school involvement projects, although these parents were satisfied with the school's role. In taped interviews, parents in the study reported feeling that teachers and principals were the primary decision makers in a child's education, and that they, as parents, were comfortable with that process. Meyers and Blacker (1987) wrote that, in a study conducted with parents who have preschoolers with severe disabilities, despite degree of active involvement with the school, the majority of parents were satisfied with the direction of the school. The implications from each of these studies seem to be that because of their own circumstances and background, some parents are not comfortable with or able to be involved in school activities, but they are nonetheless supportive of the school's function. These parents, then, may not actively participate in school activities, but expect and appreciate the school's efforts.

Linguistic and Sociocultural Background

According to Harry, Allen, and McLaughlin (1995) sociocultural differences in family life and the ways in which the schools respond to these differences result in a pattern of almost total separation of family life from the process of schooling in many instances. Social network patterns and child socialization networks, including kinship roles and the predominance of informal family-related activities which characterize certain ethnic groups, are less likely to include in their realm a formal relationship with the school. It has also noted that where sociocultural familiar patterns lie strongly outside the school, educators frequently perceive parents as being unwilling, or passive rather than active participants. Many teachers seem to perceive that the primary functions of parent involvement are to improve school attendance, discipline, and attitudes toward teachers and schools. This perception along with the notion that parents need to change to fit the school's image, may conflict with the need for educators to understand the family and community from its perspective and work within that context.

Public Law 94-142 mandated the need to communicate with families of the disabled in the language of their home. The implication here is that understanding which language is used, and in what context(s), is critical for determining the language of instruction for the child, and for deciding how best to approach and communicate with family members. Gallegos and Gallegos found, too, that letting parents choose the language for interaction influences positively the comfort and depth with which conversation takes place.

Socioeconomic Status

According to studies cited in Ovando and Collier (1985), it appears that middle class parents establish a stronger partnership with school than do working class families. The authors stated that middle class families tend to be more socially and geographically mobile, more isolated from relatives, and more dependent on school relationships than are lower class families. Also, the authors noted a greater consistency between the goals, methods, expectations, and languages of the middle class parents and schools than with working class parents. Finally, Ovando and Collier noted that teachers often attribute parents of middle class children with a higher level of interest in their children's education, though it seems that a lack of understanding of lower socioeconomic lifestyles, patterns, and values has contributed to a possible misperception.

KOREAN–AMERICAN FAMILIES OF CHILDREN WITH DISABILITIES: PERSPECTIVES AND IMPLICATIONS FOR PRACTITIONERS

Hyun-Sook Park

Introduction

A partnership between parents and schools has long been regarded as essential in the education of students with disabilities (Kroth, 1987). As our schools serve more students from culturally and linguistically different backgrounds, it is inevitable that teachers and other professionals will deal with diverse cultures which are often unfamiliar to them. In such cases, parents and families can become valuable resources to teachers and other professionals in conducting culturally sensitive educational assessment and developing programs.

Despite the importance of family involvement, however, professionals have failed to establish a successful partnership with families from nonmainstream cultural backgrounds (Delgado-Gaitan, 1991; Finders & Lewis, 1994). This is probably because these families may have not responded to the traditional methods for establishing family-school partnerships (Harry, 1993; Taylor-Gibbs & Nahme-Huang, 1989). Our current programs to involve parents have targeted mainly English-speaking, middle-class families (Lynch & Stein, 1987; Salend & Taylor, 1993). Harry (1993) found that parents from culturally diverse backgrounds possessed cultural perspectives and expectations that were different from mainstream families, which prevented them from collaborating with educational professionals. Fortunately, literature dealing with perspectives of families from diverse cultural backgrounds has begun to appear (e.g., Heller, Markwardt, Rowitz, & Farber, 1994; Shapiro & Simonsen, 1994).

Yet there is little information available on the families of Korean-American students with disabilities. Ironically, Korean-American families and students have received fair amount of attention as model immigrants and high achievers. On the other hand, Korean-American students with disabilities have been obscured by this well-publicized stereotype. Professionals, including teachers, need to have a better understanding of the Korean-American families of children with disabilities if they are to provide better service and education to such children.

The following section discusses information that will help professionals understand better where Korean-American families come from when dealing with the educational system in the U.S. And it will primarily focus on recently immigrated Korean-American families and their children. However, this section, by no means, characterizes all Korean-Americans or their families. Rather the information should serve as background information which may help professionals seek explanations of certain behaviors in Korean-American families (Park & Yount, 1994). In other words, professionals should view the following cultural perspectives as a set of frameworks that families may apply when interacting with others (Anderson & Fenichel, 1989; Salend & Taylor, 1993). In addition, implications for teachers and professionals are described.

CULTURAL TRADITION AND DISABILITY

Confucian values are among the cultural traditions that may affect perceptions and behaviors of many Korean-American families both toward a disability and toward their participation in the education of their children with disabilities. The following section discusses the influences of confucian values on the families and its implications for professionals, including teachers.

Confucian Values

Description

Confucian values are the principles observed in Confucianism, which developed from the teaching of Confucius (551–479 B.C.) and his disciples in China. Confucianism is concerned with principles of good conduct, practical wisdom, and proper social relationships (Yutang, 1994). This system of thought influenced people's attitude toward life and set the standard of social values and social order from China to Korea, Japan, and Indochina (Lee, 1993). Confucianism is not considered a religion, but is a philosophy and ideology (Lee, 1993; Wright, 1964). The principles of Confucianism are explained in the nine ancient Chinese works handed down by Confucius and his disciples. Confucian virtues include love (or translated as humanity), righteousness, propriety, integrity, and filial piety (Yutang, 1994). These virtues set a system of well-defined social relationships with one another.

> These mean love in the parents, filial piety in the children, respect in the younger brother, friendliness in the elder brothers, loyalty among friends, respect for authority among subjects, and benevolence in the rulers (Yutang, 1994, pp. 209).

A person who observes these social rules is supposed to do everything with "propriety." A person who possesses all these virtues becomes a "perfect gentleman" who achieved a perfect balance in life. The "perfect gentleman" is also supposed to achieve the "universal moral order" (Chung-yung), usually translated as "the Mean." Chung-yung places an entire "harmony" in the life of a "perfect gentleman" who finds the true central harmony and balance in his moral being (Yutang, 1994). In education, Confucius advocated "education for all without class distinction," which is remarkable for the feudal period in which he lived (Yutang, 1994).

Influences and Implications

Influenced by these Confucian virtues (social rules), many Koreans follow strict social and behavioral codes when interacting with others. These social rules are defined by a person's gender, age, and relative status. For example, a person who observes the Confucian social rules would first identify his/her position in relation to another person considering gender, age, and status. For example, a person would ask the following questions: Who is the authority figure? "Who is older?" "Is there difference in gender?" Then a person would behave strictly according to the proper rules assigned to the structure of the relationship (cf, Fiske, 1992). For example, a person would interact with an authority figure with respect and with no confrontation. He/she may not give eye contact because eye contact is considered a sign of disrespect.

It is common for many Korean-American parents of children with disabilities to follow the behavioral code given in the example above when they interact with professionals because they would regard the professionals as authority figures. They may be reluctant to express their disagreement because they consider disagreement as disrespectful confrontation. Their best purpose is to show respect and to preserve the harmony in the relationships. Therefore, it might be necessary for the professional to state that it is acceptable for the parents to express their disagreement. The professionals may also ask questions to the parents rather than expecting them to ask. It would be also important for professionals to create nonintimidating, yet respectful environments in order to encourage parents to share their input into educational programming. Professionals may ask the parents if they prefer to be addressed as Mr. ____ or Mrs. ____ rather than as their first names. In addition, using basic social phrases in Korean such as "hello" and "thank you" would serve as ice breakers and may make the parents feel less intimidated.

In addition, Confucianism mandates that Koreans retain strong ties with families and extended families. Kinship and extended families can serve as strong support networks to families of children with disabilities. On the same token, however, Park (1995) found, in her ethnographic interviews with three Korean-American families, that immigrant families of children with disabilities who did not have extended family members in the U.S. experienced more social stress than those families with extended family members in their communities. In addition, people experienced more severe social stress when they did not receive enough support from their own family members, particularly when the fathers of children with disabilities did not provide such support. Confucianism mandates distinct gender roles within the family. Therefore, the mothers of children with disabilities bear the whole responsibility for educating such children. Korean-American mothers in these situations may experience more frustration when they do not have access to the external resources available due to the cultural and language barriers (Park, 1995). Similar findings on greater stress level with Latino immigrant families have been made (Heller, Markwardt, Rowitz, & Farber, 1994).

A large number of Korean-American families expand their circles of extended families beyond their kinship and relatives, through participation in community organizations (e.g., church). However, these community organizations have not taken leadership roles in providing resources to families with disabilities. Professionals may need to utilize these community organizations more effectively. For example, professionals may provide in-service training to the community organizations in order to connect families with more resources. Teachers may include relevant members of these organizations as well as family members and significant relatives when developing an educational plan (e.g., by interviewing significant members for input and including them in the intervention plan for social-relationship building).

EXPECTATIONS FOR EDUCATION AND SOCIAL RELATIONSHIPS OF CHILDREN WITH DISABILITIES

Although many Korean-American families have high academic expectations for their children's education, the families of children with disabilities were found to have realistic views toward their children's education (Park, 1992; Cho, 1993). When they were asked about their preferences in school curricular areas, most of these families responded that functional life skills were more important than academic skills. This pattern of parental preference was parallel to findings by Hamre-Nieptuski, Nieptuski, and Strathe (1992) who surveyed Caucasian families of children with severe disabilities. In addition, Korean-American parents of lower-grade elementary school children emphasized social goals rather than academic goals as a second priority to functional skills, whereas parents with such children in upper grade levels considered academic goals as the second most important priority (Park, 1992). Korean-American parents of children with disabilities were also found to expect their children to work as hard as children without disabilities (Cho, 1993). This conflicts with Chan's (1986) previous findings that Asian parents were more permissive and had low expectations for children with disabilities. This incongruence implies that professionals may need to be cautious when attempting to apply the findings of studies with Asian families to Korean-American families.

Many Korean-American parents seem to expect their children to have friends both with and without disabilities (Cho, 1993; Park, 1995). They expect their children to have as many friends as possible to help the children socialize better and prepare them for future normalized environments. This provides important implications for teachers when facilitating socialization for Korean students with disabilities. Teachers may need to consider facilitation of various types of socialization including children with and without disabilities. Our profession has paid too much attention to friendships only between children with disabilities and those without disabilities despite the fact that some children with disabilities develop valuable friendships with peers with disabilities (Park & Harry, in press).

In addition, Korean-American children with disabilities seemed to develop their friendships with nondisabled peers at churches while developing friendships with peers with disabilities at schools (Cho, 1993; Park, 1995). Therefore, it seems that churches can provide normalized social opportunities for some Korean-American children. This finding provides teachers and other professionals with valuable implications when developing a plan for social opportunities for a Korean-American child with his/her families. Teachers and other professionals may need to encourage families who attend churches to utilize the environment for outside-of-school social opportunities for their children with disabilities. This may be practical because the families do not then need to seek the often unfamiliar social clubs, which are designed mostly for mainstream English-speaking families and take extra time away from their work and other responsibilities.

PARTICIPATION IN EDUCATIONAL SYSTEMS

Many Korean-American families of children with disabilities agree that there are more services and educational opportunities available in the U.S. than in Korea for their children with disabilities (Cho, 1993; Park, 1995). Many Korean-American families state that they immigrated to the U.S. for their children's education. Yet, their participation in the educational services seems very limited mainly because of cultural and language barriers (Cho, 1993; Park, 1995). Another reason for not participating in the service system includes lack of time due to inflexible and long work hours and other responsibilities (Cho, 1993; Park, 1995). These findings, however, do not agree with previous findings in this area with other Asian-American families. The reasons explained in the previous studies were the stigma attached to accepting services, emphasis on self-control, and subordination of self (Ishisaka, Nguyen, & Okimoto, 1985; Kinzie, 1985; Owan, 1985; Tung, 1985).

This new finding provides an important implication for the planning and coordination of services for Korean-American families. More practical assistance and considerations should be made. For example, agencies may provide child care during meetings. There is a need to train more direct professionals to work closely with families to empower families by sharing information and resources. These professionals may include case managers, teachers, or parent advocacy group coordinators. It is more culturally appropriate and practical for professionals individually to converse with Korean parents about their children rather than having the parents participate in support group meetings or seminars.

Korean-American parents may have different expectations for professionals than other mainstream English-speaking families. They may expect the professionals to provide guidance in helping their child's education. When information is shared by the professionals, they are more likely to implement the educational strategies and pursue the services more actively. In fact, some Korean-American families said that they wanted teachers to tell them what to do at home in order to help their children's progress (Cho, 1993; Park, 1995). Teachers may need to work closely with Korean-American families in order to facilitate the generalization and maintenance of appropriate skills taught to students.

TOWARD UNBIASED COLLABORATION

Although the information discussed so far helps professionals better understand the families of Korean-American children with disabilities and facilitates collaboration with such families, there is a need for a framework to which professionals can refer when working with these families. The following guidelines are to serve that purpose (refer to Table XIII). These guidelines should be helpful to professionals working with families from other different cultural backgrounds as well as with Korean-American families.

Step 1. Be familiar with information related to the culture, but only use it as background information.

Some behavioral codes and communication styles related to a particular culture (e.g., Korean culture) play important roles in helping professionals stay open-minded when encountering behaviors that are not common to the mainstream culture. However, never use such behavioral codes and communication styles as a universal approach to all people fitting a certain profile. Judge each person as an individual.

Step 2. Begin communicating with the families.

In discussions with families, ask direct questions rather than expecting the families to ask. This is the best way to obtain unbiased and valid input from the families. Explore explanations for their decisions and input. Respect their reasons and decisions. Acknowledge that you heard the information they provided.

TABLE XIII
STEPS INVOLVED IN THE UNBIASED COLLABORATION
PROCESS WITH CROSS–CULTURAL FAMILIES.

Step 1.   Be familiar with information related to the culture, but only use it as background information.

↓

Step 2.   Begin communicating with the families.

↓

Step 3.   Identify their world view using a model by Sue (1981).

↓

Step 4.   Identify barriers and solutions together with families.

↓

Step 5.   Keep communication channels with families open.

Step 3. Identify their world view using a model by Sue (1981).

The world view model helps one to understand how an individual thinks and behaves in making decisions and interpreting events. This world view consists of attitude, value, and opinions, and it is influenced by cultural heritage, life experiences, socioeconomic factors, religious belief, and gender. Sue's world view model (1981) consists of two psychological orientations: locus of control (C) and locus of responsibility (R). Each orientation has two directions of force: internal (I) and external (E) force. Therefore, there are four different types of world views when combining two orientations with two different directions of force (2 × 2 = 4): internal locus of control-internal locus of responsibility (IC–IR); internal locus of control-external locus of responsibility (IC–ER); external locus of control—internal locus of responsibility (EC–IR); and external locus of control—external locus of responsibility (EC–ER). Individuals who have an IC–IR world view believe that success is the result of their own efforts and have a strong sense of control over what happens. These individuals rely heavily on personal resources for solving problems. While many western cultures encourage this type of world view, it is not surprising to see someone from Korea has this type of world view also. For example, Changho's family has been very active utilizing community resources (e.g., church) and available support network (e.g., relatives) to help Changho participate in a normalized environment as much as possible. They believe that what they do for Changho will make a difference in his life. They have a very positive view for Changho.

Individuals with an IC–ER world view realize that they are able to affect their children's lives if given a chance. They are well aware that external barriers such as discrimination, or prejudice might still hinder their ability to succeed. Therefore, they do not participate in their children's education. For example, Soojin's parents clearly see the value of getting more involved in the educational process and they want to do so. However, they have not previously participated because they felt they did not have enough of a support system in their lives (e.g., lack of support from family). But they hope to get involved in the process in the future, which might never be possible. They tend to blame external sources rather than themselves for their lack of participation.

Individuals with an EC–IR world view accept the dominant culture's definition of self-responsibility, but do not have any control over what is happening around them. These individuals live on the margins of two cultures, not freely partaking of either (Sue, 1981). For example, Jemin's parents understand that it is their responsibility to use services and to participate in the educational process for the sake of their child's welfare. However, they are not motivated to do so probably because of their unsuccessful past experiences. They hope to regain confidence and actively participate in the system, but they are waiting to be motivated by somebody else. They take full responsibility for the outcome. They may not be aware of external barriers that can be removed so that their participation can be more easily made and successful. They are frustrated with themselves for not overcoming the difficulties. They may be too harsh on themselves.

Individuals with an EC–ER world view feel that they have no control over what is happening and feel that such obstacles are not their responsibility either. They feel helpless. For example, Tesoo's family has low self-confidence, and they do not take any responsibility either. They feel that they are the victims of the system.

Professionals can identify the world view that the families have by asking questions related to their experiences about the educational system. Examples of the questions include: What are the things you have tried in terms of working with schools? What were the outcomes? How did you feel about the outcome? Why? How do you perceive yourself participating in your child's education? What kinds of things can you think of doing? Why?

Step 4. Identify barriers and solutions together with families.

Once professionals understand how families view their participation in their children's education and their world view, they need to identify what are the barriers that prevent the families from actively participating in the education of their child. Each world view might suggest different types of solutions and collaborations. The types of solutions may vary depending on the kind of barriers that the families identify. If we take the families mentioned above as examples, professionals may only share related information with Changho' family and may not need any substantial follow-up with them. Soojin's family, on the other hand, may need tangible supports such as linking them with other community resources where they can utilize child-care services during meetings. With Jemin's parents, professionals probably need to convince the families that external variables, not the parents themselves, may be responsible for the unsuccessful experiences. They may want to identify the barriers as an initial task. Then, they can either provide tangible support if identified, or they can start with concrete action that is feasible and has a high probability of leading to success. For Tesoo's family, professionals may share many successful stories of children of similar functioning levels and may focus on simple and concrete activities that would lead to success. It is often valuable for teachers to invite parents to the school and have them observe their children performing tasks that they might never have thought the children could do. In this way, the families can gain confidence and be motivated to continue the participation. At times, it might be necessary for professionals to refer the families to other professionals or networks in order to provide tangible support.

Step 5. Keep communication channels with families open.

Professionals need to send a clear message to families that their feedback and input are always welcome and appreciated. Communication channels should be always open throughout the collaborating process even after the solution is implemented. The following communication tips are derived from the literature (Anderson & Fenichel, 1989; Brower, 1986; Finders & Lewis, 1994; Gallegos & Gallegos, 1988; LaFromboise, Graff & Low, 1989; Nagata, 1989; Ramirez, 1989; Salend & Taylor, 1993) and from the ethnographic interviews by Park (1995):

(1) Greet family in its native language, if possible.
(2) Address parents by Mr. ____ or Mrs. ____.
(3) Arrange seating so that everyone is in close proximity to everyone else (e.g., a round table is better than a rectangle table).
(4) Respect the thoughts of the parents.
(5) Be patient.
(6) Allow enough time for parents and family members to express themselves openly and freely.
(7) Provide, when necessary, an interpreter who understands the family's culture and needs (e.g., an individual from the same community as the family). Avoid asking young children to translate for their parents. It may create dysfunction within the family hierarchy.
(8) Use humor and share with your own similar experiences to establish trust and personal relationships.
(9) Don't be afraid to ask questions.
(10) State what you expect of the parents.
(11) State what you expect of the child.
(12) Realize the parents live with the child and can't go home at the end of day.
(13) Avoid the standard cliches such as "I understand how you feel," "What I hear you saying is....," or "This must be difficult for you but..."
(14) Provide a structure for the meeting and explain the agenda.
(15) Agree on the goals.
(16) Define roles.
(17) Meet parents on their own level and treat them with respect.
(18) Be sensitive to parents and have a working knowledge of the grief cycle.

(19) Accept your own feelings and limitations when working with parents and their children with disabilities.
(20) Recognize that parents are experts about their children.
(21) Take into consideration of family activities and home experiences when developing programs.

Endnote: This writer wishes to thank the Korean-American families who participated in the study. This writer also wishes to thank Beth Harry for her input into the analysis and interpretation of the ethnographic interviews with the families. This work was supported in part by Cooperative Agreement No. H086A20003, the consortium for Collaborative Research on Social Relationships, awarded to Syracuse University, by the U.S. Department of Education, Office of Special Education Programs. However, the opinions expressed herein are not necessarily those of the Department of Education, and no official endorsement should be inferred.

METHODS FOR INVOLVING PARENTS IN SCHOOL ACTIVITIES

Given the desirability of including parents of children with severe disabilities in the education of their children, and taking into consideration the unique needs of certain groups of parents, the question becomes how to achieve maximum and quality involvement.

There are two basic forms of parent involvement, direct and indirect. Direct involvement includes the active interaction between parents and the school, whereas in indirect involvement parents are basically passive recipients of information regarding school functions.

Direct Involvement

In addition to the parents' inclusion in the assessment, placement, and program processes in special education, direct parental involvement may also involve participation in training programs, parent conferences, home visits, and the use of parents as volunteers in the classroom.

Training Programs

With regard to designing parent training programs. Gaylord-Ross and Holovet (1985) have stated that professionals should build on roles that parents already carry out. According to those authors, programs should relate to areas of concern to parents as they fulfill their caretaker roles (e.g., self-help, discipline, skill-building, etc.).

In describing the development of a training program for parents of preschool children with disabilities, Sandler, Coren, and Thurman (1986) noted that since parents often consider data collection as complex and burdensome, data keeping in training programs should be kept simple and minimal. Wallar and Goldman (1979) have described successful parent training programs as including time for modeling and rehearsal of techniques being taught, provisions for direct parental involvement with problem identification and goal setting, and provisions for continued communication and feedback between program personnel and parents. Knoblock has advocated parent training programs being designed so that parents may be trained to develop new behaviors for their roles as caretakers and teachers of their children. The author has stated that these programs may be center-based or home-based, and may utilize manuals or other training materials which relate to the teaching of self-help, communication, academic, or coping skills.

Knoblock has also pointed out that educators need to be aware that there are problems associated with the program training approach. The author contended that too often the professional does all the planning of the program—the intent, meeting time and place, allowing for little parent input. Knoblock has noted, too, that low income and minority parents may be unable to attend previously scheduled events, and may find that the language of the presentation is not one they easily understand. Finally, he has insisted that the overall goal of program training should be to empower parents and to involve them in the planning and implementation of the children's education.

Parent Conferences

Hallahan and Kauffman have written of utilizing parent conferences as a teaching strategy. The authors have maintained that parent conferences can result in improved child growth by sensitizing both the home and school to one another's values, expectations, and activities.

The conference is "an individualized, personalized meeting between two or three significant persons in the child's life, with the purpose of accelerating his/her growth" (Kroth and Simpson, 1977, p. 2). Because parents who have children with severe disabilities bring with them many emotions and questions related to these disabilities and their effect on home and school behavior, the educator must be prepared to explore values and feelings and to understand both the nature and the importance of the home environment prior to suggesting a plan for action.

In preparing for the parent conference, the teacher should not only provide for time to listen actively, but should have information ready to give to the parents. This information might include samples of classroom work, samples from a cumulative folder, observational records, and comments from other teachers. The teacher may also wish to seek information from the parents which would supplement school records. This information may take the form of verbal or written observations; it may relate to personal characteristics and preferences of the child at home, family history, medical information and/or work experience of the child.

Concerning parent conferences, Baca and Cervantes (1989) spoke of the importance of providing interpreters where necessary, and understanding that cultural diversity may affect the level of comfort parents feel within the school setting. They summarized the importance of parent contact in stating that parents embody a wealth of resources and that, with the teacher, they form a team which works together for the benefit of the child.

Home Visits

Gaylord-Ross and Holovet stated that at least one visit should be made each year to the homes of families of students with disabilities. The authors have stressed the importance of seeing the family as a systematic unit and, consequently, have encouraged educators to visit homes at a time when both parents and other family members are likely to be in attendance. The authors have also proposed that the home visit should be extensive enough to provide an opportunity for the educator to observe the home environment, family interactions, and schedules.

According to Baca and Cervantes, parents of language minority children may not be accustomed to assisting in an instrumental component with the school, and need to be encouraged to feel that they are indeed important resource persons. Parents of language minority children may need guidance and specific instructional ideas (including, perhaps, demonstrations in the home) so that they become important resource persons indeed, and so that they will be able to perform the role of reinforcers. On the other hand, minority parents need to be recognized for the culturally and linguistically rich environments in which their children are raised, with the school taking information from that setting and integrating it into the school curriculum.

Parents as Volunteers

Parents who have children with severe disabilities can bring a variety of talents to the classroom. They may share their own experience in dealing with handicapping conditions, as well as their experience in areas related to hobbies, cultural activities, and linguistic ability. Parents as volunteers can serve many roles including tutoring, interpreting, preparing materials, maintaining the room, assisting with custodial tasks, supervising children, and working with other parents. Teachers and parents should outline schedules and responsibilities together. Thus teachers and parents can gain information from one another in volunteer situations, and children with disabilities will become the ultimate benefactors.

Indirect Involvement

Sometimes parents are unable to participate directly in school activities. The reasons for lack of active involvement may include conflicting work schedules, lack of transportation, baby-sitting needs, illness, or other demands of home. Additionally, lack of active or direct involvement may be due to perceptions parents have about the role of the school, and about their own roles in the home. Some parents, for example, may see themselves as caretakers not educators. Even if a family is not directly involved in school activities, it is important to maintain a communication system with its members so that both the home and school can be aware of each other's efforts in working with the handicapped child. There are several vehicles by which this information sharing may be accomplished.

In addition to sending home notices inviting families to school functions and attempting other forms of direct involvement, teachers may communicate with parents by sending information home regarding school and class activities. This information may be in the form of newsletters which come from an administrator's office, notes from the teacher, or child-made reports. Newsletters may contain information regarding school/classroom rules, calendars of events, discipline procedures, etc. A handbook made up at the administrative or local level may also serve to inform parents of school expectations. Letters to parents (which might be written by the teacher or children) also serve the purpose of communicating with the home. Hallahan and Kauffman recommend the traveling notebook where parents and professionals can write messages to one another. It is important to remember in sending home printed information, that the language of the home should be utilized. It is also important not to rely totally on print, as some parents do not read. Older children and neighbors may assist in these cases. When working with children who are capable, asking the child to inform his/her family about school activities through conversation, drawings, tape recordings or journals serves the purpose of connecting home and school.

While parents may not be able to come to the school, they may communicate information regarding the home values, routines, family characteristics and opinions, by keeping anecdotal records and sending those to school periodically. They may also utilize the telephone. Finally, parents may share information regarding family life and activities through the child, by allowing him/her to bring in items which reflect culture and tradition, shared experiences, and distinguishing characteristics (pictures of the home, family members, items from celebrations, etc). Of key importance is that contact between the school and home be maintained at whatever level possible so that agreement regarding values and methods for instruction becomes possible.

SUMMARY

Historically, families of children with disabilities have had to face issues regarding their own understanding and acceptance of the disability, and have had to seek assistance for themselves and their children. A variety of social, cultural, economic, legal, and educational variables impact on these families especially when the child is severely disabled.

There are various support systems available to these families through both community and school resources. Informing and involving parents and other family members necessitates a willingness on the part of educators to understand the child's individual needs and strengths, and to work within the context of his/her cultural perspectives and life situations. The family, for its contribution, is able to bring to the school knowledge and experience particular to the child's identity and learning style, so that the collaborative effort benefits the home, the school, community and especially the child.

DISCUSSION QUESTIONS

(1) Discuss the development of family involvement in the education of handicapped children from colonial times into the twentieth century.

(2) What characteristics of families with a disabled member must be taken into consideration prior to planning an involvement program?

(3) What impact does culture appear to have on parent's perceptions of a disability?

(4) Discuss several methods for developing communication between the home and school.

(5) What support systems are available in the local community for families of children with severe disabilities?

(6) How might parents be utilized in planning and conducting relevant counseling and instructional sessions?

(7) How might a large school district serve the needs of parents who speak a wide range of languages?

(8) Recall your own experiences working with families from cultural backgrounds that are different from yours and discuss your own feelings and barriers that you thought hindered your working relationships with those families.

(9) Discuss solutions that could have helped your working relationships with the families you discussed in the previous question.

(10) Share the names and functions of community resources available for different ethnic groups.

(11) Identify which of the Sue world views most resembles yours and discuss what might have influenced the formation of your world view.

(12) Discuss potential barriers that prevent professionals from empowering families with non-mainstream cultural backgrounds.

REFERENCES

Anderson, P. P., and Fenichel, E. S. (1989). *Serving culturally diverse families of infants and toddlers with disabilities*. Washington, DC: National Center for Clinical Infant Programs.

Baca, L. M., and Cervantes, H. T. (1989). *The bilingual special education interface*, Second Edition. Columbus, OH: Merrill.

Beckman, P. (1991). Comparison of mothers' and fathers' perceptions of the effect of young children with and without developmental disabilities. *American Journal on Mental Retardation, 95*, 585–595.

Bloom, B. S. (1964). *Stability and change in human characteristics.* New York: Wiley.

Brower, D. (1986). *The rubber band syndrome: Family life with a child with a disability.* Project Report (ERIC Document Reproduction Service No. ED280255).

Chan, S. (1986). Parents of exceptional Asian children. In M. K. Kitano and P. C. Chinn (Eds.), *Exceptional Asian children and youth* (pp. 36–53). Reston, VA: Council for Exceptional Children and Youth.

Cho, E. M. (1993). *Korean-American parents' attitudes toward their children or youth with disabilities and their education in the U.S.A.* Master's thesis. California State University, Sacramento. Sacramento, CA.

Chung, E. Y. J. (1995). *The Korean Neo-Confucianism of Yi T'oegye and Yi Yulgok: A reappraisal of the "four-seven thesis" and its practical implications for self-cultivation.* Albany: State University of New York Press.

Cobb, S. (1976). Social support as a moderator of life stress. *Psychosomatic Medicine, 38*, p. 300.

Delgado-Gaitan, C. (1991). Involving parents in the schools: A process of empowerment. *American Journal of Education, 100*, 20–46.

Doyle, P. G., Goodman, J. F., Grotsky, J. N., and Mann, L. (1979). *Helping the severely handicapped child: A guide for parents and teachers.* New York: Crowell.

Drotar, D., Baskiewicz, A., Irvin, N., Kennell, J., and Klaus, M. (1975). The adaptation of parents to the birth of an infant with a congenital malformation: A hypothetical model. *Pediatrics, 56*, 710–717.

Dunst, C. J., Trivelte, C. M., and Deal, A. (1988). *Enabling and empowering families.* Cambridge, MA: Brookline.

Finders, M., and Lewis, C. (1994). Why some parents don't come to school. *Educational Leadership,* May, 50–54.

Fiske, A. P. (1992). The four elementary forms of sociality: Framework for a unified theory of social relations. *Psychological Review, 99*, 689–723.

Gallegos, A., and Gallegos, R. (1988). *The interaction between families of culturally diverse handicapped children and the school.* Research/technical report (ERIC Document Reproduction Service No. ED 316 044).

Gallegos, A., and Gallegos, R. (1987). The interaction between families of culturally diverse handicapped children and the school. *Texas Tech Journal of Education.* Lubbock, TX: Texas Tech Press.

Gaylord-Ross, R. J., and Holvoet, J. F. (1985). *Strategies for educating students with severe handicaps.* Boston, MA: Little Brown.

Gottleib, B. H. (Ed.). (1981). *Social networks and social support.* Beverly Hills, CA: Sage.

Hallahan, D. P., and Kauffman, J. M. (1994). *Exceptional children: Introduction to special education,* 6th Ed. Boston: Allyn & Bacon.

Hamre-Nieptuski, S., Nieptuski, J., and Strathe, M. (1992). Functional life skills, academic skills, and friendship/social relationship development: What do parents of students with moderate/severe/profound disabilities value? *The Journal of the Association for Persons with Severe Handicaps, 17,* 53–58.

Harry, B. (1993). *Cultural diversity, families, and the special education system: Communication and empowerment.* New York: Teachers College Press.

Harry, B., Allen, N., and McLaughlin, M. (1995). Communication versus compliance: African American parents' involvement in special education. *Exceptional Children, 61,* 364–377.

Heller, T., Markwardt, R., Rowitz, L., and Farber, B. (1994). Adaptation of hispanic families to a member with mental retardation. *American Journal on Mental Retardation, 99*(3), 289–300.

Ishisaka, H. A., Nguyen, Q. T., and Okimoto, J. T. (1985). The role of culture in the mental health treatment of Indochinese refugees. In T. C. Owan (Ed.), *Southeast Asian mental health: Treatment, prevention, services, training, and research,* (pp. 113–135). Washington, D.C.: U.S. Department of Health and Human Services, National Institute of Mental Health.

Kinzie, J. D. (1985). Overview of clinical issues in the treatment of Southeast Asian refugees. In T. C. Owan (Ed.), *Southeast Asian mental health: Treatment, prevention, services, training, and research,* (pp. 113–135). Washington, D.C.: U.S. Department of Health and Human Services, National Institute of Mental Health.

Knoblock, P. (Ed). (1987). *Understanding exceptional children and youth.* Boston: Little Brown.

Krauss, M. W. (1993). Child-related and parenting stress: Similarities and differences between mothers and fathers of children with disabilities. *American Journal on Mental Retardation, 97,* 393–403.

Kroth, R., and Simpson, R. L. (1977). *Parent conferences as a teaching strategy.* Denver, CO: Love.

Kroth, R. L. (1987). *Mixed or missed messages between parents and professionals.* Volta Review, 89 (5), 1–10.

LaFromboise, T. D., and Graff, L. K. (1989). American Indian children and adolescents. In J. Taylor-Gibbs and L. Nahme-Huang (Eds.), *Children of color: Psychological interventions with minority youth,* (pp. 114–147). San Francisco: Jossey-Bass.

Lutzker, J. R., and Campbell, R. (1994). *Ecobehavioral family interventions in developmental disabilities.* Pacific Grove, CA: Brooks/Cole.

Lynch, E. W., and Stein, R. C. (1987). Parent participation by ethnicity: A comparison of Hispanic, black, and Anglo families. *Exceptional Children, 54,* 105–111.

Marion, R. L. (1981). *Educators, parents, and exceptional children: A handbook for counselors, teachers, and special educators.* Rockville, MD: Aspen.

Mayeski, G. W. (1973). *A study of the achievement of our nation's Students.* Washington, DC: Government Printing Office.

Meyen, E. L., and Skrtic, T. M., (Eds.). (1995). *Special education and student disability: An introduction,* 4th Ed. Denver, CO: Love.

Meyers, C. E., and Blacker, J. (1987). Parents perceptions of schooling for severely handicapped children: Home and family variables. *Exceptional Children, 53,* p. 441.

Morrow, R. D. (1987). Cultural differences—Be aware! *Academic Therapy, 23*(2), 143–149.

Nagata, D. K. (1989). Japanese American children and adolescents. In J. Taylor-Gibbs and L. Nahme-Huang (Eds.), *Children of color: Psychological interventions with minority youth*, (pp. 114–147). San Francisco: Jossey-Bass.

Ovando, C. J., and Collier, V. P. (1985). *Bilingual and ESL classrooms: teaching in multicultural contexts*. New York: McGraw-Hill.

Owan, T. C. (Ed.). (1985). *South East Asian mental health: Treatment, prevention, services, training, and research*. Washington, D.C.: U.S. Department of Health and Human Services, National Institute of Mental Health.

Park, H. S. (1992). *Korean American parents' perceptions toward educational priorities for their children with severe disabilities*. A paper presented at the International Conference of the Association for Persons with Severe Handicaps (TASH). San Francisco: CA.

Park, H. S. (1995). *A preliminary report on ethnographic interviews with three Korean families*. Consortium for collaborative Research on Social Relationships of Children and Youth with Diverse Abilities. Syracuse: Syracuse University.

Park, H. S., and Harry, B. (in press). Variations in friendships. In L. Meyer, H. Park, E. Schwartz, M. Grenot-Scheyer, and B. Harry, *Understanding the social lives of children and youth with diverse abilities*. Baltimore: Paul Brookes.

Park, H., and Yount, M. (1994). Helping English language learners socially adjust at both school and work settings. Paper presented at the Symposium for Second Language Learners in Regular and Special Education. Sacramento, CA: California State University, Sacramento.

Ramirez, O. (1989). Mexican American children and adolescents. In J. Taylor-Gibbs and L. Nahme-Huang (Eds.), *Children of color: Psychological interventions with minority youth*, (pp. 114–147). San Francisco: Jossey-Bass.

Salend, S. J., and Taylor, L. (1993). *Working with families: A cross-cultural perspective*, *14*(5), 25–32, 39.

Sandler, A., Coren, A., and Thurman, S. K. (1983). A training program for parents of handicapped preschool children: Effects upon mother, father and child. *Exceptional Children, 49*, p. 355.

Shapiro, J., and Simonsen, D. (1994). Educational/support group for Latino families of children with Down syndrome. *Mental Retardation, 32*(6), 403–415.

Sue, D. W. (1981). *Counseling the culturally different: Theory and practice*. New York: Wiley & Sons.

Taylor-Gibbs, J., and Nahme-Huang, L. (Eds.) (1989). *Children of color: Psychological interventions with minority youth* (pp. 114–147). San Francisco: Jossey-Bass.

Tung, T. M. (1985). Psychiatric care for South East Asians: How different is different? In T. C. Owan (Ed.), *Southeast Asian mental health: Treatment, prevention, services, training, and research*, (pp. 113–135). Washington, D.C.: U.S. Department of Health and Human Services, National Institute of Mental Health.

Turnbull, A. P., Barber, P., Kerns, G. M., and Behr, S. K. (1995). The family of children and youth with exceptionalities. In E. L. Meyen and T. M. Skrtic (Eds.). *Special education and student disability: An introduction*, 4th Ed. Denver, CO: Love.

Turnbull, A. P., and Turnbull, H. R. III (1990). *Families, professionals, and exceptionality: A special partnership*, 2nd Ed. Columbus, OH: Merrill.

Wallar, C., and Goldman, R. (1979). *Home, school, community interaction.* Columbus, OH: Merrill.

Yano, C. (1986). Asian families. In C. Moore (Ed.), *Reaching Out: Proceedings from a special education symposium on cultural differences and parent programs,* (pp. 39–48). Phoenix, AZ: Western Regional Resource Center. (ERIC Document Reproduction Services No. ED 284 408).

Yutang, L. (1994). *The wisdom of Confucius.* New York: The Modern Library.

Chapter 10

ISSUES RELATED TO LATINO STUDENTS

NORMA G. HERNÁNDEZ AND JORGE DESCAMPS

INTRODUCTION

Information related to the academic achievement of Latino students, particularly Mexican-Americans, is addressed in this chapter. The information is given in three sections (Table XIV): statistics on Latinos in the United States; research findings disproving prevailing stereotypes about forces that influence the learning of Mexican-Americans; and research findings that identify factors which are positively related to the achievement of Mexican-Americans.

The first section covers the demographics of Latinos in the United States: their numbers by country of origin, geographic distribution, employment statistics, and educational attainments. The second section discusses research findings disproving the assumption that low educational achievement of Mexican-Americans is caused by personal characteristics such as inferior intelligence, passivity and lack of initiative, lack of a competitive spirit, a learning style different from that used in the schools, and failure to acculturate. The third section describes research findings that identify areas or factors which, when present, impact positively on the learning and achievement of Mexican-Americans; the frequent use of English at home, the influence of well implemented bilingual education programs, a high self-concept (or positive self-perception of own abilities), internal locus of control (or inner direction), a high degree of home democratic independence training, a positive school atmosphere, and a middle-class socioeconomic home environment.

Over five hundred empirical studies were reviewed and provide the basis for the conclusions presented in this chapter. Most of the studies were conducted with Mexican American students as subjects; very few studies included other than Latino groups such as Puerto Rican Americans or Cuban Americans. Due to a disparity in the relative proportions

215

of studies focusing on the various Latino ethnic groups in the research literature reviewed in this study, conclusions relative to the under-achievement of Latino students must be applied solely to Mexican-Americans.

SECTION I
DEMOGRAPHICS OF LATINOS
IN THE UNITED STATES

When considering issues related to the underachievement of Latinos, and specifically Mexican Americans, a brief overview of statistical information such as geographical distribution, employment patterns and educational development, will accentuate the growing importance of this subculture group in the United States.

It is clear that the Latino population in the United States will increase greatly within the next fifteen years. This increase will most likely result from a large birth rate, as well as from the continued migration of people from south of the border. All of these new citizens, however, in the near future will need to achieve a greater level of education than current generations have acquired if the quality of life in our society is to remain high.

In 1990, the total population of the United States was 248.7 million, with persons of Spanish origin totaling more than 22.3 million. Of the over 22.3 million persons of Spanish ancestry, the following analysis represents a summary by national source. Of the 22.3 million, persons of Mexican origin were by far the most numerous, totaling close to 13.5 million, well over half the population of Latino origin. The next most numerous groups included were those of Puerto Rican descent, totaling 2.7 million. Cubans, whose population in the United States totaled only 1 million, comprised the smallest population of Latino origin.

While the median age of persons in the United States, in 1990, was 32.9 years, the median age of the population of Latino origin was 25.5 years. Cubans are the oldest population group of people of Latino origin, averaging 38.9 years. Persons of Puerto Rican descent average 25.7 years, while those of Mexican descent, the youngest of the groups, have an average age of 23.8 years. A breakdown by gender reveals that among Latino groups, males and females are evenly divided at approximately 11 million each, similar to the gender breakdown of the major population.

Although the nation's Latino population is relatively small as a proportion of the total U.S. population, it is increasingly visible because of its concentration in major metropolitan areas in the growing Sunbelt states. As of 1990, 91 percent of Latinos resided in only fifteen states, although Latinos can be found in every state of the country. In addition, as of 1990,

- Two-thirds of all Latinos lived in three states: 35 percent lived in California, 21 percent lived in Texas, and 10 percent lived in New York.
- Latinos comprised more than 10 percent of the state population in seven states: New Mexico (38%), California (26%), Texas (26%), Arizona (19%), Colorado (13%), New York (12%), and Florida (12%).
- In addition to clustering in certain locations, Latinos were concentrated in certain regions according to subgroup. In 1990, 74 percent of Mexican Americans lived in California or Texas; about 40 percent of mainland Puerto Ricans were in New York; and 65 percent of Cuban Americans lived in Florida.
- Latinos were the nation's most urban population, with 82 percent living in metropolitan areas.

TABLE XIV
RANK ORDER OF FIFTEEN STATES WITH HIGHEST LATINO POPULATION

State	Latino Population	% of Pop. Latino	% of U.S. Latino Pop.
California	7,687,938	25.8	34.5
Texas	4,339,905	25.5	19.5
New York	2,214,026	12.3	9.9
Florida	1,574,143	12.2	7.1
Illinois	904,446	7.9	4.1
New Jersey	739,861	9.6	3.3
Arizona	688,338	18.8	3.1
New Mexico	579,224	38.2	2.6
Colorado	424,302	12.9	1.9
Massachusetts	287,549	4.8	1.3
Pennsylvania	232,262	2.0	1.0
Washington	214,570	4.4	1.0
Connecticut	213,116	6.5	1.0
Michigan	201,596	2.2	0.9
Ohio	139,696	1.3	0.6

These data were obtained from the 1990 census.

EMPLOYMENT STATISTICS IN VARIOUS CATEGORIES

Additional employment information shows the types of employment positions Latinos generally fill. These jobs are usually in areas requiring advanced levels of education or some type of certificate or license.

As employment statistics are reviewed, it is shown that, whereas in 1980, all Latino groups were employed in various job categories in approximately equal percents, by 1990 there was a shift to higher percents in the technician/sales/administrative support and operator/laborer categories. This shows that the percents change over time, depending on the condition of national and regional economies. These percents, however, are representative of the variety and lack of professional and technical employment opportunities available to Latinos. The areas in which a majority of Latinos obtain employment are shown below and include: managerial and professional jobs, technician/sales/administrative support, crafts, equipment operational/laborer, and in rendering personal service. Table XV is a summary by ethnic distribution as well as by employment type.

UNEMPLOYMENT STATISTICS

The population, in general, in the 1990 census showed an unemployment rate of approximately 8 percent, which could fluctuate from between 5 percent to 12 percent. Latino minority subgroups in the 1980 census reflected a greater rate of unemployment than that of the general population. In the 1990 census, however, it showed that the Latino minority subgroups came close to matching the unemployment rate of the general population. Specific percents are given in Table XVI by subgroup for the year 1990.

TABLE XV
PERCENT OF POPULATION EMPLOYED IN VARIOUS CATEGORIES

	Manag./ Professional	Tech./ Sales/Admin.	Crafts	Opera./ Laborer	Service
General Population	13.0	13.0	4.8	16.1	5.4
Latino	12.6	24.1	13.2	24.6	20.1
Mexican	10.1	21.9	14.1	26.9	19.1
Cuban	23.3	34.1	10.8	16.4	14.3
Puerto Rican	15.6	30.5	12.9	21.2	18.1

TABLE XVI
UNEMPLOYMENT RATES BY ETHNICITY

Mexican	Puerto Rican	Cuban	Combined (all others)
8.2%	9.1%	7.2%	8.0%

EDUCATIONAL DEVELOPMENT OF LATINOS

While persons of Latino descent comprise the second largest minority group in the United States, second only to blacks, the group has attained educational development at a relatively low level when compared to major social groups.

The population of the United States, in general, as a group has a median of thirteen years of school completed, persons twenty-five years and older who are high school graduates comprising 76 percent of this population, and 48 percent have one or more years of college. Persons of Latino origin, aged twenty-five years and over, by comparison, have a median of twelve years of schooling completed. Of this groups, high school graduates comprise 50 percent of this population and only 29.5 percent have completed one or more years of college work. These data, however, show a significant improvement for Latinos over the 1980 census where the median for schooling completed was 10.9 years, high school graduates 43 percent and those with one or more years of college 16.5 percent.

In an analysis of the various Latino groups for comparison, it was noted that persons of Puerto Rican origin have completed a median of 12.3 years of school, with 53 percent having high school diplomas, and 28 percent having one or more years of completed college work. Persons of "other Spanish origin" (primarily Central or South American), have completed a median of almost thirteen years of schooling, with 60.6 percent of these being high school graduates, and 38.6 having one or more years of college work completed.

SECTION II
FINDINGS DISPROVING GENETIC AND CULTURAL TRAITS AS CAUSES OF UNDERACHIEVEMENT AMONG MEXICAN AMERICANS

It was during the mid-1960s that assumptions as to the causes for the lack of academic achievement of Mexican American students were initially questioned. Federal legislation addressing Lyndon Johnson's War on Poverty provided great motivation for researchers to increase their investigations into the underachievement of minority students, as well as to develop compensatory programs and materials to address the problem. Consequently, since 1970 numerous empirical studies on the academic achievement of Mexican Americans have been conducted, reexamining factors previously explored and considering additional variables such as cognitive style, locus of control, social motives, bilingual education programs, and school practices.

In 1973, Hernández conducted a review of the literature on the academic achievement of Mexican Americans attempting to identify relationships between academic success and variables hypothesized as related to increased school success such as intelligence, cultural differences, language usage, self-concept, motivation, and home environment. While research efforts on these variables were not abundant at the time, there was intense theoretical discussion, in articles, monographs and books, relative to issues related to the academic achievement of ethnic minorities.

In a ten-year update of research results on variables affecting the academic achievement of Mexican American students, Hernández and Descamps (1983) found over 500 empirical studies on the topic. These studies generally validated several theoretical postulates summarized in the 1973 review: namely, that there is no empirical evidence to suggest that a depressed intelligence, a lack of internal locus of control, a reluctance to compete, a field dependence orientation to learning, or a failure to acculturate, could be cited as general causes for the underachievement of Mexican American students. Conclusions reached in relation to these research variables are discussed below.

Intelligence

Intelligence measures have been examined in the literature since 1934 to determine their influence on the depressed academic achievement of

Mexican American students. Only in rare cases have Mexican Americans children scored on part with Anglo children (De Avila et al., 1976; Coleman et al., 1966; Carlson and Henderson, 1950; Garth and Johnson, 1987). These results have impelled researchers to question not only the test results, but the instruments themselves, test administration procedures, and the very motives for their use (Mercer, 1977; Carver, 1975; Stodolsky and Lesser, 1967).

It has not been empirically established that Mexican Americans, as a group, are less intelligent than their Anglo counterparts, nor that low IQ scores are a major cause of underachievement. Data indicate, however, that Mexican American children with high intelligence scores tend to come from less crowded homes, homes where English is the predominant language, and homes where mothers have high expectations for their children and fathers who were reared in an urban environment (Stedman and McKenzie, 1971).

Locus of Control

Fatalism and other forms of passivity have been attributed to Mexicans, and, by extension, to Mexican Americans, who are stereotyped as believing in luck, fate, and chance (Justin, 1970; Scott and Phelan, 1967; Lewis, 1961). Since data indicate that persons who score high on scales of internal control are more likely to exert control over their environment than their external counterparts, it was hypothesized that this orientation could be a casual factor in the underachievement of Mexican Americans (Nelson et al., 1980).

The claim that Mexican Americans are less internally oriented than Anglos has not received consistent research support (Cole et al., 1978). It appears that membership in an economic class, rather than an ethnic group, is a critical factor in a person's locus of control (Bender and Ruiz, 1974). Research data does not indicate that Mexican Americans live in poverty because of a cultural trait of fatalism (Cole et al., 1978). As long as a large percentage of Mexican Americans live in poverty, however, their locus of control will tend to be externally oriented.

Social Motives

Another factor suspected of contributing to the underachievement of Mexican Americans is the lack of a competitive orientation and the presence of cooperation as a social motive. Several studies compared samples of rural Mexican children with Anglo children, finding Mexican children significantly less competitive (Kagan and Madsen, 1971; Shapiro and Madsen, 1969; Madsen, 1967). Other studies indicated that urban Mexican Americans are closer to Anglos than to rural Mexicans in this measure. It also appears that cultural differences in competitiveness reported in several studies may have been inflated by noncultural factors of the populations sampled, such as SES and rural/urban settings (Kagan and Buriel, 1977; Avellar and Kagan, 1976).

Although Mexican American students appeared to have a preference for cooperation, this deceased orientation to compete was not related to decreased school achievement (Kagan et al., 1977). Recent studies further suggest that cooperative learning environments produce greater academic learning for students, in general, than do competitive learning environments (Johnson and Johnson, 1985).

Cognitive Style

A different cognitive style resulting from cultural differences was hypothesized to be a major influence on underachievement of Mexican American students (Ramirez, 1973). This position assumes that because Mexican Americans, as a group, are more field dependent than students on the majority culture and more cooperative and personal in their relationships, they possess a different mode of cognition that does not match the school's instructional practices.

Results of studies investigating the field orientation of Mexican Americans do not support this hypothesis. It was found, however, that measured field independence among Mexican Americans increases with years of schooling; females have significantly higher scores than males; scores are related to the restrictiveness of the environment of the subgroup; and field independence may appear in varying degrees, depending on the setting of the sampled population (Kagan and Zahn, 1975; Ramirez and Price-Williams, 1974). Studies have not substantiated a consistent relationship between field dependence and achievement (Buriel, 1978).

Although Mexican American children are more personal and cooperative than Anglo children, results do not indicate that these disparities create a significantly different cognitive style to justify an altered methodological or instructional approach by the schools based on a field dependent dichotomy (Kagan and Buriel, 1977).

Acculturation

It has been claimed that Mexican Americans resist acculturation, thereby failing to adjust to the majority group's norms and to school expectations. Their underachievements are thus attributed to the persistent cultural differences that do not equip them to succeed in school.

Among more frequently discussed indicators of acculturation is language usage. Studies reviewed indicate that second generation Mexican Americans and subsequent generations are shifting to English (Lopez, 1987; Patella and Kuvlesky, 1973). Continued immigration appears to be one reason Spanish is maintained as a first language. The supply of adult Spanish speakers arriving from Mexico makes Spanish necessary in certain areas. Intragenerational loyalty to Spanish and its intergenerational transmission do not appear to be less for Mexican Americans than for other immigrant groups. Mexican Americans are speaking more English while educated Mexican Americans families must struggle to have their children remain bilingual.

The nature of educational aspirations is another indicator of acculturation. Mexican Americans show high regard for schooling and see education as a means for attaining success. Frequently, however, high aspirations exist, but the knowledge of how to help children remain in school and to make the educational system responsive to their needs if unavailable to the family (Brocas, 1980; Garcia, 1973).

Other characteristics attributed to Mexican Americans, suggesting a lack of acculturation, are present-time orientation, fatalism, and low assertiveness. These traits generally are manifest among the poor, regardless of ethnic origin, in a "culture of poverty." It is important to point out that these traits are not generally manifest among middle-class Mexican Americans (Shannon, 1975, 1976; Casavantes, 1970). Societal and cultural changes such as a decrease of the extended family, a smaller number of children per family unit, and less emphasis on differentiating the roles and treatment of boys and girls, are additional indicators of acculturation (Mena, 1977).

Several variables, however, do appear to inhibit acculturation, The "barrio" with its ferment of separatism (Cardenas, 1971), proximity to the border, a person's length of stay in the United States, the degree of urbanization and economic strength, and the degree of prejudice in the community, predispose Mexican Americans to acculturate at different rates and to different degrees. Since the flow of immigrants is continuous, the Mexican American community is not a homogeneous group sharing many similarities, but rather, a collection of groups moving across a continuum of acculturation at different rates, thereby creating a very complex profile. It may be concluded that Mexican Americans, at times against their will and in an inconsistent manner, are acculturating.

Several studies have attempted unsuccessfully to find cultural differences between Mexican American and Anglo students that affect students' ability to profit from schooling. It has been found that when SES factors are controlled, few differences exist between the two groups other than differences related to family orientation, language, nurturance and interpersonal intimacy needs and a Mexican Catholic morality. These studies have found Mexican Americans neither culturally deficient nor culturally different in those factors that appear to affect achievement (Ramirez and Castaneda, 1974; Casavantes, 1970).

SECTION III
VARIABLES ASSOCIATED WITH INCREASED ACHIEVEMENT AMONG MEXICAN AMERICAN STUDENTS

That long-held negative views about Mexican Americans have been disapproved through results of research is in itself an important finding, but this fact, alone, does not help parents, educators or school policy makers in their efforts to design and implement programs that will make a difference in promoting increased academic achievement among Mexican American students. Only when factors that impact positively on learning are identified will it be possible for teachers and parents to change their practices to effect the desired outcomes. This section summarized the conclusions reached in relation to variables that contribute to the increased academic achievement of Mexican American students.

English Usage

Studies on family characteristics influencing the educational attainment of Mexican Americans have found a relationship between the amount of English used at home and school achievement (Evans and Anderson, 1973; Anderson and Johnson, 1971). Children from third generation families who experience little or no English usage at home encounter more difficulty with English instruction at school than those whose home language is English. A significant improvement in occupational levels among second-generation families has been associated with the adoption of English as an additional language in the home (Garcia, 1981). Consequently, students from families predominantly using English in the home were found to experience greater parental pressure to complete a high school degree than those from families communicating in Spanish almost exclusively. Furthermore, independence training practices in the home increase with the amount of English spoken and with an upwardly mobile occupational level of the father (Anderson and Evans, 1976).

English proficiency has been found the most consistent predictor of achievement in most minority groups, including Mexican Americans (Duncan and De Avila, 1979). On the other hand, substandard English language performance has been linked to academic underachievement (Gerace and Mestre, 1981; Duncan and De Avila, 1979; Kniet, 1975).

Bilingualism

Bilingualism, the ability to use two languages, has been found to aid in the development of greater linguistic flexibility, creativity, problem-solving skills, than monolingualism (Pearl and Lambert, 1976). It appears that in the process of becoming bilingual, for example, a person is able to conserve length at an earlier age and enter the Piagetian concrete operations stage before monolingualism. Other data available on effects of bilingualism on cognitive development and measured intelligence tip the balance in favor of the positive effects of bilingualism (Duncan and De Avila, 1979). It must be noted that a large number of studies yielding these data were conducted in Canada, northern Europe, and Israel, while a smaller number have been conducted with Mexican Americans (Ben-Zeev, 1977; Carringer, 1974; Liedtke and Nelson, 1968).

If bilingualism is desirable, should instruction be conducted in the first or second language? Some authorities claim that instruction in the child's native language is more likely to result in improved achievement, particularly when the child's language holds a high status in the home and in the community (Cohen, 1980; Cummins, 1979; Skutnabb-Kangas, 1979; Duncan and De Avila, 1979). In response to this claim school districts have designed and implemented bilingual education programs with varied and controversial results.

Bilingual Education

A number of research studies have investigated instructional methodologies and program effectiveness in bilingual education. While some studies have yielded contradictory results (AIR study, 1978), in general, the results have been favorable, indicating that students in bilingual education programs experience gains in achievement, self-esteem, and school attendance. The American Institute of Research (AIR study, 1978) on the impact of ESEA Title VII bilingual education programs reviewed thirty-eight projects to find that students in those programs scored at a lower level in English language arts than non-Title VII students, but at the same level in mathematics. Dulay and Burt (1979) found that of these thirty-eight research studies dealing with the effectiveness of bilingual instruction, only nine studies met minimum research criteria, while the remainder had serious weaknesses in research methodology. These results have been questioned repeatedly. In a related study, Troike (1978) reviewed twelve bilingual educational programs, finding evidence attesting to their effectiveness. On the other hand, it appears that some bilingual education programs lack instructional quality. As with any school innovation, bilingual education, regardless of its promise and validity, is only as effective as the competence of those implementing it (Richardson, 1980; Mace-Matluck, 1980; Troike, 1978; Balinsky and Peng, 1974; Fisher, 1974; Covey, 1973).

Self-Concept

Several studies on self-concepts of Mexican Americans and Anglo students found several inverse relationships between self-concept and academic achievement. While some researchers found evidence of a lower self-concept among Mexican American students compared to Anglo students (Evans, 1969; Anderson and Sofar, 1967; Coleman, 1966), others found no differences (McKibbin, 1977; Little and Ramirez, 1976; Lopez, 1973; De Blassie and Healy, 1970; Carter, 1968).

Male and female low SES Mexican American students do not differ significantly in overall levels of self-concept. Additionally, it was found that sex and skin color affect their perceptions of personal worth only slightly. Students from lower socioeconomic levels do not report themselves as having the degree of inferiority and worthlessness that authors have generally attributed to members of this social class (Maldonado, 1978).

School ethnic composition appears to exert a strong influence on the achievement of Mexican Americans, with higher performance scores reported in schools having a high percentage of Anglo students (McPartland and York, 1967; Coleman, 1966). Mexican American students, for example, appear more sensitive to school contextual effects than Anglos. In a study reported by Felice (1973), school racial-ethnic climate had the largest effect on dropout behavior. In a related study, Lopez (1980) found that both Anglo and Mexican American children reported higher self-concept scores when they constituted a majority in the classroom. The self-concept of Mexican Americans does not appear to increase with succeeding generations or with increasing age of the individuals. A high self-concept of ability, coupled with English usage in the home, has been found the overall best predictor of student success in school (Anderson and Johnson, 1971).

Locus of Control

Measures of locus of control appear to have the power to predict educational as well as vocational aspirations and achievement for both Anglo and Mexican American students, but especially so for Mexican Americans. A direct relationship between measures of an internal locus of control and a positive self-concept to school achievement was greater for Mexican American students than for Anglo students (Nelson et al., 1980).

Independence Training

There is a positive relationship between home independence training and academic achievement. Independence training is the result of the amount of autonomy in decision-making a child is accorded, along with the effort of parents to explain their reasons for rules and consequences. Mexican American fathers appear to be more democratic with girls than with boys, and Mexican American mothers provide their children with less independence training than Anglo mothers. In contrast with Anglo students, Mexican Americans, as a group, express more concern for adult approval of their actions than peer approval. For both groups of students, high self-concept of ability and democratic independence training are positively and directly related to academic achievement. Mexican American children perceive themselves as having much less autonomy in decision-making than their Anglo peers. They also see their parents as less willing to explain their reasons for rules and punishments. An increase in the father's education is related to increased autonomy for the child (Anderson and Evans, 1976; Evans and Anderson, 1973). The educational level of Mexican American mothers is positively associated with the use of inquiry and praise as home teaching practices and inversely related to modeling strategies (Laosa, 1987, 1977).

Among Anglos, blacks, and Mexican Americans, females score higher than males on family achievement orientation and lower on individual achievement orientation, suggesting that females may be socialized to identify with the family more than males. Mexican American males scored the second highest of the groups studied in the areas of family achievement orientation, suggesting that they are socialized to achieve both for self and for the family. Father-absent boys were found to show significantly more signs of social and emotional maladjustment than father-absent Mexican American girls (Ramirez and Price-Williams, 1976). Mothers of high-competence children viewed themselves as more hopeful, unselfish, lenient, and less aggressive. High achieving Mexican American families appeared to manifest a semantic and attitudinal structure more similar to the Anglo middle class than to low-potential families (Stedman and McKenzie, 1971).

Classroom Climate

Overall, studies reviewed on teacher practices indicate that significant disparities exist between teacher behavior directed toward Mexican American students and behavior directed toward Anglo students in the amount of praise given, the number of questions asked, and the amount of teacher contact established (United States Commission on Civil Rights, 1972; Jackson and Cosca, 1974). Low achieving, Mexican American students receive significantly less teacher contact than middle and high achieving, Mexican American students (Mendoza, et al., 1972).

Mexican American students perceive their teachers as friendly and warm, but not helpful with school work. Furthermore, for Mexican Americans, variables under teacher control such as warmth and enthusiasm, absence of authoritarianism and punitiveness, were the most influential in increasing school attendance and significantly impacted achievement. While classroom climate appears to have little effect on the success of Anglo students, it appears to be a substantial variable in the academic performance of Mexican Americans. Mexican American students need teachers who are nurturant and skillful in interpersonal relations (Engstrom, 1981; Espinosa et al., 1970).

Studies on methodology for modifying student behavior indicate that effective methods for improving Anglo students' behavior have also positively affected Mexican American students behavior (Zimmerman and Pike, 1973; Allen, 1975; Morgan, 1975).

As with studies of teacher behavior, analyses of school grouping practices also provide evidence of significant disparities between Mexican American and Anglo students. School organization patterns for grouping and tracking perpetuate school stratification patterns observed in the larger community. Poor and minority students are found in disproportionately large percentages in low-track (low achieving) high school classes, while percentages of Anglo students in such classes are lower by far. Tracking provides different educational opportunities to low and high ability students. Students tracked into low ability groups receive less attention from high school counselors than college bound students (Oakes, 1981a, 1981b; Rosenbaum, 1980a, 1980b; Amato, 1980; Esposito, 1973; Rosenshine and Furst, 1971).

CONCLUSIONS

Widely established stereotypes about Mexican Americans' inferior intelligence, external control orientation, reluctance to compete, and failure to acculturate, have been found to be false. Research results indicate that:

- Mexican Americans do not have a locus of control different from that of Anglos. Membership in a social class, and not ethnicity, is the crucial factor in a person's locus of control.
- Although Mexican Americans have a less competitive orientation than Anglos, the difference is not significantly large nor is it related to school achievement.
- It has not been empirically established that Mexican Americans, as a group, are less intelligent than their Anglo counterparts, or that low IQ scores are a major cause of underachievement.

- Mexican Americans are acculturating to the majority's group norms and school expectations.

Further results have established relationships between language usage, bilingualism, bilingual education, self-concept, locus of control, home independence training, school affective climate, and the academic achievement of Mexican American students. These findings may be classified as relating to home, school, and society.

Home

- There is a positive and direct relationship between home democratic independence training (problem-solving, nonauthoritarian orientation) and academic achievement.
- The use of English as an additional language in the home, or as the main language, is related to academic success. Substandard English performance has been linked to academic underachievement.
- English language proficiency is the most consistent predictor of academic achievement for Mexican American students.
- Bilingualism has a positive effect on the cognitive development of children.
- A high self-concept of ability and internal locus of control are strong predictors of school success.
- An increase in the parent's educational level is related to an increase in home independence training and positive parenting interactions.

School

- Teacher warmth and enthusiasm, and absence of authoritarianism and punitiveness, significantly and positively impact academic achievement of Mexican American students more so than for Anglo students.
- Students in well-implemented bilingual education programs experience greater gains in achievement and self-concept than in regular programs.
- Cooperative learning environments produce greater academic gains than competitive or individualistic learning environments for all students, but more so for Mexican Americans.

- Locus of control and self-concept measures affect school achievement to a greater degree for Mexican Americans than for Anglo students.
- Mexican American students achieve greater academic gains under teachers who are nurturant and skillful in interpersonal relations.
- Students in low-track high school classes receive less educational opportunities than students in heterogeneous groups.
- Mexican American students' academic achievement is higher in schools having a high percentage of Anglo students.

Society

- A large percentage of Mexican Americans live in a world of poverty. As long as this condition exists, their academic achievement is likely to remain substandard.
- That the self-concept of Mexican Americans does not appear to increase either with succeeding generations or with the age of the individual, suggests that these students feel they are not mastering their environment nor are they surrounded by nurturant significant others in the school or in the community.

SUMMARY OF RESULTS

In 1960, the blame for underachievement was placed on the individual whose intelligence was hypothesized to be inferior as a result of genetic and/or cultural influences. In the seventies, the focus shifted from the student to the schools, which were viewed by some as insensitive to needs of Mexican American children by not providing appropriate instruction. During those years, however, popular views relative to achievement of Mexican Americans portrayed them as a monolithic group, when in reality there are a multitude of groups evolving along several continua. Research results suggest that socioeconomic status, language skills, home and school nurturance, and independence training are key factors determining the achievement of Mexican Americans. When all these factors are held constant, differences between Anglo and Mexican American students are more a matter of emphasis, while the similarities are many.

One example of such differences is the priority that each group assigns to family and to personal future. A characteristic that cannot be overlooked when considering instructional approaches for Mexican Americans is their preference for warmth and intimacy in interpersonal relations, and their inclination toward cooperative exchanges when learning. It may be that this preference and cultural trait is a positive contribution that Mexican Americans can bring to the majority culture which at times becomes immersed in excessive competition and individualism. Research has indicated that, unlike years ago, our perceptions have changed from doubts about Mexican Americans' capacities to learn and excel in schools to a variety of positions that allow for instructional exploration, change and modification that will be, in the end, vastly more productive than attempts to implement popular strategies that are generally effective in the main, for the majority group.

DISCUSSION QUESTIONS

(1) What are some significant implications for public education associated with the high birth rate of Latinos, in the next twenty years?

(2) How will public education be funded in the next twenty years, if a significant part of the population it serves does not earn a proportional taxable income?

(3) What potentially problematic aspects of teaching special populations does the reader, who is currently teaching or is preparing to teach in an area that has a significant Latino population, foresee? What problems is the reader currently experiencing? How can these be addressed?

(4) What, if any, are some significant differences among the major Latino subgroups? Will these differences tend to affect educational achievement? Will these affect local school practices? If so, in what ways?

(5) How can non-Latino readers, aspiring to teach in an area with a significant Latino population, prepare to develop empathy for this culturally and linguistically different group? What community resources can be utilized?

REFERENCES

Allen, B. V. (1975). Paying students to learn. *Personnel and Guidance Journal, 53*(10), 774–778.

American Institutes for Research. (1978). Evaluation of the impact of ESEA title VII Spanish/English bilingual education program. *Bilingual Education Paper Series, 2*(1). Los Angeles: National Dissemination and Assessment Center, California State University, Los Angeles.

Anderson, J. G., and Johnson, W. H. (1971). Stability and change among three generations of Mexican-Americans: Factors affecting achievement. *American Educational Research Journal, 7*(2), 285–390.

Anderson, J. G., and Sofar, D. (1967). The influence of differential community perceptions on the provision of equal educational opportunities. *Sociology of Education, 40*(3), 219–230.

Avellar, J., and Kagan, S. (1976). Development of competitive behaviors in Anglo-American and Mexican-American children. *Psychological Reports, 39*(1), 191–198.

Balinsky, W. L., and Peng, S. S. (1976). An evaluation of bilingual education for Spanish-speaking children. *Urban Education, 9*(3), 271–278.

Bender, P. S., and Ruiz, R. A. (1974). Race and class as differentiated determinants of underachievement and underaspiration among Mexican-Americans and Anglos. *The Journal of Educational Research, 68*(2), 51–55.

Ben-Zeev, S. (1977). The influence of bilingualism on cognitive strategy and cognitive development. *Child Development, 48*(3), 1009–1018.

Buriel, E. (1978). Relationship of three field-dependence measures to the reading and math achievement of Anglo-American and Mexican-American children. *Journal of Educational Psychology, 70*(2), 167–174.

Cardenas, R. (1970). Three critical factors that inhibit acculturation of Mexican-Americans. University of California, Berkeley. *Dissertation Abstracts International,* 1971, 32, 661A. (University Microfilms No. 71-20, 780).

Carlson, H. B., and Henderson, N. (1950). The intelligence of American children of Mexican parentage. *Journal of Abnormal and Social Psychology, 45*(3), 544–551.

Carringer, D. C. (1974). Creative thinking abilities of Mexican youth, *Journal of Cross-Cultural Psychology, 5*(4), 492–503.

Carter, T. P. (1986). The negative self-concept of Mexican American students. *School and Society, 96*(2304), 217–219.

Carver, R. P. (1975). The Coleman report: Using inappropriately designed achievement tests. *American Educational Research Journal, 12*(1), 77–96.

Casavantes, E. (1970). Pride and prejudice: A Mexican-American dilemma. *Civil Rights Digest, 3*(1), 22–27.

Cohen, B. (1980). Issues related to transferring reading skills from Spanish to English. *Bilingual Education Paper Series, 3*(9). Los Angeles: National Dissemination and Assessment Center, California State University, Los Angeles.

Cole, D., Rodriguez, J., and Cole, S. (1978). Locus of control in Mexicans and Chicanos: The case of the missing fatalist. *Journal of Consulting and Clinical Psychology, 46*(6), 1323–1329.

Coleman, J. S., Campbell, E. O., Hobson, C. J., McPartland, J., Mood, A. M., Weingeld, F. D., and York, R. L. (1966). *Equality of Educational Opportunity,* Washington, D.C.: United States Department of Health, Education, and Welfare, Office of Education, U.S. Government Printing Office.

Cummins, J. (1979). Linguistic interdependence and the educational development of bilingual children. *Bilingual Education Paper Series, 3*(2). Los Angeles: National Dissemination and Assessment Center, California State University, Los Angeles.

De Avila, E. A., Havassy, B., and Pascual-Leone, J. (1976). *Mexican-American school children: A neo-Piagetian analysis.* Washington, D.C.: Georgetown University Press.

DeBlassie, Richard R., and Healy, G. W. (1970). *Self-concept: A comparison of Spanish-American, Negro and Anglo adolescents across ethnic, sex and socio-economic variables.* Las Cruces: New Mexico State University, Educational Resources Information Center (ERIC), Clearinghouse on Rural Education and Small Schools (CRESS).

Dulay, H. C., and Burt, M. K. (1979). Bilingual education: A close look at its effects. *Focus,* (1). Rosslyn, Virginia: National Clearinghouse for Bilingual Education.

Duncan, S. E., and De Avila, E. A. (1979). Relative linguistic proficiency and field dependence/independence: Some findings on the linguistic heterogeneity and cognitive style of bilingual children. Paper presented at the 13th Annual Convention of TESOL, Boston, Massachusetts, February 1979.

Engstrom, G. A. (1981). *Mexican-American and Anglo-American student perceptions on the learning environment of the classroom.* Technical Report No. 22. Los Angeles: University of California, Los Angeles, A Study of Schooling, Laboratory in School and Community Education, Graduate School of Education.

Espinosa, R. W., Fernandez, D., and Dornbursch, S. M. (1979). Chicano perception of high school and Chicano performance. *Aztlan, 8,* 133–155.

Esposito, D. (1973). Homogeneous and heterogeneous ability grouping: Principal findings and implications for evaluating and designing more effective educational environments. *Review of Educational Research, 43*(2), 163–179.

Evans, F. B. (1976). A study of sociocultural characteristics of Mexican-American and Anglo junior high school students and the relation of these characteristics to achievement (Doctoral dissertation, New Mexico State University, 1969). *Dissertation Abstracts International, 30,* 4826A. (University Microfilms No. 70-5911).

Evans, F. B., and Anderson, J. G. (1973). The psychocultural origins of achievement and achievement motivation: The Mexican-American family. *Sociology of Education, 46*(4), 396–416.

Felice, L. G. (1973). Mexican American self-concept and educational achievement: The effects of ethnic isolation and socioeconomic deprivation. *Social Science Quarterly, 53*(4), 716–726.

Figueroa, R. A., and Gallegos, E. A. (1980). Ethnic differences in school behavior. *Bilingual Education Paper Service,* February 1980, *3*(7). Los Angeles: National Dissemination and Assessment Center, California State University, Los Angeles.

Fisher, R. I. (1974). A study of non-intellectual attributes of children in first grade bilingual-bicultural program. *The Journal of Educational Research, 67*(7), 323–328.

Garcia, F. C. (1973). Orientations of Mexican-American and Anglo children toward the U.S. Political community. *Social Science Quarterly, 53*(4), 814–829.

Garcia, S. B. (1981). *Language Education Paper Series, 4*(6). Los Angeles: National Dissemination and Assessment Center, California State University, Los Angeles.

Garza, R. T., and Ames, R. E. (1976). A comparison of Chicanos and Anglos on locus of control. In C. A. Hernández, M. J. Haug, and N. N. Wagner (Eds.), *Chicanos: Social and Psychological Perspectives* (2nd ed.). Mosby, St. Louis.

Gecas, V. (1980). Family and social structural influences on the career orientations of rural Mexican-American youth. *Rural Sociology, 45*(2), 272–289.

Gerace, W. J., and Mestre, J. P. (1981). *Identifying learning handicaps of college age Spanish-speaking bilingual students majoring in technical subjects.* Third quarterly report, second year, NIE Grant: NIE-G-79-0094. Amherst: University of Massachusetts, Physics and Astronomy Department.

Hernández, N. G. (1973). Variables affecting achievement of middle-school Mexican-American students. *Review of Educational Research, 43*(1), 1–75.

Hernández, N. G., and Descamps, J. A. (1985). Factors affecting the achievement of Mexican-Americans. *Bilingual Education Paper Series.* Los Angeles: National Dissemination and Assessment Center, California State University, Los Angeles.

Jackson, J. B., and Cosca, C. (1974). The inequality of educational opportunity in the Southwest: An observational study of ethnically mixed classrooms. *American Educational Research Journal, 11*(3), 219–229.

Jensen, M., and Rosenfeld, L. B. (1974). Influence of mode of presentation, ethnicity and social class on teachers' evaluations of students. *Journal of Educational Psychology, 66*(4), 540–547.

Johnson, R. T., and Johnson, D. W. (1985). Student-student interaction: Ignored but powerful. *Journal of Teacher Education, 55*(2), 22–26.

Justin, N. (1970). Culture conflict and Mexican-American achievement. *School and Society, 98*(2322), 27–28.

Kagan, S., and Buriel, R. (1977). Field dependence-independence and Mexican-American culture and education. In J. L. Martine (Ed.), *Chicano Psychology.* New York: Academic Press.

Kagan, S., and Madsen, M. C. (1971). Cooperation and competition of Mexican, Mexican-American children of two ages under four instructional sets. *Developmental Psychology, 5*(1), 32–39.

Kagan, S., and Zahn, G. L. (1975). Field dependence and the school achievement gap between Anglo-American and Mexican-American children. *Journal of Educational Psychology, 67*(5), 643–650.

Kneif, L. M. (1975). Disadvantaged bilingual junior high students. Efforts to ameliorate language problems. *Urban Education, 10*(2), 150–158.

Laosa, L. M. (1977). Nonbiased assessment of children's abilities: Historical antecedents and current issues. In Oakland, (Ed.) *Psychological and Educational Assessment of Minority Children.* New York: Bruner/Mazel.

Laosa, L. M. (1978). Maternal teaching strategies in Chicano families of varied education and socioeconomic levels. *Child Development, 49,* 1129–1135.

Lewis, O. (1961). *Life in a Mexican village: Tepoztlan restudied.* Urbana: University of Illinois Press.

Liedtke, W. W., and Nelson, L. D. (1968). Concept formation and bilingualism. *Alberta Journal of Educational Research, 14*(4), 225–232.

Little, J., and Ramirez, A. (1976). Ethnicity of subject and test administrator: Their effect on self-esteem. *The Journal of Social Psychology, 99,* 149–150.

Lopez, D. E. (1978). Chicano language loyalty in an urban setting. *Sociology and Social Research, 62*(2), 267–278.

Lopez, J. T. (1980). Self-concept and academic achievement of Mexican-American children in bilingual-bicultural programs (doctoral dissertation, United States International University). *Dissertation Abstracts International, 41*, 1996A. (University Microfilms No. 80-24, 782).

Lopez, M. (1973). Bilingual-bicultural education and the self-concept of Mexican-American children (doctoral dissertation, Wayne State University). *Dissertation Abstracts International, 33*, 6019A. (University Microfilms No. 73-12, 562).

Mace-Matluck, B. J., Dominguez, D., Tunmer, W. E., Hoover, W. A. (1980). Assessing the reading readiness skills of Spanish-English bilingual children: Findings and implications. Paper presented at the meeting of the American Educational Research Association, Boston, Massachusetts.

Madsen, M. C. (1967). Cooperative and competitive motivation of children in three Mexican sub-cultures. *Psychological Reports, 20*(3), 1307–1320.

Maldonado, B. B. (1972). The impact of skin color by sex and self-concept of low socio-economic level Mexican-American high school students (doctoral dissertation, New Mexico State University). *Dissertation Abstracts International, 33*, 2716A–2717A. (University Microfilms No. 72-31, 647)

McKibbin, M. P. (1976). A study of the relationship of self-concept of reading achievement of two groups of fourth grade Mexican-American students (doctoral dissertation, The University of Nebraska). *Dissertation Abstracts International, 38*, 104A, 1977. (University Microfilm No. 77-14, 677)

McPartland, J. M., and York, R. L. (1967). *Racial isolation in the public schools*, 2 Vols. Washington, D.C.: United States Commission on Civil Rights, U.S. Government Printing Office.

Mena, C. (1977). Mexican-American cultural and language characteristics of Mexican descent children living in Boulder County (doctoral dissertation, University of Colorado). *Dissertation Abstracts International, 38*, 7119A. (University Microfilms No. 78-08, 920)

Mendoza, S. M., Good, T. L., and Borphty, J. E. (1972). *Who talks in junior high classrooms?* Report Series 68. Austin: The University of Texas in Austin, The Research and Development Center for Teacher Education.

Mercer, J. R. (1977). Implications of current assessment procedures for Mexican-American children. *Bilingual Education Paper Series, 1*(1). Los Angeles: National Dissemination and Assessment Center, California State University, Los Angeles.

Morgan, R. R. (1975). An exploratory study of three procedures to encourage school attendance. *Psychology in the Schools, 12*(2), 209–215.

Nelson, W., Knight, G. P., Kagan, S., and Gumbier, J. (1980). Locus of control, self-esteem, and field independence as predictors of school achievement among Anglo-American and Mexican-American children. *Hispanic Journal of Behavior Sciences, 2*(4), 323–335.

Oakes, J. (1981a). *A question of access: Tracking and curriculum differentiation in a national sample of English and mathematics classes.* Technical Report No. 24. Los Angeles: University of California, Los Angeles.

Oakes, J. (1981b). *Limiting opportunity: Student race and curricular differences in secondary vocational education.* Technical Report No. 28. Los Angeles: University of California, Los Angeles.

Padilla, A. M., and Ruiz, R. A. (1975). Personality assessment and test interpretation of Mexican-Americans: A critique. *Journal of Personality Assessment, 39*(2), 103–109.

Patella, V., and Kuvlesky, W. P. (1973). Situational variation in language patterns of Mexican-American boys and girls. *Social Science Quarterly, 53*(4), 855–864.

Peal, E., and Lambert, W. E. (1962). The relation of bilingualism to intelligence. *Psychological Monographs: General and Applied, 76*(27), 23 pps.

Ramirez, M., III (1973). Cognition. *Social Science Quarterly, 53*(4), 895–904.

Ramirez, M., III, and Castaneda, A. (1974). *Cultural democracy, bicognitive development, and education.* New York: Academic Press.

Ramirez, M., III, and Price-Williams, D. R. (1976). Achievement motivation in children of three ethnic groups in the United States. *Journal of Cross-Cultural Psychology, 7*(1), 49–60.

Ramirez, M., III, and Price-Williams, D. R. (1974). Cognitive styles of children of three ethnic groups in the United States. *Journal of Cross-Cultural Psychology, 5*(2), 212–219.

Richardson, J. C. (1980). Length of time in a bilingual program and academic achievement among second grade Mexican American students (doctoral dissertation, University of Houston). *Dissertation Abstracts International, 41,* 1929A. (University Microfilms No. 80-27, 022)

Rosenbaum, J. E. (1980a). Social implications of educational grouping. In C. Berlinger (Ed.), *Review of Research in Education.* Itasca, Illinois: F. E. Peacock, American Education Research Association.

Rosenbaum, J. E. (1980b). Track misperceptions and frustrated college plans: An analysis of the effects of tracks and track perceptions in the national longitudinal study. *Sociology of Education, 53*(2), 74–88.

Rosenshine, B., and Furst, N. (1971). Research on teacher performance criteria. In O. B. Smith (Ed.), *Research on Teacher Education.* Englewood Cliffs, NJ: Prentice-Hall.

Scott, J. D., and Phenlan, J. G. (1969). Expectancies of unemployable males regarding source of control of reinforcement. *Psychological Reports, 25*(3), 911–913.

Shannon, L. (1976). Age change in time perception in native-Americans, Mexican-Americans, and Anglo-Americans. *Journal of Cross-Cultural Psychology, 7*(1), 117–122.

Shapira, A., and Madsen, M. (1969). Cooperative and competitive behavior of kibbitutz and urban children in Israel. *Child Development, 40*(2), 609–617.

Skutnabb-Kangas, T. (1979). *Language in the process of cultural assimilation and structural incorporation of linguistic minorities.* Rosslyn, Virginia: National Clearinghouse for Bilingual Education.

Stedman, J. M., and Adams, R. L. (1972). Achievement as a function of language competence, behavior adjustment and sex in young, disadvantaged Mexican-American children. *Journal of Educational Psychology, 63*(5), 411–417.

Stedman, J. M., and McKenzie, R. E. (1971). Family factors related to competence in young disadvantaged Mexican-American children. *Child Development, 42*(5), 1602–1607.

Stodolsky, S. S., and Lesser, G. (1967). Learning patterns in the disadvantaged. *Harvard Educational Review, 37*(4), 546–593.

Troike, R. C. (1978). Research evidence for the effectiveness of bilingual education. *Bilingual Education Paper Series, 2,* (5). Los Angeles: National Dissemination and Assessment Center, California State University, Los Angeles.

U.S. Commission of Civil Rights (1972). *The excluded student: Educational practices affecting Mexican-Americans in the southwest.* (Mexican-American Educational Study, Report III.) Washington, D.C.: Government Printing Office.

U.S. Census (1990). *Statistical abstract of the United States,* (112th Ed.). Washington, D.C.: U.S. Government Printing Office.

Walberg, H. J. (1984). Improving the productivity of America's schools. *Educational Leadership,* 23–24.

Zimmerman, B. J., and Pike, E. D. (1973). Effects of modeling and reinforcement on the acquisition and generalization of question-asking behavior. *Child Development, 43*(3), 892–907.

Chapter 11

TEACHING ASIAN AMERICAN CHILDREN

MING-GONG JOHN LIAN

Asian American children are in one of the fastest-growing populations in American schools. It is predicted that by the year of 2050, the number of Asian Americans will increase from the current 3 percent to 10 percent of the nation's total population (Kim, 1993). Asian American children as a group may represent diverse familial and cultural backgrounds including those from Cambodia, China, Hong Kong, India, Indonesia, Japan, Korea, Laos, Malaysia, Pakistan, Taiwan, Thailand, the Philippines, Vietnam, and many other Asian countries and areas. A broader classification of the Asian American population also includes Pacific Islanders from Guam, Saipan, Okinawa, Hawaii, and other islands and areas in the Pacific Ocean (Lian, 1994).

Asian Americans were previously referred to as "Orientals," a term that may critically disadvantage Asian American children. Through the years, a stereotype of the "Orientals" has existed. Many people, for example, still tend to relate general Chinese people to illegal aliens, appearance with slanted eyes, chopsuey or chowmein-style ethnic foods, and funny speaking mannerisms, thinking of them as different from persons of "the Western World." As a result, Asian American children identified as "Orientals" in the school and community may have suffered from cultural and social discrimination and racism (Luke, 1987).

"Asian American" is a relatively new term, originating during the last ten to twenty years. Just like African Americans, European Americans, Latin Americans, and Native Americans, many persons with Asian descent are also Americans. Chinese Americans, Filipino Americans, Indian Americans, Indonesian Americans, Japanese Americans, Korean Americans, Malaysian Americans, Thai Americans, Urdu Americans, and Vietnamese Americans represent subpopulations of Asian Americans.

239

CHARACTERISTICS OF ASIAN AMERICAN CHILDREN

Asian American children may include individuals who have recently immigrated to the United States as well as those who were born or raised in this country as the second, third, fourth, or fifth generation. Some Asian American children may have limited-English-proficiency (LEP) or speak English as a second language (ESL), while others may speak only English. Some children may speak only one of the numerous Asian languages, while others may be bilingual, trilingual, or multilingual (e.g., English, Vietnamese and French). Even students who speak the same Asian language may use different dialects (e.g., Mandarin Chinese, Cantonese, Shanghainese and Taiwanese). Any of these linguistic factors could add to the complicated multicultural experience of school-age, Asian American children.

For many years, Asian Americans were ignored in American literature on ethnic relations, resulting in the general public knowing very little about this population. Wakabayashi (1977) described Asian Americans as the "least acknowledged of the national minorities" (p. 430). Many Americans developed their awareness and knowledge of Asian Americans based on false or stereotypic information eventually leading to prejudice, negative attitudes and discriminatory responses. Kim (1993) pointed out that, in the mid-19th to the mid-20th century, Asian Americans were often perceived to be "unassimilable," "inscrutable," "cunning," or "filthy." Because of the *exclusion legislation* since enacted in 1882, most Asian Americans were not allowed to become U.S. citizens until 1952. Even today, Asian American children may be perceived by their teachers or peers in schools to be foreigners or refugees (Cheng, Ima, & Labovitz, 1994) and many Asian American children and their parents, who are U.S. citizens, might be asked about their nationality or when they plan to "go back."

Since the 1960s, a new stereotypic image of Asian Americans has developed. Asian Americans are now often classified as diligent, hard-working, and high educational and economic achievers. Such overgeneralizations cause the public to overlook hidden issues and concerns among this population including poverty, limited health care, family violence, child abuse and neglect, and increased school failure and dropping out of Asian American children. As indicated by Sadker and Sadker (1994):

Despite outstanding accomplishments, the statistics hide problems that many of the new immigrants from Southeast Asia and Pacific Islands face. Cultural conflict, patterns of discrimination, lower educational achievement, and the diversity of the Asian/Pacific Americans are all hidden by the title "model minority" (p. 411).

Chen (1989) expressed the concern about the lower self-concept which may exist among general Asian American students. He listed a number of positive characteristics of Asian American students, including bilingual and bicultural experiences, long cultural history, respect within the culture for each other, strong family bonding, assertiveness, trustworthiness, higher expectations, hardworking, strong work ethics and moral values, flexibility, and adaptability. For example, Asian American students tend to be described as having "inner strength"—being flexible to bend but hard to break, especially during hardships. However, he worries that the general concern of low self-concept among Asian American students still exists.

Lian (1992) contended that the "melting pot" concept tends to force culturally and linguistically diverse students to assume the Caucasian culture and language as a priority for learning and living. If the student does not learn well, he or she may be labeled as a slow learner or even removed from the mainstreamed classroom. Such students may thus have lower self-esteem and expectations for educational achievement.

Leung (1990) indicated six major concerns related to educating Asian American students: (a) physical differences, (b) linguistic differences, (c) culture-based differences, (d) acculturation dilemma (adjustment problem), (e) identity crisis, and (f) uninformed and insensitive significant others. According to Leung, an example is provided when Asian American students speak their native language at school and other children laugh. It is not unusual for a child in this situation to say, "Mom, don't speak Chinese! It's embarrassing."

Like adults, students in the schools may face cultural differences and conflicts between the Asian American community and other ethnic populations. In American schools, maintaining eye contact with the teacher during instructional activities is emphasized whereas Asian American students are told at home that it is rude to stare at or to look into the eyes of an adult whom they respect (Lian, 1994). Direct eye contact may give Asian American parents or teachers the impression that the child disagrees or wants to argue with them, or is showing disrespect or hatred toward them. Such a response from an adult perspective, represent serious behavioral problem. At the same time, teachers may find that Asian American students show politeness by: (a) standing while parents, teachers, or elderly persons sit, (b) remaining quiet or silent when adults are talking, and (c) avoiding direct eye contact with adults.

Asian American children may exhibit learning and response patterns that appear to be unusual in American schools. In the classroom, Asian American children may feel more comfortable answering a yes-no question instead of open-ended question. Also, in addition to "yes" and "no" answers, children may select the third choice—silence, which may mean yes, no, agree, disagree, no answer, no comment, didn't understand the question, or waiting for the answer to come up by itself (e.g., the teacher or other children eventually would answer the question). Heward and Orlansky (1992) stated that "the toughest thing a teacher of Asian students must deal with is the silence; its reasons are complex" (p. 510).

Instead of showing and telling, an Asian American child in the classroom may define "sharing" as listening quietly. In addition, teachers may find that it is difficult for Asian American children to talk about their own achievement, to ask for or offer help, to ask questions in class, or to answer a teacher's question, or to express their own opinion (Brower, 1983). Teachers definitely need to avoid the conclusion that Asian American children are less active in classroom learning activities. This is especially true for a new, non- or limited-English-speaking, child who may exhibit a great deal of silence in class.

Asian American children may show one type of passive resistance. When an Asian American child is selected to represent his or her class in an activity, the child may feel that his or her friends are more deserving of the honor and decline. This passive resistance should not be interpreted as a lack of willingness to volunteer.

A general autonomy issue also exists among Asian American children. Research has indicated that Asian American children may take a few more years than European American children to become independent. For example, a fifteen-year-old, Asian American student may repeatedly ask for an adult to give directions for the next step in a routine activity such as setting up a dining table for a regular meal. Asian American parents, especially mothers, tend to provide their children with tender, loving care, which often means doing as many things for them as possible. For example, a mother of a child with a physical disability said that cleanliness and tidiness were more important than teaching her child independent self-feeding. Asian American children may also rely heavily on adults for decision-making. Many Asian American parents may expect that their child's major responsibility is to concentrate on academics, to study and to get good grades in school.

UNIQUENESS IN EDUCATING ASIAN AMERICAN CHILDREN

Asian American children have unique cultural and linguistic backgrounds. Families of these children have special traditions and values affecting their daily life, including education. Members of Asian American families generally have a strong respect for parents, the elderly, teachers, scholars, tradition, and the educational system, thinking of them as authorities. Asian American children are usually taught to be obedient and cooperative, to be dependent at home and in school, and to express unconditional loyalty to their ethnic community. As stated by Arakawa (1981), "In Western culture, individuality is praised. In Asian culture, anything that breaks homogeneity is troubling" (p. 1). Among the Asian American population, there may be an extended family orientation and a strong family central focus and tie.

Education, in the eyes of Asian American parents, is of extremely high value and is perceived to be the vehicle for upward mobility. Heward and Olansky (1992) described the influence of such perception of education:

> For many years, teachers and scholars have been revered in China and other Asian countries. For parents influenced by their traditional cultural heritage, no sacrifice is too great to obtain a good education for their children. From the child's view point, scholastic achievement is the highest tribute one could bring to his or her parents and family . . . This philosophy and work ethic has helped many Asian American students excel in schools (p. 507).

Most Asian American parents and families value and support the education of their children. In fact, Chen (1989) identified Chinese parental support and commitment as two of the major strengths and assets in the education of Chinese American children.

However, educators need to be aware of the incongruencies between non-Asian teachers' expectations and Asian American parents' expectations (Cheng, 1987). In the American school, students are encouraged by teachers to participate actively in classroom discussion and activities, while Asian American students may be told by their parents to "behave," i.e., to be quiet and obedient at school. Students may be encouraged by non-Asian teachers to be creative, while Asian American parents may think that students should be told what to do. In the American school, students learn through inquiry and debate, while Asian American students may prefer to study and place their trust in what the teacher says and what is written in the textbooks, i.e., to learn through memorization. American teachers may believe that Asian American students generally do well on their own, while Asian American parents may think that teacher's role is to teach and the student's job is to "study." In the American school, critical thinking and analytical thinking are perceived to be important, while Asian American parents may believe that it is more important to deal with the real world. Students' creativity and fantasies are encouraged by American teachers, while Asian American parents may perceive factual information to be much more important than fantasy. Problem-solving skills are emphasized in American schools, while Asian American parents may want their children to go to school to be taught the exact steps required to solve problems. In American classrooms, students need to ask questions, while Asian American parents and their children may try not to ask questions, thinking that teachers should not be challenged. The teacher may think of reading as a way of discovering, while Asian American parents may think of reading as the decoding of information and facts.

Many Asian Americans believe and follow the thoughts of Confucianism, Buddhism, and/or Christianity, in which moral behaviors and a sense of forgiveness are strictly emphasized. Asian Americans also tend to rely on the **Yin-Yang philosophy.** Yin-Yang means a contrast between two extremes such as darkness and brightness, femininity and masculinity, interior and exterior, fast pace and slow pace, and happiness and sadness. Thus, they tend to seek equilibrium between two distinct phenomena, feelings, or theories. In other words, Asian Americans may avoid either extreme or criticism of the opposite point of view. They may try to stay at the neutral-point in a controversial issue and attempt to make both sides in an argument happy—to avoid competition, conflict, and the related debate, and to work out a compromise.

Asian Americans try to avoid conflict with nature. Many tend to accept their fate and do nothing to change it or create a "new" fate. This contrasts with the fighting-for-rights effort which is prevalent in the United States. When facing the challenge of having a child with a disability, for example, Arakawa (1981) described,

> The Asian perspective is to minimize the handicap. The emphasis is on adapting and doing as little out of the ordinary as possible. This even means you avoid

legal action against discrimination. To get employment, you tough it out. If buses are inaccessible, you say it doesn't matter (p. 1).

While differences between Asian American and the majority culture may create educational obstacles, Asian American traditions and values significantly contribute to diversity in American schools and society. Heward and Orlansky (1992) stated that a great strength of the United States is cultural diversity. Our society is made up of immigrants from many lands, and we have all benefited from the contributions of the many ethnic groups. It is responsibility of the American educators to attend to the Asian American heritage and the unique educational needs of children from the Asian American population.

PARENTS OF ASIAN AMERICAN CHILDREN

Asian American parents play a significant role in education of their children. Most parents of Asian American children tend to treasure education and respect teachers and scholars highly, expecting high standards and academic achievement from educators. A Thai American parent, for example, may want his or her child to be educated to become an "ideal student" with the following virtues (Sriratana, 1995):

(1) values
- to be well-rounded and honest,
- to have confidence,
- to be trustworthy with integrity,
- to have courage and dare to attempt difficult tasks and challenges,
- to be peaceful, calm, and serene when dealing with conflict, and
- to be self-reliant and well-disciplined;

(2) giving
- to be dependable and loyal to family,
- to respect for life, property, and nature,
- to love friends and neighbors,
- to be sensitive to others' needs and feelings and to be unselfish,
- to be kind and friendly, and
- to have justice and mercy.

However, Asian American families are generally reluctant to tell when they are in need of help. Dao (1994), for example, reported that

> Hmong, Cambodian and Lao parents tend not to speak up...because of a cultural politeness and respect toward the professional, who is seen as the expert. They don't want to insult him or her by asking too much—even though they have a right and even though the question or observation might help the professional (p. 15).

Heward and Orlansky (1992) indicated that Asian American families may be reluctant in sharing information about their children's disabilities and individualized needs special attention, especially when the disability is cognitive or emotional, rather than physical. Unless the disability is severe, Asian American families may not seek special services or attention. Parents in the Asian American communities may rely on family units and totally assume the obligations of managing disordered behaviors within the family. Agencies are the last resort. Asian American families may try not to go through governmental agencies, including courts or the judicial system, to fight for their children's basic rights for education and related services.

Consumerism and advocacy may be difficult for Asian American families to understand and engage in for a person with disabilities. These families may seek to avoid underscoring a disability and focusing public attention on it. To do otherwise would be discomforting. As indicated by Arakawa (1981):

> In the last few years, attitudes about disability in the Asian Community have become more Western. But the basic values remain: be a high achiever and transcend your disability. Asians want to excel. They want to be the best (p. 1).

Asian American parents may also be unaware of how to actively participate in PTO or other school activities. Instead of concluding that these parents are less willing to volunteer for school activities, it may be more appropriate to assume that they need more time to get warmed-up or to get acquainted with the American school system, or that they might need to be informed or provided with information and opportunities before they become active volunteers to support school programs.

In the Asian American community, there is also general concern for "face." To challenge the educational system may not be acceptable because it causes trouble and, even worse, causes school administrators and teachers to lose "face." Parents and other family members may apologize repeatedly, worrying that they have bothered the school too much.

Dao (1994) listed potential barriers which may prevent Southeast Asian American parents from accessing services:

(1) fear of persecution as a result of the experience in the war against the communists in Vietnam, Laos, and Cambodia;
(2) self-reliance which may cause Asian American families to be the main caregivers of children with special education needs, to solve educational problems, and to fulfill needs within the families;
(3) limited English proficiency which may slow the assessment process and cause delay of service;
(4) tendency to trust the psychoeducational system and authority and try not to question;
(5) perception and expectation out of a disabling condition, e.g., feeling of guilt;
(6) lack of training and experience in evaluating their child's progress and achievement;
(7) cultural and custom difference, e.g., trying not to be demanding or not to advocate and trying to prevent court actions; and
(8) general misunderstanding of the Asian American families.

Asian American parents may have different perceptions of school failure. Lynch (1994) compared the three educational failure paradigms perceived by Asian American parents:

(1) **children deficit orientation** (the medical model)—the cause of failure resides within the child's physical body;
(2) **environmental deficit orientation** (the behavioral model)—since behavior is learned, children fail as a result of inappropriate or inadequate environmental circumstances in which they learn;
(3) **contextual or sociological paradigm** —learning and behavioral problems are not a result of within-child deficits or environmental inadequacies, but the product of inappropriate child-environment interactions.

Asian American parents may also misunderstand English-as-a-second-language (ESL) programs, or other educational support systems for LEP students, thinking that the ESL program is a type of special education program for slow learners and, thus, it is shameful for their children to be involved in the program. In addition, parents may be concerned that their children are missing classes in other subject areas because of the pull-out for ESL instruction. Actually, ESL program provides significant benefits for limited-English-proficient students through individualized assistance to enhance their English language skills (San, 1992).

Professionals must be sensitive to each family's values and not judge the family based upon social status-poor or rich, educated or not. Nor should they assume that the family knows the law or the educational system. Lian and Aloia (1994) recommended that teachers utilize internal and external resources to support parents with specific needs related to the education of their children. Significant **internal resources** of parents include the degree of perceived control of the parenting situation, the extended family, parental relationships, health, energy, morale, and spiritual perspectives, problem-solving skills, and available financial and related resources. School personnel may also utilize **external resources** of parents, such as friends, neighbors, professionals, and community agencies and organizations, to support parental concerns and fulfill their needs in their children's successful involvement in the school program.

SUGGESTIONS FOR TEACHERS

When teaching and learning in a culturally and linguistically diverse environment, teachers and students should try not only to prevent stereotypes and prejudice, but they should also utilize more appropriate and less restrictive approaches in their teaching and learning activities (Lian 1990a, 1990b). In schools, three different approaches may be implemented when teachers and culturally and linguistically diverse children interact with each other—aggressive, assertive, and passive approaches among which teachers and students in schools should adopt the assertive approach.

The **aggressive** approach tends to be used by teachers and students who consider certain things to be for themselves only. For example, an aggressive teacher may view a culturally and linguistically diverse student as a burden on the class or a mis-match with other students. The teacher may determine that this student should go back to where he or she belongs. Or, the student deserves a lower grade in classroom evaluations. An aggressive non-Asian student may perceive Asian American students to be followers instead of leaders. Other aggressive statements made by some members of the non-Asian populations include: "Orientals are not good at sanitation," "They are always late for their appointments," and "They speak broken English or 'Chinglish'."

Asian American students and their parents may also be aggressive. For example, parents might tell their children who are attacked by non-Asian peers that, "The only way for you to survive in this country is to fight back."

The **passive approach** is the opposite of the aggressive approach. A passive teacher or student may decide that there is no need to deal with the issue because "everything is going to be all right." Persons using a passive approach may think totally for others and blame themselves—to "swallow" the complaint or the unfair situation.

The **assertive approach** represents an effort to consider both sides— self and the counter part. Persons utilizing the assertive approach may conduct rational thinking and find the balance point to perceive and to handle issues. They engage a thoughtful evaluation of the situation, find each individual's needs and concerns, and fulfill as many personal and group considerate goals as possible.

The following are general suggestions for teaching Asian American students:

Accepting Asian American students as they are. A teacher needs to understand, accept, and appreciate students who are from Asian American cultural and linguistic backgrounds. Efforts must be made to develop an awareness of these students' specific needs, learning styles, and response patterns. Teachers must let the students work at their own pace and assure that major learning objectives are mastered. The major concepts for children to learn may be presented in different ways and then followed by the teacher giving repeated review. Teachers should avoid frustration, while encouraging students to think things out instead of supplying answers too quickly. Overall, teachers need to create learning environment which fits the student, and not to ask the student to fit the school.

Nonbiased assessment. Asian American students may be at-risk for socially, culturally, and linguistically biased assessment, educational placement, and instructional activities which may lead to misunderstandings, closed doors (less opportunity), and lower expectations. School administrators and teachers need to help these students by providing opportunities to learn and achieve their maximum potential. Cheng (1991) suggested that Asian American students be observed over time by the teacher in multiple contexts which include various interactants to obtain a better understanding of their response patterns to different individuals and situations. Maker, Nielson, and Rogers (1994), for example, suggested the use of the approaches of **multiple intelligence assessment** to prevent underestimates of culturally and linguistically diverse children's giftedness and problem-solving abilities. A **portfolio assessment** system is highly recommended for limited-English-proficient students. Examples of various types of student's work completed at different times are collected, such as art work, creative writing, math exercise, and book reports, to provide a more reliable evaluation of their ability, performance, and learning progress.

Promote meaningful communication. Teachers of new Asian American students should enunciate clearly, avoid speaking too quickly or too slowly, and use gestures to reinforce oral language, but not to replace it. Teachers should not introduce too much new information in one sentence; they should write on the chalk board or paper frequently to reinforce key terms and concepts. Also, the experiences they incorporate into lessons should be familiar to the students. Teachers should start out by asking yes-no questions and, then, work up to "wh" questions (i.e., what, when, where, why, and how). Teachers should not assume that a "yes" necessarily means that the student has understood. They should praise the student's efforts and model the correct forms in both written and oral language.

Develop new curricula. Kim (1993) suggested that teachers should develop new curricula which will focus on life experiences of Asian Americans and their structural position in the United States. Major issues such as immigration patterns, ethnic diversity among Asian American groups, socioeconomic diversity within groups, high and low educational achievement, experiences of discrimination and civil rights violations, and the complexity of family life, should be addressed.

Many local schools are still at the stage of emphasizing Asian foods and festivals as the major elements of Asian culture to which students are exposed. The multicultural education curriculum should include in-depth discussion of Asian families' traditions and values. It should be directed toward helping all students in developing more positive attitudes toward diverse cultural, racial, ethnic, and religious groups and considering the perspectives of other groups (Banks, 1989).

Cooperative learning. Children learn quickly and effectively from each other. Teachers need to facilitate opportunities and encourage learning through cooperation. Cooperative learning assignments start with concrete and simple game-oriented projects. In such projects, an Asian American student will have the chance to take the role at which he or she feels competent and comfortable. Gradually, the teacher moves onto more complicated and abstract projects by which an Asian American student can increase his or her participation, contribution, and leadership.

Collaborative teaching. Sadker and Sadker (1994) suggested that teaching be done in collaboration. Contemporary schools are more complicated than ever before, dealing with such issues as bilingual and multilingual special education services, limited English proficiency, low self-esteem, family crisis, and poverty. A teacher cannot stand alone. He or she needs to be assisted and supported by experienced educators and professionals from various disciplines, e.g., social work, counseling, nursing, and teacher education (Farra, Klitzkie, & Bretania-Schafer, 1994).

SUMMARY

Asian American children are a special group of learners who bring unique cultural and linguistic backgrounds to American schools. They have special traditions and values as well as learning styles which may significantly enrich school programs and society in general. These students may also have unique educational needs. Teachers of Asian American students will need to understand each individual student attributes and learn to implement instructional strategies and contents which provide the optimal benefits and educational outcomes for these special learners.

DISCUSSION QUESTIONS

(1) What are some stereotypes we often have of Asian American students?
(2) What are some uniquenesses of Asian American students which we have to keep in mind when teaching the students?
(3) What are some potential barriers which may prevent Southeast Asian American parents from accessing services for their children?
(4) Discuss some suggestions for teachers that the writer makes in order to work successfully with Asian American students.

REFERENCES

Arakawa, J. (1981). Minority voices: Neither part of a double disability is the whole person. *Disabled USA, 4*(8), 1.

Banks, J. A. (1989). Multicultural education: Characteristics and goals. In J. A. Banks and C. A. M. Banks (Eds.), *Multicultural education: Issues and perspectives* (pp. 2–26). Boston: Allyn & Bacon.

Brower, I. C. (1983). Counseling Vietnamese. In D. R. Atkinson, G. Morten, and

D. W. Sue (Eds.), *Counseling American minorities* (2nd ed.) (pp. 107–121). Dubuque, IA: William C. Brown.

Chen, V. L. (1989). Know thyself: Self-concept of Chinese American youths. *Asian Week*, pp. 8–9.

Cheng, L. L. (1987). *Assessing Asian language performance: Guidelines for evaluating limited English-proficient students.* Rockville, MD: Aspen Publishers.

Cheng, L. L. (1991). *Assessing Asian language performance: Guidelines for evaluating LEP students* (2nd ed.). Oceanside, CA: Academic Communication Associates.

Cheng, L. L., Ima, K., and Labovitz, G. (1994). Assessment of Asian and Pacific Islander students for gifted programs. In S. B. Garcia (Ed.), *Addressing cultural and linguistic diversity in special education* (pp. 30–45). Reston, VA: Council for Exceptional Children.

Dao, X. (1994). More Southeast Asian parents overcoming barriers to service. *PACESETTER*, p. 15.

Farra, H. E., Klitzkie, L. P., and Bretania-Schafer, N. (1994). Limited English proficient, bilingual, and multicultural special education students: Implications for teacher education and service delivery. *International Journal of Special Education, 9*(2), 128–134.

Heward, W. L., and Orlansky, M. D. (1992). *Exceptional children: An introductory survey of special education* (3rd ed.). Columbus, OH: Merrill.

Kim, S. (1993). Understanding Asian Americans: A new perspective. In J. Q. Adams and J. R. Welsch (Eds.), *Multicultural education: Strategies for implementation in colleges and universities* (pp. 83–91). Springfield, IL: Illinois Staff and Curriculum Developers Association.

Leung, E. K. (1990). Early risk: Transition from culturally/linguistically diverse homes to formal schooling. *The Journal of Educational Issues of Language Minority Students, 7*, 35–49.

Lian, M. G. J. (1990a). Book Review on E. Durán, Teaching the moderately and severely handicapped student and autistic adolescent. *Journal of the Association for Persons with Severe Handicaps, 15*(2), 118–119.

Lian, M. G. J. (1990b). Enhancing ethnic/cultural minority involvement. *TASH Newsletter, 16*(5), 1–2.

Lian, M. G. J. (1992). Project TCLDSD: Teaching culturally and linguistically diverse students with disabilities. Paper presented at the Illinois Council for Exceptional Children Fall Conference, Chicago, 1992.

Lian, M. G. J. (1994). Teaching Asian American students. In E. Durán (Ed.), *Symposium for second language learners in regular and special education* (pp. 75–85). Sacramento, CA.

Lian, M. G. J., and Aloia, G. (1994). Parental responses, roles, and responsibilities. In S. Alper, P. J., Schloss, and C. N. Schloss (Eds.), *Families of persons with disabilities: Consultation and advocacy* (pp. 51–93). Boston, MA: Allyn & Bacon.

Luke, B. S. (1987). *An Asian American perspective.* Arlington, WA: REACH Center for Multicultural and Global Education.

Lynch, J. (1994). *Provision for children with special educational needs in the Asia region.* Washington, DC: World Bank.

Maker, C. J., Nielson, A. B., and Rogers, J. A. (1994). Giftedness, diversity, and problem-solving. *Teaching Exceptional Children, 27*(1), 4–17.

Sadker, M. P., and Sadker, D. M. (1994). *Teachers, schools, and society* (3rd ed.). New York: McGraw-Hill.

San (1992). Don't misunderstand ESL. *World Journal,* June 14, p. 25.

Sriratana, P. (1995). Education in Thailand: Past, present and future. Paper presented at the Thailand Culture and Heritage Night, Illinois State University, Normal, IL.

Wakabayashi, R. (1977). Unique problems of handicapped Asian Americans. In *The whitehouse conference on handicapped individuals 1,* (pp. 429–432). Washington, DC: U.S. Government Printing Office.

Chapter 12

ISSUES IN THE EDUCATION OF AFRICAN AMERICAN STUDENTS WITH DISABILITIES

GWENDOLYN T. BENSON

INTRODUCTION

Current statistics continue to be reported concerning the disproportionate overenrollment of African American students in classes for students with mental retardation and serious emotional disturbances (Chinn & Selma, 1987). The National Black Caucus of Special Educators indicated that African American students were overrepresented in Special Education Programs in thirty-nine out of fifty states. In an investigative report by the *U.S. News and World Report* (1993), black students were found to be significantly overrepresented in special education classes when they were students in predominately white school districts; neither the number of black students nor household demographics accounted for the high percentage of black students. These statistics are cause for alarm as we focus on the resulting impact.

A large percentage of students included in reported statistics will exit school without receiving a diploma or certificate (National Education Association, 1990). This contributes to the high drop-out rate among African American students and research indicates that these youth, in particular, are at risk for teen pregnancy, problems related to drugs, and involvement in the juvenile justice system. This chapter is to discuss several issues, and more importantly, to review instructional approaches from a teacher, learner, and learning environment perspective. The issues include multicultural curriculum/African infusion, learning styles, self-esteem, and family involvement. There is evidence in many school systems throughout the nation of efforts to address the issues that continue to contribute to the ineffectiveness of the educational system for many poor and minority students. Issues tend to focus around assessment of minority students and how it is used, ineffective curriculum and instructional strategies, parent involvement, and the effects of poverty.

Though the issues may also be viewed as barriers, many trends are emerging and becoming integral components of school system efforts to teach all students. These trends include the following: multicultural curriculum/African infusion, consideration of individual learning styles, alternative schools/alternative program options, continued emphasis on self esteem, conflict resolution training, family involvement, school/ community collaboration.

TRENDS

Multicultural Curriculum/African Infusion

Until recently, special educators planned classroom instruction and developed curricula with very little consideration of the influence of sociocultural factors or the experiential backgrounds of African American learners (Ford, 1992). Hale-Benson (1986) suggested a curriculum that is relevant to Afro-American students. The goal of such a curriculum is to help children learn through experiences that are both Afro- and Euro-American. This would include language/communication skills, mathematical concepts, and Afro-American studies. The curriculum would also include strategies such as chanting, storytelling, frequent touching and hugging, frequent physical movement in both play and learning activities, group rather than individual learning, and the use of Afro-American music as a method to relax and discipline black children.

Kunjufu (1984) indicated that for a curriculum to be relevant, it must illustrate how everything we do in the classroom relates to present and future experiences, providing students with a sense of their past and present place in the world community, a sense of self-identity and pride, and a sense of purpose in daily activities.

Other researchers believe that a curriculum that focuses on cultural learning style is critical (Boykin, 1986; Cureton, 1978; Slaughter, 1988). This cultural learning style is characterized by activities involving physical movement and oral involvement.

The National Alliance of Black School Educators (NASBE) proposed a performance-based curriculum that includes African American history and culture among other academic subjects. They also recommended teaching of critical thinking skills, creativity, and problem solving (NASBE, 1984).

In 1988, the Atlanta Public Schools' system initiated a plan to reconstruct the curriculum in order to provide a comprehensive, multidisciplinary and accurate representation of human history through the infusion of African and African American historical and cultural content. At the end of the pilot year, the student outcomes tended to be positive. Teachers' perceptions were also assessed. They reported that students responded to the infusion content with special interest and showed improvements in self-esteem, group identity, motivation, and group pride.

LEARNING STYLES

Much has been written about individual learning styles. Kunjufu (1984) discussed two styles of learning: analytical and relational as they relate to African American learners. He suggests that African American children bring a higher verve to the classroom that is being labeled hyperactive rather than being considered a characteristic of learning style that indicates boredom with an irrelevant curriculum and ineffective teaching style. He also stated that African American learners are relational in their thought process, and are more oral in cognition. Boykin (1978) and Wilson (1978) document higher vibrancy, capital, and verve that black children bring into the world and which are reinforced in a highly stimulating environment.

It is well known that among African American students in general, learning styles may contrast sharply with the ways in which learning environments are typically structured in our society (Hale, 1982). Also, nonverbal communication patterns among black students differ from those of whites which might adversely affect interactions between teachers and students. However, teachers can improve the academic levels of minority students by increasing their opportunities to respond in classroom discussions (Greenwood, Preston, & Harris, 1982).

In an article in the St. Petersburg Times (1991), an interview with teachers indicated that they viewed learning styles as different but not deficient. They believed this attitude to be essential if public schools are to successfully educate all minority students. Some teachers indicated that too often, students from minority cultures are made to feel inferior because their learning styles are different from majority students. This feeling of inferiority frequently causes minority students to become discouraged and alienated.

SELF–ESTEEM

According to Kunjufu (1984), children need to know their own identity; an identity of self and family extends to the community, neighborhood, nation, race, and world. After children know who they are, they have the motivation to learn about others. Teaching self-esteem has long been discussed as a critical area for African American students for a variety of reasons. Self-esteem is to possess a favorable opinion of oneself. Each person tries to be the kind of person that he thinks his environment expects him to be. Children are extremely sensitive to the messages that are given by the people around them. Low expectations and negative attitudes toward African American students with disabilities and their families and communities can result in poor self-esteem, lack of motivation, and ultimate school failure.

There is a tremendous need to continue to place great emphasis on self-esteem for African American students. Silverstein and Krate (1975) classified over half of the African American students they studied as ambivalent. Students needed and sought teacher attention, nurturance, acceptance, constant encouragement, recognition, warmth, and reassurance to continue to participate in class activities. When students did not receive positive attention and affirmation, they often became frustrated, angry, and disruptive.

It is important that educators teach and arrange learning toward enhancing the degree of self-esteem held by students in an academic setting, while also modifying the external contingencies that influence students' self-concepts, such as the environment, teaching strategies, curriculum, and conditions of extreme poverty.

Positive expectations and emotional support are powerful tools that adults can use to shape the confidence of children and build self-esteem. This must become a major objective of all instruction, especially in early education.

FAMILY INVOLVEMENT

Despite the implementation of legislation that requires parent involvement in the education of children with disabilities, there is continued failure to secure appropriate levels of involvement from many parents of minority students. All of the reasons why parents are not involved are not known; however, Gillis-Olion, Olion, and Holmes (1986) suggested improper testing, negative perceptions of services in the community, differences in language, lack of transportation, poor communication between professionals and parents, lack of information as to how to gain access to the system, inability to locate services, and negative attitudes of professionals involved with African American parents have been listed as some of the reasons for the problem. Cultural differences in background and experiences of educators have also been cited as barriers to involvement (Dixon, 1981).

Lifestyles, values, and experiences vary a great deal within the African American community; however, members of this community have generally had the common experience of economic isolation, prejudice, and legally reinforced racism (McAdoo, 1978). Gillis-Olion, Olion, and Holmes (1986) suggest that because of their dual positions (being a black parent of a black child, and being a parent of a child with a disability), black parents of children with disabilities often may require a different approach to meet their specific needs. A number of strategies have been offered as recommended techniques to be used with black parents of children with disabilities. Among these are being a participatory listener, giving respect, developing interpersonal relations, involving fathers, and extended families, training peer parents, speaking in clear, jargon-free language, and working with other community agencies.

INSTRUCTIONAL APPROACHES

Teacher

According to Franklin (1992), culturally-sensitive teachers will identify and build on the learner's strengths and interests. African American learners' differences should not be perceived as genetic deficiencies but, rather, as sources of strength. She goes on to state that without an understanding of various cultures, well-meaning teachers may ignore cultural differences that are peculiar to the learner's cultural background. Teachers must learn to differentiate between cultural style and true misbehavior. Hilliard (1989) stated that once a teacher decides that a student is a poor achiever, several things happen: Conversation is cut short, eye contact is diminished, and the student's participation in further exercises is limited.

In summary, effective teachers of minority students have high expectations; optimize academic learning time; organize, manage, and plan well; match instructional objectives to the student's ability; use active teaching methods; and maintain a pleasant and respectful classroom environment (Irvine, 1991).

Learner

The following areas must be considered for each student entering the doors of our classrooms if we are to meet the individual educational needs of each child: Past experiences, cultural background, self-esteem, home/community environment, language pattern/verbal and nonverbal, and nature of disability.

Tharp (1989) had suggested that many African American learners have difficulty with traditional patterns of cognitive functioning because the patterns ignore the impact culture has on language, learning, and thinking. Franklin (1992) stated that many African American children are exposed to high-energy, fast-paced home environments, where there is simultaneous variable stimulation (e.g., television and music playing simultaneously and people talking and moving in and about the home freely). Hence, low energy, monolithic environments (as seen in traditional school environments) are less stimulating. This suggests when we assume that a child is hyperactive, it may be that the curriculum is too slow. Additionally, Kunjufu (1986) stated that black males often express their cognition and sensitivity through art, often learning a speech or story better through music than a book.

LEARNING ENVIRONMENT

Providing a learning environment that is stimulating, motivating, risk-free, and that honors and respects diversity is a major challenge to educators. However, if each student's individual learning needs are to be met effectively, the learning environment must be a contributing factor. Listed below are twenty components of an effective learning environment and should be considered and addressed individually.

(1) curriculum

   (2) materials
   (3) pace
   (4) school climate
   (5) peer pressure/peer support
   (6) parent/family participation
   (7) community access
   (8) generalization opportunities
   (9) opportunities to respond
 (10) instructional/educational activities
 (11) resources from learner's cultural environment
 (12) opportunity to practice new skills
 (13) open and risk-free environment
 (14) cooperative learning opportunities
 (15) inclusive schools and classrooms
 (16) small groups
 (17) stimulus variability
 (18) motivational environment
 (19) highly stimulating
 (20) use of multimedia

In preparing to address these issues head on and to provide a quality education for all students, including minority students and students with disabilities, many school systems require staff development in multicultural education, as do many college and university programs. These efforts must be continued if educators are to bring about change and have a positive impact on each and every student they have an opportunity to teach.

DISCUSSION QUESTIONS

   (1) Discuss some of the trends in working with African American students.
   (2) What are two learning styles discussed by Kunjufu as they relate to African American learners?
   (3) What does Kunjufu say about the concept of self-esteem as it relates to African American students?
   (4) Why, according to Benson, are parents of African American students not involved with the education of their children? What does Benson suggest are some strategies that can be used with the parents to get them more involved with their children?

(5) Discuss some instructional approaches Benson suggested can be used with African American students.

REFERENCES

Boykin, A. W. (1978). Psychological/Behavioral verve in academic task performance. *The Journal of Negro Education, 42*(4), 343–354.

Boykin, A. W. (1983). The academic performance of Afro-American children. In Spence (Ed.), *Achievement and achievement motives* (pp. 321–371). San Francisco: W. H. Freeman.

Chinn, P. C., and Selma, H. (1987). Representation of minority students in special education classes. *RASE, 8,* 41–46.

Cureton, G. O. (1978). Using a Black learning style. *The Reading Teacher, 31,* 751–756.

Ford, B. A. (1992). Multicultural education training for special educators working with African-American youth. *Exceptional Children, 59*(2), 107–114.

Franklin, M. E. (1992). Culturally sensitive instructional practices for African-American Learners with Disabilities. *Exceptional Children, 59*(2), 115–122.

Gillis-Olion, M., Olion, L., and Holmes, R. L. (1986). Strategies for interacting with black parents of handicapped children. *The Negro Educational Review, 37*(1), 8–16.

Greenwood, C., Preston, D., and Harris, J. (1982). *Minority issues in the education of handicapped children.* Kansas City, MO: University of Kansas, Department of Special Education.

Hale, J. (1982). *Black children: Their roots, culture, and learning styles.* Provo, UT: Brigham Young University Press.

Hale-Benson, J. E. (1986). *Black children: Their roots, culture and learning styles.* Baltimore: John Hopkins University Press.

Hilliard, A. (1989). Teachers and cultural styles in a pluralistic society. *NEA Today, 7*(6), 65–69.

Irvine, J. J. (1991). *Black students and school failure.* New York: Praeger.

Jones, R. (1989). *Black adolescents.* Berkeley, CA: Cobb and Henry.

Kunjufu, J. (1984). *Developing positive self-images and discipline in black children.* Chicago: African American Images.

Kunjufu, J. (1986). *Countering the conspiracy to destroy black boys: Volume II.* Chicago: African American Images.

McAdoo, H. P. (1978). Minority families. In J. H. Stevens and M. Matthews (Ed.), *Mother/child, Father child relationships* (pp. 177–195). Washington, D.C.: The National Association for the Education of Young Children.

National Education Association. (1990). *Academic tracking:* Report of the NEA Executive Committee/Subcommittee on academic teaching. (ERIC Document Reproduction Service No. ED 322642).

Shapiro, J. P., Loeb, P., and Browermaster, D. (1993, December 13). Separate and unequal. *U.S. News and World Report,* pp. 46–60.

Silverstein, B., and Krate, R. (1975). *Children of the dark ghetto: A developmental psychology.* New York: Praeger.

Slaughter, D. T. (1988). *Visible now: Blacks in private schools.* New York: Greenwood Press.

Tharp, R. G. (1989). Psychocultural variables and constants: Effects on teaching and learning in schools. *American Psychologist, 44*(2), 349–359.

Tuthill, D. (1991, January 5). Diversity demands "different but equal" approach. *St. Petersburg Times,* Guest Column p. 2.

Wilson, A. N. (1978). *The developmental psychology of the black child.* New York: African Research Publications.

Chapter 13

THE CULTURALLY AND LINGUISTICALLY DIFFERENT STUDENT

Elva Durán

This chapter will define the culturally and linguistically different
student and will explain some specific characteristics that distinguish the culturally and linguistically different student. Further, in this
chapter this writer will explain some ways that the culturally and
linguistically different student, more specifically the Latino student, can
be assisted in some areas which have been discussed earlier in this book.
Latino is used here as a general term that includes persons of Mexican,
Puerto Rican, Cuban, Central or South American, or other Spanish-
speaking origin. It should be recognized that there are differences among
and within these groups. In the context of this chapter and other
chapters throughout this book (where the term Latino is used) the
emphasis is on Mexican-American families.

WHO IS THE CULTURALLY AND
LINGUISTICALLY DIFFERENT STUDENT?

The culturally and linguistically different student is defined by Nuttall
(1984), Rueda (1984), Rodriguez (1979), Baca and Bransford (1982), as
the student who is a native speaker of a language other than English.
The student who is in this category also has a different culture and
values than those found among the mainstream of society (Chamot,
1984; Rodriguez, 1982). The student who is culturally and linguistically
different and is in special education because he/she additionally has
mental retardation, autism, or another disability as well, presents a
special challenge to the teacher/trainer. The student who falls in this
category may not be able to speak his/her native language due to his/her
severe disability, but has heard it being spoken at home and can understand the language when someone speaks to him/her. If the student has

only a moderate intellectual disability, he/she may be able to understand and speak some words in his/her native language.

HISTORICAL INFORMATION

In 1954, the Brown vs. Board of Education decision that led to the notion that segregation of race is unconstitutional, was one of the first decisions that helped refine the concept of equal educational opportunity (Estrada & Nava, 1976; Henderson, 1980; Cegelka, 1986). In other court decisions such as United States vs. Texas (1972), Serna vs. Portales Municipal Schools, and Lau vs. Nichols (1974) the culturally and linguistically different student was also assisted so that this particular type of student could receive a more appropriate education in his/her public school placement. In United States vs. Texas (1972), it was decided that the failure of school districts in Texas to provide bilingual-bicultural education to Spanish-speaking students violated the constitutional rights of these students (Estrada & Nava, 1976). The Serna vs. Portales Municipal Schools (1974) revealed discrimination against Mexican-American students in the schools and led Portales Public Schools to implement bilingual education programs.

In Lau vs. Nichols (1974) the United States Supreme Court ruled unanimously that San Francisco Independent School District was in violation of the Civil Rights of 1,800 non-English-speaking Chinese children, since it failed to provide instruction in their native language. The Lau decision had national ramifications, and affects every federally-supported school with culturally and linguistically different children (Estrada & Nava, 1976; Carpenter, 1983). Additionally, in Larry Pl. vs. Riles (1972), Covarrubias vs. San Diego Unified School District (1972), and Spangler vs. Board of Education (1970) the decisions have all resulted in a number of changes in the education of minority students. Most of the changes address identification and placement for special programs (Carpenter, 1983).

Further, PL 94-142, the Education for All Handicapped Children's Act of 1975, or more recently, the Individuals With Disabilities Education Act (1990) has also been responsible for promoting stronger advocacy and improved services for culturally diverse, exceptional children (Baca, 1980).

With all that has occurred with these laws and court cases to enhance the education for the culturally and linguistically different student, much remains to be done for the student with handicaps who is also culturally and linguistically different. Even more needs to be accomplished for the culturally and linguistically different student who has moderate to severe handicaps and/or autism. As this writer reviewed the literature, she was unable to locate articles and research which were directly written for the student who falls in this category. This lack of material and information in this particular area has been unfortunate, because there are growing numbers of students in special education who have cultural and linguistic difficulties, yet there is a paucity of information that can be used by teachers, parents, and trainers of these particular students.

CULTURAL IMPLICATIONS

When teaching students who also have cultural and linguistic differences, it is important to note some of the characteristics that these students may have due to their particular cultural background. According to Grossman (1984), the Latino culture often emphasizes that the people in the various groups learn by doing. Consequently, Grossman (1984) notes that such students, in many cases, learn more by touching, seeing, manipulating, and experiencing concrete objects than by discussing or perhaps reading about ideas. Some of the more direct approaches in teaching Latino students may be seen, for example, when teaching students with moderate to severe handicaps to learn various vocabulary words. The students can be shown concrete objects or pictures to help them grasp the vocabulary concept.

The idea of showing these students everything in a concrete manner is often seen at work when the trainer helps the student of moderate to severe handicaps learn how to operate an automatic dishwasher, for instance. Often it is easier for the student to learn how to operate the machine by being guided to actually push the button of the dishwasher several times before the student learns how to do this particular task on his/her own.

In addition to presenting the concept in a concrete means, very often students in various cultural groups need to hear the terms or concept spoken in Spanish or the students' first or native language. In a study done by Durán (1986), it was revealed that students of moderate to severe intellectual disabilities did better learning particular vocational tasks when the trainers cued the Mexican-American students verbally in

Spanish only. The students in the control group cued in Spanish and English were the group that learned second best. The group verbally cued in English only did not do as well as the Spanish only or the Spanish and English mixed groups.

Another cultural implication which needs to be noted is that some Latino students also believe in the supernatural—ghosts, magic, religion, saints, etc.—more than do their Anglo peers (Grossman, 1984). For example, in the Southwest along the Mexican border, students have grown up hearing stories of "La Llorona," the "crying lady" who lost her child in the Rio Grande River and spent her nights walking up and down the river area crying in despair to see if she could see or find her missing child. Teachers or instructional aides can often take some time, if they teach Mexican-American students with moderate to severe intellectual disabilities, to discover from parents and grandparents some of the cuentos or short stories that are present in the particular cultural group. This information could be included as part of the teacher's ecological or environmental inventory (Brown, 1984); asking parents or grandparents questions pertaining to what cuentos or stories the children are familiar with makes it possible for some of this information to be brought to school. Teachers could take a few minutes during the week to teach the students some of these folklore stories which are native to the cultural group. Some time could be allotted for this particular goal during reading or leisure and recreation types of activities.

Very similar to this idea of the cuentos or stories is the belief that many students coming from various cultural groups are already very familiar with songs which are particular to their culture. Teachers can often discover what some of these students enjoy listening to at home, if they once again ask the families of the students who are in their classes. One popular song among Mexican Americans, for example is the song "Las Mananitas." This particular song, which is so lively and easy to learn due to the simplicity of the lyrics, is often sung on special occasions like birthdays or for Father's and Mother's Day. Very often "Las Mananitas" is sung for a variety of other occasions. This is a song that makes up an important part of the culture of many Mexican-American students, and teachers can have the students with moderate to severe handicaps listen and perhaps learn and even attempt to sing some of the verses during leisure and recreation activities. The result may not be of concert quality, but it helps create a positive atmosphere.

Also, what may be important to bring forth in the classroom, or during home training, are some of the particular foods that are also typical of the students' family and cultural groups. Mexican-American people, for great part, enjoy tacos, flautas (rolled crisp tortillas filled with meat), fajitas (beef strips which have been marinated in special sauces and grilled and served with tortillas), and enchiladas. Students enjoy eating and preparing some of these foods, which some very often have in their homes. Thus, just as some foods, and objects from the Anglo or main group are often part of the curriculum or teacher-made lessons and materials, some additional materials from the students' culture can easily be integrated into the lessons that are part of the students' education.

City and university libraries often have stories and information about other cultural materials that can be used by teachers who teach students who are culturally and linguistically different. At U.T. El Paso and some universities in California, for instance, the libraries have sections entitled "Chicano Studies" where all kinds of materials and literature can be located for the Mexican-American student. Many teachers in El Paso, for example, are aware of this material and often use the "Chicano Studies" portion of the library to help them tie in more closely with their Mexican-American students in their classrooms. In addition, there may be story-tellers in the community who might be brought to classes for even more enrichment.

CURRICULAR IMPLICATIONS

This section, while mentioning in general terms students of other cultural and linguistic groups, will focus on giving some suggestions for teaching the student of moderate to severe intellectual disabilities who comes from the Latino and more specifically the Mexican-American group. Some of the ideas presented here have been tried in various classrooms in the Southwest, Texas, and California where this writer acts as a consultant. It has been noted in reviewing the literature that no mention has been made concerning the cultural and linguistically different student who also has moderate to severe intellectual handicaps. Except for articles authored by this writer, there is no mention of the above groups, nor is there any mention of the student with autism who comes from a different cultural group. It is vitally important to consider the cultural aspects of different groups when teaching students who have exceptional needs (Ortiz, 1984; Nuttall, 1984). More details on how to teach limited English proficient students follows in the next chapter.

FUNCTIONAL READING AND
LANGUAGE INTERVENTION

In both of these areas, the teacher or parent and/or other caregivers need to conduct an ecological inventory, and as part of this inventory, there should be some questions or information that the parent or family can generate about particular words, stories, or cuentos, etc., that could be presented to the student in class (see Table XVII). This writer has observed that many Latino parents do not know how to read or write in English and often do not respond to notes and questionnaires the teacher sends home for them to fill out. Putting the questionnaire in the home language of the family will help many parents understand more effectively what they are to do. Often if parents have a phone, or if the neighbor has a phone, then following-up on the questionnaire which was sent home can be done with a phone call; such a practice may be helpful in trying to show the parents what to do. This writer has observed in working with parents that they often do not know the importance of giving feedback to teachers, but once they understand that the teacher cares, in many instances they will open up and explain in more detail what it is that the teacher could teach at school pertaining to functional language communication.

Some particular words that may be emphasized in language and reading are those that come from family, foods, and various cultural words that are typical of the Latino group of people. In the U.T. El Paso Adult Program and in some classrooms in California schools, for example, all the words that are taught in reading or language and/or communication to students with moderate to severe handicaps and autism are from these groups noted above. The words are presented in Spanish by the teacher along with the actual or concrete object, where possible; for instance, the student learns to say "grape" and is shown a real grape. The student is told the same concept in Spanish, "uva." Many students with moderate to severe intellectual handicaps may hear only Spanish at home; they will learn the information faster if they hear the cue in Spanish and later when the English word is presented to them, it will make more sense to the student or comprehensible input will have developed for him/her.

Also, when presenting reading instruction to students with more moderate intellectual disabilities, students can be shown pictures or objects that are found in their cultural group. For example, photographs

TABLE XVII
ECOLOGICAL INVENTORY
(Inventario de la Casa, la Communidad, y de la Escuela
Tocante a la instrucción de su Hijo o Hija)

Foods (Comidas)	Name (Nombre)	
	_____	
	_____	
	_____	
	_____	
	_____	
	_____	
	_____	
Fast Food Restaurants (Restaurantes)	_____	What do you purchase most often? ¿Que compra mas frecuente vente?
	_____	
	_____	
	_____	
	_____	
	_____	

Which foods do you most often buy for your family at the grocery store? Please send the names and brands. (¿Cúales comidas compra usted in la tienda mas frecuentemente? Mande las nombres y marcas por favor) What food do you buy most often in fast food restaurants? (¿Cúales comidas compra usted para su familia en los restaurantes y tiendas? Mande las marcas de los platillas por favor)

of cultural food such as "tamales" and "tacos" could be shown so that the student could talk about what he/she saw, and later the student would read what he/she dictated orally as he/she told the teacher comments about the pictures or photographs. This technique could add a little variety to the many other story ideas or pictures that are presented to students in various classes on a daily basis. More advanced students with moderate intellectual disabilities could learn to understand the words said to them in both Spanish and English, and many could learn to spell a few words, at least in their native language. Some simple Spanish words that could be learned along with the English equivalents are "uva" (grape), "taco" (taco), "Papa" (potato), and "caldo" (soup), etc.

Parents can also be taught to help teach their verbal or nonverbal son and/or daughter new words in either or both languages, but caution should be exercised. The teacher should not send home lists of English and Spanish equivalents to the parents; when possible teachers should visit the parents of linguistically and culturally different students, in their homes, in order to teach and to model for the parents what needs to be done if the child is to have his or her learning reinforced at home.

Follow-up needs to be done by the teacher to see if what she/he suggested to the parents is being done at home. Descamps (1986) noted that many Latino parents do not come to school conferences, etc., because they feel alienated and set apart from the big school building and teachers and principals who teach in the schools. Descamps (1986) goes on to say that if teachers visit the Latino parents in their homes, or find some way to bring the parents in car pools from their homes, many of them will begin to see what they can do to help their son and/or daughter. Also, Hernández (1986) adds that it is important for teachers to know some Spanish or have bilingual interpreters present on parents' night; Latino parents would thus feel more at home and like they belong in the public schools.

In California, Texas, and Illinois, Fiesta Educativa has been instrumental in providing many services to Latino families who have children and youth with disabilities (Rueda & Martinez, 1992).

Martinez (1995), who is the founder of Fiesta Educativa in California, indicates that Latino parents and families begin to participate more when they become empowered and take leadership to provide each other with information after they have attended mini and major conferences they have helped to organize.

Having been involved directly with Fiesta Educativa in Texas and now in California, this writer feels that this is an excellent way to have Latino parents more actively participate in their son's and/or daughter's education. Where possible, more parents need to be empowered in their neighborhoods so they can become more knowledgeable with their son and/or daughters and contribute toward their education at school and at home.

Thus, in teaching language and reading to students of more moderate to severe intellectual disabilities who are also culturally and linguistically different, it is not only important to make use of familiar cultural materials that are a part of the student's family, but it is also necessary to work closely with the parents. The cooperation thus engendered should include using Spanish (or whatever the language of the home is), but it is also necessary to work closely with the parents so that they can feel that they are a part of the school environment. One way of doing this is by empowering the parents, as is done in Fiesta Educativa. Thus, the parents can be made to feel that they have something important to contribute to their son's and/or daughter's education. The strangeness that parents from a nonmainstream culture frequently feel in the "alien" community they face can also be lessened or even dissipated by getting them involved in the educational process as co-equals.

VOCATIONAL AND COMMUNITY TRAINING

Obviously, the areas of functional reading and language are important when dealing with students of moderate to severe handicaps, especially when they are of different cultural and linguistic backgrounds from the mainstream community about them. But the areas of vocational training and community training are no less vital in their education.

In coordinating several nonsheltered vocational training programs involving various school districts and also directing a postsecondary program on a university campus, this writer has become aware that many Latino parents often do not understand the value of their son's and/or daughter's participation in on-the-job training. Many parents are often reluctant to send their son and/or daughter to learn to do a job in the community because they feel that the parents will be there always to take care of the son and/or daughter, or they feel that the family member is too handicapped to do actual work.

In El Paso, in two of the school districts where the nonsheltered programming was initiated, all parents were telephoned so they could come to an instructional meeting designed to explain to each of them what nonsheltered vocational training would have to offer their son and/or daughter. The principal was asked to speak to the parents concerning the school's involvement in such programming. (It is very important to include principals and other administrators in these in-service meetings, because many Latino people tend to follow closely the advice or information of people who represent authority figures in the schools and community.) Once the parents received the explanation in their native language, they were also taken in school buses to be shown the actual setting where their son and/or daughter would participate in on-the-job training. This entire effort proved to be highly successful with the Latino parents, because they supported the entire training program once they understood it. Further, once the vocational programming was initiated, the Mexican American students were absent far less often than they had been previously.

The actual training of culturally and linguistically different students should involve some instruction in the student's native language. For instance, if a student is told, "Turn the button on," or "Push the button" in order to start a machine, the trainer should follow this particular cuing with a phrase in the student's native language. In Spanish, the client would be cued "Prenda aqui" or "Apriete este boton." Cuing the student of moderate to severe intellectual disabilities in Spanish or his/her native language is helpful so that the student can respond more easily and quickly to the trainer's directions. A tape can be made of the most important cuing in vocational training in English and Spanish (or whatever the "different" language is), so that the college student trainer, teacher, and/or aide can listen to it and follow some of this type of cuing. This material is helpful for those trainers who do not know how to speak the student's particular home language.

Just as the parents must be made a part of the vocational training for their son and/or daughter from the beginning, so too must the parents be made a part of community-based instruction. Parents must be informed by phone or letter, plus an actual meeting and/or conference of the importance of their taking their son and/or daughter to the community to shop and buy food. They must also have explained to them the importance of their family members participating in these same activities in school and in other community environments. Too often it is taken for granted that all parents see and understand the value of their son and/or daughter participating in such activities, but this is not always the case. Many Mexican American parents often do not understand that their son and/or daughter needs the exposure to other more normalized peers. Some parents, further, do not understand why their son and/or daughter should learn to use a restaurant or grocery store. All this must be explained to parents initially and be reinforced periodically so their continued support will be there for the teacher and other trainers. This writer has discovered that if parents are not shown some demonstration of how the community training is accomplished, with photographs or cards of the items that they are to have their son and/or daughter purchase, much of the instruction will never be done at home and no generalization training will occur.

Further, teachers or aides will often have to make matching-to-sample cards of the various grocery items and will have to make communication booklets for the student so that parents can use one set of these materials at home with their son and/or daughter. In order to accomplish this goal, the teacher or trainer may need to send some type of questionnaire

TABLE XVIII
FOOD AND RESTAURANT QUESTIONNAIRE
(Inventario de Comidas y Restaurantes)

Home (La Casa)	Vocabulary (Vocabulario o palabras) usuales	Stories (Dichos o cuentos)	Songs (Canciones particulares)
	_____	_____	_____
	_____	_____	_____
	_____	_____	_____
	_____	_____	_____
	_____	_____	_____
	_____	_____	_____
Community (La Communidad)	Vocabulary (Vocabulario o palabras) usuales	Places you and your family visit (Lugares que su familia frecuenta)	
	_____	_____	_____
	_____	_____	_____
	_____	_____	_____
	_____	_____	_____
	_____	_____	_____
School (La Escuela)	Vocabulary (Vocabulario o palabras) usuales		
	_____	_____	_____
	_____	_____	_____
	_____	_____	_____
	_____	_____	_____
	_____	_____	_____

Give us any other suggestions or comments about what you would like us to teach your son and/or daughter. (Denos otras sugerencias acerca de la instrucción que usted quiera decirnos que le podanos presentar a instrucción a su hijo y hija.)

in the parents' native or home language so that they can fill it out and return the information to the teacher (see Table XVIII). When the questionnaire is returned to the teacher, he/she can begin making food cards that the student in his/her class can take home and use while shopping with his/her parents and can even use while shopping independently for his/her parents. The communication booklet can also be developed to include restaurant items. Then communication booklets will have fuller usefulness at home; parents can have their son and/or daughter order what they need in restaurants when they go out to eat as a family, or when the nonverbal student is in the community on his/her own and wants to order something to eat. Thus, parents need not only to be informed of the importance of their son and/or daughter participating in community-based instruction, but they further need to be sent materials at home that they can use with their son and/or daughter in the communication. Additionally, Latino parents who do not understand the value and the techniques of such training need to be given instruction in their home language, so they can understand how to make use of the materials the teacher has made for their son and/or daughter to use at home.

In addition, it does not matter what area of the curriculum one is concerned with in teaching students who are culturally and linguistically different, the teacher must consider not only the student's home language and culture, but the parents of these students as well. Parents must be taught to use the various curricular materials; otherwise, many of these important areas of their child's education will never be used at home as part of the student's education.

DISCUSSION QUESTIONS

1. Define who is culturally and linguistically different student who also has a moderate to severe handicap.
2. What are some cultural implications that should be considered when teaching some Latino students?
3. What can be done specifically to teach the culturally and linguistically different student in vocational, community training, reading, and language?
4. Why are parents important to consider in teaching the culturally and linguistically different student?
5. How can you empower Latino parents to contribute more to their sons and/or daughters with disabilities?

REFERENCES

Baca, L. (1980). Issues of the education of culturally diverse exceptional children. *Exceptional Children, 46*(8), 583–605.

Baca, L., and Bransford, L. (1982). *An appropriate education for handicapped children of limited English proficiency.* ERIC Clearinghouse on Handicapped and Gifted Children, The Council for Exceptional Children, Reston, VA, pp. 1–22.

Brown, L. (1984). Functional skills in programs for students with severe handicaps.

(Manuscript done in cooperation with University of Wisconsin, Madison & Madison Metropolitan School District, pp. 1–6)

Carpenter, L. J. (1983). *Bilingual special education: An overview of issues,* pp. 3–56. Los Alamitos, CA: National Center for Bilingual Research.

Cegelka, P. (1986). *Educational services to handicapped students with limited English proficiency: A California statewide study.* ERIC Clearinghouse on Handicapped and Gifted Children. Reston, VA: Council for Exceptional Children, pp. 1–121.

Chamot, A., and McKeon, D. (1984). *ESL teaching methodologies educating the minority language student,* pp. 1–51. Reston, VA: National Clearinghouse for Bilingual Education Inter-American Research Associates, Rosalyn, VA.

Descamps, J. (1987). The Mexican American student: Cultural implications. (Workshop presented at U.T. El Paso during Hispanic Heritage Week).

Durán, E. (1986). Comparison of Spanish only, Spanish and English, and English only. *Reading Improvement, 23*(2), 138–141.

Estrada, L. J., and Nava, A. (1976). The long struggle for bilingualism and a consistent language policy: Early Chicano education in California and the Southwest. *Educator, 19*(1), 36–40.

Grossman, H. (1984). *Educating Hispanic students: Cultural implications for instruction, classroom management, counseling and assessment,* pp. 56–204. Springfield, IL: Charles C Thomas.

Henderson, R. W. (1980). Social and emotional needs of culturally diverse children. *Exceptional Children, 46*(8), 598–604.

Hernández, N. (1987). *The Mexican American student: Cultural implications.* (Workshop presented at U.T. El Paso during Hispanic Heritage Week)

Martínez, I. (1996). Conference call concerning setting up a local chapter of Fiesta Educativa in Sacramento, Sacramento, CA.

Nuttall, E. V. (1984). A critical look at testing and evaluation from a cross-cultural perspective. In Philip C. Chinn's (Ed.), *Education of culturally and linguistically different exceptional children.* Reston, VA: ERIC Clearinghouse on Handicapped and Gifted Children, pp. 42–63.

Ortiz, A. (1984). Language and curriculum development for exceptional bilingual children. In Philip C. Chinn (Ed.), *Education of culturally and linguistically different exceptional children.* Reston, VA: ERIC Clearinghouse on Handicapped and Gifted Children, The Council for Exceptional Children, pp. 77–100.

Rodriguez, F. (1982). Mainstreaming a multicultural concept into special education: Guidelines for teacher trainers. *Exceptional Children, 49*(3), 220–227.

Rueda, R. (1984). Cognitive development and learning in mildly handicapped bilingual children. In Philip Chinn's (Ed.), *Education of culturally and linguistically different exceptional children.* Reston, VA: ERIC Council for Exceptional Children, pp. 63–76.

Rueda, R., and Martínez, I. (1992). Fiesta Educativa: One community's approach to parent training in developmental disabilities for Latino families. *TASH, 17*(2), pp. 93–103.

Chapter 14

STRATEGIES FOR TEACHING THE
SECOND LANGUAGE LEARNERS

ELVA DURÁN

The author of this chapter will discuss some second language acquisition theories and strategies which are helpful in teaching second language learners who may be in general education classes or may be special education students who may or may not be enrolled in general education classes. This writer will additionally share some specific teaching strategies she has tried in several classrooms in northern California for the past five years.

SECOND LANGUAGE ACQUISITION INFORMATION

When students who come from another country or whose primary or first language is not English, it is necessary to keep several ideas in mind when teaching the second language learner. First, the student whose first language is not English needs to feel no anxiety when learning a second language. Students should not be pressured to speak in the new language they are acquiring until they have enough confidence to begin verbalizing in that language on their own. Many students go through a silent period when they are listening and internalizing the new language they are learning, seeing, and possibly tasting. Krashen (1994), who first talked about the *affective filter hypothesis* to learning a second language, gave us extremely important information about creating low anxiety environments so that second language learners could begin listening without feeling they had to speak in the second language immediately. The silent period could last anywhere from a few months to a year.

It is important for a teacher or parents helping the second language learner during this period to be patient and reinforcing. Praise should be given to students as they listen quietly. Praise should be continued as they become further motivated and empowered in order to continue wanting to progress and practice their new skills in the second language.

This writer has observed in various classrooms that as teachers are encouraging, warm, and positive with students who are learning English for the first time, students become highly motivated and progress even faster to learn the new language or, in this case, English. One of the greatest characteristics of a truly great teacher is his/her amazing ability to accept the student no matter at what stage or level he/she may be. There is no better way to lower the affective filter or create a low anxiety environment for second language learners than by being positive and accepting of the student's stage of language learning. Thus, a teacher or parent teaching or helping the second language learner must remember the great progress students make if they are less anxious when learning a new language.

Another important aspect to remember in teaching second language learners is that everything presented to students must be taught to them in comprehensible means. In the comprehensible input hypothesis (Krashen, 1994), the teacher in teaching second language learners must remember to present the material so that the students understand the meaning of what they are hearing and seeing. For instance, the teacher needs to remember that second language learners need to be shown concrete and visual information in order for them to understand the concept or vocabulary words that they are being presented.

Another important hypothesis that is part of second language acquisition, according to Krashen (1994), is the reading hypothesis. In the reading hypothesis, Krashen notes that the more teachers and parents read to children, the more they will hear the language sounds and the more quickly they will begin speaking the language they are learning. Also, the more books that are read to children initially and, later, the more books children read to themselves, the faster the children will learn the second language.

As part of the reading hypothesis, Krashen (1994) also noted that students must be given at least fifteen to twenty minutes daily in order for them to select books they want to see and read. During this time, the students are to observe a quiet fifteen minutes as they read their books. The sustained silent reading is also known as DEAR time, or drop everything and read (Reyes, 1995). In one of the first grade classrooms this writer observed, the teacher give a signal and the students knew it was their DEAR time or sustained silent reading time where they were to begin selecting books of their choice to quietly read for fifteen minutes. The students were silent and were very much involved in looking while some were reading or seeing pictures in their books. According to Krashen, the more students are exposed to words and sentences in books, the more they will see how language is written and the more their vocabulary and understanding will increase. Krashen (1994) also strongly believes and has researched to validate his position that as students are given time to select books they would like to read and are read to daily, the more progress they will make in acquiring a second language.

Ortiz (1994), in her Aim for the Best Program, has noted that developing shared literature units with children and having the teacher prepare reading of various stories and a variety of children's favorite literature will also help increase a child's language development. Ortiz (1994) noted that shared literature should take the following suggested format in order to insure success with the language minority student. First, the teacher should be familiar with the story he/she is going to tell or read to the students. If the students are younger, the teacher may choose stories that reflect primary through second grade focus. These can be stories that follow a simple repetition sequence such as **The Three Bears** or **Brown Bear, Brown Bear.** It is important to note that the teacher may choose simple repetition sequence stories that come from the student's language and culture. If these culturally appropriate stories are not selected initially, then the linguistically appropriate stories can be selected later in the month. The teacher should also prepare materials that are age appropriate for the children to see as he/she is reading the story. The props, the various visuals, create a motivation for the children that allows them to be further hooked into listening and chorally reading certain lines of the story.

Following the material or character development, the teacher begins to familiarize the students with the cover of the book. The teacher can ask the children, "What is the title of the story?" "Who's name(s) is on the cover?" "Who is the illustrator?" "Is the cover colorful?" the teacher may go on to ask. Again, the idea is to teach students that there are details in the front of a book as well as the cover. The teacher should continue the shared literature lesson by alerting the students to the details of the inside of the book. The children should see the author's and illustrator's names inside the first few pages of the book. The students can chorally read the author's and illustrator's names as the teacher opens the storybook to that particular part of the book.

Continuing with the instruction of the shared literature unit, the teacher begins reading from the book. The teacher carefully shows the children the visual aids he/she has developed for the story and further shows the children the various pictures or special illustrations that he/she wants the children to focus upon. As the teacher reads orally to the children, she/he can ask students questions to help build the drama or suspense of the story. Some of the questions the teacher may ask may relate directly to the story such as, "What do you think will happen next?" "Why do you feel the character is acting in such a manner?" These questions along the way help keep the students' motivation high. Questioning the students also helps the children recall details of the story.

Another part of shared literature is to ask the children how many liked or did not like the story! Along with this question, the teacher has already prepared a language chart which can be made of a large butcher paper or chart material. The chart should be displayed near the students' discussion circle or should be positioned where they can see the titles and wording of the language chart. Some suggested sections of the chart may include: "Title of the Book," "Illustrator," "Names of Characters," and "What I Liked about the Book." The teacher can lead the children in a discussion and he/she can fill in the various columns of the language chart as the students discuss answers with the teacher. The chart should be cumulative so that each of the books that the teacher reads with the students should be part of the language chart information. Keeping such a chart of various books read by the children and teacher will help additionally develop a sense of appreciation for all the various books that they read together.

In a qualitative study involving language minority students with autism who were in a fully included classroom, Durán (1995) found that language charts and shared literature were very contributing in helping southeast Asian and Asian American students increase their primary and secondary language. Also, when the students with autism were moved closer to the front of a circle and paired with general education buddies, the more the students with autism who were language minority could **cue** or pay closer attention to the various details of the different storybooks. Durán (1995) discovered that the LEP (limited proficient students of English) students with autism came running to the story circle and their attending behaviors increased as the year progressed. Thus, sharing literature and utilizing language charts with students in fully included classroom settings was a significant factor in assisting students to increase their oral language development and appreciation of books they had been read to during the school year.

In addition to emphasizing second language acquisition information so that students can acquire information presented to them in the classroom and other environments, it is necessary to know various strategies in order to teach second language learners. Some of these strategies include: total physical response approach (Asher, 1981); natural approach (Terrell and Krashen, 1994); cooperative learning (Kagan, 1994); sheltered instruction or specifically designed academic instruction in English (Walqui-vanLier, 1994); and utilizing a combination of readers' and writers' workshops/games to enhance literacy skills in second language learners. Also, some of the methodologies that have been found to be useful with second language learners include giving students much oral language development (Baca, 1989; Ortiz, 1995) as well as increasing their **line** of reading (Krashen, 1994).

TOTAL PHYSICAL RESPONSE APPROACH

The total physical response approach was a method developed by James Asher. In this method the teacher or person presenting to the students gestures and gives them commands so that they follow or try to complete a set of basic directions such as, "stand up," "sit down," "touch your hands, touch your arms." To determine if the students have learned the various commands so the teacher can go on to new curriculum information, she/he will only indicate the commands verbally and will not do the gestures as he/she is giving the oral commands to the students. If the students can perform the commands the teacher is giving them orally, then Asher suggested that comprehensible input has been achieved and the teacher can present new information to them. Asher does not have a formal curriculum for the total physical response approach, but he suggested that teachers begin with basic vocabulary and gradually move to other vocabulary around the classroom and other environments.

This writer, in assisting a variety of teachers who teach more moderate to severe students, suggests that basic vocabulary such as names of objects around the room, school, and other environments such as the home and community be presented to students. The students could further learn to point to their names or addresses, phone numbers, and other personal information. Such information is vital for the students to know, especially if they are attempting to be out in the community.

By utilizing the natural environments in order to learn vocabulary and functional information around the home, school, and community, the teacher is also stressing that the students learn the vocabulary because the students are often unable to generalize or transfer learning from one environment to the next.

When using the Total Physical Response Approach, the teacher should ask the students to demonstrate that they understand by asking them to touch the object or do the action the teacher has named but has not physically demonstrated for the children. According to Krashen (1994), true comprehension on the child's part can only come by the teacher giving the word or words orally to the child and not demonstrating the various actions that accompany the vocabulary or commands he/she is presenting to the students.

This writer has successfully used the total physical response approach when teaching university students who know only English by attempting to teach several lessons in Spanish. This is the writer's first language and she presents various demonstrations to the university students in Spanish in order for the English-only students to understand what students of other languages and cultures feel because they do not know English. The university students have told this writer that after experiencing the first vocabulary words in Spanish, they felt more tolerant of their second language learners in their classrooms. It is highly recommended that university students who are preparing to be teachers be taught in a language other than the one they know in order for them to better understand what second language learners are experiencing as they attempt to learn new vocabulary or information that is not in their first language.

THE NATURAL APPROACH

Another approach that teachers or instructional aids can successfully use to teach second language learners is the Natural Approach. The Natural Approach (Krashen and Terrell, 1981) emphasized that students will continue learning the second language, or in this case English, by having the students practice English in natural everyday talk or conversation. Krashen and Terrell (1981) stressed that the time to do the conversations must be planned in the everyday curriculum schedule, otherwise the time that is needed for the students to speak will not occur.

Some suggestions to encourage more conversation may include role playing introductions, ordering from a menu, and hearing the students answer questions about want ads or other advertisements. The teacher can have the students describe their favorite toys, animals, or events. He/she can have them explain how to get from one point or destination to another. This is a difficult task for many second language learners, but practicing pragmatics in learning a second language is important in acquiring a second language. Pragmatics, as used here, means the student can explain on a higher level, using their newly acquired language, how to go from one point to another for example. When presenting lesson demonstrations to students utilizing the Natural Approach, the teacher should demonstrate for the students. He/she may hold up a menu filled with words, fruits, and pictures, and may say, "I will order a fruit salad with iced tea." Another person can take the person's order so that a restaurant scene can be depicted for the students. The students can then role play being the waiter/waitress and another student or students can use menus in order to order their meals. Utilizing cooperative groups to have them practice ordering meals is an excellent tool in order to give different students opportunities to practice English. After the students have had opportunities to practice their role playing conversations, as in this case ordering from a menu, the teacher can check their comprehension of the activity by asking them questions about their orders. For example, the teacher may say, "Did you order furniture today, Saul?" If Saul indicates that he does not understand by responding, "Yes, I ordered furniture," the teacher will know to assist the students who were in the cooperative group who made the error in comprehension of the concept. The teacher can sit with the cooperative group where Saul is seated and he/she can participate in ordering various items from the menu. The demonstration will help the students see where they made the mistakes along with Saul.

Krashen (1994) notes that students who are second language learners will learn best to speak, read, and write if they are given the direct opportunities to do these activities in various environments. The Natural Approach gives classroom teachers many opportunities to allow second language learners the opportunities they need to learn English.

As the students learn more and more English, Krashen (1994) noted that the grammar and all its correct forms are also learned as they begin to get practice in speaking and writing. Grammar should not be emphasized, according to Krashen, in the early stages of learning English. According to Krashen, the students are often turned off to writing and speaking if their first attempts are overshadowed by correcting everything they say and write.

This writer has seen many elementary, secondary, and adult second language learners who are initially learning to speak and later write in the second language who do not feel comfortable to continue if someone is constantly reminding them of their oral or written errors. Patience and empowering the second language learners are the keys in getting these students to learn the new language. The second language learner needs to feel empowered to continue learning even if they make a few mistakes. It is a good idea to remember that learning a second language may take up to ten hours and developing oral and written proficiency may take five to seven years and in many cases up to ten years. This writer noticed that some moderately impaired students or Down syndrome children who were second language learners learned initial words and phrases after thirty-three plus hours using instruction with the students daily for thirty minutes twice a day. This writer, as a second language learner, feels that learning a second language is an ongoing process that requires patience and positive teachers who not only understand how second language learners learn other languages but it also helps if the teachers have experienced some difficulty themselves in learning a foreign language.

Similarly, the Language Experience Approach can also be utilized effectively with the Natural Approach. In the Language Experience Approach, Van Allen (1985) told us to make use of a student's experiences as someone records their words on a chart or paper. By combining the Natural Approach and Language Experience Approach, students can experience various experiences in their everyday lives and then the teacher can lead them into a discussion and begin recording some of the words and phrases they are saying. The teacher can print the words on the chalkboard or paper and have them read from left to right as he/she teaches each word. Later, the students can read back the words and phrases in a natural speech production so that they can hear the words and phrases read as conversation is naturally spoken. Students can prepare language experience booklets with the title of the story and their names on the cover of their books so they can take pride in their work as they are also authors. They can read their language experience booklets to each other or to themselves. The covers of the booklets can be illustrated for more enjoyment of their work. Thus, writing, reading, and speaking are combined with the use of the Natural Approach. All of these strategies work very nicely in fully included classroom settings.

The study done by Durán (1994 and 1995) revealed that five students with moderate disabilities who were also second language learners learned literacy skills by using a combination of the total physical response approach, natural approach, language experience, and shared literature. This study is ongoing and data will continue to be collected on the students as they progress from grade to grade. Data was further collected on five students with autism who were second language learners and were fully included in a general education classroom. One study is still in progress (1994–1995) and the results are indicating that the children with autism who are also second language learners are learning English because of a combined use of the total physical response approach and the natural approach, which the teachers and instructional aides also combine with a rich oral language development and shared literature approach (Durán, 1995).

The parents of the children in both general education and special needs enjoy social skill and language development progress which the students also enjoy in fully included classroom setting. Everyone has benefitted from this class situation.

SHELTERED INSTRUCTION/SPECIFICALLY DESIGNED ACADEMIC INSTRUCTION IN ENGLISH (SDAIE)

Sheltered instruction is generally associated with several instructional strategies designed to make academically rigorous subject matter more understandable to second language learners at intermediate fluency or above (Schifini, 1991). This is usually done by teaching new concepts in context and providing additional cues to the student. The teaching techniques geared to provide comprehensible input in the second language classroom are now also being used by content teachers (Schifini, 1991). Common cues or context clues are: gestures, visuals, props, manipulatives, audio visual aides, models, charts, graphic organizers, and teacher talk that is appropriate to the students' English language proficiency (Schifini, 1991).

According to Schifini (1991), subject matter taught in a sheltered way usually involves opportunities for careful background building and the tapping and focusing of students' prior knowledge related to the key concepts of the lesson. Texts are used as a tool to help students develop concepts.

Teachers using sheltered instruction check students' understanding of the subject matter by observation and questioning of their knowledge of the concepts. Teachers who are strong in content such as science and social studies are usually the instructors of sheltered content classes.

Students who are the candidates for this type of instruction need to have intermediate fluency in English. Generally, intermediate speakers are good candidates for sheltered classes because they have acquired many vocabulary words in English and are able to respond to questions that are asked of them orally. Additionally, many are able to engage in some discussion and would profit from various types of questions or topic themes they are presented as part of the classroom information. Students are usually in upper grades and are making transition from primary language instruction to English. The primary language may still be used when the students may be having difficulty understanding additional concepts. At no time should sheltered instruction be considered as watered-down curriculum (Walqui-vanLier, 1994). Also, the primary language may be used when the students' primary language is predominately of one particular cultural and linguistic group.

In California schools where more than seventy different languages exist in some school districts, it would not be possible to use seventy different languages in the sheltered classroom unless paraprofessionals or volunteers could come to the classroom and assist with the majority linguistic groups which would be found in the classrooms at any one time. Thus far, this has proven to be quite difficult because there are not enough translators available at any one school to help teachers when more than one or two languages exist in the various classrooms.

In a study conducted by this writer in 1994 until the present, she observed the usefulness of a teacher utilizing sheltered instruction to teach students who were in a third grade, fully included classroom in a rural town in northern California. The teacher had her bilingual/cross-cultural teaching certification and was also certified to teach in general education. She had monolingual English only speakers and had a student from a self-contained special education classroom attending half a day and additionally had limited English proficient and other students who were at an intermediate fluency and literacy level in English. The teacher had one instructional aide and several student teachers throughout the school year.

Observation data was taken twice weekly for two to two and one-half hours on the children who were limited English and those who were on a more advanced English development level. The writer shared results monthly with the classroom teacher. She wanted to know the results and also felt that she could improve the program further by adding any information to her curriculum in the classroom.

After a year, many variables were evident in academic and literacy increases in the five children whom this writer and her assistant took data on each week. One of the variables that was consistently revealed in the results was the teacher's strong use of sheltered instruction. She went out of her way to prepare materials to help all the children who needed the assistance to achieve comprehensible input. Other variables that were in evidence were the effective use of cooperative learning groups, shared literature, and reader's and writer's workshops. Data will be further collected in order to determine if the new teacher at the students' new grade level will utilize any of the variables which proved successful in the former setting. Results of this qualitative study were reported to the principal in a final report. She was able to share the results with the classroom teachers who were involved in the study. Data collection will be continued by this writer as the students move to new grade levels.

This writer has noted that once again sheltered instruction, like so many general and multilingual/multicultural strategies, has shown to be quite effective with special education students who are second language learners and also have moderate to severe disabilities. The language and literacy enrichment found in general education classrooms is very helpful to the more moderate to severe groups of students who are fully included in these particular classrooms.

Additionally, the term SDAIE (Specifically Designed Academic Instruction in English) is the newer term used to also refer to sheltered instruction in California schools (Walqui-vanLier, 1994). Because there are so many different languages found in California schools, the term SDAIE more closely explains what teachers of sheltered instruction are attempting to do in classrooms.

OTHER STRATEGIES USEFUL IN TEACHING SECOND LANGUAGE LEARNERS

Cooperative Learning

Cooperative learning consists of student-centered learning activities completed by students in heterogenous groups of two to six (Cochran, 1989). According to Cochran (1989) and Calderón (1990), students benefit from observing learning strategies used by their peers. Further, Cochran (1989) noted that limited English proficient students benefit from face-to-face verbal interactions, which promote communication that is natural and meaningful.

This writer, in conducting two qualitative studies with limited English proficient students who had autism and five other students in a second study who were at-risk for special education, discovered that one of the variables which assisted all students in both studies learn English more effectively was cooperative learning. The students with autism learned more social skills and English because of the inclusive setting they were placed in and also learned more English due to the cooperative learning groups. The students with autism stopped tantruming and were able to attend more due to the various activities scheduled in the fully included classroom.

In the third grade classroom where the other study was conducted, the teacher utilized cooperative group work for all her activities where the students needed to discuss and come up with solutions. She rotated the various roles of "leader," "recorder," "observer," and "encourager." This gave all the students an opportunity to be in charge of different activities. She also monitored each group during their discussions and while they were to complete activities. In this way, she could better see which students were not participating in the discussions or other group work.

As an observer and researcher who collected data weekly with these two groups of students, this writer was able to see that students did interact and discuss with one another as a result of the cooperative learning activities. The students with autism were able to seek others in the classroom due to cooperative learning.

It is a good idea when using cooperative learning to teach the students the various roles in which they can participate. Also, it is a good idea to teach them to have respect for each other, especially if one student says or discusses a comment that may be different from the thoughts of others in the group. If respect is not made part of the rules of the cooperative learning activities, the limited English students will become fearful of speaking and their progress to learn more English will not be realized.

According to Calderón (1990), in order for students to achieve competence in group work, certain principles must be followed:

(1) The teacher models the discourse and processes overtly, explicitly, and concretely in appropriate context of cooperative activities.

(2) Strategies for working and learning together and the range and utility of the strategies are discussed, and interventions and modifications are attempted by the students.

(3) Ineffective strategies and misconceptions about group work and individual participation are confronted.

(4) Debriefing activities where thinking is brought out into an open space where students and teacher can see it and learn from it are indicated in the cooperative learning activity.

(5) The responsibility for learning to work collaboratively and debriefing of that process should be transferred to the students as soon as they take charge. The transfer should be gradual, working on one cooperative skill at a time until it is internalized.

(6) Students should receive continuous feedback on their improvement.

(7) Just as teachers need modeling, rationale, practice, feedback, and coaching, so do students (pp. 11–12).

Thus, just putting students in groups and encouraging them to work together is not enough to produce learning gains according to Calderón (1990). Teachers must be well trained in appropriate teaching strategies and classroom management techniques for organizing critical thinking.

Finally, this writer has seen the use of direct instruction methodologies as noted by Englemann (1978) used very effectively with cooperative learning groups. In direct instruction, the teacher or facilitator uses some signaling, follow-up, and giving the students a business-like atmosphere especially when relaying to them about certain tasks which must be completed. In several classrooms in northern California where the second language learners were a part of a fully included third and fourth grade class, the teachers initially gave the students rules and explained to them that no one would laugh or not respect a different view from their opinion in the cooperative groups. The teachers would continue to use the direct instruction methodologies to follow-up and ask the students what they had said and further asked them what the rules of respect were for each student in the groups. During this portion of the information giving, direct instruction methodologies were nicely woven in with the cooperative learning group information.

It is this writer's view that no one method is the only answer to improving the students who may need additional help. Using a variety of approaches such as cooperative learning and direct instruction, for instance at the beginning of setting up rules for the groups to follow, is very helpful. Students who have severe disabilities and who are fully included in classrooms may also need additional structure that some direct instruction can insure for the learners.

INCLUSION

Since 1985 we have heard that students with more severe disabilities should be included in general education classrooms (Laski, 1994). Inclusion in our schools has made some progress since 1985, but according to many school principals, teachers, and parents, much more needs to be done before more students with severe disabilities are placed in general education classrooms for the entire school day. The key is to place students with disabilities in general education classrooms with support from the special education teacher and his/her staff. Inclusion can be of major help to students who are second language learners and who also have severe or moderate disabilities because the enriched curriculum that is seen in general education classrooms is very helpful to the students to learn English or their primary language (Durán, 1995).

Students with autism who are limited English proficient or who are learning English as a second language are enriched by being placed in fully included general education classrooms. In two general education classrooms where students with autism who were limited English or attempting to learn English for the first time and other second language learners who were more moderate in their disability were also placed in general education settings, started to increase their English language and oral language development because the teachers used a variety of whole language and other strong literature and sheltered types of instruction (Durán, 1995).

The modeling from their peers and the combination of general education practices helped the second language learners who also had severe disabilities increase their language, literacy, and social skill development (Durán, 1995).

As more and more students with disabilities are placed in general education settings which have good teacher models who are practicing and implementing a variety of curricular strategies, the more progress students who are second language learners and who have disabilities will make.

In conclusion, strategies which can be added to fully included classrooms, such as cooperative learning, some direct instruction methodologies, natural and total physical response approaches, plus a strong program which will increase literacy skills, will help to greatly enhance all students who are in fully included general education settings. The idea for teachers to use a variety of curricular strategies that are based in research and good sound practice will enhance the learning that language minority students need in order to learn English.

DISCUSSION QUESTIONS

(1) What can be done by a teacher to increase comprehensible input among the second language learners in the class?
(2) How can the Total Physical Response Approach and Natural Approach be used effectively to help second language learners who are more moderate to severe learn English?
(3) Discuss strategies that have been found effective in teaching second language learners English.
(4) Why is full inclusion effective in assisting second language learners to learn English?

REFERENCES

Ada, A. F. (1990). *A magical encounter Spanish-language children's literature in the classroom.* Compton, CA: Santillava Publishing Company.

Ambert, A. M. (1991). *Bilingual education and English as a second language, a research handbook.* New York: Garland.

Baca, L. (1989). *The bilingual special education interface* (2nd Ed.). New York: Maxwell Macmillan International.

Calderón, M. (1990). *Cooperative learning for limited English proficient students.* Washington, D.C.: Center for Research on Effective Schooling for Disadvantaged Students.

Chamot, A. U. (1985). *ESL instructional approaches and underlying language learning theories.* Washington, D.C.: National Clearinghouse for Bilingual Education.

Cochran, C. (1989). *Strategies for involving LEP students in the all-English medium classroom: A cooperative learning approach.* Washington, D.C.: National Clearinghouse for Bilingual Education.

Crandall, J. (1987). *ESL through content-area instruction mathematics, science, social studies.* Englewood Cliffs, NJ: Regent/Prentice-Hall.

Durán, E. (1988). *Teaching the moderately and severely handicapped student and autistic adolescent with particular attention to bilingual special education.* Springfield, IL: Charles C Thomas.

Durán, E. (1992). *Vocational training and employment of the moderately and severely handicapped and autistic adolescent with particular emphasis to bilingual special education.* Springfield, IL: Charles C Thomas.

Durán, E. (1993). Effective communication programming for language minority students with severe disabilities. Speeches/conference papers.

Durán, E. (1995). Inclusion and second language acquisition. Qualitative study report conducted in Sacramento City Unified School district. A report submitted to Sacramento City Unified School District, Sacramento, California.

Durán, E. (1995). Second language acquisition. Qualitative study report conducted at Valley Oaks Elementary School, submitted to school principal. Galt, CA.

Freeman, Y. S., and Freeman, D. E. (1992). *Whole language for second language learners.* Exeter, NH: Heinemann.

Krashen, S. (1981). Bilingual education and second language acquisition theory. In California State Department of Education (Ed.), *Schooling and language minority students: A theoretical framework* (pp. 51–82). Sacramento, CA: Office of Bilingual Education.

Krashen, S. (1993). *The power of reading insights from the research.* Colorado: Libraries Unlimited, Inc.

Krashen, S. D., and Terrell, T. D. (1983). *The natural approach: Language acquisition in the classroom.* Hayward, CA: Alemany Press.

Ortiz, A. (1994). How bilingual/special education came to be. Symposium for Second Language Learners in Regular and Special Education, California State University.

Ovando, C. J., and Collier, V. P. (1985). *Bilingual and ESL classrooms teaching in multicultural contexts.* New York: McGraw-Hill.

Peregoy, S. F. (1993). *Reading, writing, and learning in ESL: A resource book for K–8 teachers.* New York: Longman.

Pérez, B., and Torres-Guzman, M. E. (1992). *Learning in two worlds: An integrated Spanish/English biliteracy approach.* New York: Longman.

Reyes, R. (1995). SDAIE as part of literature stories. Presentation made to California State University faculty. Second Language Acquisition Series.

Schifini, A. (1991). *Sheltered instruction: The basics.* A training manual, pp. 1–4. Center for Language Education and Research, University of California, Los Angeles, CA.

Towell, J. (1993). *Strategies for monolingual teachers in multilingual classrooms.* Washington, D.C.: Educational Resource.

VanAllen, R. (1985). ESL instructional approaches and underlying language leaning theories. *Focus.* Washington, D.C.: National Clearinghouse for Bilingual Education.

Walqui-vanLier, A. (April, 1994). Providing access to stimulating curriculum through sheltered instruction (SDAIE). (Paper presented at California State University, Sacramento.)

Williams, S. J., and Snipper, G. C. (1990). Literacy and bilingualism. New York: Longman.

Chapter Fifteen

ADDRESSING CULTURAL AND LINGUISTIC DIVERSITY IN SPECIAL EDUCATION

PATRICIA THOMAS CEGELKA AND EUGENE C. VALLES

T he United States is characterized by its increasing cultural and linguistic diversity. Ethnolinguistic minorities are estimated to be over 32 percent of the total population by the year 2000, which translates into some 40 million persons whose primary language is other than English (Baca and Cervantes, 1989). This increasing diversity includes American Indians, immigrants from the Middle East, South Africa, Portugal, Finland, the Pacific Rim countries, South America, Central America, and Mexico, as well as many other groups. By far the greatest numbers are from Hispanic backgrounds, particularly Mexican, Cuban, and Puerto Rican. Nationally, Hispanics account for approximately half of the ethnolinguistically diverse population and 75 percent of the population who are limited-English proficient or bilingual (Baca and Cervantes, 1989).

In the near future, between 25 percent and 38 percent of all school-aged children will be culturally and linguistically diverse (Chinn and Hughes, 1987). Children of culturally and linguistically diverse backgrounds already account for over half of the school-age population in two states (California and Texas). This increasing diversity presents considerable challenges to the educational enterprise. Across the nation, schools are adopting multicultural approaches to curriculum and instruction. Bilingual education and English-as-a-Second Language programs are attempting to prepare adequate numbers of teachers to address the linguistic diversity of today's school population.

SPECIAL EDUCATION PRACTICES

Special education practices have also been dramatically affected. For many years, special education served as a dumping ground for disproportionately high numbers of culturally and linguistically diverse (CLD) students. The failure of these students to perform well on English-language intelligence tests, in combination with limited abilities in English and challenging school behaviors, resulted in children of cultural and linguistically diverse backgrounds being placed disproportionately in special education classes, most frequently classes for students with mental retardation. This was particularly true for students from Hispanic backgrounds. A 1973 study in one California city found that the enrollment of Hispanics in classes for the mentally retarded was four times greater than would be predicted statistically, given their overall representation in the community (Mercer, 1973). In this same year, in a city in Arizona where Mexican-Americans comprised 17.8 percent of the total school population, Mexican-American children constituted 67.7 percent of students placed in programs for mild mental retardation and 46.3 percent of the enrollment in programs for students with moderate to severe mental retardation (Kirp, 1973).

During the past quarter century, we have seen increased attention paid to the educational needs of culturally and linguistically diverse exceptional students (CLDE). Until very recently, the primary focus of this attention has been on issues relating to educational equity, with the objective of remedying practices that have resulted in over-representation of minority group students in special education. For this reason, the bulk of the literature, and most educational efforts, have targeted improvements in practices related to the assessment and placement of exceptional students who come from culturally and linguistically diverse backgrounds.

In addition, during this same time frame, most judicial, legislative, and policy efforts have focused primarily on the disproportional representation of CLD students in special education. Educational responses relative to program design issues, materials development, research, and personnel preparation have similarly zeroed in on assessment/identification/placement issues, frequently to the neglect of programmatic issues relating to the design and delivery of instruction. The professional literature is replete with articles reporting on the statistics of this overrepresentation, reviewing judicial decisions, critiquing assessment practices, or proposing models for culturally and linguistically sensitive assessment and for the preparation of assessment personnel.

While the gravity of these concerns cannot be overemphasized, there nonetheless remains a significant portion of students with limited-English proficiency (LEP) who do have legitimate disabilities and are in need of special education services. For example, given a total special education population of 3.6 million, and assuming that one-third of them are CLD, the incidence of such students would be approximately 1.2 million. A recent governmental report indicated that just over 64,000 LEP students are actually served in special education programs (Office of Special Education Programs, 1993). Of these, over 11,000 are students with moderate to severe mental retardation. This discrepancy may be the result of underreferral of some categories of CLDE students to special education, with educators choosing to place limited-English proficient exceptional students into bilingual education instead of special education programs (Ovando and Collier, 1985). It appears that overrepresentation is more frequently the case for minority-group children who are also limited-English proficient. In either case, the high number of CLDE students calls for systematic program development efforts if special education is to meet the needs of these students.

Because assessment concerns dominated the field for so long, scant attention was paid to issues relating to the design of instructional programs for CLDE students. It has been only since the mid-1980s that we have begun to see sustained attempts to develop instructional programs appropriate for CLDE students. And only within the past few years has much attention been paid to developing bilingual special education and ESL options for students with disabilities.

In the program design/delivery arena, as with assessment, most efforts to date have encompassed students with milder disabilities. The educational needs of CLDE students with moderate to severe disabilities has been relatively UN-addressed. This is particularly true in relationship to language minority students. For example, while bilingual special education teacher preparation programs have been springing up at universities around the nation in recent years, one review of literature identified no programs that specifically targeted the preparation of bilingual special education teachers for students with moderate to severe disabilities (Duran, 1993), while another survey found only one such program (De Leon and Gonzales, 1991). Similarly there is a dearth of literature on program structures and practices for CLDE students with moderate to severe disabilities. At the most basic level, such issues as second-language acquisition and optimal language of instruction have not been addressed for this population. Nor have the implications of cultural differences as they relate to language usage, curriculum development, and parental involvement been explored adequately. There are no published reports on program design and delivery, nor is outcome data on the adult status of such individuals available. These omissions are problematic when one considers that nationally there are approximately 542,000 students with moderate to severe mental retardation, of whom some 11,000 are estimated to have limited proficiency in English (Office of Special Education Programs, 1993).

In the remainder of this chapter, we describe a framework for educational services for CLDE students which is applicable to the design of programs for students with moderate to severe disabilities. We then discuss the unique skills and competencies needed by teachers of CLDE students and review program models for preparing special education teachers to serve these students.

DEVELOPING EFFECTIVE EDUCATIONAL PROGRAMS

The delivery of qualitative educational services to CLDE students with disabilities requires the incorporation of several programmatic components. In a statewide study of promising practices in special education, Cegelka, Rodriquez, Lewis, and Pacheco (1984) described a framework for educational delivery that included eight essential components. We have revised and expanded this framework to reflect developments over the past decade. It now includes 10 components, some of which address district and school-site support structures, while others focus on linguistic and cultural considerations, prereferral intervention, assessment, program planning, student placement and instruction, and meaningful participation by parents and community members. These core elements, which are listed below and delineated in the paragraphs that follow, include:

(1) The existence of a district-level bilingual special education program;
(2) Attention to both primary language development and English language acquisition;
(3) Cultural sensitivity and relevancy in all aspects of program design and delivery;
(4) Administrative interface between bilingual education and special education;
(5) Appropriate staff selection and development;
(6) Prereferral intervention;

(7) Appropriate assessment;
(8) Individual program planning and placement;
(9) Appropriate curriculum and instruction; and
(10) Meaningful parent participation and community involvement.

Existence of Bilingual Education Programs

There is considerable evidence that the existence within the school district of a viable bilingual education program is associated with the more effective delivery of special education to language-minority students. Districts that have bilingual education programs tend to have lower rates of referral to special education with limited-English proficient students being proportionally represented in special education (Cegelka, Lewis, Pacheco, and Rodriquez, 1987). This has been found to be true within a context of general overrepresentation of ethnic minority students (Wright and Santa Cruz, 1983; Chinn and Hughes, 1987). It appears that the existence of bilingual education programs provides a service delivery option other than special education for students experiencing academic difficulties, thereby mitigating against inappropriate referral to and placement in special education. Schools with bilingual programs are more apt to have culturally and linguistically sensitive prereferral intervention programs. In addition, it is probable that those districts already attuned to the linguistic and cultural differences of language-minority students will design special education program options that are responsive to the needs of the CLD portion of its special education population.

Attention to the Development of Two Languages

The continued development of the primary language as well as systematic attention to the acquisition of English are preferred practices in bilingual education. Providing instruction in the primary language builds conceptual and cognitive development. This permits students to continue to expand their knowledge bases while learning English.

When bilingual education is not available, as is frequently true, particularly for native speakers of languages other than Spanish, alternative approaches must be implemented. English-as-a-Second-Language (ESL) strategies have been developed to facilitate the delivery of instruction to language-minority students for whom bilingual education is not available. These strategies include the use of Total Physical Response

(TPR) and Sheltered Instruction. TPR involves the use of teacher modeling, gesturing and the use of physical prompts to assist students in responding to simple verbal commands. This approach includes repetition, body movement and extensive practice to assist in the building of a wide range of practical vocabulary (Supancheck, 1989). Sheltered Instruction uses props, visuals, media, and body language as contextual clues to clarify the meaning of new words and ideas. It has been used successfully to teach the vocabulary or technical terminology required to understand the concepts being taught, as well as the content material (math, social studies, science, etc.) itself. Both approaches are similar to many long-standing special education strategies, so it is not surprising that they have been found to be effective in the instruction of CLDE students. E. Durán (personal communication, July, 1995) has reported on the successful implementation of these strategies with CLDE students with moderate to severe disabilities.

With both bilingual and ESL approaches, the development of English language competence requires that teachers provide for extensive comprehensible input to the CLDE students. Supancheck (1989), summarizing various expert recommendations on English language acquisition, noted that teachers should employ simple, highly-contextualized language, speaking slowly and avoiding slang and idioms. The use of pictures and audiovisual materials, gestures, and facial expressions can assist in the comprehension by second-language learners. Frequent comprehension checks provide critical feedback about the quality of the student's learning. As CLDE students can benefit from exposure to a variety of adult and community language models, they need to participate in multiple language-learning environments both in school and elsewhere in the community. Peer-oriented learning structures that are congruent with the interaction patterns of the student's culture can contribute to the linguistic development of CLDE children (Kagen, 1989; Wong-Fillmore, 1986). Teachers need to establish learning environments that are supportive, caring, and accepting, where communicative intent is emphasized over linguistic structure and error correction is de-emphasized. In such environments, CLDE students feel safe to experiment with the new language.

Cultural Sensitivity

Culture is closely tied to language. For some objects, terms, and constructs, there are no direct translations into English. Differences in linguistic meanings, cultural values and attitudes, and family situations must be accounted for in the language learning process.

Researchers have documented differences among cultural groups for such characteristics as personality style, cognitive style, values, and belief systems—all variables that relate to the acquisition of new knowledge and skills (Lynch and Lewis, 1982). Cognitive styles reflect how people perceive their environment, how they receive and interpret information, and how they categorize or organize it (Ortiz, 1988). For many cultural subgroups, the cognitive or learning style is more field-sensitive than is true for the dominant culture of this country (Gollnick and Chinn, 1990). Members of these groups tend to be more group-oriented and cooperative in approach, rather than individualistic and competitive. Their interactions may be characterized as formal, courteous, and indirect. They may also evidence greater degrees of external locus of control, meaning that they tend to view outcomes as determined by external forces (luck, chance, fate, powerful others), and see little relationship between their behaviors and outcomes; internal locus of control individuals believe they are in control of their lives and that through work and effort they can accomplish desired outcomes.

Most teachers, on the other hand, are from the dominant culture; they are field-independent in approach and value self-direction and individual diligence. Their teaching tends to be more analytical, abstract, and impersonal, with a focus on independent achievement, competition, and task-orientation. They target deductive thinking and encourage analytic and reflective problem-solving.

Culturally sensitive educational practices value these differences and design instruction to be responsive to them. Awareness and acceptance of these differences by teachers and other school personnel, and responsiveness to them both affectively and instructionally, are critical prerequisites to providing effective instruction to CLDE students.

Educators must become "culturally competent," meaning that they (1) are aware of their own cultural values, beliefs, customs, and behaviors; (2) are knowledgeable about and respectful of other cultures with which they interact; and (3) have developed the skills that permit them to work successfully with individuals from other cultural backgrounds (Chan,

1990; Lynch and Hansen, 1992). In addition, they understand that while culture exerts a profound influence over one's life, this influence is mitigated by such considerations as socioeconomic status, educational level, recency of immigration, preimmigration and migration experiences, proximity to members of their cultural group, proximity to and levels of interaction with the dominant cultural group, as well as age, gender, and language proficiency (Lynch and Hansen, 1992).

School environments must acknowledge and respond to the cultures of its students in order to maximize students' participation in the learning activities (Trueba, 1989). Cummins (1991) noted that "a positive attitude and a positive self-concept are necessary ingredients for achieving maximum learning potential. A program that accepts and respects the language and culture of its students empowers them to feel confident enough to risk getting involved" (p. 1). Schools can create a facilitative climate for CLDE students in a variety of ways, as depicted in Table XIX.

TABLE XIX
CREATING A FACILITATIVE CLIMATE
FOR CLD STUDENTS AND FAMILIES

1. Reflect the various cultural groups in the school district by providing signs in the main office and elsewhere that welcome people in the different languages of the community.
2. Encourage students to use their first language around the school.
3. Provide opportunities for students from the same ethnic group to communicate with one another in their first language where possible (e.g., cooperative groups).
4. Recruit people who can tutor students in their first language.
5. Provide books written in the various languages in classrooms and the school library.
6. Incorporate greetings and information in the various languages in newsletters and other official school communications.
7. Provide bilingual and/or multilingual signs.
8. Display pictures and objects of the various cultures represented at the school.
9. Create units of work that incorporate other languages in addition to the school language.
10. Encourage students to write contributions in their first language for school newspapers and magazines.
11. Provide opportunities for students to study their first language in elective subjects and/or in extracurricular clubs.
12. Encourage parents to help in the classroom, library, playground, and in clubs.
13. Invite students to use their first language during assemblies, prize givings, and other official functions.
14. Invite people from minority groups to act as resource people and to speak to students in both formal and informal settings.

Administrative Interface

An articulated interface between various departments and programs at the school site and local district level ensures open lines of communication among programs (e.g., special education, bilingual education, migrant education) that share responsibility for educating CLDE students. Baca and Payan (1989) have identified a number of attributes of effective programmatic interface. First, program administrators must become familiar with the laws, definitions and purposes, philosophies, practices and constraints of other program areas. Strong administrative leadership across the programs must share in a common set of positive expectations for all students and staff. Formal district policies should address the needs of CLDE students and establish a mission of shared responsibility for these students. Administrators must work to establish a climate of communication and cooperation, not only at the district office level, but at the school site level as well. They need to structure their programs to facilitate teaming among staff and ensure that all staff share a common understanding of the various program areas. Through the collaborative efforts of the various staff members, articulated referral and identification procedures as well as appropriate individual educational plans and programs can be developed.

Staffing and Staff Development

If the challenge of providing appropriate and effective education for minority group students with disabilities is to be met, it is critical that persons charged with delivering that education have the necessary knowledge and skills. To the extent possible, districts should assign only staff who are fully prepared/certified in their own disciplines to teach CLDE students. When the school staff is ethnolinguistically diverse, and reflective of the school population, the probability of appropriate referral, assessment, diagnosis, placement, and educational delivery is greatly enhanced.

Districts should then ensure that staff become knowledgeable about the related programs and departments that share in the responsibility for educating CLDE students. Combined in-service educational opportunities should be provided and all special education teachers, including the bilingual special educators, should be competent in various ESL strategies and approaches.

Additional areas of teacher competence include cultural knowledge and sensitivity, familiarity with the legal mandates for educational programs, cross-cultural communication skills, understanding of the potential biases in assessment practices and familiarity with common adaptations and alternatives, adapting and utilizing effective instructional strategies and curricula, accommodating diverse learner characteristics, knowledge of language development and second-language acquisition, skills in advocacy/public relations, and the ability to work with parents from diverse backgrounds.

It is helpful if not only the teachers, but other staff as well, are reflective of the cultural, racial, and linguistic backgrounds of the student population of a given site. When the school counselors, school psychologists, site administrators, school nurses, secretaries, custodians, and lunchroom personnel reflect the diverse backgrounds of the students, the school is likely to be perceived as, and in fact *be,* more accepting, accommodating, and facilitative of the CLD students and their families.

Prereferral Intervention

Another component of the effective instructional frameworks that all teachers need to become more knowledgeable about is the preferral intervention process. While prereferral intervention is not new, it has gained recent attention when working with academically "at-risk" students as a means of preventing premature or inappropriate referral to special education. The emphasis is on making the general education environments more responsive to the diversity of learners. A comprehensive prereferral process provides support and assistance to teachers in exploring and addressing the specific learning difficulties of individual students. In addition to focusing on the individual student who is experiencing difficulties, the prereferral intervention process also affords the opportunity to explore the responsiveness of the learning environment to CLD students. Analysis of program design, physical setting, curriculum adequacy, school climate and the relationship of the school to its constituent communities can provide critical information for making school-wide responses to individual learning problems (Cloud, 1993).

This prereferral intervention process typically involves a school-wide, pre-referral intervention team comprised of teachers from various grade levels. This team, known variably as the Student Study Team (SST) or the Teacher Assistance Team (TAT), may include general education teachers, special education teachers, a school psychologist, a school nurse, a speech therapist, and, in some cases, parents. For CLD students, it is critical that a bilingual educator serve on the team as well as someone familiar with the specific cultural background of the individual student. The latter can be a professional educator or, where that is not available, a community member who is familiar with the student's backgrounds. These latter two team members can help the team to determine the extent to which the student's behaviors are a function of cultural-linguistic background variables as opposed to learning difficulties.

The team provides consultation and advice to teachers on addressing the educational needs of individual students within the context of the current placement. They recommend interventions that can be implemented in the regular classroom. Some prereferral intervention teams provide listings of potential interventions and require that teachers document their efforts with a set number of these prior to bringing a problem-situation before the team. Data collected by the teachers during the intervention process may also facilitate a more appropriate diagnosis of the student's needs. Teachers may try various interventions and report on their outcomes to the prereferral team. At this time, the team may recommend additional interventions or recommend formal referral of the student to special education.

The goal of prereferral intervention is to increase the capability of regular class teachers to meet a wide variety of educational challenges in their own classrooms. This, in turn, reduces the number of inappropriate referrals to special education.

Nonbiased Assessment and Placement

Concerns with the assessment/identification/placement processes have focused on: (1) differentiating between typical second-language acquisition processes and actual disabilities of students who are limited-English-proficient; and (2) reducing the bias inherent in much of the typical assessment processes. Differentiating between language differences and mild disabilities such as language disorders, learning disabilities, and mild mental retardation is difficult at best. Ignorance about the nature of second-language acquisition processes, coupled with inadequate assessment technology and assessment bias, have contributed to the misdiagnosis and overrepresentation of ethnolinguistically diverse students in special education. Oakland (1980) noted that with ethnolinguistically diverse populations, the potential for bias and error existed at each step of the referral-assessment-placement process. Table XX summarizes the types of bias that can occur prior to assessment, during assessment, and after assessment.

Attempts to address these concerns about assessment/identification/placement bias have included the development of new language dominance tests and other assessment instruments, the use of translators, the formal translation and reforming of existing English-language tests, the development of pluralistic norms and the use of nonverbal, criterion-referenced tests and "culturally fair" tests. Each of these efforts has had its drawbacks, which in turn has led to an increasing reliance on alternative assessment procedures and processes. One such set of procedures, described by Bernal and Tucker (1981), carefully articulates a three-step assessment process, each step of which is governed by a set of decision rules that provide for cautious interpretation of student performance. Other alternative assessment procedures abandon current standardized instrumentation and attempt to determine the learning potential of the student. They do so through the use of test-train-retest cycles that provide an indication of a student's learning potential within the context of instruction in cognitive content and cognitive skill areas (Duran, 1989). These "dynamic" assessment paradigms have evolved from the work of such researchers as Vygotsky (1978), Feurenstein (1979), and Campione and Brown (1987).

Criterion-referenced tests focus on specific skills and indicate the extent to which the individual student has mastered these skills. While the skills are selected as representative of a given curricular area, they do not mirror the specific curriculum that the student is being taught. Curriculum-based assessment (CBA), on the other hand, provides for direct measurement of performance in the specific curriculum that the individual is being taught at a given point in time. It avoids many of the pitfalls of standardized assessment approaches, e.g., their inclusion of "representative" content that may be irrelevant to the particular student's educational program and the comparing of a single student's performance to that of a broad-based "normative" group that may not be reflective of the student's linguistic and cultural background. CBA is a means by which teachers can obtain frequent and direct measure of the student's performance over time. It is useful for data gathering at the prereferral assessment level, as an evaluation of interventions, and for assessing, during the formal assessment phase, the student's actual learning. When CBAs are used daily or weekly, they provide data on learning outcomes and learning rates for individual students; this data can be

TABLE XX
BIAS IN ASSESSMENT OF MINORITY GROUP CHILDREN

Prior to Assessment	
Referral and Screening	Teacher bias and prejudice can lead to either over-referral or underreferral of members of particular groups.
Test Norms	The standardization sample upon which a test has been normed may not reflect the sociocultural characteristics of the child to be assessed.
Test Reliability	An assessment instrument may have poor reliability, with little stability in scores from one administration to the next.
Test Validity	A test may not be a valid measure of the skill for which it is designed, or it may be used for other than its intended purpose.

Bias Points During Assessment	
Child's Language Abilities	For children not proficient in standard English, results of English-language tests cannot be interpreted as indicative of child characteristics.
Test Wiseness	Some children are more "test-wise" than others, having developed test-taking behaviors that tend to optimize their performance.
Motivation, Anxiety, and Expectancy	Test results are affected by the extent to which the child being assessed is motivated to perform well, but whose anxiety over the testing situation does not interfere with test performance.
Cultural Differences	The acculturation experiences of an individual child may be qualitatively different from those of children included in the test's standardization sample.
Bias in Examiner Attitudes	Prejudice on the part of the examiner or teacher toward particular racial, ethnic, or social groups, toward particular types of behavior, or toward various home backgrounds can bias the placement decision.
Examiner Competence	A lack of technical competence in administering and scoring the test as well as the absence of cross-cultural sensitivity can adversely affect a child's performance.

Bias After Assessment	
No Intervention	Failure to provide any education interventions as indicated by the assessment results.
Erroneous Diagnosis	Misdiagnosis of student in terms of proficiency in primary language or English-language, relative to existence or nature of disability, and/or relative to types interventions required.
Inappropriate placement	Placement of student into a program that does not address linguistic, cultural, and special education needs.
No Reexamination	Failure to reassess children, evaluate their progress, and reexamine intervention placements and procedures following initial assessment.

Source: Adapted from T. Oakland (1980). Nonbiased Assessment of Minority Group Children. *Exceptional Education Quarterly*, 1(3), 31–46.

invaluable to teachers in making on-going adjustments in the instruction they are providing.

At the very least, multiple assessment materials and procedures should be employed to minimize bias in the assessment processes. The multidisciplinary assessment teams should include a broad representation of teachers, other educators, administrators, parents, and community members. At least one member of the committee should be proficient in the primary language of the child and familiar with the cultural practices of the child's home.

IEP Development and Student Placement

Once extensive assessment establishes that a CLD student has disabilities and is eligible for special education services, care must be taken to develop an individualized educational program (IEP) that provides special education interventions that are culturally and linguistically relevant. The IEP team should be comprised of individuals who are knowledgeable about the student, who can interpret assessment results relative to eligibility for services as well as instructional planning, are aware of the placement options and services available, and can interpret evaluation results. In addition to the typical membership (assessment person/school psychologist, site administrator, teachers, the parent, and, when appropriate, the student), it is important there be one or more participants who can interpret the results and make recommendations for placement and instruction that are culturally and linguistically congruent with the child's background. Parents of CLDE students may be unprepared, for reasons of language, culture or educational backgrounds, to participate fully in the IEP deliberations without assistance. When this is the case, parent facilitators, interpreters, community members, or other parties must help parents understand special education laws, programs, and options while at the same time providing valuable input to the design of linguistically and culturally appropriate special education services.

IEP forms should be available in the primary language of the family and developed in that language as well. Cegelka, Lewis, and Rodriquez (1987) found that even when non-English language IEP forms were available, the IEP content frequently was written in English only! The goals and objectives specified on the IEPs should include primary language development; second language acquisition; and cross-cultural understanding; as well as other social, personal, vocational, and academic needs. Cloud (1993) has recommended that language, culture, and disability characteristics be considered in an integrated fashion in the development of educational programs for CLDE students. Goals for first and second language development as well as cross-cultural adaptation should be included.

More inclusive educational delivery has developed in the past several years, with most exceptional students, including those with moderate to severe levels of mental retardation, receiving a significant portion of their education in general education settings. Determining how and where limited-English proficient exceptional children should receive educational services is a controversial topic. There is a paucity of bilingual special education teachers, or even special education teachers who are fluent in ESL strategies. Bilingual education and ESL instructors, on the other hand, typically are unprepared to address the unique disabilities of the CLDE student. General education teachers may be unprepared to provide optimal instruction for the LEP student or for the special education student. Hence, placement in any one of the three settings may be inadequate. To mainstream the LEP student from special education into bilingual education settings affords the advantage of enhancing the student's academic and linguistic progress, but has the disadvantage of moving the student from one restrictive setting to another. In those instances where a bilingual special education teacher is available, some find it particularly difficult to justify mainstreaming a student into a general education setting that is not responsive to the student's language development and acquisition needs.

A continuum of placement options, similar to that recommended by Collier (1989) could include a full spectrum of options, each of which would be appropriate to various periods in the student's development. These options might include full-time bilingual special education; full or part-day special education placement with a teacher proficient in ESL strategies and, possibly, regular bilingual education program placement with support from either bilingual special education, or, if that is unavailable, special education; and regular classroom placement with assistance from either bilingual special education or from bilingual education and special education personnel. Variations include assigning special education instructional aides to bilingual settings and/or bilingual instructional aides to special education settings. In both instances, it is important that these aides be monitored by fully-credentialed consulting teachers. Primary language development, ESL instruction, and/or related services may be incorporated into the IEP. Additional intermediary options could also be available to accommodate the individual student's needs within the context of available staff expertise and program structures. A flexible approach should be taken to this array of options, with changes in program placements and support services occurring as the students' language fluency and instructional needs change.

Appropriate Curriculum and Instruction

Special education instructional strategies have been generally endorsed as appropriate for bilingual special education (Kairthe, 1982), although some critics have argued that many of these strategies may be inconsistent with and in opposition to the naturalistic language development needs and field-sensitive learning styles of many CLDE students (Cummins, 1989). Bilingual education experts have criticized the systematic, skills-oriented approaches of special education, although no systematic, comparative studies of the various approaches are available.

Fradd (1987) has noted that the constricted language that special education teachers often use with CLDE students sometimes consists of brief utterances and includes repetitive practice and drill. The tendency to correct pronunciation errors, to interrupt reading to review vocabulary, and the deliberately slow pace of lessons all mitigate against the creation of a language-rich environment that promotes overall communication (Moll and Diaz, 1987).

Little data exists relative to effective bilingual special education practices. As a field, we have no clear idea as to which language is best to use instructionally with CLDE students, and when English should be introduced as the language in which instruction is conducted. There is widespread support for use of the primary language, at least until the student develops English-language proficiency. It may take seven–ten years or longer for a student with disabilities who is a native speaker of another language to develop sufficient facility with the English language to use it as a primary means of learning. For students with moderate to severe intellectual disabilities, there has been little guidance as to the most appropriate language of instruction, although there is some support for using both English and the home-language when instructing CLDE students with moderate to severe disabilities (Duran and Heiry, 1986). Some authorities have suggested that the language of instruction should reflect that of the student's family and neighborhood, meaning that for many, English-language development would not be a priority. Other authorities have recommended bilingual instruction, targeting the development of English language facility as necessary for the broader community adjustment and inclusion of these students.

Given the paucity of bilingual special education teachers, it is likely that issues of linguistic diversity will be addressed primarily through ESL strategies. Cloud (1988) suggested that special education-ESL programs for students with mild disabilities parallel the mainstream ESL programs, focusing on both oral language development and literacy development. Teachers should modify the ESL instruction in response to the student's disability, utilizing specialized teaching strategies, applying positive reinforcement, and attending to self-concept concerns. For young students with moderate-to-severe intellectual disabilities, developmental approaches to ESL instruction can help students establish self-help and communication skills in the second language. For older students, the programs should take on more of a life-skills focus, concentrating on the functional communication skills needed in the home, workplace, and community. Cloud noted that "While the need for knowledge of specialized teaching techniques, adaptive equipment, or prostheses exists for both groups of [special education] students, the need for such knowledge increases incrementally with the degree of disability" (p. 1). While individual school districts have developed some curricular programs for ESL instruction of CLDE students, there are few, if any, commercially available materials of this sort. Duran (1991) has described considerations for making functional language instruction useful for CLD students with mild to moderate disabilities. These include:

Using an Ecological Inventory to determine the words that students need to know for functioning at home, in school, and in community environments in which they participate. These should include information from families about the activities that their students participate in at home, as well as a listing of important cultural events in which each family participates. Parents should be asked to identify those words that students need to know about particular foods, celebrations and similar events, indicating the specific vocabulary terms used in the home to describe each of these.

Involving Parents in Instruction by encouraging them to share traditional legends, stories, and songs. They also should be invited to participate in classroom events, especially those that are of specific cultural relevance to them and their children. In addition, teachers should keep parents informed about classroom instruction, encouraging them to carry over school-based activities into the home.

Teaching Useful Vocabulary based on the ecological inventory. Pair the home-generated vocabulary listing with the more general one that the teacher develops for the students. These vocabulary words can be matched to both pictures and actual objects, with cueing in both English and the home language.

Instruction should be attuned to the learning styles of the students, for research has shown that this serves to reduce stress in the learners and increase achievement (Cabo, 1983; LaShell, 1986). Peer-meditated strategies, such as cooperative learning and peer-tutoring, have been recommended as a means of capitalizing on the field-sensitive, group-orientations of many CLD students. Other strategies for making instruction appropriate to learning style differences have been suggested by Carbo and Hodges (1991). These include the identification of the students' learning style strengths, de-emphasizing analytic tasks in favor of more global ones, and involving anecdotes and visual aides. Included here are activities such as listening to and reading good literature, creating models, acting in skits, and similar tactile-kinesthetic activities. Teachers should begin lessons globally by using anecdotes and visual aides to develop relevant concepts; and concrete experiences should be provided, such as skits, interviews, and model construction. Teachers should provide clear directions to students and provide flexible timelines. The learning environment itself should be highly organized; it should provide clear directions to students.

Special education programs for CLDE students should provide for rich language usage opportunities in the classroom, with teachers adding sufficient context to make instruction comprehensible. The intentional use of redundancy, the use of declarative sentences, frequent comprehension checks, and physical gestures and visual cues all assist in making communication comprehensible (Gersten and Woodward, 1995).

Few curriculum materials have been designed to meet the needs of CLDE children in the areas of basic skills and content instruction (Cegelka and Pacheco, 1984). Cloud (1988) has noted a similar dearth of ESL materials specifically designed to meet the needs of students with mild disabilities and moderate/severe disabilities. For instructional materials to be appropriate for CLDE students, they should be written in the primary language of the student, written bilingually, and/or reflect the cultural learning values and styles of the student. Table XXI lists considerations for developing/selecting appropriate instructional materials for CLDE students.

TABLE XXI
CONSIDERATIONS FOR DEVELOPING/SELECTING APPROPRIATE MATERIALS

1. Know the specific language abilities of each student.
2. Include appropriate cultural experiences in material adapted or developed.
3. Ensure that material progresses at a rate commensurate with student needs and abilities.
4. Document the success of selected materials.
5. Adapt only specific materials requiring modifications, and do not attempt to change too much at one time.
6. Try out different materials and adaptations until an appropriate education for each student is achieved.
7. Strategically implement materials adaptations to ensure smooth transitions into the new materials.
8. Follow some consistent format or guide when evaluating materials.
9. Be knowledgeable about particular cultures and heritages and their compatibility with selected materials.
10. Follow a well-developed process for evaluating, the success of adapted or developed materials as the individual language and cultural needs of students are addressed (Hoover and Collier, 1989, p. 253).

PARENT PARTICIPATION AND COMMUNITY INVOLVEMENT

The meaningful involvement of parents and other community members in the education of CLDE students can play a critical role in the provision of effective educational programs. Parents can provide important input at the prereferral, assessment, program planning, implementation and evaluation stages. However, there are a number of barriers to meaningful partnerships between CLD parents and special educators.

Parents of CLDE children may be unaware of the rights and services available to them. They will need to have the basic tenets of the federal Individuals with Disabilities Act (PL 101-476) and, if they have preschool children with disabilities, the Education of the Handicapped Act Amendments of 1986 (PL 99-457) which provides for early interventions services for children from birth through age three who either have a disability or are at risk for one, explained to them in their native language. A series of studies designed to identify barriers to parental participation in special education revealed that the participation and input of CLD parents was frequently limited to providing consent for special education services, as opposed to assuming assertive partnership roles in planning and monitoring educational delivery.

Within some cultures, an attitude of respectfulness for educators precludes "interference" from the home. This may, in effect, discourage active parent participation in the schools. Parents may feel uncomfortable about involvement with the schools and reluctant to participate in the absence of clear invitation to do so. However, when minority group parents do become involved in their children's education, they appear to develop a sense of efficacy that they communicate to their children.

Strategies to promote greater parent participation include providing all school information to the parents in their own language, posting signs in the main office and elsewhere that welcome people in different languages, increasing the numbers of bilingual school personnel, holding special informational meetings in the language of the parents, employing parent facilitators who are culturally and linguistically congruent with the backgrounds of the parents, inviting these parents to serve as classroom assistants and participate in various school activities, and to teach students about their native cultures. And, of course, cross-cultural communication skills on the part of school staff are essential to the meaningful participation of CLD parents.

BILINGUAL SPECIAL EDUCATION TEACHER COMPETENCIES

Those bilingual special education teacher competencies that have been identified as effective are drawn from current literature on effective teaching in general education, special education, bilingual education, and bilingual special education. In addition to those embedded in the components of the expanded frameworks discussed previously are high academic expectations (Slavin, Karweit, and Madden, 1989); emphasis on basic skills (Tickunoff, 1985); emphasis on task completion (Tickunoff, 1985); reduced classroom distractions and interruptions (e.g., Kerr and Nelson, 1990); effective lesson presentation skills (Rieth and Evertson, 1988; Sullivan, 1992); consultation involving paraprofessionals and other professionals (Idol, Paolucci-Whitcomb, and Nevin, 1986; Harris, 1991); and a variety of specialized cultural and linguistically appropriate instructional strategies (Hoover and Collier, 1985). Yates and Ortiz

(1991) also identified the need for bilingual special education teachers to comprehend, speak, read and write both the target language and English.

In addition to these competencies, Baca and Amato (1989) reviewed the literature and identified seven general competencies for bilingual special education teachers. These competencies were:

(1) The desire to work with CLDE students.
(2) The ability to work effectively with the parents of these students.
(3) The ability to develop appropriate IEPs for these students.
(4) Knowledge about and sensitivity toward the languages and cultures of the students.
(5) The ability to teach English as a second language to the students.
(6) The ability to conduct non-biased assessment with CLDE students.
(7) The ability to use appropriate methods and materials when working with CLDE students.

As teacher training programs are developed to help meet the needs of the CLDE students, program developers should pay close attention to insure that these competencies are addressed within the program coursework. For some programs, it may be simply a matter of infusing these competencies into the existing coursework; for other programs, it may mean restructuring the existing program to insure that prospective teachers have been exposed to and assisted in acquiring the necessary competencies.

Program Models

Historically there has generally been a dearth of teachers from diverse cultural and ethnic groups in education (Justiz and Kameen, 1988; Haberman, 1989; National Forum on Personnel Needs for Districts with Changing Demographics; 1990; Macias, 1988) as well as special education (Baca and Cervantes, 1989). Special education teacher preparation programs have been slow to respond to the need to incorporate ESL strategies or to offer bilingual special education program options. In 1991, De Leon and Gonzales identified a total of twenty-one programs, in the United States training in bilingual special education and the related areas of bilingual school psychologists, bilingual educational diagnosticians, and bilingual speech and language pathologists. Of this number, only one program was identified as having bilingual special education training for teachers serving the severely handicapped. Two programs were identified nationally that concentrated on training bilingual teachers to meet the needs of the learning handicapped. There also is a paucity of special education programs with specific bilingual special education coursework and with bilingual special education curriculum (Baca and Cervantes, 1989). Recently, two additional models of preparation have been identified. Given both the dearth of bilingual personnel in education, as well as the move toward integrated educational delivery models, these models provide training for all teachers to work with CLDE students.

One model of special education teacher preparation incorporates ESL methodologies and multicultural content into the special education teacher training curriculum (Fradd and Correa, 1989). A program at California State University, Sacramento, combines the certification requirements for general education certification with those for special education as well as for the Cultural and Language Academic Development (CLAD) credential. This two-year graduate program provides students with an option of either elementary or secondary general education with special education options in either mild or moderate to severe disabilities. In addition, candidates complete requirements for the new CLAD certification.

In another model developed at the University of Florida, Gainesville (Fradd, Weismantal, Correa, and Algozzine, 1988), there is a course offered at the undergraduate level the provides all students an opportunity to learn about handicapping conditions and all education majors are required to take a mainstreaming course as part of their training. In addition, students in the Department of Special Education, are exposed to bilingual special education through coursework in the core curriculum. Bilingual/ESL materials have been infused into all courses taught by the department faculty. Students may also take bilingual/ESL special education courses that focus on content not infused into the core curriculum of special education. These courses are Language Development, Language Assessment, Teaching within a Multicultural System, and Foundations of Bilingual/ESL Special Education. If students want, they may also be involved in special projects that focus on some element of bilingual/ESL special education. As another option, individuals may take one of the four new courses during the summer institutes that are offered at a time when school personnel may attend. The final option is offered to students as an academic year fellowship. Five scholarships are offered each semester to advanced degree candidates in special education who are interested in an in-depth emphasis on bilingual/ESL special education.

An alternative credential model currently being implemented at San Diego State University utilizes the Internship Credential option available in California. This option requires a high level of collaboration between one or more local education agencies and a university. They must jointly design the program, apply for approval from the state, and then collaboratively manage all aspects of the program. The Internship Credential provides teachers with a formal credential status that is good for two years. During this time, Interns complete all requirements for their Specialist Credential in special education. They work as fully paid teachers in their own classrooms, where they receive intensive support and assistance from both university and district personnel. Once they complete the program and are employed by the district under the authorization of their Specialist Credentials, the time spent as an Internship teacher counts toward tenure within the district.

In the San Diego program, bilingual certified teachers are recruited from their districts and assigned as special education teachers. The cohort of interns take the required core curriculum coursework for the special education credential and receive specialized training in bilingual/ESL methodologies, second language acquisition, and curriculum based assessment. Specific courses that emphasize bilingual special education instruction include the following: Ethnolinguistic Diversity in Special Education, Education Adaptations for Ethnolinguistically Diverse with Disabilities, and Assessment of Ethnolinguistically Diverse Special Education Students, as well as a series of topical courses in adapting ESL strategies for special education, peer-mediated learning, curriculum-based assessment, and second language acquisition.

A strong feature of this program is the support and assistance provided to each of the interns as they transition into becoming special education teachers. Each of the school districts involved is committed to providing their interns with placement in a bilingual special education classroom and a designated district resource teacher or on-site mentor, whose job it is to assist the teachers in their classrooms, is provided. These resource teachers may provide support in IEP development, assessment, classroom management, working with parents, and material selection or development. The university also provides faculty supervision and support for the interns in their own classrooms. At the conclusion of their training the interns receive the Specialist Credential in Special Education.

An in-service preparation model in California, described by Baca and Amato (1989), implemented a three-year effort aimed at changing the perceptions about the culturally and linguistically diverse students by the school staff. It included the components of creating an awareness within the entire school staff of the needs of the linguistically diverse students, provided training for meeting those needs, assisted in the implementation of the new strategies developed by the staff, and instituted an ongoing evaluation of the process. During the awareness portion of the training all staff perceptions about the need for services were discussed and a direction for the training was determined. Awareness sessions were provided on the referral process, IEP development with culturally and linguistically appropriate goals, effective teaching strategies, parent education and involvement, the use of interpreters, and research was presented on CLD students in general and CLDE students. The awareness phase of training was followed by training and implementation phases.

The training and implementation phases where conducted as one because the two were determined to be interdependent. During this portion of the process, training was presented on theory and research, demonstration, guided practice, and peer coaching. As in the awareness portion of the training, national experts in the field were brought in to assist with the training. These experts were not used in the typical one time fashion but were retained to assist in the ongoing training strands which allowed for professional relationships to develop between the experts and the teachers in the school.

Since the district had been identified by the state as being out of compliance in various areas of the state's regulations, the evaluation process was ongoing. This allowed for the state to monitor for compliance with state regulations. Surveys with the staff and school community also provided feedback to the school district. Additional information was gathered from achievement test scores, mainstreaming data, time to transition into English data, prereferral modifications and interventions, and transition into the world of work data. After four years of work, the district received a state award for the services provided for the bilingual exceptional student.

Designing a program to meet the needs of the CLDE student will require that the institution of higher education review the literature on existing program models and take into consideration the makeup of its service delivery area. Knowing the communities and the languages that the prospective teachers will work in will greatly enhance the preparation that the teachers receive. Knowledge of identified effective teacher skills necessary for working with CLDE populations will help ensure that the needs of all exceptional students will be met.

SUMMARY

A great deal of progress has been made in recent years toward the goal of providing individuals with exceptional needs a free and appropriate public education. With the increase in the number of individuals from other countries immigrating to the United States, it is inevitable that there will be an increase in the number of children attending our schools who are from culturally and linguistically diverse groups. It should also stand to reason that statistically some of these children will require educational programming that more closely resembles that provided for exceptional students. What is not clear is whether the existing educational system is prepared to deal with this diversity. Our public schools have to face this problem directly, with perhaps a less than adequately prepared staff. Institutions of higher education, responsible for preparing teachers to meet the challenges of the future, are faced with the task of preparing competent and qualified teachers to meet this diversity.

As potential candidates for teacher training programs are recruited, extra effort should be made to select individuals who speak, read, write, and comprehend the target home language, as well as English. The program should insure that these individuals receive training in the following areas: Working with the parents and families of the students in ways that meaningfully involve them, their culture and community; pre-referral interventions, non-biased assessment that includes multiple assessment procedures, classroom organization and management, program planning that incorporates appropriate cultural and linguistic IEP goals, second-language issues, curriculum design and instruction. Components of instruction should include ESL and ESOL methodologies, Sheltered Instruction strategies, and teaching that focuses on language arts and mathematics skills in the child's native language, so that children continue to develop necessary cognitive concepts as they acquire English.

Teacher training programs must be sure to incorporate the components and competencies identified here. Educational administration programs should prepare future administrators to provide appropriate administrative support to teachers as they work in the different programs within the schools. It is important that programs be designed with an eye to the future. As the linguistic and cultural diversity of the school population changes, so should educational practices. In the United States, the public schools are expected to provide students with much of the knowledge and skills they need to participate fully in society, regardless of their cultural and socioeconomic background, their native language, the geographic area in which they live and study, or their disability.

DISCUSSION QUESTIONS

(1) What is the rationale for the increasing attention given to addressing the ethnolinguistic needs of special education students from diverse backgrounds?

(2) Discuss the importance of a prereferral process that includes attention to the ethnolinguistic of the student.

(3) Based on the information presented in this chapter, as well as other information that you may have, briefly describe situations in which it would be appropriate, as well as situations in which it would be inappropriate, to include primary language development goals in the IEPs of LEP students with disabilities.

(4) Identify and describe the strengths of various program models for preparing special education teachers to serve culturally and linguistically diverse exceptional students.

REFERENCES

Baca, L., and Amato, C. (1989). Bilingual special education training issues. *Exceptional Children, 56,* 168–172.

Baca, L. M., and Cervantes, H. T. (Eds.). (1989). *The bilingual special education interface* (2nd Ed.). Columbus, OH: Merrill.

Baca, L. M., and Payan, R. (1989). Development of the bilingual special education interface. In L. M. Baca and H. T. Cervantes (Eds.), *The bilingual special education interface* (2nd Ed., pp. 79–99). Columbus, OH: Merrill.

Bernal, E. M., and Tucker, J. A. (1981). *A manual for screening and assessing students of limited English proficiency.* Paper presented at The Council for Exceptional Children Conference on the Exceptional Bilingual Child, New Orleans. (ERIC Document Reproduction Service NO. ED 209785).

Cabo, M. (1983). Research in reading and learning style: Implications for exceptional children. *Exceptional Children, 49,* 486–494.

Carbo, M., and Hodges, H. (1991). Learning style strategies can help students at risk. *Eric Digest.* Reston, VA: The Council for Exceptional Children, ERIC Clearinghouse on Handicapped and Gifted Children.

Campione, J. C., and Brown, A. L. (1987). Linking dynamic assessment with school achievement. In C. S. Lidz (Ed.), *Dynamic assessment: An instructional approach to evaluation of learning potential* (pp. 82–115). New York: Guilford Press.

Cegelka, P. T., Lewis, R., and Rodriguez, A. M. (1987). Status of education services to handicapped students with limited English proficiency: Report of a statewide study in California. *Exceptional Children, 54,* 220–227.

Cegelka, P. T., and Pacheco, R. (1984). *Special education curriculum materials for Mexican American and Asian American handicapped students: Final Report.* San Diego: San Diego State University, Department of Special Education.

Cegelka, P. T., Rodriguez, A. M., Lewis, R., and Pacheco, R. (1984). *Promising Practices.* Unpublished monograph. San Diego, San Diego State University, Department of Special Education.

Chan, S. Q. (1990). Early intervention with culturally diverse families of infants and toddlers with disabilities. *Infants and Young Children, 3*(2), 78–87.

Chinn, P. C. (1979). Curriculum development for culturally different exceptional children. *Teacher Education and Special Education, 2*(4), 49–58.

Chinn, P. C., and Hughes, S. (1987). Representation of minority students in special education classes. *Remedial and Special Education, 8*(4), 41–46.

Cloud, N. (1988). ESL in special education. *Eric Digest.* Washington, D.C.: Center for Applied Linguistics, ERIC Clearinghouse on Languages and Linguistics.

Cloud, N. (1993). Language, culture and disability: Implications for instruction and teacher preparation. *Teacher Education and Special Education, 16*(1), 60–72.

Collier, C. (1989). Mainstreaming the bilingual exceptional child. In L. Baca and H. Cervantes (Eds.), *The bilingual special education interface* (2nd Ed., pp. 280–293). Columbus, OH: Merrill.

Cummins, J. (1989). A theoretical framework for bilingual special education. *Exceptional Children, 56*(2), 111–119.

Cummins, J. (1991). Empowering culturally and linguistically diverse students with learning problems. *ERIC Digest,* Reston VA: The Council for Exceptional Children. Clearinghouse on Handicapped and Gifted Children.

De Leon, J., and Gonzales, E. (1991). An examination of bilingual special education and related training. *Teacher Education and Special Education, 14*(1), 5–10.

Durán, E. (1991). *Functional language instruction for linguistically different students with moderate to severe disabilities* (ERIC Digest No. E501). Reston, VA: The Council for Exceptional Children Clearinghouse on Handicapped and Gifted Children.

Durán, E. (1993, April). Strategies for teaching limited English proficient students with severe disabilities. Paper presented at the California Association for Persons with Severe Handicaps, Burbank, CA.

Durán, E., and Heiry, T. J. (1986). Comparison of Spanish only, Spanish and English and English only cues with handicapped students. *Reading Improvement, 23*(2), 138–141.

Duran, R. P. (1989). Assessment and instruction of at-risk Hispanic students. *Exceptional Children, 56,* 154–159.

Feurestein, R. (1979). The dynamic assessment of retarded performers: the Learning Potential Assessment Device. *Theory, instruments and techniques.* Baltimore: University Park Press.

Figueroa, R. A., Fradd, S. H., and Correa, V. I. (1989). Bilingual special education and this special issue. *Exceptional Children, 56*(2), 174–178.

Fradd, S. H. (1987). Accommodating the needs of limited English proficient students in regular classrooms. In S. Fradd and W. Tikunoff (Eds.), *Bilingual education and special education: A guide for administrators* (pp. 133–182). Boston: Little, Brown.

Fradd, S. H., and Correa, V. I. (1989). Hispanic students at risk: Do we abdicate or advocate? *Exceptional Children, 56*(2), 105–110.

Fradd, S. H., Weismantal, J., Correa, V. I., and Algozzine, B. (1989). Developing a personnel training model for meeting the needs of handicapped and at-risk language-minority students. *Teacher Education and Special Education, 11*(1), 30–38.

Gersten, R., and Woodward, J. (1994). The language-minority student and special education: Issues, trends, and paradoxes. *Exceptional Children, 60*(4), 310–322.

Gollnick, D. M., and Chinn, P. C. (1990). Multicultural education in a pluralistic society (3rd Ed.). Columbus, OH: Merrill.

Haberman, M. (1989). More minority teachers. *Phi Delta Kappan, 70,* 771–776.

Harris, K. C. (1991). An expanded view on consultation competencies for educators serving culturally and linguistically diverse exceptional students. *Teacher Education and Special Education, 14*(1), 25–29.

Hoover, J. J., and Collier, C. (1985). *Educating minority students with learning and behavior problems. Strategies for assessment and teaching.* Lindale, TX: Hamilton.

Idol, L., Paolucci-Whitcomb, P., and Nevin, A. (1986). *Collaborative consultation.* Rockville, MD: Aspen.

Justiz, M., and Kameen, M. (1988). Increasing representation of minorities in the teaching profession. *The Peabody Journal of Education, 66,* 49–101.

Kagen, S. (1986). Cooperative learning and sociocultural factors in schooling. In Bilingual Education Office, California State Department of Education (Eds.), *Beyond Language: Social and cultural factors in schooling language minority students* (pp. 231–298). Los Angeles: California State University Evaluation, Dissemination and Assessment Center.

Kiraithe, J. (1981, December). Second language acquisition: Implications for assessment and placement. In A. Ochoa and J. Jurtado (Eds.), *Special education and the bilingual child* (pp. 38–55). San Diego, CA: National Origin Desegregation Assistance (Lau) Center; San Diego State University.

Kerr, M. M., and Nelson, C. M. (1990). *Strategies for managing behavior problems in the classroom.* Columbus, OH: Merrill.

Kirp, D. L. (1973). Schools as sorters: The constitutional and policy implications of student classification. *University of Pennsylvania Law Review, 121*(4), 705–797.

LaShell, L. (1986). *An analysis of the effects of reading methods on reading achievement and locus of control when individual reading style is matched for learning disabled students.* Unpublished doctoral dissertation, Fielding Institute, Santa Barbara, CA.

Lynch, E. W., and Hansen, M. J. (1992). *Developing cross-cultural competence: A guide for working with young children and their families.* Baltimore: Paul H. Brookes.

Lynch, E. W., and Lewis, R. B. (1982). Multicultural considerations in assessment and treatment of learning disabilities. *Learning Disabilities, 1,* 93–103.

Macias, R. (1988). *Bilingual teacher supply and demand in the United States.* Claremont, CA: The Tomas Rivera Center and University of Southern California, Center for Multilingual, Multicultural Research.

Mercer, J. (1973). *Labeling the mentally retarded.* Berkeley: University of California Press.

Moll, L. C., and Diaz, E. (1987). Change as the goal of educational research. *Anthropology and Education Quarterly, 18,* 300–311.

National Forum on Personnel Needs for Districts with Changing Demographics, (1990). *Staffing the multilingually impacted schools in the 1990s.* Washington, D.C.: U.S. Department of Education: Office of Bilingual Education and Minority Language Affairs.

Oakland, T. (1980). Nonbiased assessment of minority group children. *Exceptional Education Quarterly, 1,* 31–46.

Office of Special Education Programs, (1993). Limited English proficient students with disabilities. *Fifteenth annual report to Congress on the implementation of the Individuals with Disabilities Act,* Appendix F, pp. F-1 through F-35.

Ortiz, A. (1988). *The influence of locus of control and culture on learning styles of language minority students.* In M. J. Johnson and B. A. Ramirez (Eds.), American Indian Exceptional Children and Youth. Report of a Symposium (Albuquerque, NM, February 6–8, 1985). (ERIC Reproduction Services No. ED 322 706).

Ovando, C., and Collier, V. (1985). *Bilingual and ESL classrooms: Teaching in multicultural contexts.* New York: McGraw-Hill.

Rieth, H., and Evertson, C. (1988). Variables related to the effective instruction of difficult-to-teach children. *Focus on Exceptional Children, 20,* 1–8.

Slavin, R., Karweit, N. E., and Madden, N. A. (1989). *Effective programs for at risk students.* Boston: Allyn and Bacon.

Sullivan, T. (1992, Fall). Sheltered English techniques in the mainstream class: Guidelines and techniques for teachers. *Focus on Diversity, 2*(1). (Published by the National Center for Research on Cultural Diversity and Second Language Learning).

Supancheck, P. (1989). Language acquisition and the bilingual exceptional child. In L. M. Baca and H. T. Cervantes (Eds.), *The bilingual special education interface* (2nd Ed., pp. 101–123). Columbus, OH: Merrill.

Tickunoff, W. J. (1985). *Descriptive study of significant bilingual instructional features.* San Francisco: Far West Laboratory for Educational Research and Development.

Treuba, H. (1989). Cultural embeddedness: The role of culture on minority students' acquisition of English literacy. In *Competing visions of teacher knowledge: Proceedings from an NCRTE seminar for education policy makers, Vol. 2: Student diversity.* East Lansing, MI: Michigan State University, National Center for Research on Teacher Education.

Vygotsky, L. S. (1978). *Mind in society: The development of higher psychological processes.* Cambridge, MA: Harvard University Press.

Wright, P., and Santa Cruz, R. (1983, Fall). Ethnic composition of special education programs in California. *Learning Disability Quarterly, 6*(4), 387–394.

Wong-Fillmore, L. (1986). Research currents: Equity or excellence? *Language Arts, 63,* 474–481.

Yates, J. R., and Ortiz, A. A. (1991). Professional development needs of teachers who serve exceptional language minorities in today's schools. *Teacher Education and Special Education, 14*(1), 11–18.

Chapter 16

CROSSCULTURAL LANGUAGE AND ACADEMIC DEVELOPMENT

BRUCE A. OSTERTAG

Our democratic society reflects a diverse student population. In many parts of our country, "minorities" represent the majority of students attending our schools. Our nation's bilingual population is distributed throughout the states with heavier concentrations in the southwest and northwestern regions. The highest concentration of language different students is in the larger urban areas. By the year 2000, the United States population will be one-third African American, Latino American, or Asian American (Díaz-Rico and Weed, 1995).

Languages, cultures, beliefs, and home backgrounds of all students are intrinsic to the implementation of our school programs. Different language and cultural experiences of students from nonmainstream backgrounds must not be viewed as deficits but rather as assets to be incorporated in a curriculum that empowers and benefits all students. Unfortunately, school practices have often tended to perpetuate inequalities in educational opportunity for students based on their culture, language, gender, perceived abilities, and social economic status. The U.S. Department of Education has acknowledged that students with limited English proficiency are often inappropriately identified as disabled and placed in special education classrooms with low expectations (Riley, 1995). Add into this equation disparities faced by students who actually have physical involvements and/or learning differences and you have an even more complex situation, particularly given their estimated unemployment rate of 79 percent (Bolt, 1995). Educators need to critically analyze school practices that perpetuate such inequalities and be provided with a pedagogy that reaches and promotes equity for all students that are traditionally less well served by schools. Teachers must adopt, incorporate, and practice a pedagogy that reflects the changes

321

necessary to provide students with these differences an equal opportunity to realize their full potential.

Despite efforts at the state and national levels to meet the need for teachers trained to teach Limited English Proficient (LEP) and Non-English Proficient (NEP) students, the demand continues to be greater than the supply. In California, the California State Department of Education has identified nearly one million LEP or NEP students currently in its public schools and projects that the number will continue to rise if past trends continue. Table XXII illustrates the increase of language different students in California between 1980–1992.

TABLE XXII
NUMBER OF K–12 LEP AND NEP ENROLLMENT, 1980–1992

Language	1980	1982	1984	1992	1992%
Spanish:	257,003	322,526	355,560	1,804,536	35.3
Non-Spanish:	68,715	108,923	132,185	552,934	10.9
(Asian)	(30,791)	(51,809)	(56,667)	(407,652)	(8.0)
(Filipino)	(6,658)	(8,569)	(10,941)	(117,153)	(2.3)
(All Others)	(31,266)	(48,545)	(64,577)	(28,129)	(0.6)
Total:	325,748	431,449	487,835	2,357,470	46.2

Source: Legislation Analyst Report California State Legislature, 1992.

Spanish-speaking students make up the largest majority of LEP and NEP students. The latest available California State Department of Education (CDE, 1994) special education pupil count, in terms of ethnicity, continues to indicate a significant rise in language minority students. Spanish speakers increased by 142 percent during this time period. Asian languages and others also increased 80 percent. These increases persist despite the fact that the average time in a bilingual class is less than three years for LEP and NEP students. Table XXIII presents these statistics. While no information was available on precisely how many other LEP and NEP students are in need of special education, extrapolating from the percentage of the general student population in California, it can be conservatively estimated that 12 percent, or over 100,000, LEP and NEP students need special help. Approximately 3,000 public schools had more than 100 LEP students enrolled at their site (Bilingual Education Office, 1994).

At this time, few states are equipped to handle this population of at-risk students. Only two states (Hawaii and Maryland) even have a

TABLE XXIII
CALIFORNIA K–12 ETHNIC ENROLLMENT PUPIL COUNT:
GENERAL AND SPECIAL EDUCATION
(September, 1994).

	Native	Asian	Pacific	Filipino	Hispanic/ Latino	African- American	White	Total
All	43,459	432,140	29,616	126,878	1,951,57	455,954	2,227,652	5,267,277
%	.83	8.20	.56	2.41	37.05	8.66	42.29	100
Special Education	4,848	19,427	2,196	6,047	190,428	68,963	261,267	553,176
%	.88	3.51	.40	1.09	34.42	12.47	47.23	100

Source: California Department of Education, Special Education Division (1994)

definition for bilingual special education and only sixteen have an official position (Smith and Luckasson, 1995). Specific funding for these bilingual/bicultural is virtually nonexistent with just Maryland and Washington D.C. having set aside monies (Smith and Luckasson, 1995).

A recent study (Children Now, 1993) projects a growth in the special education population of nearly 40 million students by the year 2000. The national demand for teachers who will be able to teach non-English speaking students in special education is tremendous. The supply will not be able to keep up with the need in the foreseeable future.

TABLE XXIV
DIVERSITY OF LANGUAGES IN SACRAMENTO COUNTY SCHOOLS

English	Burmese	Ilocano	Pashto
Spanish	Croatian	Indonesian	Polish
Vietnamese	Dutch	Italian	Assyrian
Cantonese	Farcy	Punjabi	Gujarati
Korean	French	Russian	Mien (Yao)
Pilipino	German	Samoan	Rumanian
Portuguese	Greek	Serbian	Taiwanese
Mandarin	Guamanian	Thai	Lahu
Japanese	Hebrew	Turkish	Marshallese
Lao	Hindi	Tongan	Other Chinese
Arabic	Hmong	Urdu	Other Filipino
Armenian	Hungarian	Visayan Sign Language	Native American Languages

Source: Sacramento County Office of Education (1993).

A microcosm of this national situation can be seen in the Sacramento-Stockton area in the Northern Central Valley of California. This region has experienced a steady growth of diverse language minority communities (as noted in Table XXIV) that require a continuous supply of teachers with competencies to serve LEP/NEP students. Sacramento and Stockton are surrounded by rural farm areas. Approximately 27,000 LEP and NEP students are enrolled in the area schools, representing over four dozen languages, including: Spanish, Vietnamese, Cantonese, Mandarin, Korean, Filipino, Portuguese, Japanese, Khmer, Lao, Punjabi, Hmong, and Mien (Sacramento County Office of Education, 1993). The Latino population in California is nearly 26 percent of the state's population with its Asian population ten times as large as that of any other state (Diaz-Rico and Weed, 1995). One in every six children in Sacramento County speaks a language other than English at home (*Sacramento Bee*, Diversity Poll, 1991). Special education teachers are not specifically trained to serve any of these language groups. Many needs of the children and parents of these children go neglected because teachers have not received the training necessary in working with students who are language different.

As stated above, our schools are facing an ever-escalating shortage of qualified teachers in the area of special education (Doorlag, 1993). This shortage is occurring at a time when the number of special education programs provided for students is increasing dramatically; projections for this trend indicate a continuation, particularly in California which represents nearly one-eighth of all students in the United States (Children Now, 1993). A large percentage of California's special education teachers do not possess special education credentials (see Table XXV). These numbers run as high as 40 percent (Doorlag, 1993). This percentage is consistent with other states. A U.S. Department of Education report indicates that as many as 30 percent of the special education teachers do not meet the special education teacher certification standards for their state (Schrag, 1989). These teachers often have minimal training and experience related to special education, let alone at-risk students who are also English language learners. This situation is exacerbated among those teachers who work with students who have severe disabilities. In California, school districts employ special education teachers under "emergency" credentials after verifying for the Commission on Teacher Credentialing (CTC) that they have searched for, and failed to find, a fully credentialed educator. School districts resort to employing substitute teachers on long-term contracts to staff special education classrooms. Additionally, many California districts are now requiring all educators

TABLE XXV
A SUMMARY OF THE DATA ON SPECIAL EDUCATION TEACHER SHORTAGE IN CALIFORNIA, 1984–85 TO 1991–92.

Summary of Data Related to Special Education Teacher Shortage

Type of Authorization	1984–85	1985–86	1986–87	1987–88	1988–89	1989–90	1990–91	1991–92	8 Year Change	1 Year Change
Emergency Special Education (Up to one year in a district)	1180	1629	2042	2317	2422	2835	2875	3501	197%	22%
Special Education Specialist Internship Credentials	35	56	142	228	343	169	179	220	528%	22%
State Board Waivers (Up to one year in a district)	240	261	309	384	484	589	798	885	268%	11%
Supt. Public Inst. Waivers (40+ days)	180	261	324	624	688	1026	1209	1611	795%	33%
Total Special Education Intern,	1635	2207	2817	3553	3937	4619	5061	6217	280%	23%
Emergency & Waiver Credentials Supt. Public Inst. Waivers (20+20 days)	N/A	N/A	N/A	N/A	1204	N/A	N/A	N/A	N/A	N/A
Unfilled Openings (Vacant Positions)	N/A	N/A	N/A	N/A	N/A	N/A	N/A	N/A	N/A	N/A
Number of Classrooms Staffed by Subs (Each Serving < 20 days)	N/A	N/A	N/A	N/A	N/A	N/A	N/A	N/A	N/A	N/A

Summary of Breakdown by Percent of SPED Teachers Serving on Waivers

Type of Authorization	1984–85	1985–86	1986–87	1987–88	1988–89	1989–90	1990–91	1991–92	8 Year Change	1 Year Change
Total Number Special Education Teachers Employed on Waivers	420	522	633	1008	1172	1615	2007	2496		
Percent of Non-credentialed Teachers employed on Waivers	26%	24%	23%	28%	30%	35%	40%	40%		

Source: Doorlag, D. (1993). Department of Special Education, San Diego State University.

to have a Crosscultural, Language, and Academic Development (CLAD) emphasis to maintain or obtain a teaching position.

WHAT IS CLAD?

The Crosscultural, Language, and Academic Development (CLAD) emphasis certification is different than the Bilingual/Crosscultural, Language, and Academic Development (B/CLAD) credential. As the titles imply, CLAD is an emphasis certification, not a credential. California's CTC has identified six domains of knowledge and skill required for educators who wish to obtain a B/CLAD credential; recipients of the CLAD emphasis certificate only need to complete the first three of those domains and experience learning a second language (CTC, 1994). The required domains for the CLAD emphasis certification are:

(1) language structure and first- and second-language development;
(2) methodology of bilingual, English language development, and content instruction; and
(3) culture and cultural diversity. The domains also required of B/CLAD credential educators are;
(4) methodology for primary language instruction;
(5) knowledge and skills related to the culture associated with the bilingual teacher's language of emphasis; and
(6) proficiency in the language of emphasis.

Persons receiving a CLAD emphasis are not fully qualified to teach in bilingual education programs.

The structure of California's university credential programs contributes to the shortage of trained special educators and CLAD emphasis regular educators. CTC guidelines mandate that most special education teaching credentials must be built upon a prior regular education (or basic) teaching credential. Thus, teachers interested in a career in special education must complete an entire program in special education after finishing the basic credential program. A typical special education training program requires three semesters of full-time study following a bachelor's degree and a two-to-three semester general education credential. Add to that time-frame another year of coursework in obtaining the CLAD emphasis certification. In all, it is not unusual for a special educator to have completed seven or eight years of college courses prior to receiving their final credential. Given that special education teachers are paid no more than regular educators, the present university structure of credential programs constitutes for many a disincentive in pursuing a career in special education. The situation is made worse by the current shortage of qualified general education personnel. It takes a very dedicated person to turn down a paying general education position to pursue additional study in special education.

To respond to these concerns, California State University, Sacramento (CSUS) has created a combined teacher credential training program. The ultimate goal of the credential program (discussed in further detail below) is to train initial-level teachers in a brief-yet-efficient manner to provide services to Limited English Proficient (LEP) and Non-English Proficient (NEP) special education students. It trains preservice teachers in methodologies for meeting the needs of these English language learners with mild/moderate or moderate/severe learning involvements. Each teacher candidate receives multiple credentials in elementary and a specified special education area, and a CLAD emphasis certificate. This enables the teacher candidate to provide appropriate services for LEP or NEP students in special education settings.

The outlined combined credentials program decreases significantly the number of semesters necessary to train a person for entrance into the special education classroom. This program increases the number of trained special educators and CLAD emphasis teachers. Benefits of the combined credentials program do not accrue to special education alone. One result will be to enhance the general education classroom teacher's skills in teaching children who experience difficulties in learning and/or may be English language learners. This program also benefits those teachers who do not choose to teach in special education programs but rather want to gain additional competence in teaching all children who experience difficulties in a general classroom.

By combining the teacher credentials training program, university faculty are able to make use of their unique skills and content backgrounds in a coordinated fashion without sacrificing quality; it also allows for exciting opportunities to co-teach. The combined credentials program is based on the same CTC approved competencies that are imbedded in the California's traditional Multiple Subject (MS), Learning Handicapped (LH), Severely Handicapped (SH) credential, and a Crosscultural, Language, and Academic Development (CLAD) emphasis programs. Potential teacher candidates in the combined credentials program must demonstrate all of the same competencies required of their peers in traditional university teacher credential programs for elementary, and severely or learning handicapped special education classes.

The combined teacher credentials training program represents a collaboration of three CSUS departments: Teacher Education; Bilingual/ Multicultural Education; and Special Education, Rehabilitation, and School Psychology. The program was developed by faculty from these departments, community members representing parents and school district professionals, and passed successfully through the review and approval processes stipulated by the School of Education and University policy. In 1989, the initial MS/LH credentials program was named an Exemplary Program by the California State Department of Education. It was the first time a preservice teacher preparation program in California was so honored. Since then, CSUS had successfully developed, implemented, and received CTC approval for MS/SH, MS/LH/CLAD, and MS/SH/ CLAD credentials programs. These programs serve as the models for the suggested combined teacher credentials training program blueprint outlined below.

A BLUEPRINT FOR A COMBINED TEACHER CREDENTIALS PROGRAM

The two teacher training programs are fairly similar. Both the MS/LH/CLAD and MS/SH/CLAD allow the teacher candidates to receive training for a Multiple Subject (K–8th grade) credential and CLAD emphasis (K–12th grade CLAD setting) certificate. The MS/ LH/CLAD program also trains candidates for a Learning Handicapped (LH, Life-span) credential. Typically, students in these programs have mild/moderate disabilities (identified federally as students with specific learning disabilities, educational retardation, emotional disturbances, or traumatic brain injuries). The MS/SH/CLAD program differs in only that their trainees are recommended for the Severely Handicapped (SH, life-span) credential. As the name implies, teachers in these programs have students with more moderate/severe disabilities (IDEA labels would be seriously emotionally disturbed, traumatic brain injuries, severely mentally handicapped, trainable mentally handicapped, multihandicapped, or autistic). Certain categories overlap with eventual special education student placement occurring based upon the severity of involvement and student need (CTC, 1995).

The combined MS/LH/CLAD credentials program consists of sixty-eight semester units of study sequenced over four semesters. Approximately thirty students are admitted each year. The similar MS/SH/CLAD program has seventy-four units of study also completed in four semesters and admits approximately twenty-five students every two years. Both programs run parallel to the traditional MS, LH, SH, and CLAD programs. The traditional MS program consists of thirty-five units with most students completing their studies in two-to-three semesters. The traditional LH program consists of forty-two units which may be completed in three semesters of intensive study. The SH program consists of forty-one units which also takes three semesters of intensive study. A CLAD emphasis adds an additional eighteen units. Thus, the combined credentials program saves at least two semesters in the training of special educators. A third semester is "saved" if a student is given permission to be supervised in a paid special education internship position during the last semester of the combined program. Students are eligible for the MS credential and CLAD emphasis following successful completion of the third semester of the combined programs; students earn the LH or SH credential following successful completion of the fourth and final semester. Tables XXVI and XXVII outline courses taken for the combined MS/LH/CLAD and MS/SH/CLAD programs. A brief course description is included with these outlines.

The combined programs are competency-based per the standards identified by CTC for beginning teachers (CTC, 1995). All courses in the programs have bilingual and bicultural elements firmly embedded within their structure. This policy is deemed critical given the variety of languages and ethnicities basic to our public school programs; it is imperative that teachers have the basic skills for implementing methodologies, evaluation, etc. consistent with the students in their programs. For example, assessing a potential special education student whose primary language is other than English solely in English invalidates any subsequent test results, as well as being illegal (CDE, 1995). The additional CLAD courses and teaching experiences further the skills necessary for future educators to deliver appropriate services to their diverse population of students.

The first level of the combined programs concentrate upon academic content. The pedagogy underlining general and special education programs, positive behavioral management, legal considerations, collaborative consultation skills, and curriculum and instruction in basic skills

TABLE XXVI
**BRIEF COURSE DESCRIPTIONS OF THE COMBINED MULTIPLE
SUBJECT/LEARNING HANDICAPPED SPECIALIST/CROSSCULTURAL
LANGUAGE AND ACADEMIC DEVELOPMENT EMPHASIS
CREDENTIALS PROGRAM (MS/LH/CLAD)**

LEVEL I		SEMESTER UNITS
EDS 280	*Legal Aspects and Socio-Humanistic Factors in Education*	3
	• Legal, organizational and financial aspects of schools	
	• Philosophical and sociological bases of education	
	• Legal, professional and ethical aspects of the role of the teacher	
	• Individual Education Plans (IEPs)	
	• Special Education legislative and case law	
EDS 281	*Introduction to Learning/Foundations of Special Education*	3
	• Psychology of learning and classroom implications of learning theories (i.e., applied behavioral analysis)	
	• Etiology and educational implications of mild and moderate disabilities	
	• Instructional models	
EDS 282	*Behavior Management in Inclusive/Supportive Educational Environments*	3
	• Approaches, theories and applications of behavior management systems	
	• Development of behavior management strategies that are effective in a school environment across a broad range of pupil behaviors and classroom situations (i.e., applied behavior analysis)	
EDS 283	*Language and Literacy in General and Special Education*	6
	• Principles, techniques, procedures, and curricular materials for developing reading programs	
	• Principles, techniques, procedures, and curricular materials for developing language arts programs	
	• Alternative and augmentive communication devices	
	• Methods and materials for instruction in language skill areas for pupils with mild/moderate learning needs	
	• Methods and materials for instruction in reading skill areas for pupils with mild/moderate learning needs	
EDS 292	*Cultural and Linguistic Diversity in Inclusive/Supportive Educational Environments*	2+1
	• Psychology of learning and classroom implications of learning theories (i.e., applied behavioral analysis)	
	• Cultural diversity in General and Special Education (theories, issues, cultural fairness of materials and assessment practices)	
	• Methods of language instruction (i.e., audiolingual, naturalistic, and total immersion)	
	• Etiology and educational implications of mild and moderate learning needs	

TABLE XXVI (Continued)

- Instructional models (i.e., ICSM)
- Field placement synthesizing and implementing above elements

		SEMESTER UNITS
LEVEL II		
EDBM 170	*Introduction to Bilingual Education*	3

- Analysis and development of curriculum with emphasis on multicultural student populations
- Principles, approaches, and techniques of bilingual education
- Principles of second language acquisition
- Identification elements of public schools which effect the achievement of bilingual students
- Historical development of bilingual education
- Federal and state mandates for limited English proficient students
- Principles for the selection and development of curriculum materials

EDS 202	*Collaborative Consultation Skills in Inclusive/Supportive Educational Environments*	3

- Issues and problems in consultation
- Best practices in consulting with general educators, other school professionals and staff
- Understanding and working with families from diverse cultural backgrounds
- Understanding and working with multiple agencies
- Consulting with families and agencies to make transitions work
- Case management
- Group process problem-solving skills
- Negotiation skills
- Interpersonal communication skills
- Leadership and bringing about change

EDS 284	*Assessment in Education*	3

- Assessment methodologies, principles and practices
- Assessment procedures for pupils with mild/moderate learning needs
- Application and interpretation of formal assessments
- Development application and interpretation of informal assessments (i.e., CBA)
- Application and interpretation of informal assessments
- Non-biased, culturally-fair assessment issues and practices

EDS 285	*Curriculum and Instruction in Math, Science, and Computers*	6

- Meaning approach to math
- Teaching science in classroom and lab
- Microcomputer usage/software for a wide-range of pupils
- Methods and materials to teach math/science to pupils with mild/moderate learning needs

EDS 380	*Seminar I: Issues in General and Special Education*	1

TABLE XXVI (Continued)

	• Practicum seminar covering topical elements of student teaching in general and LH-designated classrooms	
EDS 420	*Student Teaching: Multiple Subjects and Students with Mild/Moderate Learning Needs*	5
	• Practicum experience at an elementary school site split between a general education classroom and a Special Day Class-LH designation or an integrated classroom	

SEMESTER

LEVEL III   *UNITS*

EDBM 272A	*Language and Literacy for the Bilingual Child-Spanish*	
	or	3
EDBM 272B	*Language and Literacy for the Bilingual Child-Asian*	

• Models for instruction in a bilingual setting with emphasis on Spanish-/Asian-speaking students
• Techniques and approaches for first and second language development with emphasis on Spanish-/Asian-speaking students
   • Procedures and curricular materials for developing general programs with emphasis on Spanish-/Asian-speaking students
• Language assessment procedures and bilingual lesson delivery approaches with emphasis on Spanish-/Asian-speaking students
• Focus on language acquisition theories with emphasis on Spanish-/Asian-speaking students
• Principles, techniques, procedures and curricular materials for developing reading and language arts programs with emphasis on Spanish-/Asian-speaking students

EDS 286	*Social Science in Teacher and Special Education*	3
	• Curriculum and teaching strategies in social studies education	
	• California social studies framework	
	• Content and methodologies of social studies for pupils with mild/moderate disabilities	

| EDTE 307 | *Seminar in Student Teaching: Teacher Education* | 1 |
| | • Practicum seminar covering topical elements of student teaching in a CLAD-designated classroom | |

| EDTE 420B | *Student Teaching: Teacher Education CLAD–Designated Setting* | 10 |
| | • Practicum experience at an elementary school site in a general education, CLAD-designated classroom | |

Multiple Subject and Crosscultural Language and Academic Development Emphasis Credential Earned

SEMESTER

LEVEL IV   *UNITS*

EDS 277	*Advanced Seminar in Special Education: Severe Emotional Disorders*	[3]
	• Prerequisite is *EDS 276 Education of Students with Serious Emotional and Behavioral Disorders.* Only to be taken with *EDS 472E* or *EDS 421* in SED placement.	
EDS 472	*Student Teaching/Internship: LH*	
	• Practicum experience at an elementary—high school site in an	

TABLE XXVI (Continued)

	inclusive general education, Special Day Class-Learning Handicapped, or Resource Specialist Program designation class	
	• Placed with a mentor teacher or internship, based upon availability, past experiences, success in coursework, availability of position, and recommendation of university instructors	
	or	10
EDS 472E	*Student Teaching/Internship: Severe Emotional Disorders Setting*	
	• Practicum experience at an elementary—high school site in an inclusive general education, SED designated classroom	
	• Placed with a mentor teacher or internship, based upon availability, past experiences, success in coursework, availability of position, and recommendation of university instructors	

Learning Handicapped Specialist Credential (and optional Serious Emotional Disturbance Certificate) may be Earned

	TOTAL SEMESTER UNITS	68

NOTES		SEMESTER UNITS
	Pre- or requisite Course (or Equivalencies)	
ANTH 101	*Cultural Diversity*	3
	• Partially meets CTC CLAD Domain 3 requirements	
ENG 110	*Studies in Linguistics*	3
	• Partially meets CTC CLAD Domain 1 requirement	
	One year second language	6
	• Meets CTC CLAD second language acquisition requirement	
HS 136	*School Health Education* (to be completed within five years)	3
	• Meets CTC requirements for a clear credential	

are highlighted (some of these courses are switched in the programs for logistical reasons and may appear in Level II). Level I also offers a unique course that specifically focuses upon cultural and linguistic diversity in special education. This course highlights an underlying philosophy of the combined teacher training programs of offering services for at-risk students in inclusionary environments. Theory is also supplemented with field-based experiences throughout the two programs where trainees are required to synthesize and implement their coursework in real-life settings.

Level II continues this trend with more courses on curriculum and instruction in myriad skill areas as well as the beginning of specific CLAD-content coursework. Another common element for the MS/LH/CLAD and MS/SH/CLAD is the first supervised student teaching experience. This experience is split between a general education class-

TABLE XXVII
BRIEF COURSE DESCRIPTIONS OF THE COMBINED MULTIPLE
SUBJECT/SEVERELY HANDICAPPED SPECIALIST/CROSSCULTURAL
LANGUAGE AND ACADEMIC DEVELOPMENT EMPHASIS
CREDENTIALS PROGRAM (MS/SH/CLAD)

		SEMESTER
LEVEL I		UNITS
EDS 202	*Collaborative Consultation Skills in Inclusive/Supportive Educational Environments*	3
	• Issues and problems in consultation	
	• Best practices in consulting with general educators, other school professionals and staff	
	• Understanding and working with families from diverse cultural backgrounds	
	• Understanding and working with multiple agencies	
	• Consulting with families and agencies to make transitions work	
	• Case management	
	• Group process problem-solving skills	
	• Negotiation skills	
	• Interpersonal communication skills	
	• Leadership and bringing about change	
EDS 222	*Behavior Management in Teacher and Special Education*	3
	• Approaches, theories and applications of behavior management systems	
	• Development of behavior management strategies that are effective in a school environment across a broad range of pupil behaviors and classroom situations (i.e., applied behavior analysis)	
EDS 220	*Foundations of Teacher Education in Inclusive/Supportive Educational Environments*	3
	• Psychology of learning and classroom implications of learning theories (i.e., applied behavioral analysis)	
	• Etiology and educational implications of moderate and severe disabilities	
	• Instructional models (i.e., ICSM)	
EDS 221	*Curriculum and Instruction in Math, Science, and Computers*	6
	• Meaning approach to math	
	• Teaching science in classroom and lab	
	• Microcomputer usage/software/assistive devices/Internet for a wide-range of pupils	
	• Methods and materials to teach math/science to pupils with disabilities	
EDS 292A/B	*Cultural and Linguistic Diversity in Inclusive/Supportive Educational Environments*	2+1
	• Psychology of learning and classroom implications of learning theories (i.e., applied behavioral analysis)	
	• Cultural diversity in General and Special Education (theories, issues, cultural fairness of materials and assessment practices)	

TABLE XXVII (Continued)

- Methods of language instruction (i.e., audiolingual, naturalistic, and total immersion)
- Etiology and educational implications of mild and moderate learning needs
- Instructional models (i.e., ICSM)
- Field placement synthesizing and implementing above elements

		SEMESTER UNITS
LEVEL II		
EDBM 170	*Introduction to Bilingual Education*	3

- Analysis and development of curriculum with emphasis on multicultural student populations
- Principles, approaches, and techniques of bilingual education
- Principles of second language acquisition
- Identification elements of public schools which effect the achievement of bilingual students
- Historical development of bilingual education
- Federal and state mandates for limited English proficient students
- Principles for the selection and development of curriculum materials

EDS 201	*Legal Aspects of Special Education*	3

- Legal, organizational and financial aspects of schools
- Philosophical and sociological bases of education
- Legal, professional and ethical aspects of the role of the teacher
- Individual Education Plans (IEPs)
- Special Education legislative and case law

EDS 210A/B	*Assessment Strategies, Assistive Technologies, and Positioning*	3+1

- Techniques for Students with Moderate/Severe Learning Needs
- Assessment methodologies, principles and practices
- Assessment procedures for pupils with moderate/severe disabilities
- Application and interpretation of formal assessments
- Development, application and interpretation of informal assessments
- Non-biased, culturally-fair assessment issues and practices
- Assistive devices/technology for pupils with physical and/or communicative needs
- Positioning techniques for students who are medically-fragile, physically-in-need
- Field placement synthesizing and implementing above elements

EDS 225A/B	*Reading and Language Arts I: Teacher Education*	2+1

- Principles, techniques, procedures and curricular materials for developing reading programs
- Principles, techniques, procedures and curricular materials for developing language art programs
- Field placement synthesizing and implementing above elements

EDS 420	*Student Teaching: Multiple Subjects and Students with Moderate/Severe Learning Needs*	5

TABLE XXVII (Continued)

- Practicum experience at an elementary school site split between a general education classroom and a Special Day Class-SH designation or an integrated classroom

		SEMESTER UNITS
LEVEL III		
EDS 226A/B	*Instructional Design and Strategies I: Early Childhood Education for Students with Moderate/Severe Disabilities Learning Needs*	2+1

- Early exceptional childhood developmental curriculum
- Design models and early childhood curriculum (i.e., ICSM)
- Self-help skills and functional academics for the primary grades
- Management of disabilities (i.e., positioning, toileting, feeding)
- Transitions from home to community, school and agencies
- Parents as partners and case managers
- Working with parents from diverse cultural backgrounds and the young exceptional child
- Field placement synthesizing and implementing above elements

EDS 227	*Social Science in Teacher and Special Education*	3

- Curriculum and teaching strategies in social studies education
- California social studies framework
- Content and methodologies of social studies for pupils with moderate/severe disabilities

EDS 228	*Reading and Language Arts II: Strategies and Applications for Students with Moderate/Severe Learning Needs*	3

- Continuation of the principles, techniques, procedures and curricular materials for developing reading programs
- Continuation of the principles, techniques, procedures and curricular materials for developing language arts programs
- Methods and materials for instruction in language skill areas for pupils and moderate/severe disabilities
- Methods and materials for instruction in reading skill areas for pupils with moderate/severe disabilities
- Skills sequences (pre-language, language acquisition)
- Individual Critical Skills Model (ICSM) and communication skills training
- Alternative and augmentive communication devices

EDBM 272A   *Language and Literacy for the Bilingual Child—Spanish*

or

EDBM 272B   *Language and Literacy for the Bilingual Child—Asian*

- Models for instruction in a bilingual setting with emphasis on Spanish-/Asian-speaking students
- Techniques and approaches for first and second language development with emphasis on Spanish-/Asian-speaking students
- Procedures and curricular materials for developing general programs with emphasis on Spanish-/Asian-speaking students
- Language assessment procedures and bilingual lesson delivery approaches with emphasis on Spanish-/Asian-speaking students
- Focus on Language acquisition theories with emphasis on Spanish-/Asian-speaking students

TABLE XXVII (Continued)

- Principles, techniques, procedures and curricular materials for developing reading and language arts programs with emphasis on Spanish-/Asian-speaking students

EDTE 307	*Seminar in Student Teaching: Teacher Education*	1

- Practicum seminar covering topical elements of student teaching in a CLAD-designated classroom

EDTE 420B	*Student Teaching: Teacher Education CLAD–Designated Setting*	10

- Practicum experience at an elementary school site in a general education, CLAD-designated classroom

Multiple Subject and Crosscultural Language and Academic Development Emphasis Credential Earned

		SEMESTER
LEVEL IV		UNITS
EDS 230A/B	*Instructional Design and Strategies 2: Transition Curriculum and Independent Life Skills*	2+1

- Transitions through school and adulthood
- Trends and techniques in career awareness, prevocational and vocational education
- Models, implementation and management of community-based site placements
- Development and implementation of: community living skills, social behavior, daily living and recreational skills
- Techniques to achieve integration
- Achieving interagency collaboration in providing services to adolescents, young adults with moderate and severe disabilities and their families
- Management of disabilities with older students (i.e., positioning) moderate/severe disabilities
- Field placement synthesizing and implementing above elements

EDS 231	*Clinical Seminar on Students with Moderate/Severe Learning Needs*	3

- Review of case studies for students with disabilities
- Describe intervention strategies in working with students with disabilities
- Analyze process of inter-disciplinary and interagency cooperation used in each of the case studies
- For each case study, formulate recommendations for further assessment

EDS 412	*Student Teaching/Internship: SH (SH setting)*	10

- Practicum experience at a DCH, elementary school site in a Special Day Class—SH-designation, or fully-included general education class with SH-designated students
- Placed with mentor teacher or internship, based upon availability, past experiences, success in coursework, availability of position, and recommendation of university instructors

Severely Handicapped Specialist Credential Earned
TOTAL SEMESTER UNITS   74

TABLE XXVII (Continued)

NOTES		UNITS
Pre- or requisite Course (or Equivalencies)		
ANTH 101	*Cultural Diversity*	3
	• Partially meets CTC CLAD Domain 3 requirements	
ENG 110	*Studies in Linguistics*	3
	• Partially meets CTC CLAD Domain 1 requirement	
	One year second language	6
	• Meets CTC CLAD second language acquisition requirement	
HS 136	*School Health Education* (to be completed within five years)	3
	• Meets CTC requirements for a clear credential	

room (K–6th) and either a designated LH or SH designated program. A concerted effort is made to place student teachers in public schools with model, inclusive general education classrooms. Differences in programmatic implementation also occur in Level II where more special education-specific courses begin. For example, trainees in the MS/SH/CLAD program take a course that looks at positioning techniques and assistive device technology that may be more appropriate to the moderate/severe level of involvements and needs faced by their future special education population. A course on assessment also differs to an extent according to the level of disabilities to be faced in a specific setting between the MS/LH/CLAD and MS/SH/CLAD groups.

By the third level, the two programs again have more similarities than differences. A CLAD-specific course on language and literacy is offered to both groups. Content in social sciences, a seminar for student teachers, and student teaching in a general education CLAD-designated classroom are also matriculated. The only significant difference is found in an instruction and curriculum course in early childhood special education for the MS/SH/CLAD program. Once more, the severity level and needs of future special education students and state mandates dictate the necessity of this course for trainees in the MS/SH/CLAD program.

Finally, Level IV sees a significant departure of programmatic design for the two groups. Trainees in the MS/SH/CLAD program take an additional clinical seminar specific for their future special education population and another strategies course pertaining to independent life skills and transition curriculum. Though both programs have a third semester of student teaching (or interning) full-time in a special education setting, the class designation of LH or SH differs. Depending on the trainees area of interest, he/she also have the option of teaching in a class designated for the Severely Emotionally Disturbed (SED); however, because of California's CTC mandates, the MS/LH/CLAD trainee must have also taken a prerequisite course on students with behavioral disorders and severe emotional disturbance as well as a concurrent seminar on this topic with their student teaching. The MS/SH/CLAD program already have the competencies for teaching students identified as SED built into their courses. It does become quite complex given the structure of California's teacher credential system. A standard joke regarding California's credentialling of teachers is that if you understand the system, then you don't understand the system.

Critical to the successful implementation of the above program is the development of program coordinators and working committees. The program coordinators are responsible of the actual workings of the programs. Some of their responsibilities may include student advisement, recruitment, programmatic and student teaching logistics (scheduling, placements, etc.), service of related committees, reports, etc. A committee that oversees the on-going development of the programs in terms of currency, applicability to the field, long-term goals, and program philosophy is useful. Membership should include program coordinators, faculty, departmental administrators, local district personnel, and parents of students with exceptionalities. Periodic meetings of perhaps twice a year are recommended. Another recommended committee could be ad hoc in nature and designed to deal with programmatic logistics and guidance for the MS/LH/CLAD and MS/SH/CLAD program coordinators. Initially, this group may meet every other week to deal with immediate issues. Once the programs are up and running, these meetings will occur less frequently. University program coordinators, departmental and school administrators, and involved faculty are recommended for this ad hoc group.

There are several other recommended components for the successful implementation of the above MS/LH/CLAD and MS/SH/CLAD programs. Develop student support services in cooperation with the university that will include tutoring, skills development, and language development for trainees who may need those services. This factor has been shown to be of great assistance particularly in the recruitment and retention of bilingual and/or bicultural students. Initiating a mentor program in which each program participant is assigned to a faculty member who will assist and supplement in a personalized way other student service efforts. Cooperative student mentors may also be of a great assistance. Introduce staff development activities/seminars, visiting scholar lecturers, scholarly papers, etc., that emphasize the cultural, folklore, and research of culturally and linguistically different students for the respective faculty involved in teaching the prospective candidates. The trainees of the program should be invited to these sessions to participate and/or offer their perspectives. And as a final suggestion, involve university faculty across departments in the development and implementation of the various components of the combined teacher training programs.

SUMMARY

There are many more specifics to the above blueprint for developing a combined teacher training program that meets the needs of the educational community. As previously stated, there is a critical need for general and special educators who are trained to work with students representing cultural and linguistic diversity. To meet the national shortage of these qualified personnel, the above programs offer a model for teacher-training institutions that is time- and cost-effective. Different states may have other mandates and requirements for teacher candidates, but the basic need is the same: teaching all students so that they can achieve their full potential. We can move in this direction of ensuring success for diverse students by working to create a system that creates an integrated, coherent, and comprehensive teacher training program.

DISCUSSION QUESTIONS

(1) Define the acronyms NEP, LEP, ELL, CLAD, and BCLAD.
(2) What are the required domains for a CLAD emphasis?
(3) How many language different students attend your local K–12th public school system? How many students are enrolled in special education programs? Approximately, how many special education students also have a primary language other than English?
(4) What teacher credential programs are available at your local university? How might a combined general and special education teacher training program be implemented? How might a CLAD emphasis certificate be integrated into these existing programs?

REFERENCES

Baca, L., and Amato, C. (1989). Bilingual special education: Training issues. *Exceptional children, 56*, 168–173.

Bilingual Education Office (1994). *LEP/FEP enrollment—district summary (by language, by grade)*. Sacramento, CA: California Department of Education.

Bilingual Education Office (1994). *LEP enrollment in instructional programs—school/ district summary*. Sacramento, CA: California Department of Education.

Bolt, W. (1995). ADA makes little difference for the severely disabled. *Sacramento Bee, B7*. Sacramento, CA: McClatchy Publications.

California Commission on Teacher Credentialing. (1994). *CLAD/BCLAD Certificate Handbook*. Sacramento, CA: Author.

Cegelka, P., MacDonald, M., and Gaeta, R. (1987). Promising programs: Bilingual special education. *Teaching Exceptional Children, 20*, 48–50.

Children Now (1993). *California: The state of our children 1993*. Oakland, CA: Author.

Children Now (1993). *California: The state of our children 1993—data supplement*. Oakland, CA: Author.

CSUS (1994). *CSUS Catalog, 1992–1994*. Sacramento, CA: California State University, Sacramento.

Díaz-Rico, L., and Weed, K. (1995). *The crosscultural, language, and academic development handbook: A complete K–12 reference guide*. Boston, MA: Allyn and Bacon.

Doorlag, D. (1993). *A summary of the data on special education teacher shortage in California*. San Diego, CA: Department of Special Education, San Diego State University.

Durán, E., and Ostertag, B. (1993). *Multiple subjects/special education specialist/crosscultural, language, and academic development emphasis credentials preservice program proposal*. Sacramento, CA: Department of Special Education, California State University, Sacramento.

Durán, E., and Ostertag, B. (1995). *Multiple subjects/special education specialist/crosscultural, language, and academic development emphasis credentials preservice program continuation application*. Sacramento, CA: Department of Special Education, California State University, Sacramento.

Jasmine, J. (1995). *Addressing diversity in the classroom*. Westminster, CA: Teacher Created Materials, Inc.

Kozol, J. (1990). *Savage inequalities: Children in America's schools*. New York: Crown.

Lynch, E. W., and Hansen, M. J. (1992). *Developing cross-cultural competence*. MD: Paul H. Brookes.

National Council on Disability (1993). *Meeting the unique needs of minorities with disabilities*. Washington, D.C.: Author.

Ortíz, A. A., and Garcia, S. B. (Eds.). (1988). *Schools and the culturally diverse exceptional student: Promising practices and future directions*. Reston, VA: Council for Exceptional Children.

Ostertag, B., and Durán, E. (1994). *CTC proposal: Multiple subjects/learning handicapped specialist/crosscultural, language, and academic development emphasis credentials preservice program*. Sacramento, CA: Department of Special Education, California State University, Sacramento.

Ostertag, B., and Durán, E. (1994). *CTC proposal: Multiple subjects/severely handicapped specialist/crosscultural, language, and academic development emphasis credentials preservice program.* Sacramento, CA: Department of Special Education, California State University, Sacramento.

Riley, R. (1995). *Letter to the speaker of the house of representatives.* Washington, D.C.: United States Department of Education.

Rueda, R. (1987). Social and communicative aspects of language proficiency in low-achieving language minority students. In H. Trueba (Ed.), *Success or failure? Learning and the language minority student.* New York: Newbury House.

Salend, S., and Fradd, S. (1986). Nationwide availability of services for limited-English proficient handicapped students. *Journal of Special Education, 20,* 127–135.

Schrag, J. (1989). *Department of education report, 1989: Special education division.* Washington, D.C.: United States Department of Education.

Smith, D., and Luckasson, R. (1995). *Introduction to special education: Teaching in an age of challenge.* Boston, MA: Allyn and Bacon.

Special Education Division, California Department of Education (1995). *California special education programs: A composite of laws* (17th ed.). Sacramento, CA: Author.

Special Project in Bilingual Special Education (1994). *Improving services for language minority students with disabilities.* Austin, TX: University of Texas, Austin.

United States Department of Education (1992). *The condition of education in the nation.* A report from the secretary of education to the president and the Congress, Washington, D.C.

University of Texas at Austin (1991). Individuals with Disabilities Education Act challenges educators to improve the education of minority students with disabilities. *Bilingual Special Education Perspective, 10,* 1–6.

U.S. Bureau of the Census (1992). *Statistical abstract of the United States* (112th ed.). Washington, D.C.: U.S. Government Printing Office.

Chapter 17

A PROACTIVE ASSESSMENT FRAMEWORK TO MEET THE CHALLENGE OF DIVERSITY

Elba Maldonado-Colón*

Evaluation that is responsive to shifts in demographics produces useful information. As cultural and linguistic diversity increase among those referred for special education services, teachers and evaluators should prepare to meet the challenge. Because diversity extends beyond disability to include sociocultural and linguistic background, a comprehensive approach is necessary to strengthen informed educational planning.

This chapter proposes a framework for those evaluating culturally and/or linguistically diverse (CLD) students. Aspects to be discussed include: (1) concerns in assessment, (2) a framework to enhance learning opportunities: A proactive perspective, and (3) recommendations for instructional planning.

CONCERNS IN ASSESSMENT

Traditional assessment involving culturally and/or linguistically diverse (CLD) students tends to fall into a pattern best characterized by the famous poem, "The blind men and the elephant," in which each man feels a different part of the elephant and assumes that it represents the whole domain. The understanding that the whole is greater than the sum of the parts seems to escape assessors' perception given the comments appearing in the evaluation reports of CLD students (Maldonado-Colón, 1984; in press). Evaluators seem to be satisfied with the perception that indeed parts do represent totality. For example, the administration of one or several measures, or a few measures and an observation, may be accepted as sufficient to satisfy the quest for information on the origins

*The author wishes to recognize the contribution of a colleague, Professor Gilbert Guerin, from San Jose State University, in providing editorial comments for the enhancement of the chapter's content.

343

or nature of a disability, or more seriously, as adequate to distinguish the effects of cultural and/or linguistic difference from the effects of a disability. Maldonado-Colón (in press) noticed that evaluators are prone to disregard the need for specific information about a child's home and classroom once the evaluator has obtained test results suggesting developmental delays. This practice frequently results in the misidentification of CLD children and minimally effective instruction within special education programs (Cummins, 1984; E. Durán, 1988; Wilkinson and Ortiz, 1986).

Children of limited English proficiency, who are developing English as their second language, with or without disabilities, live in a rich and diverse world, one that once understood by professionals can lead to more accurate interpretation of the results of both screening and diagnostic measures of development and accomplishment. A quote, referring to the rationalization of origins (Logan in Volk, 1995), [with a subject adaptation] seems very appropriate to the approach this chapter advocates,

> [A child's potential]... is written in that vast book which stands forever open before our eyes, I mean the universe; but it cannot be read until we have learned the language and become familiar with the characters in which it was written (p. 151).

The impact of context on observed and/or tested behaviors must be taken into consideration. The context of the home and immediate cultural community is as important as the context of teaching and classroom practices. Evaluators, teachers and parents need to interpret "the language" (attitudes, behaviors and expectations of the home and community) and become familiar with the socio-linguistic conditions underlying behaviors which seem to impact on academic progress. Neither the results of an academic examination nor a classroom observation approximate the totality of a child's experiences and understanding. CLD children with disabilities, particularly those with moderate to severe challenges, require comprehensive study and analysis in order to determine the conditions that optimize learning. The following subsections raise concerns and caveats related to the evaluation process.

UNDERSTANDING THE ONTOGENY OF THE CURRENT EDUCATIONAL CONDITION

An understanding of the background, or development, of a learning problem merits careful study of the factors which might have influenced or promoted current patterns of performance. Two ecologies are critical to this understanding, the home and the school. Actions within the home environment impact on school and vice versa; each sphere of influence affects the students' learning opportunities.

BACKGROUND OF THE CASE: THE ECOLOGY OF THE HOME

The child does not live in a vacuum. Knowledge of the child's language models, socioeconomic conditions and the family's expectations is important to the interpretation of problems and to the interpretation of findings. Regardless of the severity of a disability, every child functions in a world outside of school which can be quite different from, or quite similar to, the world of the school. Heterogeneity profiles of multiple cases should be developed to assist professionals later on in the interpretation of data.

Language. Language is a critical variable in the interpretation of many problems for which children are referred. Socio-linguistic heterogeneity characterizes the group profile of CLD children. While some children come from homes where a language other than English is the only one used, others reside in environments where English and another language coexist in varying functions and proportions. For example, English is used by siblings, the other language by adults; or English is used for daily communication among nuclear family members while the other language is used when older relatives and/or relatives and friends not proficient in English visit the family. Other children experience English speaking environments where the proficiency of the models available to them ranges from limited to full competence; for example, the father barely speaks it, the mother is proficient in basic communication, and the older sibling is developing it. Understanding the child's language experiences and challenges help to explain difficulties with learning and related behaviors. Evaluators and teachers should recognize and document such variation in background and learning opportunities, and most importantly, address it when interpreting prior learning and current test performance.

While some professionals hold the perspective that in cases of moderate to severe disabilities, the presence of the disability overrules issues related to dual language or non-English language use, such a perspective limits a full appreciation of the child's condition. The child does not live in a sociolinguistic vacuum: He or she has a family which has cared for him or her, who may have immersed the child in a primary language other than English, or who has added English to the other language. Efforts to assist the child need to include attention to the child's most meaningful, linguistic environments in order to gain the understanding and the support needed to facilitate academic progress. An extensive linguistic profile must be developed.

Thus, at the prereferral stage, professionals should take time to study and analyze the linguistic environments in which the child lives, gathering specific information to assist with interpretation. De León (1990) developed several surveys related to language usage, within an advocacy-oriented process, which seeks information about how the first and second language are used within the home. These surveys which will be discussed later can be useful assessment tools.

Experiential Background. Organization for learning includes attitudes, behaviors and expectations which affect the processing and assimilation of new information. While many children arrive at school prepared to tackle new learning challenges with organization strategies geared for success, others do not. Some children by virtue of restricted economic conditions and other limiting circumstances arrive at school without the organization necessary to succeed in academic learning. Another group of children enter school with a disability which affects their potential to learn; among this group are some second language learners who in addition to a natural disability bring limited language skills and experiential background to the classroom (Reed and Sauter, 1990).

Hence, while conducting prereferral screenings and/or later diagnostic assessment, it is important to distinguish between students,

(1) whose experiential and linguistic background reveal patterns of limited performance due to linguistic and socioeconomic difference, possessing no disability, and

(2) those whose disability interferes with their opportunity to learn regardless of their linguistic and socioeconomic background.

Reduction of inappropriate referrals, support for children at risk of academic failure, and augmentation of teacher understanding and facilitative teaching strategies are desirable goals at the prereferral stage.

Perspectives About Disability. Regardless of socioeconomic level, parents all over the world have the potential of having a child with a disability. Cultures differ in their perspectives on, and the potential of children with disabilities (Lynch and Hanson, 1993). Thus, attitudes toward a disability are going to impact on the availability and quality of the child's opportunities to learn. The family's attitude toward such issues as promoting readiness to learn and patterns for independent living (such as feeding, greeting, dressing, engaging participation with others) can be critical to the success of the child and important in understanding problems in schools. Investigation of perspectives about disability and genuine efforts to understand such perspective make parents active partners in the evaluation process (Harry, 1992) and improve the quality of data available to interpret the problem and to draft recommendations.

Background of the Case: The Ecology of the Classroom

Lack of academic progress as well as the presence of a moderate to severe disability trigger referrals to special education. Teachers seek assistance and/or support in promoting changes in order to facilitate transformations in learning patterns which can result in leaps in learning, increased motivation, adoption of helpful strategies and ultimately, increased academic success. Thus, an assessment of the ecology of the home and the school is critical to develop knowledge needed to process new experiences and learning. A discussion of the elements of language, experience, intervention and expectations within the classroom is the focus of this section.

Language. Most children with or without disability who are second language learners receive instructional services through what is often their emerging and weakest language (English). The presence of a moderate to severe disability often trigger a set of arbitrary assumptions concerning the language of instruction (Ortiz in conference): Evaluators and teachers often feel that given the presence of a disability, the child should be taught through the school system's preferred language (English). To ignore the influence of the native language can severely limit the usefulness of the evaluation, can lead to a reduction of the child's learning opportunities and can negatively affect the parent-child or family-child relations.

Determination of the child's ability to use language to communicate within his/her immediate community is critical to the evaluation. Of particular interest are previous efforts to facilitate language acquisition and development, documentation of precise efforts to reduce communication barriers, their effects, and the level of the youth's functional language in the classroom.

Experiential Background. Many CLD children come from homes where experiences directly related to the school curriculum can vary significantly from the homes of non-CLD children. When these children begin school, they have to deal with the linguistic and curricular demands of the classroom environment. The lack of, or limited familiarity with, routines, habits and expectations of the school system can lead to student confusion and eventual school failure, placing children within a zone of high risk regardless of having or not having a disability. While many children share common experiences that make schooling familiar to them, such as opportunities to interact with adults and toys, as well as to engage in some form of pretend play, or to visit places like libraries and museums, such experiences might be absent from the lives of many CLD children. Yet, these children may have other equally valuable experiences which rarely are included in the curriculum taught in the classrooms and in instructional activities. Understanding the difference in experience can enhance the interpretation of problems with learning as well as testing outcomes, and help with differentiation between individual difference and specific disability. Further, this background information can assist the professional distinguish between degrees of severity. Cultural experiences influence the learning process.

Previous and Current Interventions. It is useful to determine what has been done, if anything, to assist the child in transitioning from native language to English language. Is there a relationship between the language of the home and the language of instruction? Have the English and home language proficiencies been evaluated recently? How do they compare to proficiencies at school entry? What has been done to bridge the language of the home and the language of the school? Has the child participated and benefitted from a specialized language development program (i.e., English Language Development)? Can learning gaps be traced back? What does the evidence indicate or suggest? These types of data can reduce misinterpretation of testing outcomes. De León (1993) has developed a survey that promotes understanding of the relationship of experiences to literacy development.

Expectations. Teachers' expectations are powerful determinants of children's progress. Expectations impact on attitudes, behaviors, and the availability and quality of the learning opportunity. Classroom observations should not focus solely on the youth but should include teacher-student interaction, instructional modifications, appropriateness of materials, and teachers' expectations concerning the culture of the child and his/her first language (or the language of the home).

Summarizing, in order to become familiar with the conditions underlying an apparent or real disability among culturally diverse individuals, teachers and evaluators need to study both, home and classroom ecologies focusing on language use, quality and type of experiential background, perspective of a disability, and teachers' expectations. Such an approach would enable professionals to make changes to increase transformations (learning), or to proceed with greater and stronger confidence to the diagnostic stage. Data gathered at this point, as well as the insights developed, are essential for interpretation at all stages of the evaluation and instructional planning processes. The next section presents a framework for examining the process of assessment and the cultural and linguistic features that are important considerations in a proactive program.

A PROACTIVE PERSPECTIVE

When a child is not accomplishing as expected, whether at home or school or both, a referral for evaluation can be helpful to determine the nature of the problem and possible solutions. Finding the best fit between the youth's needs and possible interventions can promote his/her strengths and ameliorate weaknesses. To facilitate the quest for information, scholars and researchers (Barona and Barona, 1987; Cummins, 1984; Duran, 1989; Ortiz and Wilkinson, 1990) have proposed various models of intervention which roughly include three stages: modification, diagnosis and prescription. Special features of these models will be examined briefly in an effort to assist professionals to understand the conditions that interfere with academic development.

Modification Stage

At the modification stage information is sought about the home and school ecologies in an attempt to understand the degree of appropriateness between the curriculum, its delivery, and the child's current characteristics and needs. This prereferral stage is called the preventive stage by Ortiz and Wilkinson (1990) since it is the point where resolution eliminates the need for further study. Elements critical to this stage have been addressed in the preceding section.

Before a student becomes eligible for special education evaluation and services, every effort should be made to assist him/her within the framework of the regular classroom (Adelman in Ortiz and Wilkinson, 1990). At this point inclusion in everyday classroom activities ensures exposure to same-age/grade models, authentic interaction with grade-level peers on numerous grade-level materials and routines, and most important, the development of a positive self-esteem. Ortiz and Wilkinson propose that when a student's academic performance falls below expectations rather than proceeding to a formal evaluation and consideration for placement, it is more beneficial to study the child's background (linguistic and experiential) as well as previous and current interventions and to provide alternatives within the regular curriculum and placement. They believe that planned modifications to existing conditions can improve the opportunity to learn and can increase the learning rate (transformations) of the student. Thus, they endorse teacher support teams such as Chalfant and Psysh's (1981) Teacher Assistance Teams (TAT) which focus on exploring and suggesting alternatives or adaptations to current instructional delivery. The approach provides opportunities for teacher consultation as well as for specialized support such as experts in the education of second language learners, personnel familiar with the language and culture of the student, and personnel conversant with instructional modifications for students with disabilities. TAT's can provide a wealth of support for the teacher, and can help increase appropriate learning opportunities for the student. A proactive program should plan to build CLD expertise into its capacity development plan.

At the modification stage consideration should be given to De León's (1990) **Survey of Factors Which Might Affect Test Performance [of CLD Students] and [Its] Interpretation.** It addresses language and cultural mismatches, as well as gaps between the students' pre-academic experiences and the expectations of the curriculum. The survey's twenty-seven items are divided into issues related to the family/home background, the child's most immediate community, the school's ecology (overall and classroom) and the student (self-image and language competence). A companion instrument, the **Student First and Second Language**

Oral and Literacy Skills, enables evaluators to gather informal data on the student's "language proficiency and classroom language demands" (p. 65).

A critical question to be considered at this stage was raised by Fradd and Hallman (1983): Has the child had the opportunity to develop competencies appropriate to the school's learning environment?

Also of particular concern with CLD children is transfer of knowledge and strategies from one context to another. Greenlee suggests that checking for transfer become an automatic habit in teachers of CLD students; therefore, it should also be considered during the modification stage. How did teachers plan and check for transfer? These considerations guide the interpretation of previous limitations in effectiveness as well as the selection of alternative instructional approaches. The instruments and questions suggested can be part of an ecological assessment plan, reserved for youth with limited success in learning the academic curriculum. Both ecobehavioral assessment and the assessment of instructional environments would support inclusion of such qualitative data to enhance the interpretation of the problem. Ecobehavioral assessment involves the collection of data to substantiate how students spend their time in school, with particular attention to opportunities to learn and academic engaged time. The second, studies both the home and the school in their role as educators, focusing on the presence and quality of the components of effective instruction (Salvia and Ysseldyke, 1995).

Many researchers and evaluators (Ambert, 1982; Barona and Barona, 1987; Braden, 1989; Fradd, Barona and Barona, 1989) endorse observation and interviewing as processes that enable observers to identify: what the child does know and can act upon, what seem to be effective enabling strategies, what promotes learning in a linguistically and/or culturally different environment, what reduces blockages to learning, and what explains unexpected behavior(s). Gaining information through observation is an ongoing practice in the teaching profession, but consistently and systematically recording such observations is different (Guerin and Maier, 1983). Behaviors to be observed have to be "defined in terms of its observable attributes (Salvia and Ysseldyke, 1995, p. 201). Once behavior, goals, context(s), procedures and caveats have been identified, teachers, evaluators and parents can conduct systematic observations which can be supplemented with informal less structured notes such as those kept by teachers on Post-its" or index cards. The purpose for which observational data are collected will determine the method that is selected (Guerin and Maier). Ongoing systematic observation should be habitual in cases where students are not progressing as expected or when children have moderate to severe disabilities. Observations of CLD children should address the classroom ecology, particularly delivery of instruction, as well as the student's behavior(s)/response(s). Readers interested in conducting quantitative behavioral observations should review Alberto and Troutman's (1990) and Guerin and Maier's (1983) texts. Observers studying CLD youth must be alert to personal bias, children's background and familiarity with schooling procedures as instituted in the schools across the United States, the length of stay in this country, peer discrimination toward the student, and the family's cultural practices should be considered when evaluating observed performance. Accurate and thorough observations supported by technical equipment facilitate modification of learning opportunities (Boehm and Wainberg, 1977).

Language, background experiences and educational interventions have special relevance at the modification stage as stated previously.

Language Evaluation. In spite of a disability every child is immersed in a language milieu. Questions about usage, modeling, and proficiency are critical at this level since they can guide in the selection of alternative instructional approaches. Key aspects to consider among CLD children include: amount and quality of exposure to English, dialectal variations, the influence of one language (L1) on the other (L2), language loss, reasons for code-switching, interference, motivation to learn, self-image, and reason(s) for referral or teacher consultation. For specific suggestions on studying the child's language proficiency(-ies), see Ambert, 1982; Barona and Barona, 1987; Ortiz and Garcia, 1988; and Ruiz, 1988. A promising practice for language skills evaluation, in process of development across the world is the collection of language and work samples in portfolios. Portfolios enable professionals to gather data directly related to the students' performance. Salvia and Ysseldyke (1995) note that, "portfolios are intended to facilitate judgements about student performance. They are collections of products used to demonstrate what a person has done and, by inference, what a person is capable of doing" (p. 243). Data collected in portfolios is considered to be a better representation of the student's abilities and limitations since it is based on the student's actual classroom performance. Portfolio material can support or challenge standardized data thus, providing a broader base for educational decision-making.

The content of a portfolio should respond to a specified purpose; for example, a language and literacy portfolio for a second language learner can include materials that document second language progress or lack of it in the areas of oral and written production, through language samples, creative writing, response to dictation, cloze tests developed from children's literature (narratives, poems and expository prose) and written or oral interpretation of stories read or heard.

Part of the portfolio can be a collection of taped natural conversations, interviews and retelling samples, accompanying written samples (if the youth can write or draw) or video-tapes with signing (if the child can sign), which can be used to assess language and previously identified aspects of academic development. For specific ideas on content of portfolios see Tierney, Carter and Desai (1991) and Hart (1994). Even though the value of portfolio assessment continues to be debated (Salvia and Ysseldyke, 1995), as professionals work toward a more precise definition of content of portfolios, scoring criteria and procedures, interater reliability, less complexity and greater comparability, it is nevertheless, a promising practice representing discipline specific information portraying the students' strengths and weaknesses in daily endeavors.

Sociocultural Background. Orientation to learning is culturally bound. Learning is facilitated when the child's learning style, language and culture are taken into consideration. De León (1990) proposes that information about how these factors have impacted on the learning opportunity be gathered during this stage since they are important for the identification of mismatches and later on for determining instructional modifications.

Language impacts on literacy development, thus, expectations and attitudes toward language and literacy development at home and school should be compared also to determine the student's unmet needs.

Previous Academic Interventions. The construction of knowledge is incremental. Thus, underachievement needs to be investigated to determine whether poor achievement is the result of instructional opportunity, or problems with learning (executing transformations and transfers). Studying instructional opportunities includes both, exposure to content, and to language models, and opportunity to practice and develop within the youth's time needed to learn. Modifications to instructional delivery must be considered in relation to the child's status, for example, non-English speaker, second language learner, dialectal speaker, culturally diverse. Thus, if the child is a second language learner of limited English proficiency, the quality of the modifications that were made to enhance comprehension when English, the weakest language, was used as the medium for instruction and learning need to be investigated.

Another aspect requiring documentation would be the child's experiential background in relation to classroom curriculum. For example, how did the teacher handle culturally-biased readings given the youth's limited exposure to certain sociocultural experiences critical to the understanding of such stories, or to the strategies they exemplify? Previous efforts to assist the child with learning English both in school and at home must be also thoroughly documented. If the child was a non-English or limited English speaker, or a dialectal speaker, at the time of enrollment in school, documentation of efforts to assist the child augment linguistic competence to enhance opportunities for literacy development must be sought. Have his/her teachers understood the difference between Cummins' (1984) two dimensions of linguistic demands, BICS (Basic Interpersonal Communication Skills) and CALP (Cognitive Academic Language Proficiency)? If affirmative, have they adjusted their teaching and expectations accordingly to facilitate communication, comprehension and academic learning?

According to Cummins (1981), language proficiency is more than an ability to communicate socially at interpersonal levels. It involves the application of linguistic knowledge and intuition, developed through experiences in meaningful contexts, to higher order thinking skills such as generalization, analysis, synthesis and abstraction. To distinguish between these two dimensions which can and do affect academic performance, Cummins (1980) utilized the analogy of an iceberg. Like it, in language there is a contextualized, perceivable, more concrete dimension which can be readily noticed by those involved in the exchange. This perceptible dimension, or Basic Interpersonal Communication Skills (BICS), relies on a visible highly interactive context and is usually supported by other aspects of language such as nonverbal and paralinguistic cues. Like the submerged part of the iceberg, there is another aspect of language that is readily perceived, it is hidden within itself, context reduced in comparison with BICS. It is the abstract dimension of formal conceptualization, abstraction, higher order cognitive processing, advanced reading, writing and oral expression: Cummins (1980) named it Cognitive Academic Language Proficiency (CALP). Examples would be, the language of the textbooks from second grade on, of short stories, novels and advanced poetic forms; the language of debate, oral discussion and explanations in classes where no visual referents are used; the language of word problems in mathematics: Their message is encoded in complex syntactical constructions forcing the reader to go beyond language. In studies reported by Cummins (1981, 1984), instructors who do not understand these two dimensions as well as the time they require to develop, and the conditions that favor their development, refer second language learners for psychological evaluation believing that a disability exists in the learner which prevents him/her from achieving higher levels of academic performance in spite of his/her progress in the acquisition of English language skills.

A promising approach to assessment and interpretation of academic achievement for CLD students can be curriculum-based evaluation, since analysis of patterns of strengths and weaknesses can be cross-validated with information available on language proficiency, experiential background and previous interventions. Curriculum-based measures can be locally developed tools comparing the student's behavior samples to established performance standards (Howell, Fox and Moorehead, 1993). Confidence in evaluation emerges from the authenticity of the material or tasks selected by relating it to the curriculum taught in the school, and to the standards promoted by the district. Specific skills as well as deficits are readily identifiable providing material for educational planning. Simplicity, practicality and flexibility characterize this type of assessment. For specific suggestions and models, see Howell, Fox and Moorehead (1993).

The process of modifications to instruction should be continuous and consistent in classrooms and particularly in those where cultural diversity exists. Longitudinal monitoring has been suggested by Cummins (1987); the approaches suggested in the preceding sections make this periodic checking viable and fruitful. Such considerations are in tune with the central theme proposed in this chapter, that evaluators need to study the youth in all his/her ecologies in order to learn about his/her challenges and to become familiar with the nature of the problem. Alternative ways should be explored to resolve or ameliorate the learning gap (limited transformations) which is the purpose that triggers referrals and assessment.

Diagnostic Stage

When the repertoire of strategies appropriate to an inclusive environment have been exhausted, with limited evident academic progress, or the severity of the disability consistently interferes with learning, an indepth, or diagnostic evaluation is appropriate. Barona and Barona (1987) propose that careful consideration be given to the evaluation stages. At the diagnostic stage, three aspects need to be investigated and cross-referenced with the extensive information gathered in the modifications stage. Both formal and informal assessment should focus on communication, intelligence, achievement and other specific behaviors, depending on the nature of the problem. Comprehensive approaches are necessary at this stage. Assessment profiles should include, "data that are representative of student performance across time, contexts, contents, subjects and skills . . . [and across languages]" (Ortiz and Wilkinson, 1991, p. 41). Selective administration of subcomponents, modification of instruments, testing the limits, dynamic assessment, and other measurement strategies for CLD children are critical in order to obtain non-biased or limited-bias profiles.

Communication Assessment. Communicative competence is judged by the effectiveness of exchanges of information. In cases involving CLD children, the identification of language dominance is critical. Language dominance needs to be established from analysis and comparison of profiles in both the first (L1) and the second (L2) language. A profile of abilities and skills must be developed **before** the administration of intellectual and academic tests, since it will enable the evaluator to make necessary adjustments to assure reliable and valid results. Effective verbal communication throughout the process is necessary in order to obtain an accurate profile of the child's potential, strengths, and developing competence, as well as frustrations with the learning process. Both receptive and productive aspects of language competence need to be determined in evaluating communication. Specific suggestions on how to approach this process and/or strategies to use can be found in Ambert (1982), Barona and Barona (1987), Canale (1984), Damico (1991), De León (1990), Durán (1984), Fradd, Barona and Barona (1989), Hernández (1994), Pike and Salend (1995), Russell and Ortiz (1988, 1989). Analysis of data gathered in the modifications stage can reveal areas to pursue with diagnostic procedures at this stage.

Intellectual Assessment. The ability to learn (intellectual ability) is critical to the educational process. While the definition of intelligence continues to evolve (Cummins, 1984; Gardner, 1983; Kaufman and Kaufman, 1982), the measures to evaluate it and the learning potential remain rather static, restricted and limited in perspective, particularly for CLD children. Formal measures continue to be required by most state agencies as part of the evaluation process to identify learning disabilities. Given such requirements, careful use and cautious interpretation of testing outcomes are recommended. Approaches that rely solely on standardized verbal or nonverbal measures are not fully endorsed since they have been found consistently to be culturally biased (Salvia and Ysseldyke, 1995).

Salvia and Ysseldyke (1995) conclude that, "intelligence is an inferred entity, a term or construct we use to explain differences in present behavior and to predict differences in future behavior" (p. 331). While predictions have proven to be erroneous quite often in cases involving CLD youth (Cummins, 1984; R. Durán, 1989; Figueroa, 1989; García, 1985) professionals continue to measure limited parts (for example, questions on general knowledge, receptive vocabulary, context reduced applications) to predict the whole. To remediate this limitation, several options to traditional intellectual assessment practices have emerged through which youth are evaluated on, and provided opportunities to demonstrate, their knowledge and abilities through different mediums (Gardner, 1983) and/or direct and active participation (Hernández, 1994). A dynamic assessment process, engaging and participatory, incorporating observation, intervention and guidance followed by evaluation seems to be a most promising practice for CLD children (Cummins, 1984; R. Durán, 1989) in spite of criticism because of its demands on time. Rate of learning, quality of learning, and effort to learn are critical variables in the evaluation of intelligence and the estimation of potential to learn and accomplish.

While tests of intellectual ability or functioning might indicate weaknesses in general information and/or in processing of information, other criticisms endorsed by R. Durán (1989) include, providing limited information on the most pressing concerns of the teachers or parents; the instruments lack the ability to identify what the child is ready to learn. Cummins (1984) and Holtzman, Jr. and Wilkinson (1991), for instance, propose alternative interpretations of the WISC–R subtests and testing the limits as avenues to gain additional information necessary for interpretation and remediation. Also, Cummins underscores the evaluator's cultural sensitivity as critical to the intellectual assessment process since many test items and procedures might appear unnatural to children from other socio-cultural groups. Thus, data gathered during the diagnostic stage needs to be cross-referenced with instruments such as De León's (1990) **Survey of Factor Which Might Affect Test Performance and Interpretation** and **Students' First and Second Language Oral and Literacy Skills,** in order to reduce bias in interpretation and to increase the possibility of appropriate placement and interventions.

Specific Assessments. Once the influence of culture, language and the intellectual potential have been estimated, an evaluation for disabilities requires assessment of academic-related knowledge. Combinations of formal and informal assessment are common (Cloud, 1991). Today's professionals have access to a gamut of informal evaluation strategies (See Pike & Salend, 1995 for examples). Currently, approaches such as Curriculum Based Assessment (CBA) (Glicking, 1981; Howell, Fox & Moorehead, 1993), Portfolio assessment (Hart, 1994; Tierney, Carter, & Desai, 1991; Wolf, 1989) and the development of frameworks for authentic literacy assessment (Paris et al., 1992) seem to promise more accurate information of what the students know, and what they are ready to learn. Informal strategies enhance the holographic image: They include interviews, work sample study, analysis of performance on teacher-developed tests, and comparative performance analysis on measures such as informal reading inventories. In addition, norm-referenced and standardized test results continue to be required in most programs. Hence, experienced evaluators attempt to gather a variety of data from multiple sources in order to increase accuracy and to facilitate appropriate instructional decision-making.

Certain students, in addition to, or in lieu of, measures of achievement, require evaluation of other aspects of individual functioning, such as motor, social and attitudinal behavior (Barona & Barona, 1987; Chamberlain & Medeiros-Landurand, 1991). For these students, selection of procedures and/or instrumentation, and interpretation of assessment outcomes requires cross-validation with knowledge about norms within the child's socio-cultural group to prevent errors in interpretation. Evaluation of social behaviors and motor behaviors should be from a multiple perspective approach in order to benefit from the expertise that several fields can contribute (i.e., physical therapy, occupational therapy and developmental diagnosticians). For example, observations, frequency counts, time samplings are important in determining and interpreting the importance of behaviors of autistic children. Functional analysis provides the opportunity to replace negative behaviors with more positive and efficient ones (Koegel and Koegel, 1995). Ecological inventories can be culturally and linguistically relevant tools to identify and plan for functional needs (E. Durán, 1989).

Overall, the process of assessment should, as Ortiz and Wilkinson (1991) propose, yield data that enable special educators and evaluators to **simultaneously** [emphasis added] address disability and critical background characteristics. It is in the hands of professionals that such a process remain open to learning, limiting bias, and yielding increased understanding of the youth (a whole child) under study. Fragmentation and compartmentalization might be appropriate for administrative and accountability purposes, but they have no place in the evaluation of a CLD student. An organized, integrated and collaborative approach among professionals is necessary to optimize the learning opportunity of CLD youth (Gersten, Brengelman and Jiménez, 1994). Potential bias must be monitored because of its impact on hypothesis generation and eventually in the selection or design of appropriate interventions. A case study approach proposed by Barona and Barona (1987) would facilitate organization of data collection and data, interpretation and recommendations for instructional planning.

The previous sections of this chapter aimed at raising consciousness and directing professionals to considerations, caveats, instrumentation and procedures to promote greater understanding of the CLD youth. Table XXVIII summarizes key aspects of a proactive approach to assessment and evaluation of CLD youth. The next section suggests considerations for instructional planning.

Prescriptive Stage

Teachers seek for support in effecting transformations (learning) when they approach referral. They expect the outcome of the process to be an educational plan that identifies what has or is causing the learning challenge, and suggestions on how to reduce or eliminate the learning gap. According to PL 94-142, the individual educational programs (IEPs) emerging from the data collected through multiple approaches throughout the modifications and diagnostic stages should be the blueprint for instruction. Thorough and appropriate assessments of the strengths and weaknesses of CLD youth, cross-validated with informal data on language and socio-cultural background as well as previous

TABLE XXVIII
A PROACTIVE MODEL FOR THE ASSESSMENT OF CLD YOUTH

Stage	Information Needed or to be Utilized
Pre-referral Modification(s)	• Language abilities and background profile • Socio-cultural profile • Experiential profile (pre-academic and academic experiences, record of performance in relation to local curriculum) • Cross-validation analysis
Referral Diagnostic	• Multidimensional profile developed in previous stage (Includes results of all three profiles plus the text of the deliberations) • Stronger analytical profile of challenges the student is facing • Intellectual or learning potential assessment • Other assessments • Cross-validation analysis
Placement Prescriptive	• Multidimensional profile • Diagnostic profile

interventions, yield robust data for evaluation and planning of educational programs for CLD students. Annual goals and short term objectives flow from carefully interpreted available data and specially, from curriculum-based assessment, and in cases of mild to moderate disabilities, from students' portfolios. The evaluator uses the available information to formulate interpretations necessary for the development of goals and objectives, and the recruitment of supportive services. Salvia and Ysseldyke (1995) underscore that, appropriate goals and objectives direct the selection of instructional opportunities, methods and "the least restrictive *appropriate* [emphasis added] environment" (p. 307).

Transformation of a noneffective learning opportunity is the ultimate goals of the assessment and evaluation processes in schools. Identification of strategies which promote high functioning in order to challenge an underdeveloped potential, capitalizing on strengths and strengthening weak areas is an expected outcome of the assessment process. It is what parents and teachers expect too. Variation of instructional opportunities and methods of instruction, concern with the student's self-image, consideration for inclusion in diverse supportive efforts, awareness of time to accomplish objectives, degree of proficiency and use of languages would be expected of professionals involved in planning programs for CLD youths.

Overall, today's intervention approaches are characterized by higher expectations for students, highly interactive learning opportunities, integrated instruction and a holistic perspective concerned with the whole child. Current focus on intervention include interactionist (Cummins, 1984), collaborative and integrative (Ruiz, 1989) approaches aimed at increasing communication, motivation, improving self-esteem (empowerment) and ultimately, academic performance. Instructional planning should also take into consideration what is known about language acquisition and development (both L1 and L2) of second language learners, skills transfer and modification to instruction for these students. Today's teachers strive harder to promote in students abilities that enable them to generate their own knowledge. For appropriate adaptations for CLD children see Ortiz and Wilkinson (1989) and Ruiz (1989).

CONCLUSION

Today's schools focus on identification and development of appropriate curriculum frameworks that enable all students to advance in their learning. A comprehensive assessment framework facilitates the match between the curriculum framework and the CLD student's profile. This chapter provides suggestions to facilitate this effort in consonance with Johnston's (in Allington, 1994) suggestion that the evaluation of student learning, or exploration of their learning difficulties, become a personalized process relying on close, careful examination of a student's work, [background and previous efforts].

A broader assessment of second language learners is necessary, not optional, and constitutes the message of this chapter. Teachers and evaluators must seek as much information as possible to be able to understand the behaviors and limitations they observe in these learners. The richer the database, the sounder the interpretation of observed behaviors and performance in formal and informal assessment tasks. The heterogeneity of the population requires it, professional ethics (i.e., The Council for Exceptional Children Code of Ethics, 1991) demand it.

DISCUSSION QUESTIONS

(1) What are some concerns we have in assessment at the present?
(2) What are some considerations we should make when attempting to assess a cross-cultural and linguistically different student?

(3) What are some informal types of assessment we can do with culturally and linguistically different students? Discuss a few the writer mentioned in her chapter.

REFERENCES

Alberto, P., and Troutman, A. (1990). *Applied behavior analysis for teachers* (3rd Ed.). Columbus, OH: Merrill.

Allington, R. L. (1994). The schools we have. The schools we need. *The Reading Teacher, 48*(1), 14–29.

Ambert, A. (1982, Fall). The identification of LEP children with special needs. *Bilingual Journal,* 17–22.

Barona, A., and Barona, M. S. (1987). A model for the assessment of LEP students referred for Special Education Services. In S. H. Fradd and W. J. Tikunoff (Eds.), *Bilingual education and bilingual special education: A guide for administrators,* (pp. 183–209). Boston: College-Hill.

Boehm, A. E., and Weinberg, R. A. (1977). *The classroom observer: A guide for developing observation skills.* New York: Teachers College.

Braden, J. P. (1989). Organizing and monitoring data bases. In S. H. Fradd and M. J. Weismantel (Eds.), *Meeting the needs of culturally and linguistically different students: A handbook for educators,* (pp. 14–33). Boston: College-Hill.

Canale, M. (1984). A communicative approach to language proficiency assessment in a minority setting. In C. Rivera (Ed.), *Communicative competence approaches to language proficiency assessment: Research and application,* (pp. 107–122). Clevedon, England: Multilingual Matters.

Chamberlain, P., and Medeiros-Landurand, P. (1991). Practical considerations for the assessment of LEP students with special needs. In E. V. Hamayan and J. S. Damico (Eds.), *Limiting bias in the assessment of bilingual students,* (pp. 111–156). Austin, TX: Pro-ed.

Cloud, N. (1991). Educational assessment. In E. V. Hamayan and J. S. Damico (Eds.), *Limiting bias in the assessment of bilingual students,* (pp. 219–245). Austin, TX: Pro-ed.

Cummins, J. (1980). The construct of language proficiency in bilingual education. In J. E. Alatis (Ed.), *Georgetown University roundtable on languages and linguistics.* Washington, D.C.: Georgetown University Press.

Cummins, J. (1981). The role of primary language development in promoting educational success for language minority students. In California State Department of Education (Eds.), *Schooling and language minority students: A theoretical framework,* (pp. 3–49). Los Angeles, CA: Evaluation, Dissemination and Assessment Center.

Cummins, J. (1984). *Assessment of bilingual exceptional students: Issues in assessment and pedagogy.* Clevedon, England: Multilingual Matters.

Cummins, J. (1987). The role of assessment in the empowerment of minority students. In E. Bayardelle et al. (Eds.), *Assessment: From policy to program,* (pp. 2–3). Rochester, NY: New York State Education Department.

Damico, J. S. (1991). Descriptive assessment of communicative ability in limited English proficient students. In E. V. Hamayan and J. S. Damico (Eds.), *Limiting bias in the assessment of bilingual students*, (pp. 157–217). Austin, TX: Pro-ed.

De León, J. (1990, Summer). A model for an advocacy-oriented assessment process in the psychoeducational evaluation of culturally and linguistically different students. *The Journal of Educational Issues of Language Minority Students, 7,* 53–67.

Durán, E. (1989). Functional language instruction for the handicapped or linguistically different students. In *Reading Improvement, 26*(1), 265–268.

Durán, R. P. (1984). Some implications of communicative competence research for integrative proficiency testing. In C. Rivera (Ed.), *Communicative competence approaches to language proficiency assessment: Research and application*, (pp. 44–58). Clevedon, England: Multilingual Matters.

Durán, R. P. (1989). Assessment and instruction of at-risk Hispanic students. *Exceptional Children, 56*(2), 154–158.

Fradd, S. H., Barona, A., and Barona, M. S. (1989). Implementing change and monitoring progress. In S. H. Fradd and M. J. Weismantel (Eds.), *Meeting the needs of culturally and linguistically different students: A handbook for educators*, (pp. 63–105). Boston: College-Hill.

Fradd, S. H., and Hallman, C. L. (1983). Implications of psychological and educational research for assessment and instruction of culturally and linguistically different students. *Learning Disabilities Quarterly, 6,* 468–478.

Fradd, S. H., and Weismantel, M. J. (1989). Developing and evaluating goals. In S. H. Fradd and M. J. Weismantel (Eds.), *Meeting the needs of culturally and linguistically different students: A handbook for educators*, (pp. 34–62). Boston: College-Hill.

Gardner, H. (1983). *Frames of mind: The theory of multiple intelligences.* New York: Basic Books.

Gersten, R., Brengelman, S., and Jiménez, R. (1994). Effective instruction for culturally and linguistically diverse students: A reconceptualization. *Focus on Exceptional Children, 27*(1), 1–16.

Greenlee, M. (1981). Specifying the needs of a "bilingual" developmentally delayed population: Issues and case studies. *NABE Journal, 6*(1), 55–76.

Guerin, G. H., and Maier, A. S. (1983). *Informal assessment in education.* Palo Alto, CA: Mayfield.

Harry, B. (1992). *Cultural diversity, families, and the special education system: Communication and empowerment.* New York: Teachers College.

Hart, D. (1994). *Authentic assessment: A handbook for educators.* Menlo Park, CA: Addison-Wesley.

Hernández, R. D. (1994). Reducing bias in the assessment of culturally and linguistically diverse populations. *The Journal of Educational Issues of Language Minority Students, 14,* 269–300.

Holtzman, Jr., W. H., and Wilkinson, C. Y. (1991). Assessment of cognitive ability. In E. V. Hamayan and J. S. Damico (Eds.), *Limiting bias in the assessment of bilingual students*, (pp. 247–280). Austin, TX: Pro-ed.

Howell, K. W., Fox, S. L., and Moorehead, M. K. (1993). *Curriculum-based evaluation: Teaching and decision-making* (2nd ed.). Pacific Grove, CA: Brooks/Cole.

Koegel, R. L., and Koegel, L. K. (Eds.). (1995). *Teaching children with autism: Strategies for initiating positive interactions and improving learning opportunities.* Baltimore: Paul H. Brookes.

Maldonado-Colón, E. (1984). *Profiles of Hispanic students placed in speech, hearing and language programs in a selected school district in Texas* (Doctoral dissertation, The University of Massachusetts, 1990). (University Microfilms No. 84-10309).

Maldonado-Colón, E. (1995). *Multiple perspectives analysis of second language learners of Mexican-descent identified as learning disabled: Issues of concern in the development of their language and literacy.* Manuscript submitted for publication.

Ortiz, A. A., and Wilkinson, C. Y. (1989). Adapting IEP's for limited English proficient students. *Academic Therapy, 24*(5), 555–568.

Ortiz, A. A., and Wilkinson, C. Y. (1991). Assessment and intervention model for the bilingual exceptional student (AIM for the BEst). *Teacher Education and Special Education, 14*(1), 35–42.

Paris, S. G., Calfee, R. C., Filby, N., Hiebert, El H., Pearson, P. D., Valencia, S. W., and Wolf, K. P. (1992). A framework for authentic literacy assessment. *The Reading Teacher, 46*(2), 88–95.

Pike, K., and Salend, S. J. (1995). Authentic assessment strategies: Alternatives to norm-referenced testing. *Teaching Exceptional Children, 28*(1), 15–20.

Ruiz, N. T. (1988). *Crosscultural special education. The nature of bilingualism: Implications for special education.* Sacramento, CA: Resources in Special Education.

Ruiz, N. T. (1989). An optimal learning environment for Rosemary. *Exceptional Children, 56*(2), 130–144.

Russell, N. L., and Ortiz, A. A. (1988, Fall). Assessment and instruction within a dialogue model of communication: Part I. *Bilingual Special Education Newsletter, 8*, 1, 3–4.

Russell, N. L., and Ortiz, A. A. (1989, Spring). Assessment and instruction within a dialogue model of communication: Part II. *Bilingual Special Education Newsletter, 8*, 1, 3–6.

Salvia, J., and Ysseldyke, J. E. (1995). *Assessment* (6th ed.). Boston: Houghton Mifflin.

Tierney, R. J., Carter, M. A., and Desai, L. E. (1991). *Portfolio assessment in the reading-writing classroom.* Norwood, MA: Christopher-Gordon.

Wilkinson, C. Y., and Ortiz, A. A. (1986). Reevaluation of learning disabled Hispanic students: Changes over three years. *Bilingual Special Education Newsletter, 5*, 1, 3–6.

Wolf, D. P. (1989, April). Portfolio assessment: Sampling student work. *Educational Leadership,* 35–39.

AUTHOR INDEX

A

Acuesta, Yvonne, 134
Ada, A.F., 290
Adams, G.L., 116
Adams, J.O., 252
Adams, R.L., 237
Adelman, 350
Aguirre, Thelma, xvii
Ahlgren, S., 3, 25
Alatis, J.E., 362
Alberto, P., 55, 58, 70, 352, 362
Algozzine, B., 313, 319
Allen, B.V., 229, 232
Allen, N., 193, 212
Allington, R.L., 361, 362
Aloia, G., 248, 252
Alper, S., 8, 25, 252
Alva, Art, xvii
Amato, C., 229, 312, 314, 317, 341
Ambert, A.M., 251, 290, 352, 356, 362
Ames, R.E., 234
Anderson, 28
Anderson, B., 176
Anderson, J.G., 224, 225, 226, 227, 228, 233, 234
Anderson, P.P., 195, 204, 210
Anderson, S., 164, 169, 176
Arakawa, J., 243, 244, 246, 251
Asher, James, 280
Atkinson, D.R., 251
Aveliar, J., 222, 233

B

Baca, Leonard M., v, ix, xvii, xix, 164, 176, 186, 207, 211, 263, 264, 274, 280, 290, 292, 300, 312, 313, 314, 317, 318, 320, 341

Baldwin, M., 180
Baldwin, V., 161, 171, 172, 176, 178
Balinsky, W.L., 226, 233
Balla, D.A., 164, 181
Ballantyne, D., 74, 92
Baltaxe, C.A.M., 140, 142, 158
Bambura, L.M., 52, 71
Banks, C.A.M., 251
Banks, J.A., 250, 251
Barber, Lou, xviii, 134
Barber, P., 186, 213
Barona, A., 164, 176, 349, 351, 352, 356, 358, 359, 362, 363
Barona, M.S., 164, 176, 349, 351, 352, 356, 358, 359, 362, 363
Barone, Cathy, 134
Barraga, N.C., 176
Barth, Robert S., 15, 25
Baskiewicz, A., 186, 211
Battle, C., 171, 172, 181
Baumgart, 122, 123, 124, 138
Bayardelle, E., 362
Beckman, P., 188, 211
Behr, S.K., 186, 213
Bellamy, T.G., 67, 73, 95, 99, 115
Bender, P.S., 221, 233
Benson, Gwendolyn T., v, xxiv, 254, 260, 261
Benz, M.R., 76, 92
Ben-Zeev, S., 225, 233
Berlinger, C., 237
Bernal, E.M., 303, 317
Best, C., 176
Beyer, B.K., 130, 139
Biklen, D., 7, 25, 63, 64, 70
Biklen, S., 154, 158
Billingsley, F.F., 165, 180
Birch, J., 7, 29
Black, J., 165, 178, 192, 212
Bloom, Benjamin S., 191, 211

Blum, L., 169, 177
Bobath, B., 167, 176
Bobath, K., 167, 176
Boehm, A.E., 352, 362
Bogand, 154
Bogdan, R., 158
Boigon, S., 164, 176
Bolduc, M., 163, 172, 176
Bolt, W., 321, 341
Bond, D.E., 169, 176
Booth, T., 65, 71
Borphty, J.E., 228, 236
Boyd, Cheryl, xviii
Boykin, A.W., 255, 256, 261
Boyle, P., 172, 180
Braden, J.P., 351, 362
Bradley-Johnson, S., 163, 176
Brady, M.P., 20, 25
Bransford, L., 263, 274
Branston, M.B., 165, 177
Brengelman, S., 359, 363
Bretaniá-Schafer, N., 252
Bricker, D.D., 164, 172, 176
Brigance, A., 164, 176
Brocas, 223
Browder, D.M., 117, 139
Brower, D., 204, 211
Brower, I.C., 242, 251
Browermaster, D., 261
Brown, 163
Brown, A.L., 303, 317
Brown, Ann, 130
Brown, F., 176
Brown, Lou, v, xvii, 3, 25, 56, 61, 65, 67, 69,
	71, 72, 74, 86, 87, 92, 95, 96, 104, 106,
	109, 115, 117, 120, 126, 135, 139, 142,
	151, 158, 165, 172, 266, 274
Brown, W.H., 3, 20, 25
Bullis, M., 172, 174, 177
Bullo, 65
Bunch, G., 6, 29
Burgemeister, 169, 177
Buriel, E., 222, 233, 235
Burnette, J., 20, 29
Burt, M.K., 226, 234
Bush, George, 10
Butterworth, J., Jr., 92
Byrnes, M., 7, 26

C

Cabo, M., 309, 317
Calculator, S.N., 64, 71
Calderón, M., 287, 288, 290
Calfee, R.C., 364
Campbell, E.O., 221, 233
Campbell, K., 66, 71
Campbell, R.C., 66, 71, 187, 212
Campione, J.C., 303, 317
Canale, M., 356, 362
Carbo, M., 309, 317
Cardenas, R., 223, 233
Carlson, H.B., 221, 233
Carpenter, L.J., 264, 275
Carr, E., 142, 143, 158
Carringer, D.C., 225, 233
Carter, T.P., 226, 333, 253, 358
Carver, R.P., 221, 233
Casavantes, E., 223, 224, 233
Castaneda, A., 224, 237
Cavallaro, C.C., 52, 71
Cegelka, Patricia Thomas, v, xxv, 264, 275,
	292, 295, 296, 303, 309, 317, 318, 341
Certo, N., 165, 177
Cervantes, H.T., 164, 176, 186, 207, 211, 292,
	312, 313, 317, 318, 320
Chacon, Katherine Wellborn, xviii
Chadsey-Rusch, J., 94, 116
Chalfant, 350
Chamberlain, P., 358, 362
Chamot, A.U., 263, 275, 290
Chan, S.Q., 198, 211, 298, 318
Chen, V.L., 241, 243, 252
Cheney, C.O., 140, 158
Cheney, S.B., 19, 26
Cheng, L.L., 240, 243, 249, 252
Cherry, J., 171, 177
Chinn, Philip C., 211, 254, 261, 275, 296, 298,
	318, 319
Cho, E.M., 198, 199, 200, 211
Chung, E.Y.J., 196, 211
Chung-young, 196
Cicchetti, D.V., 164, 181
Cline, Mark, xviii
Cloninger, C.J., 172, 177, 178
Cloud, N., 301, 306, 308, 309, 318, 358, 362
Cobb, B., 79, 80, 81, 82, 93
Cobb, S., 189, 211

Cochran, C., 287, 290
Cohen, B., 225, 233
Cohen, D., 139
Cole, D., 221, 233
Cole, S., 221, 233
Coleman, J.S., 221, 226, 227, 233
Collier, 193
Collier, C., 306, 311, 318, 319
Collier, V.P., 291, 294, 320
Connolly, J., 17, 26
Connolly, T.T., 172, 179
Coon, M.E., 122, 139
Coren, A., 206, 213
Correa, Vivian I., v, xxii, 160, 166, 167, 173,
    177, 179, 181, 313, 318, 319
Cosca, C., 228, 235
Cote, K.S., 163, 177
Covey, 226
Crandall, J., 290
Cress, P.J., 161, 177
Crossley, R., 63, 71
Cummins, J., 64, 225, 234, 299, 307, 318, 344,
    349, 354, 355, 357, 361, 362
Cureton, G.O., 255, 261

D

Damico, J.S., 356, 362, 363
Daniloff, J., 58, 71
Dantona, R., 171
Dao, X., 246, 247, 252
Davern, I., 165, 178
Davidson, R., 161, 177
Davis, K., 164, 176
Davis, W.E., 6, 26
Dayan, M., 56, 61, 71
Deal, A., 189, 211
DeAvila, E.A., 221, 225, 234
De Blassie, Richard R., 226, 234
DeBriere, T.J., 161, 177
DeCaluwe, S.M., 172, 180
De Leon, J., 294, 312, 318, 346, 348, 350, 353,
    356, 358, 363
Delgado-Gaitan, C., 194, 211
Delk, M., 182
Dempsey, P., 165, 178
Dennis, R., 172, 178
Deno, E., 12, 26

Desai, 353, 358
Descamps, Jorge, v, xxiii, 215, 220, 235, 270,
    275
Dewey, M., 142, 158
Diaz, E., 307, 320
Diaz-Rico, 321, 341
Dixon, 258
Donaldson, J., 17, 27
Donnellan, Ann M., 139, 167, 177
Dominguez, D., 236
Dodlag, D., 324, 325, 341
Doreck, Fred, xviii
Dornbursch, S.M., 229, 234
Dowdry, C.A., 19, 23, 28
Doyle, A., 17, 26
Downs, J.P., 170, 180
Doyle, P.G., 188, 190, 211
Drew, C., 8, 26
Drotar, D., 186, 211
Dubose, R.E., 163, 172, 179
Dulay, H.C., 226, 234
Duncan, S.E., 225, 234
Dunlap, W.C., xvii, 172, 177
Dunst, C.J., 189, 211
Durán, Elva, v, ix, xi, xiv, xx, xxi, xxii, xxiv,
    50, 74, 84, 85, 92, 94, 100, 102, 107, 110,
    115, 117, 140, 143, 145, 148, 154, 157,
    158, 252, 263, 265, 275, 276, 279, 284,
    289, 291, 294, 297, 303, 308, 318, 341,
    342, 344, 349, 356, 359, 363
Durán, R.P., 307, 318, 357, 363
Durand, M., 158
Duxstad, J., 3, 25

E

Edelman, S., 172, 178
Egan, M., 8, 26
Ekwall, E.E., xvii, 152, 158
Ellis, D., 160, 161, 176, 177, 179, 181
Englemann, 288
Engstrom, G.A., 229, 234
Espinosa, R.W., 229, 234
Esposito, D., 229, 234
Estrada, L.J., 265, 275
Evans, F.B., 224, 225, 226, 228, 234
Evans, I.M., 178
Evertson, C., 311, 320

F

Falvey, M., 117, 118, 120, 139, 149, 158, 165, 178
Farber, B., 194, 197, 212
Farra, H.E., 252
Fassbender, L.L., 177
Feeley, D., 171, 180
Fein, G.G., 17, 28
Felice, L.G., 227, 234
Fenichel, E.S., 195, 204, 210
Fernandez, D., 229, 234
Fernández, Sylvia, xviii
Ferrell, K.A., 165, 166, 178
Feurenstein, R., 303, 318
Fewell, R.R., 164, 178
Figueroa, R.A., 234, 318, 357
Filby, N., 364
Finders, M., 194, 204, 211
Firling, J.D., 61, 69, 71
Fisher, R.I., 226, 234
Fiske, A.P., 196, 211
Ford, A., 165, 178
Ford, B.A., 255, 261
Forest, M., 7, 22, 27, 29
Fox, J.J., 20, 21, 25, 27
Fox, L., 8, 26, 167, 170, 172, 182
Fox, Melvin, xviii
Fox, S.L., 355, 358, 363
Fradd, S.H., 176, 307, 313, 318, 319, 342, 351, 356, 362, 363
Franco, Barbara, xviii
Franklin, M.E., 258, 259, 261
Fredericks, H.D., 171, 178
Freeman, D.E., 291
Freeman, Y.S., 291
Furst, N., 229, 237

G

Gaeta, R., 341
Gallegos, Anne Y., xxii, 192, 193, 204, 211
Gallegos, E.A., 234
Gallegos, R., 192, 193, 204, 211
Garcia, F.C., 223, 225, 234, 352, 357
Garcia, S.B., 234, 252, 341
Gardner, H., 357, 363
Gardner, Paula M., xix, 13, 14, 16, 21, 22, 26
Garth, 221

Gartner, A., 6, 7, 8, 26, 27
Garza, R.T., 234
Gast, D.L., 178
Gaylord-Ross, R.J., 26, 206, 207, 211
Gecas, V., 235
Gee, K., 166, 167, 172, 178, 180
Gentry, D., 164, 178
Gerace, W.J., 225, 235
Gerber, M., 7, 26, 27
Gersten, R., 309, 319, 359, 363
Geruschat, D.R., 172, 178
Giangreco, M.F., 172, 177, 178
Gillis-Olion, M., 258, 261
Glick, J., 27
Glicking, 358
Goetz, L., 56, 166, 172, 178, 180
Gold, M., 104, 116
Goldman, R., 206, 214
Gollnick, D.M., 298, 319
Gonzales, E., 294, 312, 318
Good, T.L., 228, 236
Goodman, J.F., 188, 190, 211
Gottleib, B.H., 188, 211
Gottlieb, J., 5, 22, 26
Graff, L.K., 204, 212
Graham, M., 178
Greenlee, M., 351, 363
Greenwood, C., 256, 261
Grenot-Scheyer, M., 213
Gresset, G., 163, 172, 176
Griffiths, R., 164, 178
Grossman, H., 265, 266, 275
Grotsky, J.N., 188, 190, 211
Gruenewald, L., 3, 25, 165, 177
Guerin, Gilbert H., 343, 351, 352, 363
Guess, 65
Guess, C., 72
Guess, D., 143, 159, 169, 171, 172, 178, 180
Gullo, D.F., 71
Gullo, J.C., 71
Gumbier, J., 236

H

Haberman, M., 312, 319
Hale, J., 256, 261
Hale-Benson, 255, 261
Hallahan, D.P., 4, 7, 26, 27, 183, 188, 189, 206, 209, 211

Halle, J.W., 51, 53, 54, 55, 71
Hallman, C.L., 351, 363
Halpren, A.S., 76, 92
Halvorsen, A.T., 19, 26
Hamayan, E.V., 362, 363
Hamre-Nieptuski, S., 177, 198, 211
Hanline, M.F., 8, 26
Hansen, M.J., 299, 319, 341
Hardman, M., 8, 26
Haring, N.G., 65, 72
Harkins, J.E., 161, 182
Harley, R., 167, 178
Harrell, R., 167, 178
Harris, J., 256, 261
Harris, K.C., 311, 319
Harris, William Mateer, xx, 30
Harry, B., 193, 194, 198, 212, 213, 347, 363
Hart, D., 353, 358, 363
Hasbury, D., 22, 27
Haug, M.J., 235
Havassy, B., 221, 234
Healy, C.W., 226, 234
Heiry, T.J., 307, 318
Heller, K., 7, 26
Heller, T., 194, 197, 212
Helmstetter, E., 163, 169, 171, 172, 180
Henderson, N., 221, 233
Henderson, R.W., 264, 275
Hernández, M.J., 235
Hernández, Norma G., vi, xvii, xxiii, 215, 220, 235, 270, 275
Hernández, R.D., 356, 357, 363
Hetherington, E.M., 28
Heward, W.L., 171, 179, 242, 243, 245, 246, 252
Hiebert, El H., 364
Hill, E.W., 179
Hill, J., 104, 116
Hill, M., 165, 167, 178
Hilliard, A., 258, 261
Hiskey, M., 169, 179
Hobbs, N., 7, 26
Holland, 9
Hobson, C.J., 221, 233
Hodges, H., 309, 317
Hoffman, Stacey, 134
Holmes, R.L., 258, 261
Holovet, J.F., 206, 207, 211
Holtzman, W., 26

Holtzman, Jr., W.H., 357, 363
Hoover, J.J., 310, 311, 319
Hoover, W.A., 236
Howell, K.W., 355, 358, 363
Huebner, K.M., 171, 179
Humphrey, Herbert, 3
Hughes, S., 296, 318
Hunt, J., 181
Hunter, D., 12, 28

I

Idol, L., 18, 27, 311, 319
Ima, K., 240, 252
Irvin, N., 186, 211
Irvine, J.J., 259, 261
Isaev, D.N., 141, 158
Ishisaka, H.A., 199, 212

J

Jabin, T., 28
Jackson, J.B., 228, 235
Jacobs, L.A., 172, 180
Jacobson, J.W., 179
Janicki, M.P., 179
Jasmine, J., 341
Jenkins, J.R., 27
Jensema, C., 165, 169, 172, 181
Jensen, D.L., 172, 180
Jensen, M., 235
Jenson, W., 91, 92, 136, 139
Jewell, M., 27
Jiménez, R., 359, 363
Joffee, E., 167
Johnson, 221
Johnson, D.R., 20, 28, 74, 93
Johnson, D.W., 222, 235
Johnson, F., 3, 25
Johnson, J.L., 161, 177
Johnson, Lyndon, 220
Johnson, M.J., 320
Johnson, P.A., 177
Johnson, R., 20, 28
Johnson, R.T., 222, 235
Johnson, S.M., 21, 27
Johnson, W.H., 224, 227, 233
Johnston, 361
Jonwa, E., 161

Jorgensen, J., 3, 25
Jose, P.T., 163, 177, 178
Jurtado, J., 319
Justin, N., 221, 235
Justiz, M., 312, 319

K

Kagan, 280
Kagan, S., 222, 233, 235, 236, 297, 319
Kagan, V.E., 141, 158
Kairthe, J., 307, 319
Kaiser, A.P., 52, 73
Kameen, M., 312, 319
Kampschroer, E., 3, 25
Kanner, 140
Karchmer, M.A., 182
Karweit, N.E., 311, 320
Kaufman, 357
Kauffman, J.M., 4, 7, 26, 27, 183, 188, 189,
    206, 209, 211
Kawahara-Matsuo, Linda, 134
Kennedy, John F., 3
Kennell, J., 186, 211
Keogh, B., 7, 27
Kerns, G.M., 186, 213
Kerr, M.M., 311, 319
Kilman, B., 140, 158
Kim, S., 239, 240, 250, 252
Kinzie, J.D., 199, 212
Kiraithe, J., 307, 319
Kirchner, C., 162, 171, 179
Kirp, D.L., 293, 319
Kitano, M.K., 211
Klaus, M., 186, 211
Kleinhammer-Tramill, J.P., 93
Klitzkie, L.P., 252
Knief, L.M., 225, 235
Knight, G.P., 236
Knoblock, P., 183, 184, 206, 212
Koegel, L.K., 359, 364
Koegel, R.L., 359, 364
Kozol, J., 341
Krashen, S.D., 277, 280, 281, 282, 283, 291
Krate, R., 257, 262
Krauss, M.W., 188, 212
Kropka, B.I., 168, 179
Kroth, R., 194, 207, 212
Kukla, D., 172, 178

Kunjufu, J., 255, 256, 257, 259, 260, 261
Kuvlesky, W.P., 223, 237

L

Labovitz, G., 240, 252
Lambert, W.E., 225, 237
Langley, B., 163, 172, 178, 179
Langley, M.B., 164, 167, 170, 172, 178, 179
Laosa, L.M., 228, 235
LaShell, L., 309, 319
Laski, 289
La Vigna, G., 147, 158
Lee, Roseanna, xviii, 195
LeFromboise, T.D., 204, 212
Leiter, R.G., 169, 179
Lesser, G., 221, 238
Lettick, A.L., 110, 111, 112, 114, 116, 151, 159
Leung, E.K., 241, 252
Levi, David E., 8, 10
Lewis, C., 194, 204, 211
Lewis, Michael John, xviii
Lewis, O., 221, 235
Lewis, R.B., 295, 296, 298, 305, 317, 318, 319
Lian, Ming-Gong John, vi, xxiii, 239, 241, 248,
    252
Lidz, C.S., 317
Lieberman, L., 27
Liedtke, W.W., 225, 235
Lilly, S., 7, 27
Lipsky, D.K., 6, 7, 8, 26, 27
Lipton, Diane, 9, 27
Little, J., 226, 235
Lloyd, J.W., 7, 26
Logan, 344
Loeb, P., 261
Long, E., 3, 25
Lopez, D.E., 223, 226, 227, 236
Lopez, J.T., 236
Lopez, M., 236
Lorge, 169, 177
Lovaas, Ivar O., 54, 67, 72, 111, 112, 114, 116,
    135, 139
Low, 204
Lucero, Josephine Durán, xviii
Luckasson, R., 323, 342
Luethke, B., 170, 179
Luiselli, J.K., 172, 180
Luiselli, T.E., 172, 180

Luke, B.S., 239, 252
Lutzker, J.R., 187, 212
Lynch, E.W., 194, 212, 298, 299, 319, 341
Lynch, J., 247, 252

M

Macdonald, C., 163, 180
MacDonald, M., 341
Mace-Matluck, B.J., 226, 236
MacFarland, 172
Madden, N.A., 311, 320
Madsen, M.C., 222, 235, 236, 237
Maier, A.S., 351, 352, 363
Maker, C.J., 249, 253
Maldonado, B.B., 227, 236
Maldonado-Colón, Elba, xxv, 343, 344, 364
Manding, 54
Mangold, P., 164, 181
Mangold, S., 164, 181
Mann, L., 188, 190, 211
Marias, R., 312, 319
Marion, R.L., 186, 188, 212
Marks, S.B., 171, 180
Markwardt, R., 194, 197, 212
Marozas, D., 4, 27
Marshall, 54, 55
Martin, J.E., 122, 139
Martine, J.L., 235
Martinez, I., 270, 275
Matthews, M., 261
May, D., 4, 27
Mayeski, G.W., 191, 212
McAdoo, H.P., 258, 261
McCarthy, P., 76, 93
McDonald, Anne, 63
McEvoy, M.A., 21, 27
McKenzie, R.E., 221, 228, 237
McKeon, D., 275
McKibbin, M.P., 226, 236
McKinney, 7
McLaughlin, M., 193, 212
McLean, M., 170, 173, 180
McPartland, J.M., 227, 233, 236
McQuarter, R., 54, 72
Medeiros-Landurand, P., 358, 362
Mena, C., 223, 236
Mendez, A., 170, 173, 180
Mendoza, S.M., 228, 236

Mercer, J.R., 221, 236, 293, 320
Mesaros, R.A., 167, 177
Mesibox, G.B., 110, 116, 144, 159
Messick, S., 26
Mestre, J.P., 225, 235
Meyen, E.L., 186, 187, 212, 213
Meyer, L.H., 148, 159, 165, 178, 213
Meyers, C.E., 192, 212
Mirenda, P.L., 167, 177
Moll, L.C., 307, 320
Mood, A.M., 233
Moore, C., 214
Moorehead, M.K., 355, 358, 363
Morgan, E.C., 172, 180
Morgan, R.R., 229, 236
Morrison, A., 180, 192
Morrow, R.D., 212
Morten, G., 251
Mulligan, M., 171, 172, 180
Murphy-Herd, M.C., 169, 171, 172, 180
Musselwhite, C.R., 57, 65, 72
Myles, B.S., 63, 64, 72

N

Nagata, D.K., 204, 213
Nahme-Huang, L., 194, 212, 213
Nava, A., 264, 275
Neary, T., 19
Neel, R.S., 165, 180
Nelson, C.M., 311, 319
Nelson, L.D., 221, 225, 227, 235
Nelson, W., 236
Nevin, A., 311, 319
Nguyen, Q.T., 199, 212
Nielson, A.B., 249, 253
Nieptuski, J., 198
Nietupski, H.S., 50, 72, 118, 139
Niswander, P.S., 170, 180
Norris, Tasha, 134
Northam, J.K., 161, 177
Northern, J.L., 170, 180
Nuttall, E.V., 263, 267, 275

O

Oakes, J., 229, 236
Oakland, T., 302, 304, 320
O'Brien, J., 27

Ochoa, A., 319
Okimoto, J.T., 199, 212
Olion, L., 258, 261
Olley, G.J., 147, 159
Olsen, G.O., 129, 139
Orelove, F.P., 160, 163, 166, 180, 181
Orlansky, M.D., 242, 243, 245, 246, 252
Ortiz, A.A., 161, 180, 267, 275, 278, 280, 291,
        298, 311, 320, 341, 344, 347, 349, 350,
        352, 356, 360, 364
Ostertag, Bruce A., vi, xviii, xxv, 321, 341, 342
Ovando, C.J., 193, 213, 291, 294, 320
Owan, T.C., 199, 212, 213

P

Pacheco, R., 295, 296, 309, 318
Padilla, A.M., 237
Paolucci-Whitcomb, P., 311, 319
Paris, S.G., 358, 364
Park, Hyun-Sook, vi, 134, 194, 195, 197, 198,
        199, 200, 204, 213
Pascual-Leone, J., 221, 234
Patella, V., 223, 237
Patton, J.R., 19, 23, 28
Payan, R., 300, 317
Peal, E., 237
Pearl, 225
Pearson, P.D., 358, 364
Peck, C.A., 17, 27
Peng, S.S., 226, 233
Peregoy, S.F., 291
Pérez, B., 291
Perske, M., 22, 28
Perske, R., 22, 28
Peterson, R., 162, 179
Pezzoli, M., 17, 27
Phelan, J.G., 221, 237
Phelps, A.L., 74, 93
Phillips, J.A., 129, 130, 134, 139
Pike, E.D., 229, 238
Pike, K., 356, 358, 364
Pious, C.G., 27
Poe, Maurice, xviii
Polloway, E.A., 19, 23, 28
Poulson, C., 166
Preston, D., 256, 261
Price-Williams, D.R., 222, 228, 237
Prickett, J.G., 171, 179

Prior, 64
Prizant, B.M., 57, 67, 72
Psysh, 350
Ptasnik, Joe, xvii
Pumpian, I., 165, 177

R

Radach, Charlene, xvii
Rainforth, B., 163, 180
Ramirez, A., 222, 224, 226, 228, 235
Ramirez, B.A., 320
Ramirez, M. III, 237
Ramírez, O., 204, 213
Rasche, D., 28
Razo, Rick, xviii
Reed, 346
Reichle, J., 165, 180
Reiman, J.W., 177
Reyes, R., 277, 291
Raynell, J., 164, 180
Reynolds, Maynard, C., 5, 6, 7, 12, 28, 29
Richardson, J.C., 226, 237
Rieth, H., 311, 320
Rikhye, C.H., 167, 179
Riley, R., 321, 342
Rimland, B., 64, 72, 112, 116
Risley, T.R., 52, 72
Rivera, C., 362
Rivest, L., 17, 26
Roberts, S., 169, 171, 172, 180
Rodriquez, A.M., 295, 296, 305, 317, 318
Rodriquez, F., 263, 275
Rodriguez, J., 221, 233
Rogers, J.A., 249, 253
Rogers-Warren, 54
Rosen, S., 167, 179
Rosenbaum, J.E., 229, 237
Rosenberg, R., 167, 178
Rosenfeld, L.B., 235
Rosenshine, B., 229, 237
Ross, Anne, xviii
Rothstein, L., 3, 4, 5, 28, 29
Rowitz, L., 194, 197, 212
Rubin, K.H., 17, 28
Rueda, R., 263, 270, 275, 342
Ruiz, N.T., 352, 360, 364
Ruiz, R.A., 221, 233, 237
Rusch, F.R., 74, 93, 94, 116

Russell, N.L., 356, 364
Ryndak, D.L., 8, 25
Rynders, 20, 28

S

Sadker, D.M., 240, 251, 253
Sadker, M.P., 240, 251, 253
Sailor, W., 8, 26, 28, 61, 67, 72, 84, 86, 88, 93, 117, 118, 120, 126, 139, 143, 151, 159, 172, 180
Salend, S.J., 194, 195, 204, 213, 342, 356, 358, 364
Salvia, J., 351, 352, 353, 357, 360, 364
Salzburg, C., 166, 177
Salzinger, E., 27
San, 247, 253
Sandler, A., 206, 213
Sanschagrin, S., 163, 172, 176
Santa Cruz, R., 296, 320
Sauter, 346
Schaeffer, B., 57, 69
Schafer, 143
Schein, J., 182
Schifini, A., 284, 291
Schildroth, A.N., 182
Schleifer, 189
Schloss, C.N., 252
Schloss, P.J., 5, 28, 104, 116, 252
Schmidt, B., 28, 120
Schnoor, R., 165, 178
Scholl, G.T., 165, 178, 179, 180, 182
Schopler, E., 64, 110, 116, 141, 144, 159
Schrag, J., 12, 28, 324, 342
Schubert, A., 63, 70
Schuler, A., 142, 159
Schwarz, P., 3, 25
Schwartz, E., 213
Scott, J.D., 221, 237
Selma, H., 254, 261
Semmell, M., 27
Shane, K.G., 163, 179
Shannon, L., 223, 237
Shapira, A., 237
Shapiro, J.P., 194, 213, 222, 261
Sheridan, M.D., 172, 181
Shores, R.E., 21, 27
Sigafoos, J., 165, 180
Silberman, R., 173, 181

Silverstein, B., 257, 262
Simon, M., 79, 80, 81, 82, 93
Simonsen, D., 194, 213
Simpson, R.L., 63, 64, 72, 207
Sims-Tucker, B., 165, 169, 172, 181
Singer, J., 7, 28
Singer, K., 71
Sisco, F.H., 169, 176
Sizemore, A.C., 161, 177
Skelly, M., 58, 72
Skrtic, T.M., 5, 28, 186, 187, 212, 213
Skutnabb-Kangas, T., 225, 237
Slaughter, D.T., 255, 262
Slavin, R.E., 20, 28, 311, 320
Slovic, R., 123, 139
Smith, A.J., 11, 28, 72, 163, 177, 179
Smith, D., 323, 342
Smith, O.B., 237
Smith, T.E., 16, 19, 23, 24, 28
Smithey, L., 19
Snell, M.E., 66, 73, 117, 139, 167, 172, 177, 178, 181
Snipper, G.C., 291
Snow, J., 22, 27
Snow, P.S., 172, 180
Snyder, L.K., 61, 73
Sobsey, D., 160, 161, 163, 165, 166, 169, 170, 180, 181
Soderhan, A., 21, 28
Sofar, D., 226, 233
Sparrow, S.S., 164, 181
Spellman, C.R., 161, 177
Spence, 261
Spon-Shevin, M., 6, 28
Spradlin, D., 54, 55, 71
Sriratana, P., 245, 253
Stainback, S., 4, 6, 7, 28, 29, 165, 181
Stainback, W., 4, 6, 7, 28, 29, 165, 181
Stedman, J.M., 221, 228, 237
Stein, R.C., 194, 212
Sternberg, L., 116
Stevens, J.H., 261
Stillman, R., 164, 171, 172, 181
St. Louis, K., 57, 72
Stodolsky, S.S., 221, 238
Strathe, M., 198, 211
Stratton, D., 176
Strauch, J.D., 92
Stremel-Campbell, K., 178, 180

Sue, D.W., 201, 202, 213, 252
Suillivan, T., 311, 320
Supancheck, P., 297, 320
Swallow, R., 164, 181

T

Tally, R.C., 20, 29
Taylor, L., 194, 195, 204, 213
Taylor-Gibbs, J., 194, 212, 213
Terrell, T.D., 280, 281, 291
Terry, B.G., 172, 180
Tharp, R.G., 259, 262
Thibodeau, J., 163, 172, 176
Thompson, Anneke, 158, 159
Thurman, S.K., 206, 213
Tickunoff, W.J., 311, 320
Tierney, R.J., 353, 358, 364
Tikunoff, W., 176, 319, 362
Tompson, Lynn, xviii
Torres-Guzman, M.E., 291
Towell, J., 291
Tramill, J., 93
Trivette, C.M., 189, 211
Troike, R.C., 226, 238
Troutman, A., 352, 362
Trueba, H., 299, 320, 342
Tucker, J.A., 303, 317
Tung, T.M., 199, 213
Tunmer, W.E., 236
Turnbull, A.P., 161, 165, 184, 186, 188, 189, 192, 213
Turnbull, H.R., III, 3, 4, 29, 161, 165, 184, 186, 188, 189, 192, 213
Tuthill, D., 262

U

Udvari-Solner, A., 325
Utley, B., 172, 180
Uzgiris, I.C., 181
Uzgiris-Hunt, 164

V

Valdespino, Loretta, xviii
Valencia, S.W., 364
Valles, Eugene C., vi, xxv, 292
Valletutti, P., 181

VanAllen, R., 283, 291
Vandenberg, B., 17, 28
Van-Deventer, P., 3, 25
van Dijk, J., 172, 173, 181
Van Wallenghem, J., 122, 123, 138
Volk, 344
Vowell, Jack, xvii
Vulpe, S.G., 164, 181
Vygotsky, L.S., 303, 320

W

Wagner, N.N., 235
Wainberg, 352
Wakabayashi, R., 240, 253
Walberg, H.J., 5, 6, 7, 12, 28, 29, 238
Wallar, C., 206, 214
Walqui-vanLier, A., 280, 285, 286, 291
Wang, Margaret C., 5, 6, 7, 12, 20, 28, 29
Ward, M.E., 182
Ward, M.J., 161, 162, 171, 181
Warren, A.K., 50, 65, 66, 69, 73
Warren, S.F., 50, 52, 65, 66, 69, 73
Warren, D., 54, 160, 182
Watkins, S., 172, 180
Watts, J., 172, 180
Waugh, Ruth, xvii
Weed, K., 321, 341
Wehby, J.H., 21, 27
Wehman, Paul, 67, 73, 74, 76, 93, 103, 109, 116
Weinberg, R.A., 362
Weingeld, F.D., 227, 233
Weismantal, J., 313, 319
Weismantel, M.J., 362, 373
Welsch, J.R., 252
West, F., 18, 27
West, John, xviii
Westling, D.L., 167, 170, 172, 182
Whaley, Susan L., vi, 100, 116, 128
Whiren, A., 21, 28
Wiesner, Kenneth, xviii
Wilcox, Barbara, 61, 65, 67, 86, 93, 158, 159
Wilen, W.W., 129, 130, 134, 139
Wilkerson, C.Y., 344, 349, 350, 356, 357, 360, 363, 364
Will, Madeleine, 5, 6, 7, 8, 29
Williams, C., 168, 179
Williams, S.J., 291

Wilson, A.N., 256, 262
Wing, J.K., 72, 148
Woessner, Kelly, xvii, 157
Wolery, M., 178
Wolf, 358
Wolf, B., 8, 26
Wolf, D.P., 364
Wolf, K.P., 364
Wolfe, E., 161, 182
Wolfensberger, 117
Wolff, Anne, xviii
Wolf-Schein, E.G., 161, 162, 165, 169, 170, 181
Woodward, J., 309, 319
Wright, P., 296, 320
Wong-Fillmore, L., 297, 320
Wright, 195

Y

Yano, C., 214
Yates, J.R., 161, 180, 311, 320
York, J., 163, 165, 180
York, R.L., 227, 233, 236
Yount, Michael R., vi, 128, 195, 213
Yutang, L., 195, 196, 214
Ysseldyke, J.E., 351, 352, 353, 357, 360, 364

Z

Zaharie, Pam, 134
Zahn, G.L., 222, 235
Zambone, A.M., 161, 171, 181
Zimmerman, B.J., 229, 238
Zollers, 7, 25

SUBJECT INDEX

A

ADA of 1990, application of, 45
Adaptive Learning Environment Model
(ALEM), description, 20
Adaptive Performance Instrument of Gentry,
164
Adolescent students with autism (*see* Autistic
adolescent students)
Adult transition program
beginning of, 84
description of, 84–85
funding source for, 84
African American students with disabilities
education issues, 254–260
African infusion, 255
curriculum initiated in Atlanta, 256
discussion questions, 260–261
family involvement, 257–258
instructional approaches, 258–259
student, 259
teacher, 258–259
learning environment, 259–260
components of, 259–260
learning styles, 256–257
multicultural curriculum, 255–256
overrepresentation in special education
programs, 254
prognosis of, 254
self-esteem, 257
trends emerging, 255
AIDS, qualifications under IDEA, 46
Aim for the Best program, 278
America 2000: Educate America Act
children included in, 10–11
description of, 10
features of, 11–12
goals of, table, 11
supports for, 15
themes of, 10

American Indian Sign or gestures, 58
Americans With Disabilities Act, content of,
31, 185–186
Asian American Children, 239–251
characteristics of, 240–243
cultured differences and conflicts,
241–243
new stereotypic image of, 240
positive characteristics of, 241
stereotype, 239
collaborative teaching, 251
concerns related to educating, 241
cooperative learning, 250
demographics of, 239
discussion questions, 251
exclusion legislation, 240
increase expected in future, 239
internal and external resources of parents
and teachers, 247–248
lack understanding school programs, 247
language spoken by, 240
meaning of silence to questions, 242
parents of, 245–248
difficulty seeking special services, 246
educational failure seen by, 247
potential barriers from accessing services,
247
reluctance to ask for help, 246
unaware participation PTO, etc., 246
virtues desired in child, 245
previous attitudes Americans toward, 240
suggestions for teachers, 248–251
accept students as they are, 249
aggressive approach to teaching, 248
assertive approach to teaching, 249
develop new curricula, 250
nonbiased assessment, 249–250
passive approach to teaching, 249
promote meaningful communication, 250

Asian American children (*Continued*)
  summary, 251
  uniqueness in educating, 243–245
    attitudes parents toward education, 243
    attitudes toward handicapped children,
      244–245
    differences attitudes toward classroom
      behaviors, 244
    non-Asian teacher expectations—parent
      expectations, 243–244
    reliance on Confucianism and Yin-Yang
      philosophy, 244
    use of term Orientals, 239
Assessment, Evaluation, & Programming Systems Measurement (0–3 yrs.), 172
Auditory Behavior Index, 170
Augmentative Communications Systems, 174
Autism
  learning English proficiency, 289–290
  learning English as second language,
    289–290
  shared literature unit benefits with, 279–280
  use cooperative learning, 287
Autistic adolescent students
  adolescent students with in vocational
    training, 110–115
    conclusion, 114–115
    difficulties placing, 110
    handling autistic adolescents, 110–111
    handling inappropriate behavior of
      students, 111–112, 112–113
    keeping students on task, 112
    methods used to teach, 113
    role of teacher, 114
  advantages full inclusion students, 101
  characteristics of, 140
  discussion questions, 157–158
  functional reading, 151–153
    methods used, 151–153
    purpose of, 157
  inclusion and second language acquisition
    by, 153–157
    fully included site, 155–157
    pre and post data of study, 153–154
    pre-test data in self-contained site,
      154–155
    relationships with general education
      children, 156–157
    variables or characteristics, 156

independent skill training, 148–149
intensified symptoms at puberty, 141
language and/or communication, 142–144
  functional language, 142–143 (*see also*
    Functional language)
  role of parents in, 144
  teaching alternative form of, 143
  use of photographs, 143–144
management of adolescent, 146–148
  guidelines for, 146–148
problems focusing on task, 101
  use of reinforcers, 102
self-help skills, 149–151
social skills, 144–145
  participation of parents, 145
  use of role play to teach, 144
staying on the job, 101
students in the community-based
  instruction, 135–138
  handling behavior problems, 137
  supervision during trips into community,
    127
  teaching compliance, 135
  teaching crossing the street, 136–137
  use of praise, 135–136
unusual behavior of students on buses,
  118–119
  case illustration, 119
  cost of transportation, 119

B

Basic Interpersonal Communication Skills
  (BICA), 354
B/CLAD (*see* Bilingual/Crosscultural,
  Language, & Academic Development)
Behavior disorders, 4
Bilingual/Crosscultural, Language, & Academic
  Development (B/CLAD) (*see* CLAD)
  domains of knowledge and skill required for,
    326
Bilingual Cultural Language Academic Development (B/CLAD) (*see* CLAD)
Bilingual education programs
  bilingual special education (*see* Bilingual
    special education)
  development of two languages, 296–297
  English-as-a-Second-Language strategies,
    296–297

Bilingual education programs (*Continued*)
  existence of, 296
  percent school-aged children with diverse
      backgrounds, 292
  use special education instructional strategies,
      307
Bilingual special education
  lack teachers for, 306
  mainstreaming LEP student into, 306
  placement SEL students, 306–307, 308
  skills-directed approaches, 307
  teacher competencies, 311–315
    description models, 313–314
    in-service preparation model, 314–315
    Internship Credential program, 314
    lack training programs, 312
    listing of, 311–312
    program models, 312–315
    Specialist credential program, 314
  teachers lack preparation for, 306, 308
  timing introduction English, 307–308
  use special education instructional strategies,
      307

C

Callier-Azusa instrument, 164, 172
Children with disabilities
  definition, 33
  medical services considered appropriate, 35
  services interpreted as appropriate for, 35
Circle of Friends
  activities of, 22–23
    example, 22–23
  use of, 22
Civil Rights Act of 1871 Section 1983, 32
Civil Rights Movement, 3
  foundation for, 30–31
CLAD (Crosscultural, Language, and Aca-
    demic Development), 321–340
  CLAD emphasis certification (*see* Com-
      mission on Teacher Credentialing)
  combined teacher credentials program
      blueprint, 328–340
    competency-based programs, 329
    course descriptions of MS/LH/CLAD
        program, table, 330–333
    course descriptions of MS/SH/CLAD
        program, table, 334–338

  criticisms of combined program, 339
  differences in programs, 328
  first level of combined programs, 329,
      333
  for Multiple Subject credential with
      CLAD emphasis, 328
  for MS/LH/CLAD, 328
  for MS/SH/CLAD, 328
  fourth level of combined programs,
      338–339
  recommended components for combined
      program, 339–340
  second level of combined programs, 333,
      338
  third level of combined programs, 338
  units of study required, 329
  definition, 326
  discussion questions, 340
  diverse students as assets, 321
  diversity of languages in Sacramento County
      Schools, 323–324
    table, 323
  domains required for, 326
  ethnic pupil count in California, 322–323
    table, 323
  increase in language difference students in
      California, 322
    table, 322
  special education students increase
      projected, 323
    demand for teachers, 323
  special education teacher shortage data, 324,
      326
    table, 325
  summary, 340
  teacher credential training program, 327
    benefits of, 327
  teacher shortage and credential programs,
      325–326, 326–327
  unemployment rate students with physical/
      learning differences, 321
Cognitive Academic Language Proficiency
    (CALP)
  definition, 354
  examples, 354–355
Columbia Mental Maturity Scale, 169
Commission on Teacher Credentialing of
    California (CTC)
  CLAD emphasis requirement, 325–326

Commission on Teacher Credentialing of
   California (CTC) (*Continued*)
   combined credential programs, 326–327
      advantages of, 327
      basis of, 327–328
      goal of, 327
   domains required for, 326
   MS/LH/CLAD training program, 328
   MS/SH/CLAD training program, 328
   credential programs, 328
   teacher shortage for special education, 324,
      326
   table, 325
Communication board, 59–61
   organization of, 60
   use environmental inventory, 60–61
Communication booklets, 61–63
   case illustration, 61–62
   use of, by adolescents with autism, 61–63,
      140–141
Community-based instruction, 117–138
   considerations to make in implementing,
      117–122
      acceptance of student with disability,
         120–121
      basis in normalization, 117
      costs to consider, 119–120
      definition, 117
      discussion questions, 138
      environments used by students, 117, 121
      factors in developing, 118
      insurance coverage for students off
         campus, 118
      methods of teaching students, 121–122
      partial participation of some students,
         120
      supervision students off campus, 118–119
      teacher factors in, 121
      time students spend in, 122
      training students to utilize community,
         120
   model community based transition program,
      128–134
      benefits experience of students, 133–134
      capacity to thrive, 128
      characteristics students, 129–130
      competence demonstrated by student,
         129
      cooperation parents, 133

domestic skills, 133
gaining control of decision making, 129
independence obtained from opportunity to participate, 128–129
participation by parents, 133
role recreation and leisure activities, 133
student's need for critical judgment, 129
teaching critical thinking skills, 129
teaching students to make choices,
   128–134
thriving in environments, 128
using metacognitive process, 130 (*see*
   Metacognitive process)
patterns used, 122–124
   consultants utilized, 122–123
   related staff, 123–124
   staggered implementation of, 124
   substitutes or paraprofessionals, 124
   team teaching, 124
   volunteers and peer tutors, 123, 127
staffing strategies useful in, 122–128
   follow-up on, 127–128
   importance of, 122
   inservice outline, table, 126
   inservice training for trainers, 125
   need for adequate student supervision,
      128–129
   practical experience for students, 125
   role of coordinator, 127
   scheduling students in, 125–126
summary, 134
use concrete activities in teaching, 130–131
Community-based vocational education (*see*
   Vocational Education)
Cooperative learning, 287–289
   description, 287
   effectiveness of, 287
   principles followed, 287–288
   use direct instruction methodologies,
      288–289
Cultural Language Academic Development (*see*
   CLAD)
Cultural and linguistic diversity in special
   education, 292–317
   appropriate curriculum and instruction,
      307–310
      considerations for developing/selecting
         appropriate materials, 310

Cultural and linguistic diversity in special education (*Continued*)
    for bilingual special education, 307–308
      (*see also* Bilingual special education)
    involvement parents in instruction, 308–309
    knowledge of specialized teaching technique needed, 308
    language of instruction, 307–308
    learning style differences strategies, 309
    modification ESL instruction, 308
    need for ESL materials for basic skills, 309–310
    peer-mediated strategies, 309
    teaching useful vocabulary, 309
    use ecological inventory, 308
bilingual special education teacher competencies, 311–315
creation facilitative climate for, 299
    table, 299
developing effective educational programs, 295–310
    administrative interface, 300
    appropriate curriculum and instruction, 307–310
    attention to development of two languages, 296–297
    components of, 295–296
    cultural sensitivity, 298–299 (*see also* Cultural sensitivity)
    culturally competent educators, 298–299
    culture and language, 298
    developing bilingual and ESL options, 294
    existence of bilingual education programs, 296
    IEP development and student placement, 305–307
    nonbiased assessment and placement, 302–305
    prereferral information, 301–302
    staffing and staff development, 300–301
    Student Study Team use, 301–302
    Teacher Assistance Team (TAT), 301–302
discussion questions, 317
existence of bilingual education programs, 296

incidence of, 294
increasing growth of, 292
majority as Hispanic, 292
nonbiased assessment and placement, 302–305
    assessment instruments, 303
    bias in, table, 304
    curriculum-based assessment, 303
    focus of, 302
    purpose criterion-referenced tests, 303
    team members, 305
    types of bias, 302–303
parent participation and community involvement, 310–311
preferral intervention, 301–302
    advantages of, 301
    emphasis of, 301
    goal of, 302
    team for, 301–302
proactive assessment framework for, 343
special education practices, 292–295
    disproportional representation CLD students in, 292–293
    focus on educational equality, 291
    LEP students in special education, 294
    limited-English proficiency (LEP) students, 293–294
    results intelligence tests in English, 293
summary, 316
Culturally and linguistically different student, 263–274
advantages use native language with student, 265–266
characteristics students, 265
cultural implications, 265–267
definition, 263
functional reading and language intervention, 268–271
    ecological inventory, illustration, 269
    use ecological inventory, 268
    use familiar cultural materials, 270–271
    use photos with reading instructions, 268–269
historical information, 264–265
Latinos and (*see* Latino students)
learning by doing, 265
legislation for, 264–265
past court decision, 264
purpose being in special education, 263–264

Culturally and linguistically different student
(*Continued*)
   teaching in concrete manner, 265
   vocational and community training,
      271–274
      consideration student and parents, 274
      helping student shop, 272–274
      explanation via field trip to parents, 271
      parents as part of community-based
         instruction, 272
      parents lack understanding importance
         of, 271
      questionnaire to prepare student to shop,
         273
      use some instruction in native language,
         271–272

D

DASI, 164
Deaf-blind impairments (*see* Dual sensory
   impairments)
DEAR time, 277–278 (Drop everything and
   read)
Disabilities, definition, 45
Disabilities, persons with (*see also* Persons with
   Disabilities)
Discussion questions, 25, 47–48, 70, 92, 115,
   138, 157–158, 175–176, 210, 232, 251,
   260–261, 274, 290, 317, 340, 361–362
Dual sensory impairments and multiple
   disabilities
   approach to, 172
   assessment, 171–172
   communication for non-English speaking
      student, 173
   communication systems for, table, 174
   instruments used for, 171–172
   intervention, 172–174
   prevalence, 161, 171
   role of teacher, 173
   steps to van Dijk approach, 172–173

E

Easement, Evaluation, and Programming
   System Measurement for Birth to
   Three Years, 164

Educate America Act (*see* America 2000: The
   Educate America Act)
Education of the Handicapped Act in 1970
   (EHA) (*see* IDEA)
Education, as a property right, 32
Education for All Handicapped Children Act
   of 1975 (EAHCA), 264
English as a second language (ESL)
   definition, 240, 247
   strategies developed, 296, 297
   strategies for teaching, 276–290 (*see also*
      Second language learners)

F

Facilitated communication, 63–64
   attitudes toward, 63–64
   definition, 63
   questionable future of, 64
Fair Labor Standards Act
   and students in vocational programming,
      80–83
      documentation necessary for students,
         83
      employment relationship maximum
         hours, 82
      guidelines for, 81–82
      students covered by, 82–83
      use community-based placements, 81
      wages for students covered, 83
   contents of, 80
Federal Rehabilitation Act of 1973, Section 501,
   content of, 31–32
Fiesta Educativa, help given by, 270
Fingerspelling, 174
Florence County School District Four v.
   Carter, 43–44
Full inclusion (*see also* Inclusive education)
   definition, 8
Functional language, 50–70
   considerations teaching students severely
      handicapped, 67–70
      following sequence of instruction, 69
      noun labels to teach, 69
      role parents working with child, 68–69
      use age appropriate materials, 67–68
   delay procedure, 54–55
   developing attending skills, 66–67
      attending skills defined, 66

Functional language (*Continued*)
  discussion questions, 70
  eliminating inappropriate behaviors, 66–67
  for adolescents with autism, 142–143
  incidental teaching, 51–52 (*see also*
      Incidental teaching)
  mand model (*see* Manding)
  manding, 52–54 (*see also* Manding)
  meaning of, 50–51
  nonvocal communication approaches, 55–70
      (*see also* Nonvocal communication)
  prelanguage training goals, 67
  teaching of, 50–51
  vocal systems, 64–66 (*see also* Vocal systems)
Functional Speech and Language Program
  case illustration, 65–66
  parts of, 65
  uses of, 64–65
Functional Vision Inventory, 263
Functional Vision Screening for Severely
  Handicapped Children, 163

G

Glove Method of Palm Writing, 164, 174
Griffiths Mental Development Scales, 164

H

Hearing impairments
  assessment, 169–170
  categories of, 168–169
  causes of, 168
  classification of, table, 169
  intervention, 170
  tests used to assess, 169
Hiskey Nebraska Test of Learning Aptitude,
  169
HIV positive, qualifications under Rehabilitation Act, 46–47
Honig v. Doe, 38

I

IDEA–Individuals With Disabilities Education
  Act, 264
  components of, 79–80
  due process and the IEP, 35–39 (*see also*
      Individualized educational plan)

exclusions from, 35
free appropriate public education, 33–35
  appropriate defined, 34
  definition, 33
  free defined, 33–34
  IEP for student, 34
  related services defined, 35
  purpose of, 31
  requirements of, 4, 9, 31
inclusion transition service requirements, 79
least restrictive environment (*see* Least
  restrictive environment)
mainstreaming (*see* Mainstreaming)
modifications academic programs, 46
provisions included, 79
relationship location child's school to home,
  42
stipulations in, 185
vocational exploration, 79
IEP (*see* Individualized educational plan)
Informal Assessment of Developmental Skills
  for Visually Handicapped Students, 164
Incidental teaching
  definition, 51
  effectiveness of use, 52
  examples of, 51
  responses handicapped students to, 51–52
Inclusive, supportive education, definition, 40
Inclusive classrooms
  barriers to, 23–24
  benefits of, 24
  collaboration, 18
  cooperative, 20
  curriculum adaptation and supportive
      instructional practices, 19
  least restrictive environment, 4–5 (*see also*
      Least restrictive environment)
  of Individuals With Disabilities Education
      Act, 9
  peer acceptance, 16–17
  peer relationships, 20–22
  role of teacher, 13–14, 15
Inclusive communities, 3–25
  and educational reform, 3
  barriers to building inclusive classrooms,
      23–24 (*see also* Inclusive classrooms)
  basic components of, 8

Inclusive communities (*Continued*)
  benefits of, 24
    for typically developing children, 24–25
  building inclusive communities, 13
    principles of, table, 14
    recommendations, 13
  building peer relationships, 20–22 (*see also*
    Peer relationships)
  Circle of Friends, 22–23
  Civil Rights movement, 3
  collaboration, assumptions, 18
  continuum of services, 12
  cooperative inclusion, 20
    Adaptive Learning Environments model,
      20
  curriculum adaptation, 19
  definition terms used for, 8
  discussion questions, 25
  Educate America Act, 10–12 (*see also*
    Educate America Act)
  guidelines, table, 19
  inclusion considerations, table, 16
  Individuals with Disabilities Education Act,
    9
  least restrictive environment, 4–5 (*see also*
    Least restrictive environment)
  legislation, 3–4
    right to education for all children, 4
    right to least restrictive environment, 4
  peer acceptance, 16–17
  promoting, understanding, celebrating indi-
    vidual differences, 15
  role of general education teacher, 15
  special education reform efforts, 5–8 (*see also*
    Special education)
  support systems, 17
    steps in planning, 18
  supportive instructional practices, 19
  teacher acceptance, 13–14
  value of differences, 15
Inclusive schooling definition, 8 (*see also*
  Inclusive education)
Individual Family Service Plan (IFSP), stipulations of, 185
Individualized Educational Plan (IEP), 34–35,
  305–307
  and CLD student placement, 305–307
    language used on forms, 305–306
    placement LEP and ESL students, 306

    team members, 305
  contents of, 36–37
  development and student placement,
    305–307
    forms used, 305–306
    helping parents understand, 305
    lack qualified teachers, 306
    placement options, 306–307
    team membership, 305
  due process and
    contents of, 36–37
    hearing for, 37–38
    involvement parent/student in, 35–36
    members IEP team, 36
    parental consent necessary, 37
    settling disagreements, 37
    stages due process, 35–36
  effect of, 37
  members of team, 36
Individuals With Disabilities Education Act
  (*see* IDEA)
INSIGHT Developmental Check List, 172
Intelligence
  assessment of, 356–358
  criticisms of, 357
  definition, 357
  interpretations subtests and evaluator
    sensitivity, 357–358
Irving Independent School District v. Tatro,
  35

                    K

Korean-American families of children with
  disabilities, 194–195
  Confucian values, 195–198
    behavioral codes, 196–198
    definition Confucianism, 195
    description, 195
    influences and implication, 196–198
    social rules, 196
    virtues of, 196
  cultural tradition and disability, 195
    Confucian values, 195–198
  differences mainstream families and, 194
  direct parent involvement, 205
    home visits, 207–207
    parent conferences, 206–207
    parents as volunteers, 208

Korean-American families of children with disabilities (*Continued*)
    training programs, 207–208
    expectations for education and social relationships, 198–199
    indirect parental involvement, 208–209
    need for understanding school and, 195
    participation in educational systems, expectations role professionals, 200
    reasons not to participate, 199
    toward unbiased collaboration, 200–205
        guidelines, 200
        steps involved in, table, 201

L

Labeling students with disabilities, 7
Language
    crosscultural academic and language development (*see* CLAD)
    functional (*see* Functional language)
    intervention strategies (*see* Functional language)
Latino students, issues related to, 215–232
    belief in supernatural, 266
    demographics of in U.S., 216–217
        current status Latino, 217
        expected increase in Latino population, 216
        recent changes in, 216
        states with highest population of, table, 217
    discussion questions, 232
    educational development of, 219
        statistics regarding, 219
    employment statistics, 218
        percent employed by categories, table, 218
    inability read/write in English by many, 268
    learning by doing, 265
    teaching students in Spanish, 268
    studies reviewed, 215
    underachievement among Mexican Americans (*see also* Mexican Americans)
    unemployment statistics, 218
        rates by ethnicity, table, 219
    use of term, 263
    working with parents at home, 270
Lau vs. Nichols, 264

Learning, how children learn, xiii
Learning handicapped teacher training (LH), 328–329
Least restrictive environment, 4–5
    legislation leading to, 4
    Public Law 94-142 and, 4–5 (*see also* Individuals with Disabilities Act)
    requirements of IDEA, 39–40
Legal system and persons with disabilities, 30–48
    discussion questions, 47–48
    intent of law, 30
    types legislation impacting, 31
        IDEA (*see* IDEA)
Legally blind, definition, 162
Leiter International Performance Scale, 169
Limited English Proficient (LEP)
    definition, 240, 247
    lack trained teachers for, 322
    number Californian students enrolled 1980–1992, 322
        ethnic enrollment, table, 323
        primary language, 322
        table, 322
    use CLAD to train teachers, 327
Linguistically different student (*see* Culturally and language different student)
Low birth weight and hearing impairment, 168

M

Mainstreaming
    Daniel R R v. State Board of Education, 41–42
    definition, 40
    indications for, 41
    Mand model technique (*see* Manding)
Manding, 52–54
    definition, 52
    uses of, 52–54
Manual communication, 55–57
    conditions for use of, 55–56
    considerations in teaching, 56, 57
    definition, 55
    environmental inventory used, 56
        table, 56
    purpose of, 55
    systems used, 57–64
        American Indian Sign, 58

Manual communication (*Continued*)
  communication board, 59–61
  communication booklets, 61–63
  facilitated communication, 63–64
  pointing and natural gestures, 58–59
  signed English, 57
  signed Exact English, 57–58
  techniques used to teach, 55–57
Merrill Palmer Performance tests, 169
Metacognitive process of Brown
  action portion of, 131–132
    table, 134
  awareness outline, 130
    table, 134
  thinking out loud process, 132
Mexico-American group (*see* Latino)
Mexican American's increased achievement, 224–232
  bilingual education, 226
  bilingualism, 225
  classroom climate, 228–229
  conclusions, 229–230
    home, 230
    school, 230–231
    society, 231
  English usage, 224–225
  independence training, 227–228
  locus of control, 227
  self-concept, 226–227
  summary of results, 231–232
Mexican American's underachievement, 220–224
  acculturation, 223–224
    factors inhibiting, 223–224
    fatalism, 223
    language usage, 223
    low assertiveness, 223
    nature of educational aspirations, 223
    present-time orientation, 223
  cognitive style, 222
  discussion questions, 232
  disproving genetic and cultural traits as causes of, 220–224
  intelligence, 220–221
  locus of control, 221
  review of research results, 220
  social motives, 221–222
  summary of results, 231–232

Mills v. Board of Education of District of Columbia, 4, 33
Morse Code, 174
Multiple disabilities students, 160–175
  conclusion, 174–175
  definition, 160
    by IDEA, 160
  discussion questions, 175–176
  dual sensory impairments, 161, 171–174
  hearing impairments, 168–169
  orientation and mobility training, 166–167
  prevalence, 160–162
  sensory impairments
    dual sensory, 171
    incidence, 162
  visual impairments (*see* Visual impairments)
Multiple Subject Teacher Training, 328–329

N

National Alliance of Black School Educators (NASBE), curriculum proposed, 255–256
Non-English Proficient
  number California students enrolled 1980–1992, 322
    ethnic enrollment, table, 323
    primary language, 322
    table, 322
  use CLAD to train teachers, 327
Nonsheltered vocational training
  age students beginning, 109–110
  doing environmental or ecological survey, 106–107
  information for job employers, table, 107
  locating job sites, 109
  necessity of, 106
  placement students in, 95–97
    jobs on campus, 96–97
    payment of, 95–96
    sites of jobs, 97
  starting of, 106
  training principals and teachers, 107–108
  use ecological or environmental inventory, 96
  work with parents of students, 108–109
Nonvocal communication approaches, 55–70
  manual communication, 55–57
Normalization, definition, 117
Norrie's disease, 168

O

Optic nerve atrophy, definition, 162
Oregon Project for Visually Impaired and Blind Preschool Children, 164
Orientals (*see* Asian American children)
Otitis media and hearing impairment, 168

P

Parent and family issues, 183–210
    characteristics parents and families of children with severe disabilities, 186–188
        acceptability of disability defined, 187
        effects of stress on families, 187–188
        reaction to a disability, 186–187
        variables affecting reaction to a disability, 186–187
    concerns regarding parent involvement, 192–194
        linguistic and sociocultural background, 193
        socioeconomic status, 193–194
    considerations related to involving parents in children's education, 191–205
        Korean-American families and (*see* Korean-American families of children)
        rationale for parent involvement, 191–194
    discussion questions, 210
    historical and legislative perspective, 183–186
        attitudes toward disabled in past, 183
        Americans With Disabilities Act, 185–186
        attitudes toward child with a disability, 183–184
        characteristics families by economics, 183
        Education for All Handicapped Children Act, 184 (*see also* IDEA)
        feeling parents as source of child's disability, 184
        Individuals With Disabilities Education Act (IDEA), 183–184
        P.L. 94-142 amendments, 185
        summary, 186
        vocational Rehabilitation Act of 1973 passed, 184
    methods for involving parents in school activities, 205–209
        direct involvement, 205–208
        indirect involvement, 208–209
    need for support from school and community, 188–190
        legal support, 190
        practical support, 190
        professional support, 189–190
        social support, 189
    summary, 209–210
Partially sighted children, definition, 162
Peer relationships
    Circle of Friends meeting, 22–23
    general education teacher behaviors, 20–22
    peer acceptance, 16–17
Pennsylvania Association for Retarded Children v. Commonwealth of PA, 4, 32–33
Persons with disabilities
    Education Act, 32–33 (*see also* IDEA)
    legal system and (*see* Legal system and persons with disabilities)
Pointing and natural gestures communication, 58–59
Postsecondary programming, 84–91
    beginning adult transition program, 84–85 (*see also* Adult transition program)
    for persons with severe handicaps, 86–91
        acceptance of students by others, 89–90
        communication necessary, 90
        conferences for review progress, 87
        funding of, 90–91
        job placement, 88–89
        results of, 87, 88
        review objectives of, 89
        role of parents, 87–88
        started community-based program, 86–87
        types jobs learned, 87
        work as volunteers, 87, 91
    results of, 85–86
    skills needed by students entering, 85
Proactive assessment framework to meet diversity challenge, 343–362
    characteristics intervention approaches, 361
    concerns in assessment, 343–344
        misidentification CLD children, 344
    conclusion, 361
    diagnostic stage, 356–361
        communication assessment, 356

Proactive assessment framework to meet diversity challenge (*Continued*)
  focus formal and informal assessment, 356
  formal measures to identify learning disabilities, 357
  intellectual assessment, 356–358
  purpose assessment process, 359
  specific assessments, 358–359
discussion questions, 361–362
ecology of the classroom, 347–349
  expectations, 349
  experiential background, 348
  language, 347
  previous and current interventions, 348–349
ecology of the home, 345–349
  distinguishing between students, 346
  experiential background, 346–347
  language, 345–346
  perspectives about disability, 347
goals of, 360
key aspects of to assessment/evaluation of CID youth, 359
  table, 360
modification intervention model, 349
  Basic Interpersonal Communication Skills, 354
  Cognitive Academic Language Proficiency, 354
  curriculum-based evaluation, 355
  inclusion in everyday classroom activities, 350
  language evaluation, 352–353
  language proficiency, 354
  prereferral state, 350
  previous academic interventions, 353–355
  process of, 355
  sociocultural background, 353
  Teacher Assistance Team focus, 350
  teacher support teams, 350
transfer of knowledge with CLD children, 351
  use *Student First & Second Language Oral & Literacy Skills*, 351
  use *Survey of Factors Which Might Affect Test Performance & Interpretation*, 350
prescriptive stage, 359–361

proactive perspective, 349–352
  diagnostic stage, 356–359
  modification stage, 349–355
  prescriptive stage, 359–361
stage and information needed, table, 360
summary, 349
understanding ontogeny of current educational condition, 345
Puerto Rican (*see* Latino students)

R

Regular education initiative (REI), 5–8
  disadvantages of, 6–7
  dual system use, 5–6, 7
  labeling students with disabilities, 7
  objective, 6
  problem areas affecting current model, 6
  proponents attitude toward, 6, 7–8
  pull-out approach, 6
  students included in, 8
Rehabilitation Act of 1973, Section 504, 9
  application of, 45
Retinopathy of prematurity, definition, 162
Reynell-Zinkin Scales, 164
Rh factor and hearing impairment, 168
Roncker v. Walter decision, 40–41

S

S-1 v. Turlington decision, 38
School
  effect changing demographics on, xiii–xiv
  goal of full inclusion, xiii
  how children learn, xiii
School Board of Nassau County v. Arline, 47
Second language learners teaching strategies, 276–290
  acquisition information, 276–280
    affective filter hypothesis, 276
    Aim for the Best program, 278
    comprehensible input hypothesis, 277
    DEAR time, 277–278
    guidelines for, 276
    need to praise student, 276–277
    reading hypothesis, 277
    shared literature unit, 278–279
  cooperative learning, 287–289 (*see also* Cooperative learning)

Second language learners teaching strategies (*Continued*)
discussion questions, 290
inclusion, 289–290
learning English, 289
Language Experience Approach, 283
sheltered instruction, 284–286 (*see also* Sheltered instruction)
Specifically Designed Academic Instruction in English, 284–286
strategies used, 280
the natural approach, 281–284
Total Physical Response Approach, 280–281
Sensory impairments
deaf-blind (*see* Deaf-blind impairment)
dual (*see* Dual sensory impairment)
hearing (*see* Hearing impairment)
prevalence, 161, 162, 171
visual (*see* Vision impairments)
Serna vs. Portales Municipal Schools, 264
Severely Disabilities Progress Inventory, 172
Severely handicapped teacher training, 328–329
Sheltered Instruction, 284–286, 297
illustration, 285
new term for, 286
student candidates for, 285
techniques used, 284
uses of, 286, 297
Sheltered vocational training
description, 94–95
problems with, 95
tasks performed, example, 94
Sheltered workshops (*see* Sheltered vocational training)
Sign systems, 174
Signing Exact English, 57–58
Signed English, 57
Simultaneous communication (*see* Manual ommunication)
Southeastern Community College v. Davis, 47
Special education
as a support service, 44
bilingual (*see* Bilingual special education)
combination CLAD, special and general education, xiv
cultural and linguistic diversity in (*see* CLD special education)
curriculum relevant to Afro-American students, 255

data on shortage teachers in California, 324, 326
table, 325
definition, 33
demand for qualified teachers, 323, 324
reform efforts, 5–8
regular education initiative and reform efforts of, 5–8
students increase projected, 323, 324
teacher shortage data, 324, 326
table, 325
Special education cultural and linguistic diversity in, 292–317 (*see also* CLAD)
Special needs children
early treatment of, xiii
first acceptance at school, xiii
Specifically Designed Academic Instruction in English (SDAIE), 286
Student Study Team, 301–302
STYCAR Battery, 163

T

Tadom Method of communication, 174
Teacher Assistance Team (TAT), 301–302
focus of, 350
Telephone Communication Systems, 174
Total communication (*see* Manual communication)
Total Physical Response Approach
description, 296–297
to teach second language, 280–281
presentation basic vocabulary, 280–281
Transition
components essential to, 75
definition, 74
Transition programming, 74–91
adult transition program (*see* Adult transition program)
discussion questions, 92
Fair Labor Standards Act (*see* Fair Labor Standards Act)
postsecondary programming, 84–91 (*see also* Postsecondary programming)
vocational transition programming, 75–78 (*see also* Vocational transition programming)
Typing and script writing, 174

U

United States vs. Texas, 264
Usher's syndrome, 168
Uzgiris-Hunt Ordinal Scales of Psychological
    Development, 164

V

Vineland Adaptive Behavior Scales-Expanded,
    164
Viral infections and hearing impairment, 168
Vision, maximizing residual vision, 166
Visual impairments and multiple disabilities,
    162–168
    approach to, 162, 163
    assessment, 163–165
        case illustration, 164–165
        implications for, 164
        instruments used, table, 164
        of functional vision, 163
    causes of, 162
    definition terms used, 162
    intervention, 165–168
        decreasing maladaptive behaviors,
            167–168
        early intervention, 165–166
        maximizing residual vision, 166
        orientation and jobility, 166–167
        steps to developing vision program, 166
        types of, 165
    persons supporting teacher of, 162–163
    prevalence, 161
    steps to developing vision program, 166
Vocal systems of communication, 64–66
Vocational education
    cooperative vocational education, 81
    vocational assessment, 79–80

vocational exploration, 79
vocational training, 80
Vocational Rehabilitation Act (1973), passage
    of, 184
Vocational Training, 94–115
    age and success on, 102
    autism students in (*see* Autism students in
        vocational training)
    discussion questions, 115
    full inclusion students in regular classrooms,
        100–101
    for persons with moderate to severe
        handicaps, 94–115
    nonsheltered (*see* Nonsheltered vocational
        training)
    sheltered (*see* Sheltered vocational training)
    starting student to do a job, 101
    trainers need to be low-key, 100
    techniques used, 97–100, 103–106
        achieving production, 104
        acquisition, 103–104
        error correction, 105
        follow-up, 105, 106
        reinforcement strategies used, 102–103
        role of trainer, 98–99
        skill maintenance, 104
        starting student on job, 101–103
        work endurance, 103
        work evaluation, 105
        work quality, 104–105
        workshops for trainers, 99–100
Vocational transition programming, 75–78
Vulpe Assessment Battery, 164

W

WISC–R for the Hearing Impaired, 169